Modern Jewish Plays

Shooting Magda •

• Hand in Hand

• The Murder of Isaac

Reading Hebron •

Masada •

• The Trials of John Demjanjuk

Modern Jewish Plays

- *Masada*
- *The Murder of Isaac*
- *The Trials of John Demjanjuk: A Holocaust Cabaret*
- *Hand in Hand*
- *Shooting Magda (The Palestinian Girl)*
- *Reading Hebron*

edited by Jason Sherman

Playwrights Canada Press
Toronto • Canada

Playwrights Canada Press
The Canadian Drama Publisher
215 Spadina Avenue, Suite 230, Toronto, Ontario CANADA M5T 2C7
416-703-0013   fax 416-408-3402
orders@playwrightscanada.com • www.playwrightscanada.com

Financial support provided by the taxpayers of Canada and Ontario through the Canada Council for the Arts and the Department of Canadian Heritage through the Book Publishing Industry Development Programme, and the Ontario Arts Council.

Cover concept by Jason Sherman, design by JLArt.
Production Editor: JLArt

Library and Archives Canada Cataloguing in Publication

Modern Jewish plays / selected and edited by Jason Sherman.

Includes two Israeli plays translated into English from Hebrew.
Contents: Masada -- The murder of Isaac -- The trials of John Demjanjuk: a holocaust cabaret -- Hand in hand -- Shooting of Magda (the Palestinian girl) -- Reading Hebron

ISBN 0-88754-734-6

1. Canadian drama (English)--Jewish authors. 2. English drama--Jewish authors.
3. Israeli drama--20th century--Translations into English. 4. Canadian drama (English)--20th century. 5. Canadian drama (English)--21st century. 6. English drama--20th century. 7. Jewish drama. 8. Jews--Drama. I. Sherman, Jason, 1962-

PN6120.J4M63 2006   822'.9140808924   C2006-901596-1

First Edition: April 2006
Printed and bound by AGMV Marquis at Quebec, Canada.

Publisher Acknowledgments and Production Rights Information

Masada
Arthur Milner

Playwrights Canada Press
(see copyright page for contact information)

The Murder of Isaac
Motti Lerner
translated from the Hebrew
by Anthony Berris
© 1999 Motti Lerner
American Premier:
Centerstage, Baltimore, Maryland

Lescher & Lescher, Ltd.
Carolyn Larson
47 East 19th Street, New York, NY 10003 USA
212-529-1790   fax 212-529-2716
cl@lescherltd.com

The Trials of John Demjanjuk:
A Holocaust Cabaret
Jonathan Garfinkel

Playwrights Canada Press
(see copyright page for contact information)

Hand in Hand
Simon Block

Nick Hern Books
14 Larden Road, London W3 7ST
fax +44 (0) 208-735-0250
info@nickhernbooks.demon.co.uk

Shooting Magda (The Palestinian Girl)
Joshua Sobol
translated from the Hebrew
by Miriam Shlesinger

Professionals and amateurs are hereby warned that performances of *Shooting Magda* are subject to royalty. It is fully protected under the copyright laws of the United States, Canada, United Kingdom and the rest of the British Commonwealth, and of all countries covered by the Berne Union for the Protection of Literary and Artistic Property, the Pan American Copyright Convention, the Universal Copyright Convention, and of all countries with which the United States has reciprocal copyright relations. All rights, including professional/amateur stage rights, motion picture, recitation, lecturing, public reading, radio broadcasting, television, video, or sound recordings, all other forms of mechanical or electronic reproduction, such as CD Rom, CD-1, information storage and retrieval systems and photocopying, and the rights of translation into foreign languages, are strictly reserved. Particular emphasis is placed upon the matter of readings, permission for which must be secured in writing.

International Creative Management, Inc.
Buddy Thomas
40 West 57th Street, New York, NY 10019 USA
212-556-5600   fax 212-556-5665
www.icmtalent.com

Reading Hebron
Jason Sherman

Kensington Literary Representation
Michael Petrasek
54 Wolseley St., Toronto, Ontario
M5T 1A5 CANADA
416-979-0187   kensingtonlit@rogers.com

Table of Contents

Masada

Arthur Milner

• Arthur Milner •

Arthur Milner lives in Val-des-Monts, Quebec. He was resident playwright at the Great Canadian Theatre Company from 1984 to 1991, and then Artistic Director until 1995. He has taught theatre at Concordia and Carleton universities, and has worked as a dramaturg for the Manitoba Association of Playwrights, Banff Playwrights Colony and Playwrights Workshop Montreal. His articles on social, economic and arts issues have appeared in *Saturday Night* magazine and *The Globe and Mail*, and he is a member of the editorial board of *Inroads, the Canadian Journal of Opinion*. His published plays include *Zero Hour, Learning to Live with Personal Growth, It's Not a Country, It's Winter, Crusader of the World* and (with Allen Cole and Estelle Shook) *Joan Henry*. *Facts,* a murder mystery set in the occupied West Bank, was produced in Winnipeg in July 2005.

• Playwright's Notes •

Masada is a play for one actor, male or female, 40-50 years old. The play takes place in a Canadian city and is a lecture delivered by an Israeli historian, to a meeting organized by the education committee of a Jewish community organization. A lectern, a table, a jug of water and a glass may be of use. A few books and documents, from which the actor occasionally reads, are necessary.

Readers of *Masada* will notice that, towards the end of the play, the character of the historian appears to alter radically. A note of clarification may be of help.

The character change is best understood as having two components: a shift from critic of Zionism to extreme supporter; and a shift from reason to passion or from rational to irrational.

The historian has come to speak to a group of people—North American Jews— who are strong supporters of Israel, but who, she (or he) knows, increasingly have misgivings about Israeli policy. Because she undercuts many of the myths of Zionism, she seems to be a critic. But her logic should be clear: if objectionable behaviour was required to establish Israel, then we can have no qualms about further objectionable behaviour in support of further expansion. ("If you are unwilling to face what was necessary in the past, you will be unable to do what is required of you in the future." [p. 20]) Her history of Zionism may intersect with a critical history, but its goal is completely different.

The second apparent change—from rational to irrational—is more complex, because the historian is unconscious of the shift. She reduces history to a simple case of winners and losers. Winners, she believes, are rational, think strategically, and are unencumbered by morality. She takes pride in her cold detachment and sees her father's moral restraint as a tiresome impediment to the attainment of Zionist goals. But her rationalism leads to overconfidence, to arrogance, and ultimately to a sense of invincibility. This sense of invincibility eliminates the flexibility—the willingness to compromise—required for strategic thinking. So while she starts out decrying the fanaticism of the Zealots, she nonetheless becomes fanatical. The Zealots' sense of invincibility resulted from their confidence that God was on their side; the historian's from amoral rationalism. In both cases, the loss of the willingness to compromise is the dangerous consequence of fanaticism—dangerous to Israel in that fanaticism has nothing remotely to do with practical security needs.

She loves political ideas and debate, and loves the power that comes from entertaining and challenging an audience. She feels she is in complete control of the situation and, with respect to the use of apparently dovish arguments to reach extreme conclusions, she is. But she is largely unaware of the increasing irrationality of her arguments.

• Acknowledgements •

I would like to thank Robert Bockstael, Steven Bush, Douglas Campbell, Neil Caplan, Neil Freeman, Peter Froehlich, Simon Malbogat, Patrick McDonald, Henry Milner, Gil Osborne, Gary Reineke, Simon Rosenblum, Sally Singal, Rabbi Reuben Slonim and Tamar Weinstein for their comments on early drafts; Naomi Campbell for her research; and Vincent Chetcuti for assistance in preparing this publication; the National Arts Centre Playwrights' Circle for making three script workshops possible; and the Great Canadian Theatre Company for its overall and continuing support. None of them bear any responsibility for the "facts" or opinions expressed.

• Note •

This play is a work of fiction. The "historian," the "father," "Walid," "Yossi" and "Shabtai" do not exist, nor are they based on any persons, living or dead. The attributed quotations are, of course, actual quotations (in most cases adapted for clarity and brevity), and are taken from the publications listed in the bibliography.

Masada is dedicated to Palestinians, Israelis and compromise.
—A.M., *27 January 1990*

• **Production History** •

Masada was first produced at the Great Canadian Theatre Company, Ottawa, in January 1990, with the following company:

Sally Singal

Directed by Steven Bush
Set, Costume and Lighting Design by Roy Robitschek
Stage Manager: Mary Burns
Assistant to the Director: Kate Wilkinson
Production Dramaturg: Naomi Campbell

• Characters •

One actor, male or female, 40-50 years old.

• *Masada* •

The Book of Genesis, chapter twenty-two: (*reads*) "And it came to pass after these things that God tested Abraham and said unto him: 'Abraham,' and he said: 'Here I am.' And He said: 'Prithee, take thy son, thine only son, whom thou lovest, Isaac, and get thee unto the land of Moriah, and offer him up there for an offering on one of the mountains which I will tell thee of.' And Abraham rose up early in the morning and saddled his ass, and took two of his young men with him and Isaac, his son, and chopped the wood for the offering and rose up and went—"

I have always had difficulty with this story. God said, "I want a human sacrifice of your son." Abraham said, "Yes."

I asked myself, what kind of person would kill his child because God said, "Kill him"? I wanted to know, if God did not stop him, would Abraham really kill Isaac? Maybe Abraham was going to count, (*holds up arm as if with an axe*) "One, two, three… three and a half…" and at the final moment say to God, "No, I'm sorry, but no. I will obey you most of the time, but I won't kill my son to prove that I believe that you are the one God, the only God, the most powerful God, King of the Universe—besides, what kind of God would ask such a thing?" I would like to believe that this is what Abraham would have done.

What would he do?

We also know Abraham moved from Sumer, where the Hebrews lived then, to *Canaan*—in English, Canaan—because God said, "Go to *Canaan*." And we are told, in Genesis, that before he left Sumer, and on the way to *Canaan*, Abraham smashed idols. I can imagine Abraham's neighbours praying, and they have a look-out who says, "Here he comes, hide the idols." What kind of person goes around smashing other people's religious articles? My point is, a man who destroys other people's idols, is probably the kind of man who would kill his young child because God told him.

And this is the beginning of monotheism, the belief in one, indivisible, all-powerful God—the beginning of Judaism, Christianity and Islam.

Of course, I am neither a biblical scholar, nor a theologian. Some might question my expertise, and prefer to consult with Rabbi Hirsch.

• • •

Shalom. I want to thank each of you for coming this evening, despite the snow and the cold and the hockey game. Especially the young people. Sometimes we Israelis are afraid the young Jews of America are impatient with our problems.

I want to thank also Rabbi Hirsch, a generous host, a learned and liberal man, with whom I have had, since my arrival, many stimulating conversations.

I have been asked by my friend and colleague, Dr. Maslik, to express his regrets. A personal matter of some urgency has made it impossible for him to be here today, and, as you can see, the pleasant, if unexpected, duty of speaking to you has fallen to me.

I must thank, too, Ms. Wynowski, who, as head of your Education Committee, has taken upon herself the task of increasing discussion and knowledge of matters of great import to Jews today.

I am informed by Ms. Wynowski that a few of you here may be unaware of Dr. Maslik's change in plans, and you may, therefore, be anticipating a lecture entitled "The Dead Sea Scrolls, New Findings." I am not an archaeologist, and it is my hope that my subject, "The Miracle of Zionism," will be of no less interest.

As you know, I am a historian. My father was a Zionist, he went from Poland to what was then Palestine in nineteen hundred and twenty-two, at the age of seventeen. When I was still a child we left Israel. I returned to Israel in nineteen sixty-seven, where I live to this day.

• • •

To understand modern Israeli history, one must begin with ancient Israeli history, and I hope that this fortunate coincidence will alleviate the disappointment felt by those aficionados of archeology with us this evening.

Israel, Palestine, *Canaan*, the Promised Land, the Holy Land, Land of Milk and Honey: *Eretz Yisrael*.

The first people in *Canaan* were the Canaanites. Then came Abraham and his followers among the Hebrews. Then Egypt took it over, then the Hyksos. Egypt again, the Hittites, the Hebrews again—except now we're Israelites. The Babylonians, the Persians, the Greeks, Egypt again, the Seleucids, the Israelites again—but now we're Jews. Even the Armenians for a short time were the owners of Palestine. Then Romans. Arabs. Turks. Crusaders. Mamelukes. Turks again. Great Britain. And then the Jews. But now we're Israelis.

For promising to obey Him, God gave this land to Abraham and his descendants. Why would God give the Jews this desert of a land through which, for thousands of years, walked every army in the world? This is a reward? Perhaps it was a joke—perhaps God has a dry sense of humour. Or perhaps Abraham was given a choice and he asked for *Canaan*. Myself, I would have asked for France.

There is a story that Moses stuttered and that after leaving Egypt, God asked where he wanted to go. Moses said, "ca-can-can," so God led them to *Canaan*, but really Moses meant Canada.

The Canaanites disappeared, and the Hyksos and the Akkadians, and the Sumerians, and hundreds of other peoples have disappeared. The Jews have remained.

• • •

So. Zionism.

We should all know—you're very intelligent people, you must know—history is written by the winners. There are many excellent histories written from the point of view of the losers, but these, nobody reads. Losers whine about this, and whining is unbecoming. This does not mean the losers are wrong. But, losers are losers. And writing the history is part of the reward for winning.

So.

There are short facts and long facts. The short facts of Zionism were best expressed by Moshe Dayan—who I'm sure you all know, maybe the young people don't— Israeli general and politician, hero of the Six-Day War, the one with the patch. *(touches eye)* In nineteen seventy, Moshe Dayan said, "We took an Arab country and made it a Jewish one."

If anyone asks you what happened in Palestine from nineteen hundred to nineteen forty-eight, you can say, "We took an Arab country and made it a Jewish one."

Why does this piece of land, this desert, this crossroads, mean so much to the Jews? Is it because in Israel we can walk on the same ground where Abraham and King David walked? Is it because there we find the last wall of the Temple, the archaeologists will tell you it isn't that wall, but who cares. Is it because Masada is there, and the spirit of the Zealots' heroic defeat is still in the air? Are the Danish so attached to Denmark because there they can walk in the footsteps of Hamlet and Ophelia?

Or—the land. Is there something very deep, or personal, perhaps spiritual, those shadows that historians ignore, that has nothing to do with history because it is felt by Jews who know nothing of David and Solomon, but a feeling that exists in the air, that lives in the hearts of Jews, that has lived in our hearts for three thousand years, one has only to stand in the hills of Judea or on the shores of the Dead Sea to feel in one's heart. The land of Israel. *Eretz Yisrael.*

Or, maybe the historians are right and it is more simple. Think of the Turkish exile who goes to Turkey, where he's never been, and feels something special because for the first time he is where Turks are in charge. Turkey isn't perfect. He knows this. But nobody in Turkey is telling Turks what to do except other Turks. Israel is where Jews are in charge. In Israel, no Gentile tells a Jew what to do. It's a nice feeling for Turks and Danes. It's a nice feeling for Jews.

• • •

Zionism was the return of the Jews to Palestine. To return, they must first leave. Why did they leave? One thousand, eight hundred and sixty years ago, the Romans threw them out. Why?

Rome ruled Palestine for almost seven hundred years. As rulers, in that time, they were not so bad. Jews could own land, they could be dentists and play hockey, they didn't have to—and this was an exception the Romans made only for the Jews—Jews did not have to pray to Roman idols. We were even allowed to collect our own tax for the Temple. Then the Romans made a big mistake, they put a new man in charge, whose name was Quietus. Quietus stole the money for the Temple. And he didn't allow Jews to be circumcised. The Romans thought circumcision barbaric, but

Quietus forbade it. Circumcision was part of the agreement between God and Abraham. It was important to the Jews. In fact… an uncircumcised Jew… is a woman. Jewish leaders went to Quietus to talk. Nothing. They appealed to Rome. More nothing. What could the Jews do? How could a few Jews fight the most powerful empire in the world?

There were some Jews, the Zealots—they were a bit religious—the Zealots said, "Jews are commanded to obey God. Therefore obeying anyone else is a sin. Therefore obeying Romans is a sin." The Zealots began to kill Roman soldiers, only one or two at a time, but the Romans became upset. The Romans started killing Jews, but not just Zealots because they did not always know which Jew was a Zealot and which was not.

There were three main groups of Jews. It's not important but it is interesting to know we were divided then just like now. The Sadducees were the priests and the economic elite. They said the Torah should be followed word by word. But, as is common with elites, they did not always do what they recommended to others. The second group, the Pharisees—to them the Torah was like a philosophy, to be discussed and improved. The Pharisees were interested in the teachings of other peoples. They studied Aristotle, even though Aristotle prayed to idols. The third group, the Essenes, were like monks. They owned no property and lived without women, they thought women unclean. They took young boys from other Jews and taught them to be Essenes.

The leaders of the Sadducees, the Pharisees and the Essenes had a meeting and they agreed that this new group, the Zealots, must be stopped and Rome must be convinced to replace Quietus. If not, there would be a war and the Jews would lose.

The Zealots thought, "Lose? How can we lose if we obey God?" The Zealots said any Jew who thinks the Jews can lose is a sinner and a traitor. So the Zealots killed Jews, too. And the Zealots killed Romans and the Romans killed Jews, so more Jews joined the Zealots and the Zealots killed more Romans and the Romans killed more Jews and more Jews joined the Zealots and it turned into a full-size revolt.

The Jews fought with great determination but Palestine was the only way to go by land from Europe to Africa, so the Romans, too, were determined. It took time for the fresh Roman battalions to reach Palestine—when they did, the Jews lost. The last Zealots escaped to Masada, an abandoned fortress high above the Dead Sea, where they lived for three years, the Roman army all around, sitting, waiting. When the end came near, their leader, Eleazar ben Shimon or Shimon ben Yair—we don't know which is right—made a speech. Very few people know that this speech was tape-recorded. This is the speech, word by word:

(reads) "My loyal followers, long ago we resolved to serve neither the Romans nor anyone else but only God. Now the time has come that bids us prove our determination by our deeds. At such a time we must not disgrace ourselves— hitherto we have never submitted to slavery, we must not choose slavery now.

God has given us this privilege, to die nobly and as free men. This, our enemies cannot prevent.

"From the very first, we ought to have read the mind of God and realized that His once beloved Jewish race had been sentenced to extinction. For if He had remained gracious or only slightly indignant with us, He would not have shut His eyes to the destruction of so many thousands or allowed His most holy city to be burnt to the ground by our enemies. These things are God's vengeance for the many wrongs that we dared to do.

"For those wrongs let us pay the penalty not to our bitterest enemies, the Romans, but to God. Let our wives die unabused, our children without knowledge of slavery."

What would you do? Kill your children or let them live in slavery?

The Zealots were not convinced. Eleazar ben Shimon—or Shimon ben Yair—continued.

(reads) "I made a sad mistake in thinking I had the support of loyal followers in the struggle for freedom. You are not a bit different from the common herd, you, who fear death even when it means the end of utter misery."

He talked for hours. He praised them. He insulted them. He complimented them. He berated them. He told them that death was like sleep, only better. He told them God wanted them to die. And that they deserved to die.

In the end, his followers agreed. Each man killed his family. Ten men were picked to kill the other men. Then one man killed the nine and then himself. Nine hundred and sixty men, women and children, dead.

• • •

History tells us three things are of great importance in war: weapons, soldiers, and perhaps first among these, determination. The Zealots had plenty determination, but the Romans, too, were determined. The Zealots did not count weapons and soldiers because they believed they possessed, in God, the ultimate weapon. They believed that they were invincible. This is always a dangerous belief and this belief made the Zealots excellent soldiers but poor generals.

We can see here a kind of tension that still exists among Jews, the tension between the rationalists, like the Pharisees, who look at a situation, measure the good against the bad, on one hand and on the other hand, full of doubts, always ready to negotiate and to compromise. And then, on the other side, the Zealots. Passionate. Brave. Confident. For whom compromise is treason.

I had last night an interesting discussion with Rabbi Hirsch. He asked, "Is it good to give this interpretation to what happened at Masada?" Rabbi Hirsch was concerned that the spiritual value of the story of Masada would be lost—lessons of humility, of devotion to God, of putting the tribe before the individual. Rabbi Hirsch also is concerned with justice and morality: were the Jews not right to rebel against the oppressor?

History is like a great window through which we can see wonderful things. But we must not look with one eye closed.

History is not concerned with morality. The Zealots were wrong to rebel because they lost.

Thousands of Jews died in what is known as the Great Revolt. The Temple was destroyed, Jews were expelled from Jerusalem. Only from Jerusalem.

• • •

What did the Jews learn from this defeat at the hands of the Romans?

Sixty years after, there was another revolt, led by a man named Bar Kokhba. The great Rabbi Akiba said Bar Kokhba was the Messiah. The great Rabbi was wrong. The Jews lost again, and this time the Romans had enough and expelled them from all of Palestine.

In exile, in the Diaspora, the Jews abandoned rebellion, and turned to compliance. Not conformity, not assimilation, but compliance. They waited quietly for God to send the Messiah, and they said one to another, "The law of the land is the law." Jews, they believed, would return to Palestine—but only when God was ready. Each new year they said, "*Le shanah haba-ah beyerushalayim,*" next year in Jerusalem. But it was not a plan, it was a prayer.

I should say that the Roman expulsion was not complete and a few thousand Jews remained in Palestine. But for eighteen centuries, nothing changed in the relationship of Jews to Palestine. During this time, Jews divided in two: the Ashkenazi, those who settled in Europe; and the Sephardi, who settled in North Africa and Spain, and the Middle East.

• • •

Why suddenly, after so many years, did Jews decide to return to *Eretz Yisrael*?

My father came from a religious family in Poland. At the age of seventeen, against the wishes of his parents, he went to Palestine. Why did he choose to go?

Western Europe, Eastern Europe. The second half of the nineteenth century. Forgive me if I speak about things which some of you already know.

Western Europe. Jews are becoming full citizens. They are doctors and lawyers and historians, and they work in factories. In England, a Jew has tea with the prime minister.

Eastern Europe. Very different. There are pogroms, random violence against Jews. Jews must move from one village to another, sometimes they are killed. Jews are restricted to certain occupations. They are not permitted to own land. There are limits on Jews admitted to universities. But. I hope Rabbi Hirsch will forgive me for this—these Jews cherished their separateness. They lived in their little villages—their *shtetls*, walked in long dark robes and studied the Torah and the commentaries on the Torah and the commentaries on the commentaries. Ahad Ha-am, a Russian Jew, a writer and early Zionist, wrote that he was not allowed to look at the letters of the

Russian alphabet because, *(reads)* "My mother's father had heard from a great religious leader that the sight of a foreign letter made the eyes unclean."

One could say that the Jews of Eastern Europe were still living in the Dark Ages. One could say that in this period, before nineteen hundred, all of Eastern Europe was still in the Dark Ages. What does that mean, the Dark Ages? It was a period of the absolute dominance of religion. Only when it became conceivable that God did not control every single act and event, did the Dark Ages become a little lighter.

Not all the Jews of Eastern Europe were living in the Dark Ages. Many, including my father some years later, became adherents of a very new, very modern, very bright religion—socialism. Nineteen seventeen was, of course, that great triumph over darkness, the Russian Revolution.

I have left out the Jews of North Africa and the Middle East who had nothing to do with Zionism—yet.

So. Where did Zionism begin? Naturally, it began with oppressed religious Jews of Eastern Europe who longed to return to Jerusalem. No.

We go to France, eighteen-eighty-six. A Jewish soldier, Alfred Dreyfus, is accused of treason, found guilty, and sent to Devil's Island. The old stories come out. "You cannot trust Jews." "Jews will never be loyal citizens." "Jews eat Christian babies." Theodore Herzl, an Austrian journalist reporting on the trial for his Viennese newspaper, decides the Dreyfus affair proves that Jews will never be accepted. He writes a pamphlet, *Der Judenstaat*, The Jewish State. "What we need," said Herzl, "is a homeland for the Jews." Modern Zionism is born.

It is not easy to convince the Jews of Germany and Austria and France. Imagine the conversations. Herzl: "This proves..." His friend interrupts: "It proves nothing." Herzl: "Newspapers write the Jews are disloyal. All Jews are called traitors." "Look, Teddy," his friend says, "our enemies have always said, 'Jews are different.' By calling for a separate country for Jews, it is you who is saying 'Jews are different.' You are giving ammunition to our enemies." We Jews are always concerned about giving ammunition to our enemies. But imagine someone saying that Zionism itself was giving ammunition. Still, Herzl persisted: "Jews," he said, "will never be accepted. We need a state."

Years later, Herzl's friend sent a postcard: "Dear Teddy. Now that Dreyfus has been not only acquitted but also awarded the *Légion d'Honneur* by the *gouvernement de France*, have you changed your mind?"

In fact, there was no postcard and by this time Herzl was dead.

Every Jew learns—I hope—about the Dreyfus affair and how it proved that Jews were not accepted in Europe. Very few Jews know that Dreyfus was given the *Légion d'Honneur*. The Zionists won, they write the history.

• • •

This debate between the Zionists and the anti-Zionists persisted for many years.

Twenty years after Herzl's book, in nineteen seventeen, Lord Edwin Samuel Montagu, a British Jew and a British cabinet minister, wrote a memorandum to his fellow ministers:

(reads) "I lay down with emphasis four principles. One. I assert that there is not a Jewish nation. It is no more true to say that a Jewish Englishman and a Jewish Moor are of the same nation than it is to say that a Christian Englishman and a Christian Moor are of the same nation. Two. Zionism seems to me a mischievous political creed, untenable by any patriotic citizen of the United Kingdom. If a Jewish Englishman longs for the day when he will shake British soil from his shoes, he seems to me to have acknowledged aims inconsistent with British citizenship. Three. Palestine plays a large part in Jewish history, but so it does in modern Mohameddan history and, surely, it plays a larger part than any other country in Christian history. Four. When Jews are told that Palestine is their national home, they will drive out Palestine's present inhabitants and take all the best in the country."

What do you think? Are Jews better off inside other countries, or outside, with their own country? At one time this was a great debate. One can understand it as the recurring tension between the forces of progress, represented by Lord Montagu, and Herzl's passionate belief that this progress was a mirage, that the Dark Ages of intolerance and persecution would return and return and return.

Jews are modern people. On every subject we are rational, we are children of enlightenment. Except. About Jews. About Israel. The unending struggle between darkness and light. The ego and the id. Between knowledge and superstition. Science and religion. Thinking and feeling. The Pharisees and the Zealots. Theocracy and democracy. The brain, the heart. Passion, reason. Anti-Semitism and tolerance. Herzl and Montagu. In every one of us. The darkness and light at war.

Every Jew feels as if we are members in a club but the membership card has a stamp, "may be cancelled without notice." We all say to ourselves, and we teach our children, "The Jews of Germany were Germans, they were proud of being Germans. They were the most cultured, the most assimilated, the most successful Jews. But, for the Nazis, this was nothing. Even the Jews who converted. Even the Jews who didn't know they were Jews."

Six million methodical, pre-meditated murders. Of three and a half million Jews living in Poland, seventy-four thousand were alive after the war. This is the Dark Ages.

The first religions were based on cycles, the endless repetition of rain and sun and the seasons, prosperity and hunger and freedom and slavery. We Jews invented the idea of progress, of a future that would be different from and better than the past— no more floods, no more slavery, no more wandering in the desert. The coming of the Messiah meant a better future. And the idea that the Messiah would come only when the Jews deserve Him meant that people could control their destiny. Now, Jews again see history as endlessly repeating—pogroms and persecution and wandering. And Nazis always waiting, ready to continue the cycle.

Only Israel could break this cycle. Only in a Jewish state with power to defend themselves, only then would Jews be secure. This was Herzl's conclusion in eighteen-ninety-six. This was what the Nazis confirmed forty-five years later.

• • •

So. "Zionism is an American Jew giving money to a British Jew for a Polish Jew to go live in Palestine." Jews in America and Western Europe did not want to give up their microwave ovens for malaria and swamps and back-breaking toil awaiting them in Palestine. But to Polish and Russian Jews, going to Palestine was more attractive. That is who went to Palestine. Not the religious Jews of Eastern Europe, who believed Zionism a great sin, but the socialist Jews, like my father.

The Zionists had a slogan: "A land without people for a people without land." "A land without people for a people without land." The Jews were a people without land. But was Palestine a land without people? In nineteen hundred, the northern half of Palestine—the south, as you know, is desert—had a density of forty people per square kilometre. There are today twenty-three people per square kilometre in that part of your country called Prince Edward Island. But the Jews of Europe never heard of Prince Edward Island.

My father borrowed money and in nineteen hundred and twenty-two, he arrived in Jaffa. He worked on a plantation. He had never worked with his hands, it was very hard. Many of these young Zionists were surprised that all the arable land was taken, and many were leaving. My father's best friend became sick with malaria and returned to Russia. My father joined a socialist party which believed that Jewish and Arab workers must together fight British imperialism to build a socialist country. One day, my father heard that, with money from Zionists in Europe, his party bought some land and was starting a collective farm. The work was hard. But with new, European, scientific methods of agriculture, they were making the land more productive.

A heroic story.

There is another story, about an Arab—we'll call him Walid. Like his father and his father before him, Walid was an olive farmer. One day, a stranger, a Zionist, perhaps my father, told Walid, whose family had worked this land for many generations, that he must leave. Walid left with his family and found work on a plantation, perhaps the same plantation where my father had worked.

You see, Walid did not own his land. In eighteen-fifty-eight, the Ottoman empire decreed that all land must be registered. So, a few Arabs who lived in the cities rushed to sign documents, and became the legal owners of land they perhaps had never seen. For fifty years this made no difference—the legal owners didn't want to live on this land and there was no one to purchase it. Then the Zionists came. The Zionists saw. The Zionists bought land.

When my father came to claim his new land, and when Walid was leaving, I ask myself, "Did for a moment their eyes meet? What did they think, the one looking to the future, the other to the past?"

Walid, and many like him, lost their land. They were angry. They attacked Jews. But who is to blame—the Zionists who bought the land or those Arabs who grew wealthy from selling it?

We were Europeans. When Europeans move into a Third World country, there are always unpleasant side effects.

. . .

"We took an Arab country and made it a Jewish one." This is a very important statement. You are all familiar—I hope—with the Passover service, where we say, "We shall remember the Exodus from Egypt all the days of our lives." The rabbis discuss at great length if "all the days of our lives" refers to only the days or the nights as well. There is a long tradition in Jewish learning of looking at the text very carefully, word by word. The word that interests me in Dayan's statement is a simple one, four letters, "took." "We took an Arab country." The Zionists had to overcome malaria and the British, and the Arabs of Palestine, and then, in nineteen forty-eight, when they proclaimed the State of Israel, they fought the armies of six Arab states that invaded the tiny, newborn country. All these obstacles the Zionists overcame. We often speak of this as a miracle. We compare it to David's defeat of Goliath. Tiny Israel, against all odds, defeated the mighty Arab countries. About all this, Moshe Dayan says, "We took."

Was it a miracle, or did we "take"?

Ben Gurion wrote—perhaps the young people don't know Ben Gurion. His first name was not "Ben." Ben Gurion means "son of a lion"—like many Zionists he adopted a Hebrew name—and he was a great leader and the first Prime Minister of Israel. The one with the hair. Ben Gurion wrote, in nineteen forty-eight:

(*reads*) "Three things have happened up till now. A, invasion by the armies of the Arab states. B, our ability to withstand these armies. And C, the flight of the Arabs. I was not surprised by any of them."

Does this sound like a man who has just witnessed a miracle?

More from the young lion.

(*reads*) "The strategic objective of the Jewish forces was to destroy the urban communities, which were the most organized and politically conscious sections of the Palestinian people. This was done by the conquest and destruction of the rural areas surrounding the towns. Deprived of transportation, food, and raw materials, the urban communities underwent a process of disintegration, chaos, and hunger. This technique led to the collapse and surrender of Haifa, Jaffa, Tiberias, Safed, Acre, Beit-Shan, Lydda, Ramleh, and Beersheba."

Does this sound like a man who has just witnessed a miracle?

The young lion makes it sound easy. It was not so easy. Many thousands of lives were lost.

Still, we took. We were Europeans. We went to a small, Third World country, and we took it. And we had help, in the beginning, from Great Britain, not the pathetic country it is now, but, at that time, the strongest power in the world.

The religious Jews of Eastern Europe were waiting for a miracle. The Zealots demanded miracles. If the Zionists expected miracles, there would be no Israel.

· · ·

We know the story of Exodus, yes? A great drought in *Canaan* drove the Israelite tribes to Egypt. For a few hundred years they live in peace, but then a new Pharaoh makes of the Israelites slaves. Moses remembers the promised land, and implores the Egyptians to "let my people go." The Egyptians refuse. The God of the Israelites inflicts horrible acts of terror on the Egyptians, many kinds of biological warfare—these are not the words of Exodus but how else can we describe grasshoppers sent to destroy crops, water turned to blood, a pestilence against cattle, and the killing of the Egyptians' first-born sons?

I wonder if you are troubled, Rabbi Hirsch, by these events. They raise significant theological questions, yes? Is terrorism permitted in the struggle for freedom? Does God believe that the ends justify the means?

I have a great deal of respect for my prime minister, Yitzhak Shamir. We have our differences, but in nineteen forty-three, Mr. Shamir wrote:

(reads) "Terrorism is for us a part of the political battle being conducted under the present circumstances, and it has a great part to play. Neither Jewish ethics nor Jewish tradition can disqualify terrorism as a means of combat."

Perhaps this Jewish tradition of which Mr. Shamir was speaking refers to what God did to the Egyptians.

The Israelites escape from Egypt and wander in the desert forty years. Then, led by Joshua, the Israelites enter *Canaan*. In the beginning, the Twelve Tribes are separate but the threat of invasion forces the tribes to join together and Israel is born. Under kings David and Solomon, Israel becomes a small superpower, with merchant ships and international trade. Israel reaches its greatest size, on both sides of the Jordan River. This was three thousand years ago. This Kingdom of Israel lasted for seventy-three years.

Why do I tell this story?

When the Zionists came to Palestine, this was Palestine. This was the dream, this was *Eretz Yisrael*—both sides of the Jordan River.

· · ·

So Zionists start arriving. What do the Arabs think? The Arabs of Palestine knew Jews, a few thousand Jews had always lived side by side with Arabs. But the Jews of Palestine wore long black robes and big hats. These new Jews could be seen farming the land, which the Jews of Palestine would never do. The women worked, they wore trousers, and men worked without shirts, which the Jews of Palestine would never do. To the Arabs of Palestine, these new immigrants were Europeans, not Jews. But the Zionists were different from other Europeans who came to control, to take money, and to leave. These new Europeans came to stay.

Nineteen fourteen. There begins a fight among the countries of Europe for colonies—the First World War. Nineteen seventeen. The British Government issues the Balfour Declaration. Nineteen eighteen. The Ottoman Empire is defeated, the British take Palestine, the war ends.

The Balfour Declaration was perhaps the first major victory for Zionism.

The Balfour Declaration said, *(reads)* "His Majesty's government view with favour the establishment in Palestine of a national home for the Jewish people..."

"A national home." Does "a national home" mean a place where Jews can go, or does it mean a Jewish state in Palestine?

Nahum Sokolov, President of the World Zionist Organization, said in nineteen twenty-one:

(reads) "The Jewish State was never part of the Zionist programme. The determination of the Jewish people is to live with the Arab people on terms of concord and mutual respect, and together with them, to make the common home into a flourishing community."

But two years before, an American commission reported that, *(reads)* "the Zionists looked forward to a practically complete dispossession of the non-Jewish inhabitants." And that, *(reads)* "Every British officer consulted by the commissioners believed that the Zionist programme could be carried out only by force of arms."

• • •

In nineteen twenty, the British create a new country. The reasons are not important for us. But they take the part of Palestine, of *Eretz Yisrael*, on the east side of the Jordan River, and make Transjordan.

What can the Zionists do? They accept it. But not all. The right-wing Zionists were against.

I know what you are thinking. "Right-wing Zionists? You said the Zionists were socialists."

Of the left-wing Zionists, there were many different groups. One said socialists work with their hands in the soil, another that socialism is not possible without an urban working class. One group said we must speak Yiddish, another said we must speak Hebrew—even though there was no word for tractor. One group wants socialism with the Arabs, another without.

There is also a right wing, small, the Zionist Revisionists. The Revisionists were admirers of Benito Mussolini. In nineteen thirty-one, they founded a newspaper whose editor called himself a fascist. A Revisionist spokesman wrote, *(reads)* "Were the Hitlerites to remove hatred of Jews from their programme, we, too, would stand by their side."

Jewish fascists? Why should Jews be different from other people?

The Revisionists said *Eretz Yisrael*, the whole land of Israel, belonged to the Jews. Palestine was stolen from the Jews by the Romans. The Arabs were living on stolen land. Every inch belonged to the Jews.

The socialists were flexible. Did this principle stand in the way? Get rid of it. Did this goal appear unrealistic? Change the goal. We can't have Transjordan? We will survive.

• • •

Let us go back. You're a Polish Jew, like my father. Do you agree with Lord Montagu that Jews are better off as Englishmen or Germans or Poles? Or—do you go to Palestine?

Remember, it is nineteen twenty-two. You don't know about the death camps.

If you stay in Poland we have no story and no Israel. So, like my father, you have joined the Zionists and have gone, at great sacrifice, to this poor, primitive country. Like most Zionists, like my father, you are a socialist and you believe without question in the equality of all people. But once in Palestine, you find out you can't move without upsetting the Arab peasants. What do you do now? Go home?

My father had to decide.

He stayed. And he agreed there had to be a Jewish state, because if Jews don't control the state, they don't control immigration. And if they don't control immigration, how can Palestine be a refuge for the Jews?

So. You're in Palestine and you want a Jewish state. The Revisionists call for armed struggle, but you are not a Zealot, so you know that you cannot win a war against the British Empire. What do you do?

David Ben Gurion was a smart man. This is what the young lion thought: "One day the British will leave Palestine. If Jews are a majority when the British leave, it will be a Jewish state. If not, it will be an Arab state. There are nine times as many Arabs in Palestine as Jews. The key to creating a Jewish majority is to convince the British to allow more Jewish immigration."

But the British were not so easy to convince. The Arabs of Palestine believed—knew—that the Zionists wanted a state, and there were strikes and riots and attacks on British soldiers. Other Arab countries were complaining and the British liked their "sun which never sets" to shine over a peaceful empire.

The British looked for compromise. They restricted Jewish immigration, not enough to please the Arabs, but more than enough to upset the Zionists.

More decisions for you, the Zionist. The British say immigration will depend on "absorptive capacity," which means, "Are there jobs for Jewish immigrants?"

So you have to make sure there are jobs for Jewish immigrants. A number of suggestions are made. First, our new union will be open only to Jews. "This is unjust," you say. "Look," you are told, "we need a separate union so that we can force Jewish employers to hire only Jews." Every socialist blood cell in your socialist bloodstream cries out in pain.

Some Zionists return to Russia, the new socialist paradise.

Another problem. A fund existed from which Jews in Palestine borrow money to buy land for settlement. Sometimes the settlements fail, the settlers sell the land. Sometimes they sell the land back to Arabs. So a condition of borrowing from this fund is that the land may never be resold except to Jews. This, too, you don't like. What do you do, return to Poland?

Zionists, young men and women, eighteen, nineteen, twenty-five years old, had to make these decisions. What do you have to decide? To wear brown pants or blue?

You must look with both eyes open. You who love Israel must not hide behind misunderstandings, behind convenient distortions, behind the beautification of history. If you are unwilling to face what was necessary in the past, you will be unable to do what is required of you in the future.

• • •

My father did not like to talk about his activities as a Zionist. Every word was like pulling water from a stone. "*Abba*," I'd ask, "why did we leave Israel?" "Because it was time to leave." I asked my mother, "*Ima*, why did we leave?" "Your father decided."

In nineteen sixty-seven, after months of troop movement and fist-waving, the Arab countries blocked shipping in the Gulf of Eilat—an act of war. Israel retaliated, and for six days my father listened to the radio. When Israel won, he was not happy. Relieved, yes, very relieved. But not happy. Some days later, he told me a story.

He was twenty-two years old, living on a kibbutz. He was a member of the Labour Party and taking military training. One day, a man named Yossi said to him, "We have a job for you. Don't cut your hair." "You want me to be Samson?" "Yes."

A few months later, my father was called to a meeting in Tel Aviv. There were six people, he was the youngest. Yossi told them that an ultra-Orthodox Jew was spying for the Arabs. Yossi said, "He must be killed." There was shouting and screaming, "Are we sure?", "How can we kill a Jew?" But, in the end, all agreed. Yossi looked at my father. "You are from an ultra-Orthodox family. You can pass for one of them."

My father went to the religious district of Jerusalem. It was as if a Jewish village had been lifted from Poland. The smells, everyone dressed in black, the women looking at the ground. And the same divisions. One group sings and dances. For another, singing and dancing is a sin until the Messiah comes. My father knew from Yossi which group to look for. He approached an old man and asked if he could join them for prayers. He had to be careful to speak only Yiddish. He said he wanted to study the Torah. They accepted him. They wanted to arrange a marriage, he said he was not opposed. With a word here and another there, my father let it be known he believed the Zionists were bringing trouble on all Jews.

Weeks passed. One day, a man named Shabtai came and asked about his family in Poland, about why my father had come to Palestine. A few days later, Shabtai said he needed help—he had a truck, the driver was sick. My father said, "I don't know how to drive." Shabtai said, "You can learn." They loaded empty crates on the truck. My father drove slowly, like someone beginning. Shabtai spoke. "The rabbis say that when the Messiah comes, only then will Israel be redeemed. The Zionists believe they can force the Almighty to do as they please. They have made of Palestine an idol. It is Palestine they worship in the place of the Almighty."

My father drove while Shabtai slept. When they arrived in the Arab market, a man approached. Speaking together in Arabic, he and Shabtai walked down a path and away from sight. Two Arab boys helped my father load the produce on the truck. Soon Shabtai returned. My father drove back to Jerusalem and Shabtai slept.

For a few more weeks my father prayed and studied. He met the girl they had chosen for him. Shabtai spoke of his respect for the Arabs. He said they were a pious people, not like the Zionists.

Then Shabtai asked my father to drive again. In the truck, my father asked, "If Zionism is to be stopped, what can we do?" Shabtai slept.

They reached the same Arab village. Again Shabtai left, again the two Arab boys helped my father to load the produce. Shabtai returned and they set off. Shabtai said, "Before the Zionists came, Palestine was quiet. In the beginning, I believed nothing will come of it. But each day there are more Zionists. Only the Arabs can stop Zionism. We must give them information about the activities of the Zionists. To do this we need spies in the Zionist organizations." My father said, "It would be a blessing to do such work." Shabtai didn't answer. My father asked, "How would I report to you?" Shabtai said, "Why would you report to me? Why not to the Arabs?" My father panicked. Was he suspicious? "I don't speak Arabic," he said. Shabtai said, "It is not a decision to be made in haste." A moment later, Shabtai slept.

They came to an empty part of the road. My father stopped the motor, and pushed the accelerator until he smelled petrol. Then he held the ignition until Shabtai woke. They got out of the truck. Shabtai took a screwdriver and opened the front. Shabtai reached into the engine. My father pulled the front down and at the same time stuck a knife into his side.

My father hid Shabtai's body under the produce. He cleaned up the blood and waited until the motor was clear of petrol. He drove to a different Arab village and, making expressions and moving his hands, he explained he would pay two men to do some work. They drove into Jerusalem and stopped by a café. My father motioned for the Arabs to wait. He entered the café, left from a back door, and went to a safe-house. He cut his hair and burned his clothing.

The next day, two Arabs were arrested for the murder of an Orthodox Jew. Yossi was pleased. Shabtai's friends would know that he was not killed by an Arab. At the same time, the Zionists demanded that the British deal with Arab violence against Jews.

My father said, "I befriended a man, then I killed him. And, as we had planned, the blame fell on the Arabs."

Two weeks later, two weeks after the nineteen sixty-seven war, I returned to Israel.

• • •

Nineteen thirty-seven. The British come up with a new idea. Partition. They will divide Palestine. A Jewish state, an Arab state.

The Zionists have already lost Transjordan. Now we are asked to give up more.

The left wing, the Labour Party, didn't like partition but they thought, "Part of Palestine is better than all of nothing." The right wing were one hundred percent opposed.

The Arabs of Palestine also did not want partition. The Zionists said, "You Arabs, you have so many countries." The Arabs of Palestine said, "Egypt is not ours. Iraq is not ours. We have only one country. This one." The British said, "Look at the poor Jews. Look how they have been treated." The King of Saudi Arabia said, a few years later, *(reads)* "What injury have the Arabs done to the Jews of Europe? Amends should be made by the criminal. Give the Jews and their descendants the choicest lands and homes of the Germans."

If you were an Arab, what would you say?

Canada has ten states, yes? Give this Prince Edward Island to the Palestinians. It is a small part of your country. The citizens of Prince Edward Island could learn Arabic or they could move to Montreal.

• • •

Then the Second World War begins.

And ends.

The British, still confused, gave their problem to the United Nations and, in nineteen forty-seven, the United Nations voted to partition Palestine into a Jewish state, an Arab state, and an international zone around Jerusalem. The Arabs of Palestine fought against partition and, as we know, they lost. On May fourteen, nineteen hundred and forty-eight, the Jewish State was proclaimed. The next day, the armies of Egypt, Lebanon, Jordan, Syria, Iraq and Saudi Arabia invade.

One must look at history with both eyes. The Zionists did not want war but they expected war and they were prepared. For many years, the Zionists trained a militia and, in this war, the Zionists had more men and women with weapons than did the six Arab states together. And the Arab countries were not one united force. Golda Meir—who became Prime Minister of Israel—negotiated with King Abdallah of Jordan. About these negotiations she wrote: *(reads)* "It was agreed that Abdallah would control Arab Palestine if he did not interfere with efforts to set up a Jewish state."

Jordan had the largest army of the Arab states. And Golda Meir says they made a deal. There would be no war between Jordan and Israel. And there would be no Palestinian state.

Should we be ashamed that instead of being weak and relying on miracles we put our faith in strength of arms and secret negotiations?

In front of whom should Jews be ashamed?

Like many of the world's people, Jews have been victims. But sometimes, a people can make history.

It is sometimes good to appear weak, but never to be weak.

Israel exists because the Zionists counted soldiers and weapons and determination.

• • •

(reads) "The first room was dark, everything in disorder, but there was no one. In the second, amid all sorts of debris, I found some bodies, cold. Here, the cleaning up had been done with machine guns, then hand grenades. It had been finished off with knives, anyone could see that. The same thing in the next room, but as I was about to leave, I heard something like a sigh. I turned over all the bodies, and eventually found a little girl of ten, mutilated by a hand grenade, but still alive. I gave orders for the bodies to be loaded on the truck, and went on to the next house. Everywhere it was the same horrible sight. I found out there had been about four hundred people in the village of Dir Yassin. About fifty escaped. All the rest had been deliberately massacred in cold blood."

From the report of Jacques de Reynier, Head of International Red Cross in Palestine.

More from Monsieur de Reynier: *(reads)* "The affair of Dir Yassin had immense repercussions. A general terror was built up among the Arabs, a terror astutely fostered by the Jews. Driven by fear, the Arabs left their farms, villages, and whole towns."

It was the right-wing Zionists—a small group, a hundred men—who carried out the events at Dir Yassin, yet my father said, "We must all bear the shame."

Of course, it is easy to bear shame. It is more difficult to refuse the opportunities presented.

Joseph Shectman, a Zionist involved with land distribution, wrote: *(reads)* "Twelve hundred square miles of Arab-owned land was deserted as a result of the Arab flight. In addition, seventy-three thousand rooms in abandoned houses became ownerless in towns and villages. It is difficult to overestimate the tremendous role this abandoned Arab property played in the settlement of thousands of Jewish immigrants."

All wars create refugees. The Arab-Israeli war of nineteen forty-eight turned seven hundred and fifty thousand Palestinian Arabs into refugees. When the war ended, these refugees were not permitted to return to their homes in Israel.

My father said Israel should let the Arab refugees return. What would you have done?

My father said, "If the Jews are fighting for freedom, is it permitted to kill the first-born sons of the Egyptians?"

My father could have returned to Poland as soon as he stepped from the boat in Jaffa and saw that Palestine was not a land without people.

In nineteen fifty-six, Moshe Sharett resigned as Prime Minister of Israel. *(reads)* "I have learned that the state of Israel cannot be ruled in our generation without deceit and adventurism. In the end, history will justify both the stratagems of deceit and the acts of adventurism. All I know is that I, Moshe Sharett, am not capable of them, and I am therefore unsuited to lead the country."

The new Israel was filled with men like my father and Moshe Sharett.

My father left Israel.

So what did the Zionists get in nineteen forty-eight? The eastern half of *Eretz Yisrael* was already Jordan. Judea and Samaria went to Jordan. Gaza went to Egypt. They got half of Jerusalem. They got half a country.

The right wanted to keep fighting. *(reads)* "The partition of the Homeland is illegal. It will never be recognized. It will not bind the Jewish people. Jerusalem was and will forever be our capital. The land of Israel will be restored to the people of Israel. All of it. And forever."

In the first election after independence, the right-wing party, the Herut, received twelve percent of the vote. Israelis were tired from fighting.

• • •

This is where history might have stopped. If the Palestinians had forgotten Palestine, if the Arab countries accepted defeat, we too might have forgotten our dream, of an Israel in all of the land ruled by King David.

But the Arabs did not forget. And Israel's decisive victory in the nineteen sixty-seven war and our capture of Judea and Samaria, and Gaza, of all the land between the Jordan River and the sea, reawakened the dream.

Two changes came together to ensure that this time, the dream would not die.

In Eastern Europe, as we know, most religious Jews opposed Zionism, believing that Zionism delayed the Messiah's coming. But now, through perhaps a miracle, many religious Jews have decided that the Messiah is waiting at the door, and that if we abandon even one inch of *Eretz Yisrael*, He will not enter.

Remember the Sephardic Jews, the Jews of Northern Africa and the Middle East? We forgot about them. But now they come back. Israel was a new country. She needed people. The Zionists believed that hundreds of thousands of Jews from Europe and America would come to Israel when the state was declared. Did you go? Did your parents go? Even the Jews in the displaced persons camps of Europe preferred America. The socialist Zionists said we need people, so we will bring the Jews of North Africa and the Middle East to Israel. And they came. But what should the socialists do with these Jews who they believed were primitive and uneducated? They didn't want them in their kibbutzim. They were kept in tents while the immigrants from Europe were put in the abandoned houses of the Arabs. These Sephardic Jews, kept from the mainstream of Israeli life, gave their support to the other group kept from the mainstream, the right-wing Herut. The oppressed masses chose the right wing instead of the socialists.

• • •

My father is no longer alive. But he would say today, "If we sit and talk with the Palestinians, we can live together in peace." My father would want to be just and fair.

Zionism was successful, not because it was just and fair, but because it was smart and strong. They talked and they planned and they argued and they discussed but they did what was necessary. Now, these old men sit and talk about the original goals of Zionism—which they abandoned; about their principles—which they changed when they were not convenient. They sit and talk and they ask what went wrong.

What went wrong? I will tell you. Were the Zionists wrong to accept partition? At the time, Ben Gurion said there was no choice—I believe him. At the same time, the young lion said, *(reads)* "I do not see partition as the final solution to the Palestine question." He said, *(reads)* "After the formation of a large army in the wake of the establishment of the state, we will abolish partition and expand to the whole of Palestine."

What went wrong? For twenty years the dream was buried. Even the young lion, when he was old, abandoned the dream. Now it is reawakened—should we be ashamed?

"It isn't fair," calls my father from his grave.

History is not the result of what is fair, but simply what has happened. The Zionists were wonderful people but in the end they did what needed to be done and fairness shrivelled beside the practical necessities. The Zionists are not alone. They were not special. The Spanish and the French and the British murdered and enslaved whole nations and took whole continents. We want only a few hectares. Is it fair? Why don't you return your country to the Indians? The only difference is that you took their land a hundred years ago. You live here, you're not leaving, you will not return this land to its fair owners. These are facts. In a hundred years, Israel, in its proper borders, will be a fact. A hundred years later, whatever happened before is fair. As long as you're the winner.

• • •

Do the Palestinians have a right to a country? Yes. Of course. They have simply to take it from us.

The great Jewish humanitarians, the intellectuals, the artists—those who say, "Negotiate," "Give up Judea and Samaria," "Live with the Arabs"—let them be generous and compassionate and have love for all living things. They will be remembered, these tender poets, and the Gentiles will speak of their wisdom and their gentle voices. And we, who refuse to abandon the dream, will lead Israel to victory after victory. Perhaps we will be cursed, perhaps forgotten. But we will have created a strong Israel, *Eretz Yisrael*, a fact.

The old Zionists did what was needed. Their time is passed. We don't need their approval and their regrets and their excuses.

Compromise with the Arabs? Live side-by-side in peace—a Jewish state, a Palestinian state? Compromise—is for the weak as miracles are for the weak.

It's very simple. What the Arabs want they cannot have, not one foot, not one inch. Judea and Samaria is ours. Gaza is ours. Jerusalem is ours. And will never be negotiable.

Compromise—is for the weak as miracles are for the weak. Jews are no longer weak. We need neither compromise nor miracles.

We are the inheritors of the Zionist struggle. We have made a decision and will not be stopped. We have soldiers with determination. We have weapons of great power. And we have excellent generals.

We will do what must be done. The uprisings will end when the Arabs learn that Jewish rule in *Eretz Yisrael* is a fact. If they don't like it, they will leave.

And we will not beg the approval of the Gentiles. What do we expect—that suddenly the Gentiles will like what Jews do?

If they want to help us—fine. If it fits in with their strategic interest, we will take what they give. If the United States offers weapons and dollars, we won't refuse. But if the United States decides its interests are better served by Syria or Saudi Arabia, we will take care of ourselves.

If the whole world is against us, is this something new for Jews? We will take care of ourselves.

• • •

The Zionist enterprise was based on the love of Jews for the land of Israel. They took that longing and love and coupled it with negotiations and deals and compromises, but the love underlay it all. And the love remains. Not for any country, but for Israel. Not for any Israel, but for *Eretz Yisrael*, every inch of it. If you love a person, you love a whole person, not a wrist and a thigh. If we love Israel, we love the whole of Israel, not just Tel Aviv and Eilat and half of Jerusalem. Judea and Samaria as much as Haifa and Tiberias. And the Gaza and yes, the East Bank of the Jordan is also part of the land of Israel, we must say it, the whole of Israel as King David ruled it.

Let the Arabs send their armies against us. If we are resolute, if we are ready to sacrifice, we shall not be defeated. We shall take strength from the land.

Yes, we want peace and we shall have peace—on our terms. We shall choose a never-ending war over an Israel cut up and divided. We shall not shrink from the methods God used to rescue us from Egypt. If we fight with the courage and determination of the Zealots—and if we are willing to die a thousand deaths—we cannot be defeated.

The descendants of King David shall again rule all of ancient Israel. The land of Israel belongs to the people of Israel. All of it and forever.

• • •

I want to thank again, Rabbi Hirsch for his hospitality, and Ms. Wynowski for allowing me this opportunity to speak. *Shalom.*

End.

• Bibliography •

*(This bibliography, by no means complete, consists of books and articles
I found particularly useful or provocative. —A.M.)*

Avishai, Bernard. *The Tragedy of Zionism: Revolution and Democracy in the Land of Israel*. New York: Farrar, Straus, Giroux, 1985.
Avnery, Uri. *My Friend, the Enemy*. Chicago: Chicago Review, 1987.
Begin, Menachem. *The Revolt*. London: W.H. Allen, 1979.
Clausewitz, Carl Von. *On War* and especially the introduction by Anatol Rapoport. London: Penguin Books, 1988.
Cohn-Sherbok. *The Jewish Heritage*. Oxford: Basil Blackwell, 1988.
Eban, Abba. *My People: The Story of the Jews*. New York: Random House, 1968.
Flapan, Simha. *The Birth of Israel: Myths and Realities*. New York: Pantheon Books, 1987.
Grossman, David. *The Yellow Wind*. New York: Farrar, Straus, Giroux, 1988.
Halevi, Ilan. *A History of the Jews: Ancient and Modern*. London: Zed Books, 1987.
Harkabi, Yehoshafat. *The Bar Kokhba Syndrome: Risk and Realism in International Politics*. Chappaqua, New York: Rossel Books, 1983.
———. *Israel's Fateful Decisions*. London: I.B. Tauris & Co, 1988.
Josephus. *The Jewish War*. Harmondsworth, England: Penguin Books, 1987.
Khalidi, Walid, ed. *From Haven to Conquest: Readings in Zionism and the Palestine Problem until 1948*. Washington: Institute for Palestine Studies, 1987.
Morris, Beni. "Revising Zionist History." *Tikkun*, 3, 6 (Nov/Dec 1988).
———. "The Eel and Zionist History." *Tikkun*, 5, 1 (Jan/Feb 1990).
Oz, Amos. *In the Land of Israel*. New York: Harcourt-Brace-Jovanovich, 1983.
Said, Edward and Christopher Hitchens, eds. *Blaming the Victims: Spurious Scholarship and the Palestinian Question*. London: Verso, 1988.
Said, Edward. *The Question Of Palestine*. New York: Times Books, 1979.
Shalom, Moshe Ish. "The Problem with Halakhic Ethics." *Tikkun*, 4, 2 (March/April 1989).
Shamas, Anton. "The Morning After." *New York Review of Books*, 35, 14 (September 29, 1988).
Slonim, Reuben. *To Kill a Rabbi*. Toronto: ECW Press, 1987.
Teveth, Shabtai. *Ben Gurion: The Burning Ground: 1886-1948*. Boston: Houghton-Mifflin, 1987.
Weizman, Ezer. *The Battle for Peace*. Toronto: Bantam Books, 1981.

The Murder of Isaac
a play in two acts

Motti Lerner

translated from the Hebrew by Anthony Berris

• **Motti Lerner** •

Motti Lerner was born in Israel in 1949. He studied mathematics and physics at the Hebrew University, Jerusalem. He studied theatre in various theatre workshops in London and San Francisco. In 1976-1979 he wrote and directed plays for experimental and street theatres, and in 1979-1984 he was a director and dramaturg at the Khan Theatre in Jerusalem. Since 1984 he has been a freelance playwright and screenwriter for the major theatres and TV channels in Israel. His plays have been produced in the U.S., England, Germany, Switzerland, Austria, and Australia. He currently teaches Political Playwriting at Tel Aviv University.
In 1992 Motti Lerner was writer in residence at The Centre for Postgraduate Hebrew Studies in Oxford. In 1994 he won the Prime Minister of Israel Award for Writers, and in 1997 he was Visiting Professor at the Drama Department, Duke University, North Carolina. In 2000 he participated in the International Writers Program at the University of Iowa. He frequently lectures at European and American Universities on various issues regarding Israeli theatre and especially about Israeli theatre and the Israeli-Palestinian conflict.

• Location •

The action takes place in an Israeli Ministry of Defense rehabilitation centre for post-traumatic stress disorder (PTSD) cases, some of whom have been there since the 1948 War of Independence. The centre is run as a closed hospital but there is no military atmosphere. A number of patients are allowed to come and go as they please, but the majority are not allowed out as they are incapable of functioning on the outside. Some are not allowed out as they might constitute a danger to those around them when suffering an anxiety attack. Although the centre is a state institution, there is an obvious desire to do as much as possible for the patients. The atmosphere is supportive and pleasant. The patients are treated by psychiatrists and psychologists, and cared for by male and female nurses. The treatment is quite effective and many of the patients live in the hope of being discharged one day and going back to living a normal life, but among them are cases who have been treated at the centre for many years. The majority of the patients are visited by their families, especially those whose parents are still alive, but the older patients whose parents have died and whose friends have returned to the routine of their lives, have been forgotten and are only visited under exceptional circumstances. The centre's administration is constantly trying to improve treatment and ease the patients' suffering. The majority undergo medicinal treatment and conventional psychological therapy, but every now and again they also undergo non-conventional treatment—group therapy, psychodrama, and various other relaxation techniques. This is how the play performed by the patients is born—a play that the administration views as a means of helping them to cope with the reality outside the centre's walls.

• The Time •

One evening in 1998, when the patients perform the play they have written before an audience of family members, the centre's medical staff and the other patients.

• The Set •

The centre's hall. The stage is empty except for the patients' beds. This emptiness imbues the place with a non-realistic atmosphere that creates the sense of a nightmare. Most of the actors are onstage during the greater part of the play, follow what is happening and react to it. In most cases where the script indicates that a character exits, it means that he leaves the acting area, but remains onstage. The actors will exit the stage to behind the scenes only if there is a particular justification for it.

•The Music •

Despite the fact that the music is performed by the patients, it is rich, theatrical, and for the most part its gaiety contrasts starkly with the pain that is the play's subject.

• Note •

As noted above, *The Murder of Isaac* is constructed as a play-within-a-play. The dialogues written and rehearsed by the patients are printed **in this font**, while those created as the play is staged due to the various snags and interruptions appear <u>in this one</u>.

• Production History •

The Murder of Isaac was first produced at Heilbronn Municipal Theatre, Germany, in November 1999, with the following company:

Principal roles   Peter Anger
                      Ingrid Richter-Wendel
                      Henning Kohne

Directed by Johannes Klaus
Designed by Thomas Pekny
Music by Heinrich Huber

. . .

The Murder of Isaac had its American premiere at Centerstage, Baltimore, Maryland in February 2006 with the following company:

Shulamit	Lise Bruneau	Binder	David Margulies
Talia	Charlotte Cohn	Avi	Chaz Mena
Female Guard	Kelli Danaker	Avner	Tzahi Moskovitz
Lola	Mia Dillon	Yigal	Benjamin Pelteson
Musician	Daniel Feyer	Eliahu	Jeffrey Ware
Yuda	Olek Krupa	Mendel	Gordon Joseph Weiss
Boris	Dan Manning	Natan	Joe Zaloom

Artistic Director: Irene Lewis
Managing Director: Michael Ross
Directed by Irene Lewis
Music composed and directed by Eric Svejcar
Scenic design by Christopher Barreca
Costumes designed by Candice Donnelly
Lighting designed by Mimi Jordan Sherin
Sound designed by David Budries

• **Characters** •

BINDER - A 67-year-old amputee who plays the murdered Prime Minister. He was wounded in the battle for Jerusalem in 1948 but has been at the centre since 1954. On the face of it, he shows no signs of mental disability. He has maintained his intellectual capacity, keeps up with world events and continues to formulate his worldview in accordance with the changes taking place in the world. However, he suffers from severe anxiety as he feels that somebody is going to assassinate him at any time. The other patients respect him despite his limitations and accept his leadership because of his wisdom. He led them through the play's writing process and it is he who emcees it to ensure that it reaches its conclusion.

LOLA - A 67-year-old widow and bereaved mother who plays the Prime Minister's Wife. Both her sons were killed in the Yom Kippur War of 1973. Her husband died soon after and since then she has been a volunteer matron at the centre. She is a strong, motherly woman who is devoted to the patients and has even established a choir of which she is the conductor.

NATAN - He is 53, blind, wears dark glasses and uses a cane. He plays the Head of Security Services and a Bereaved Father. In 1973 he served as a private in a home front unit, but was caught in a bombardment and wounded. He has been at the centre for 25 years. Deep down he feels that despite his blindness he can see the truth more clearly than the sighted. In recent years he has lived in total isolation. Nobody visits him.

AVNER - He is 35 and wheelchair-bound. He plays the Attorney General, a Mourner, and a Poet. He was a medic in an infantry unit. He suffered Post-Traumatic Stress Disorder (PTSD) during an air raid on our forces in 1982 and has been at the centre ever since. Despite the fact that his legs were not injured, he is incapable of standing; his only way of coping with the severe anxiety in which he lives is by constantly dozing.

TALIA - 28 years old. She wears a short skirt. She is a former opera singer. She has been at the centre since 1996 after suffering severe body burns and losing her hair when the bus she was on was blown up. She wears a wig. Most of the patients are unaware of this. In the course of the play she occasionally exposes her body to tease the audience. She plays an Announcer and the Girlfriend of a young man murdered in a terrorist outrage. Her family visits her very rarely.

YUDA - 51 years old, plays the Leader of the Opposition. He was wounded in the battle for Jerusalem in 1967 and also suffered PTSD. He was single when he was wounded but is still a ladies' man. His anxiety level is high. Weeping and shouting arouse terror in him. He is considered a dangerous patient who cannot be allowed outside the centre for fear that he will harm those around him. Despite this he is convinced that he has been hospitalized by mistake. For years he has tried vainly to be discharged from the centre and return to the army. He is charismatic, impulsive and belligerent.

SHULAMIT - A 38-year-old religious woman who plays a Settler. Up to 1994 she lived in a settlement. Her husband fought in Lebanon in 1986 and returned home suffering from PTSD, but was never hospitalized. In 1994 a terrorist broke into their home and murdered her husband and two of their children. Since then she has been hospitalized at the centre. Her two young children who survived the attack were given over to custody in another settlement. Over the years her children have broken off contact with their mother. Due to her severe anxiety she is not allowed out of the centre. She is embittered and resentful, yet is still a compulsive giggler.

AVI - He is 36 and a "born again" Jew. He plays a Rabbi, an Assistant Rabbi, an Activist in the National Party, a Settler, and a Settler Leader. Throughout the play he carries a suitcase containing cans of peanuts. With the outbreak of the Lebanon War in 1982 he deserted from the front, but was handed over to the army by his father. He then served as a guard in a POW camp. During a riot there he lost control and shot 28 prisoners. On his first leave he went home and killed his father. He has lived at the centre ever since. He suffers from asthma and frequently uses an inhaler.

MENDEL - A 55-year-old ex-colonel in the armoured corps. He plays an Activist in the National Party and a Settler. He was taken prisoner in 1973 and repatriated in serious physical and mental condition after nine months of torture. He has been at the centre since 1974. Over the years he has lost contact with his family. He clutches onto his rank as the last proof of his status.

ELIAHU - A 50-year-old ultra-Orthodox Jew who was born in Jerusalem's Me'ah She'arim quarter. He is married and has ten children. He plays a Settler Rabbi. He was a gravedigger who served in a special unit for locating the body parts of war and terrorist action casualties. He has been at the centre since 1996 after suffering severe trauma in the wake of a terrorist attack. Since suffering the trauma he is constantly immersed in finding ways of reforming and saving the world. His contact with his family has been severed.

YIGAL - About 30, wears a yarmulke, and plays the Prime Minister's Murderer. Carries a "theatre" pistol. Has been at the centre since 1988 after being wounded by a roadside bomb in Lebanon. Since then he has become more religious, but at the same time he is filled with anxiety that God has abandoned him. He is hostile towards Binder because Binder is a complete atheist and because he feels that Binder derides him.

BORIS - About 55, a guard at the centre. He is fat and strong. He has worked at the centre for about 20 years and is armed with a baton and a pistol. The patients are frightened of him because he uses excessive force when called to restore order. He follows the play with which he is very familiar, and as he is an excellent singer, every now and again he joins in the songs from the guard post where he sits.

MUSICIANS - According to the possibilities and needs. They, too, have suffered PTSD in the various wars.

• Characters in the Play-Within-the-Play •

PRIME MINISTER *played by Binder*
PRIME MINISTER'S WIFE *played by Lola*
PRIME MINISTER'S MURDERER *played by Yigal*
HEAD OF SECURITY SERVICES *played by Natan*
BEREAVED FATHER *played by Natan*
ATTORNEY GENERAL *played by Avner*
MOURNER *played by Avner*
POET *played by Avner*
ANNOUNCER *played by Talia*
GIRLFRIEND *played by Talia*
LEADER OF THE OPPOSITION *played by Yuda*
SETTLERS *played by Shulamit, Avi, Mendel*
SETTLER LEADER *played by Avi*
SETTLER RABBI *played by Eliahu*
HEAD OF TORAH SAGES *played by Eliahu*
RABBI *played by Avi*
ASSISTANT RABBIS *played by Avi, Mendel*
ACTIVISTS *played by Avi, Mendel*

• *The Murder of Isaac* •

Act One
Scene I

*As the lighting comes up the stage is almost empty. In the far corner
BORIS the guard is sitting on his chair drinking tea. Enter ELIAHU.*

ELIAHU. We'll be starting right away, Boris... *(He looks for somebody in the
audience.)* Yes. With God's help.... We'll be starting right away.... In just
a moment... *(thinks he has recognized somebody)* Excuse me, sir... *(realizes his
mistake)* I'm sorry. I thought you were... *(Again, he thinks he has recognized
him.)* Sir, are you really sure you're not the...? *(reconsiders)* Sorry, it's just that
you look like him...

> *Enter SHULAMIT carrying a broom. She sweeps the stage vigorously to
> conceal her excitement.*

(to SHULAMIT) You've already swept it a dozen times...

SHULAMIT. I've swept it and you've dirtied it...

ELIAHU. That's how you sweep? *(takes the broom from her and demonstrates)*

SHULAMIT. *(She takes the broom. He gives up. She turns to the audience.)* I also do
my own laundry. And I don't touch their food either. They served meat one day
and said it was lamb, but I could see it was pork right off... *(laughs)*

> *Meanwhile ELIAHU continues looking at the audience. As he does
> so, YIGAL enters and sits down on a bed at the far end of the stage.
> MENDEL, who is frightened by the audience, peeps from behind
> the scenes every now and again, and immediately hides. Enter TALIA
> wheeling the dozing AVNER in his wheelchair. She parks him in his
> place, blows a noisy kiss to BORIS and addresses her mother who is in
> the audience.*

TALIA. Mother! It's me. Your daughter. *(lifts her skirt showing her behind)*
Remember now? *(to an enthusiastic member of the audience)* You can come and
see me after the play. *(to her mother)* And don't leave in the intermission,
Mother. I want to show you who I fuck here. One of the doctors. And the
administrator. And the cook. And two guards. And there are the four soldiers
who came a couple of months ago. Nineteen years old. If I didn't give them
a blow-job once a week they'd have killed themselves a long time ago... *(turns
back to the enthusiastic member of the audience)* I receive guests in Room 4,
Entrance 2, darling... *(exits)*

SHULAMIT. There are drugs for that, but they don't give them to her... *(laughs)*

ELIAHU, who put his hands over his ears during the "show", addresses someone in the audience.

ELIAHU. You, sir, are the minister of defense. Aren't you? You probably didn't want to draw attention to yourself. But you can't fool me. I saw you once, when you were a general...

SHULAMIT. *(to the audience)* All his life he's been waiting for the minister of defense...

ELIAHU. Isn't he the minister of defense?

SHULAMIT. No... *(laughs)*

ELIAHU. *(to the "minister")* I beg your pardon, sir...

SHULAMIT. We'll be starting right away. They're getting ready...

MENDEL. *(peeps out, to the audience)* Nobody's getting ready. They're all sitting in the lounge, watching news of the war... *(hides for a moment and then peeps out again)* They're waiting for the names of the dead. There's nine already... *(hides for a moment and then peeps out again)* How can we put on a play on a day like this?

Enter TALIA leading blind NATAN to his place next to AVNER's wheelchair. As she does so, she again notices the excited member of the audience and reveals her shoulder to him.

TALIA. Don't forget, darling. Entrance 2, Room 4... *(shows a leg)* You can bring some friends too, honey... *(exits)*

ELIAHU. *(to the "minister")* Mr. Minister, I would like to speak to you after the ceremony. I know you don't have much time, but I have a few ideas I'm sure will be of interest to you...

NATAN. *(scans the audience with his blind eyes)* There's no minister here, Eliahu, I don't see him...

SHULAMIT. *(to the audience as she sweeps)* And he thinks he can see... *(laughs)*

As she speaks, enter AVI, carrying his suitcase. He approaches ELIAHU and whispers something to him.

ELIAHU. *(angrily)* Out of the question. No way. No way. I don't care what they say...

NATAN. What's going on over there?

AVI. There's not going to be any play. We shall not make a mockery of the dead... *(to the audience)* Perhaps they're our relatives? First we should know their names...

MENDEL. *(peeping out)* First we must rend our clothes. First we must mourn...

ELIAHU. *(angrily)* Many died yesterday. Many will die tomorrow. Only after the Day of Judgment will there be no more dead... *(hurries to the "minister" in the audience)* Mr. Minister, you must issue a clear order... we will not keep silent...

(starts trembling) Mr. Minister, these are difficult times for all of us…. Yesterday the sun stopped in its orbit for a full hour… the Day of Judgment is nigh…

> *Enter LOLA who hurries over to him, sits him on one of the beds and sits down next to him.*

LOLA. Sit down. Do you want a glass of water? Do you want to go back to your room? *(He calms down.)*

MENDEL. *(peeps out)* We must dig graves. We must bury the dead… *(hides)*

NATAN. Ladies and gentlemen, please remain seated. We'll be starting right away…

MENDEL. *(peeps out)* And then get into the tanks and start the engines… *(hides)*

NATAN. All of us are ready…

AVI. There's no play! Go home! Go! *(He loses his breath.)*

MENDEL. *(peeps out)* And then we must load the cannons… *(hides)*

LOLA. *(to AVI)* Sit down… *(She sits him down then speaks to the audience.)* Good evening. My name's Lola and I've been a volunteer here for twenty-five years. Ever since my two sons fell in the war. I know what mourning is and I think that even on a day like today we can and we should…

AVI. *(gets up and shouts to the electrician)* Turn off the lights…. Turn off the lights…

> *He has difficulty breathing. LOLA hurries over to him, takes the inhaler from his pocket and puffs the medication into his mouth. Enter BINDER, limping, leaning on his cane. MENDEL plucks up his courage and enters after him.*

BINDER. We're starting!

AVI. Who'll listen to us on a day like this, Binder…

BINDER. People who don't want any more days like this…

MENDEL. We're shaming our dead…

BINDER. We're honouring them… *(to the audience)* We know there's a war going on outside. We've seen the numbers of the dead. They died because nobody took the trouble to stop this damn war. Nobody on our side, nobody on theirs…. There are also three times more wounded… and there are many more who you only think have survived… *(gestures at those around him)* Look at us. You can't tell us: "Wait until the war is over." Our war will never be over… *(signals the orchestra to start playing)*

> *The orchestra starts playing, LOLA organizes some of the patients into a choir and she conducts.*

CHOIR. We are the living dead
Showing you our faces,
Faces defeated and miserable,
Faces that are invisible.

We have been the stain on your war diaries
Since the war of forty-eight, since the war of fifty-six.

These are faces that hide from the light
In a place where black is blacker than night,
A place where blue flows stronger than the Flood,
And red is redder and more bitter than blood.

We have been the stain on your war diaries
Since the war of sixty-seven, since the war of seventy-three.

Here the sounds are scarred and pungent
The notes are rough and strident
Here the words are coarse and unforgiving
Because fear of death is easier than fear of living.

We have been the stain on your war diaries
Since the war of seventy-three, since the war of eighty-two.

We have no skin in which to hide
Our empty eyes into yours stare wide
Look at us and see who you are
Our dejected faces are yours.

We have been the stain on your war diaries
From then till now…

> *Applause. The singers bow. TALIA uses her bow to reveal a shoulder and then a thigh.*

SHULAMIT. *(to the audience)* She was completely burnt in the suicide bombing by the opera house. She left the building after her singing, and boom!!! When she was brought here she shut herself up in her room. A year later she came out and started with this vulgarity…

NATAN. *(to the audience)* I can also hear from miles away. I've still got some shrapnel in my head that they can't get out. It transmits the sounds to my brain…

> *Helped by LOLA, BINDER gets onto one of the beds. In front of them stand AVNER, NATAN and TALIA as three "security men."*

TALIA. *(announces, singing)* I now present the Prime Minister
Thousands have gathered in the city square
Waiting to hear him an end to war declare…

BINDER. My dear friends. I have just returned from a journey around the world with an agreement in my hands… *(takes out a scroll)* In every country I've presented it, I've met grateful people. They are grateful to us because we have given them hope. Because we have proved to them that even after a hundred years of killing, it is still possible to find wisdom and compassion in Man. Because we have proved to them that wisdom and compassion can overcome bloodthirsty hatred. That Man can find victory in compromise. That he can prefer life over martyrdom. That his good sense can overcome his fanaticism. That his survival can be more meaningful to him than land. The whole world has accepted this agreement. Now you must accept it...

> LOLA, NATAN and TALIA applaud. YUDA, who has been following the action from a corner of the stage, signals the orchestra to play and gets onto the bed that is his stage.

MENDEL. Ladies and gentlemen, the Leader of the Opposition... *(applause)*

YUDA. Thank you. Thank you very much. My dear brothers... *(to the audience)* I too have seen the numbers of the fallen this evening. All of us here send our condolences to the bereaved families. We all face death together and will do everything to loosen its grip around our neck... *(takes the agreement from BINDER)* My dear Mr. Prime Minister. We are grateful to you for this agreement. We congratulate you for it from the bottom of our hearts. *(to the audience)* Our prime minister is a wise man. He was a general too. If he promises us peace, then who are we to doubt him? Despite the fact that we face death every now and again. On the borders. In the streets. On buses. Despite the fact that we are all asking one another "What has happened to our enemies?" Have they come to love us overnight? But he promises peace and we must believe him. After all, he's been a soldier all his life. He would surely not put us at the mercy of these enemies. But perhaps because he has fought all his life, he isn't prepared to go on fighting? Perhaps he has become feeble and no longer able to go on fighting? And if he can't fight he won't bring us peace, because we will only achieve peace through war... *(tears up the agreement)*

MENDEL. Through war!

YUDA. And who will lead you into war? Him? *(points at BINDER)* He no longer believes in war. He doesn't even want to win it. He is afraid of war. That's why he's making *you* afraid of war. And that's why he won't lead you into war.

AVI. You will lead us into war...

SHULAMIT. Into the holy war...

YUDA. Each of our wars has made us stronger and so will this one. Those who *ask* for peace will never achieve it. Only those who *give* peace will achieve it. And so we shall continue fighting until *our enemies* ask for peace...

> Applause.

YUDA. *(to the audience)* They won't manage there much longer without me. Tomorrow they'll call me back to my unit, a machine gun in my hands, grenades on my belt. Burst will follow burst. It's an easy run. Fire from the right! Fire from the left! And I forge ahead. A scratch on my forehead. Never mind. Shrapnel in my shoulder. Don't worry. Forward between burned-out tanks. Jump into the trench, pull out a knife and stab. And stab. Up to the hilt in blood. And the Land will rest for a hundred years...

AVNER, who has opened his eyes, suddenly sees the audience. He is alarmed and calls out.

AVNER. Doctor... call a doctor... morphine, morphine.... call a doctor.... Have some water.... Don't move.... Calm down. Don't move...

YUDA. *(startled)* Shut up already... *(moves away)*

AVNER. My legs, doctor... my legs...

LOLA hurries to him and soothes him. MENDEL addresses one of the doctors in the audience.

MENDEL. Doctor, you promised us we'd be able to go out for a few days after the play. I'm a colonel. I shouldn't have to plead like a private...

LOLA. You'll go out, Mendel, I promised you...

MENDEL. I'm not in prison. I was a POW for nine months...

AVI. We're going to the cup final, doctor... *(gestures at MENDEL)* We've bought tickets...

LOLA. You'll go out too...

TALIA. *(to the doctor)* I haven't been taking pills for two months.

NATAN. I don't go out. I like it here. It's a wonderful place. Nice people. Sometimes they even bring us ladies... *(laughs)*

BINDER. *(soothing them)* You'll all go out. Not for two days, not for three, but four days. I don't envy anybody who comes back earlier. He'll have to talk politics with me from morning till night... *(to the orchestra)* Music!

Scene 2

The home of the chairman of the Judea and Samaria rabbis committee. Enter RABBIS A and B played by AVI and MENDEL. ELIAHU, who plays RABBI C, the committee chairman, looks at them. They are silent.

RABBI C. He's come back with an agreement? *(silence)* He's come back with an agreement or without an agreement? *(Silence. He understands.)* Did he give them everything? *(silence)* Everything?

SHULAMIT. Everything...

RABBIS A and B tear their shirts as a sign of mourning. RABBI A goes to RABBI C and tears his shirt too. RABBI C realizes that the peace agreement has been signed.

SHULAMIT. *(to the audience)* The rabbis warned him not to sign. Even the Almighty warned him... *(laughs)*

RABBI C. Oy, Land of Israel. Oy, Mother. Oy, Hebron and Bethlehem.... Your sweet breasts...

RABBI A. What do we do, Rabbi?

RABBI C. *(weeping)* Oy, Jerusalem, Jerusalem. The first word my lips uttered. Oy, Jerusalem... Jerusalem. Widowed. You have no consolation...

SHULAMIT. I can hear Jerusalem weeping all the time...

RABBI A. What do we do, Rabbi?

RABBI C. *(cries)* Oy, the Temple. The Temple. Where shall we worship you, O Father in Heaven? Father. Oy, Father.... Your children trample you...

RABBI B. Rabbi...

RABBI C. We are orphans. Our crown is fallen. The Holy One hides his countenance from us. The Divine Spirit is weeping.... The Messiah is silent...

SHULAMIT. He isn't silent. He is weeping too...

RABBI B. What do we do, Rabbi?

RABBI C. *(stops weeping all at once)* Everything.... We do everything.... Everything.... Everything...

RABBI A. "Everything" meaning "everything"?

RABBI C. *(forcefully)* Everything.... Everything.... Everything.... Everything.... Everything.... Everything...

RABBI B. You mean really everything?

SHULAMIT. Everything... everything...

RABBI C. *(in a rage)* Everything.... Everything.... Everything.... Everything.... Everything.... Everything.... Everything!

> *At the height of RABBI C's ecstatic outburst YIGAL pulls out a gun and aims at BINDER.*

YIGAL. Everything! *("fires" three shots)* Blessed art thou, O Lord our God, who wreaks our vengeance.

BINDER. *(in a terrible panic)* Ahhhhh... *(He shields his head with his arms.)*

NATAN. *(frightened)* My ears are ringing, Lola...

LOLA. *(angrily, to YIGAL)* Sit down until it's your turn. And put that gun in your pocket. *(to BINDER)* Calm down, Binder, he got confused, that's all...

BINDER. Did you check everyone at the entrance? Their bags too?

LOLA. Yes... *(to AVI)* Bring him some water...

BINDER. Are the doors locked? Are the guards outside?

LOLA. Yes... *(She takes out a tissue and wipes his nose.)*

SHULAMIT. *(to the audience)* When *we* get scared like that she doesn't run after us...

BINDER. *(to the audience)* They're trying to kill me. By running me down. By poisoning me. By throwing me out of a window…

LOLA. These people have come to hear us. We can't continue without you…

BINDER. *(to LOLA)* They'll do anything to shut me up. Just so I won't remind them what war is all about… *(to the audience)* War is a sting on your shoulder. A burning sting! In the dark. Like a hornet's sting. What is it? What's this sting? I've been shot. Who dares? You shout and no one answers. You're all alone in the world. And there's another sting. On the cheek. God, what a terrible noise. And there's nowhere to run. Now there's a flash of lightning and the rumble of thunder. And you're covered in dust and smoke. And you choke and retch. You want to stand up but can't. You try again and fall down. And more lightning and more thunder. And suddenly you feel a dull pain. And the pain slowly spreads. You look to the side. It's hard to see in the darkness. There's something lying there, right next to you. Something weird. Suddenly you understand. *(slaps his artificial leg)* It's your leg. Your leg that has been ripped from your body. And it's still wearing your boot… *(He chokes on his words, LOLA holds his hand.)*

NATAN. *(to TALIA)* Sing, Talia…. Sing your song…. Now…

TALIA. Now?

LOLA. Yes, now.

TALIA. *(looks for her mother in the audience)* Where's my mother?

NATAN. She's right there…

The orchestra plays, TALIA sings.

TALIA. If I'd said the cannon was red hot
You would have said, "Cease fire!"
If I'd said the tank had lost a track
You would have said, "Hold back!"

If I'd said we're out of ammo
You would have said, "Hold on!"
If I'd said the radio's out
You would have said, "Hold fast!"

But I say that our heart is weak
I say that our blood has frozen
I say that our breath has stopped
And you say "Fire! Fire! Fire!"

I say our skin has worn thin
I say that our flesh has crumbled
I say that our bones are feeble
And you say "Fire! Fire! Fire!"

I say that wisdom is hiding
I say our purpose is over

I plead to you, "Let us live"
And you say "Fire! Fire! Fire!"

BINDER. *(to the audience)* I sometimes go out of here…

LOLA. Let's continue, Binder…

BINDER. They take me to see this country of ours. I walk through the streets. I look at the passersby and don't see any pain in their faces. I see people hurrying by. I see people working. People walking. Enjoying themselves. Loving. Quarrelling. But I know. That one's brother is dead. This one's father. That one's son was blown up. This one hides a scar running the length of his belly. That one hides his burn-scarred hand in his pocket. This one hasn't slept since a bomb landed next to him and ripped five people to shreds…

LOLA. Binder…

BINDER. *(indicates SHULAMIT)* Her husband and two children were murdered. Pain is a danger signal. If we cover it up, we won't see the danger coming…

> *LOLA brings the play back on track. She takes a bulletproof vest and offers it to BINDER. Now she's playing the Prime Minister's wife.*

BINDER. I won't wear a bulletproof vest.

LOLA. Didn't you hear, Isaac? The rabbis ordered them to do everything.

BINDER. Nobody will do a thing.

LOLA. The security people told you to wear it…

BINDER. Those rabbis are all talk…

LOLA. But the murderer can hear them…

BINDER. A vest won't deter a murderer. It will only cause damage.

LOLA. What damage?

BINDER. People watch me. Once they see the vest, they'll think I'm afraid…

LOLA. Aren't you afraid?

BINDER. No…

LOLA. If you weren't afraid, you wouldn't be so concerned about hiding it.

BINDER. I wouldn't hide anything from you.

LOLA. You've always listened to me. What's happened? If you're so afraid of being seen as a coward, then say that I'm the coward. Put the vest on, and say I made you wear it.

BINDER. And then they'll say I'm ruled by my wife's fears.

LOLA. They've declared war on you, Isaac! You won't escape them with blind eyes…

BINDER. Blind eyes? With these eyes I can see for another thousand years. A new world. A world without fanaticism. Without nationalism. Without religions. Without borders…

LOLA. Is such a world really possible? Will people truly want it?

BINDER. If we show them its advantages, they'll want it...

LOLA. People are like children. They need religion and nationalism. They certainly need borders...

BINDER. They'll grow up and mature. With these eyes I can already see them. In a world without soldiers. Without wars. Without fear. Without violence. Without hatred. If I can see all that, do I need a bulletproof vest?

Meanwhile, YUDA is trying to flirt with TALIA. Her patience snaps.

TALIA. If you touch me once more I'll cut your prick off...

SHULAMIT. *(to TALIA)* He didn't touch you. Why are you talking nonsense?

YUDA. You should be thankful that somebody comes anywhere near you...

BINDER signals the orchestra to play. Music.

Scene 3

ELIAHU, who plays a SETTLER RABBI, is standing at a lectern on which there is a thick volume of the Talmud. YIGAL addresses the audience.

YIGAL. *(to the audience)* Before I begin, I'd like to tell you that a disaster is about to happen here. A terrible disaster. Hundreds of thousands will die. All the rivers will flow with blood. The sea will be flooded...

BINDER. Not now...

YIGAL. I won't tell you how I know, but I know. I write to the prime minister every day and that stupid idiot doesn't reply. He doesn't care that so many people will die...

BINDER. Okay. They've got it. Begin...

YIGAL. And if we know and do nothing, then God gets even more angry. Because he wants us to prevent the disaster. He wants us to save ourselves. And not one of you has any idea what God does in his wrath...

BINDER. I asked you to begin...

YIGAL. *(determined)* God's lost his patience. Anyone who's killed here today is a warning signal. And when I think what God might do to us tomorrow, my heart starts pounding like a helicopter...

BINDER. *(angrily)* Do you want to go back to the closed ward?

YIGAL. Like that helicopter that rescued me from the fire. Pounding and pounding. And I can't breathe, and I'm sweating, and we continue falling into the abyss, and I'm not sure I can rescue you, but I can't hide any longer from God who keeps forcing me to speak…

BINDER. *(yelling)* Stop it already!

> *YIGAL falls silent. He gradually regains his composure and addresses the RABBI.*

YIGAL. Honoured Rabbi…

RABBI. *(without stopping his study)* Is it you?

YIGAL. Yes, Rabbi.

RABBI. Was it you who asked for an urgent meeting?

YIGAL. Yes, Rabbi.

RABBI. *(closes the book)* Welcome. *(kisses him)* Tell me, if you would be so kind. Don't you have a rabbi?

YIGAL. I do, but lately he hasn't been answering any urgent questions.

RABBI. And how do you know that I'll answer them?

YIGAL. They say that you are a master of erudition on the laws of war.

RABBI. Is that what they say?

YIGAL. So what is the answer?

RABBI. What is the question?

YIGAL. In the matter of heretics, Maimonides says that killing them is our religious duty. If we can kill them by the sword in public, they should be killed right away—and if not, they should be pursued with cunning until they can be killed…

RABBI. That's the answer…

YIGAL. But how can I know if a man is a heretic?

RABBI. He's a heretic because he denies the Torah…

YIGAL. And how can I know that he denies the Torah?

RABBI. If he denies the existence of the Almighty, then all the more so he denies the Torah, which was given to us by the Almighty…

YIGAL. Yes, but how can I know that he denies the existence of the Almighty?

RABBI. If he abandons the holy land of the Almighty, which was given to the Chosen People by the Almighty, then he certainly denies the existence of the Almighty…

YIGAL. Even though he is a Jew?

RABBI. He is a Jew, but the spawn of a beast.

SHULAMIT. And if he is the spawn of a beast, he is not of the seed of Adam…
(laughs)

RABBI. Only we who observe the commandments are of the seed of Adam. And if he is not of the seed of Adam, then the commandment, "Thou shalt not kill" does not apply to him...

YIGAL. *(kisses his hand)* Thank you very much, Honoured Rabbi. *(turns to exit)*

RABBI. Wait a minute. Where are you going? I haven't said a thing. And if they ask you what I said, or didn't say, you say I didn't say what I said. Because if you say that I said what I said, or what I didn't say, then the commandment, "Thou shalt not kill" will not apply to you either...

> But YIGAL leaves. ELIAHU suddenly turns to the "minister of defense" in the audience.

ELIAHU. Your Excellency the Minister of Defense. Now you'll finally hear what I've been waiting so impatiently to tell you...

BINDER. Eliahu, where do you see a minister of defense?

ELIAHU. *(continues)* Now Your Excellency is probably asking himself what a believer such as myself is doing in a place like this...

BINDER. Are you out of your mind? Who told you that the minister of defense was supposed to be here?

ELIAHU. Can't you see I'm speaking to him? *(to the "minister")* I'm one of those black crows who carry plastic bags and fly to your shattered corpses in the killing fields. I'm one of those who collect spilled eyes, amputated fingers, ripped-out tongues and crushed testicles. I'm one of those who try to join a head to its neck, a shin to a thigh and a hand to its arm. I create your dead so you can have bones to weep over...

BINDER. There's no minister here, Eliahu!

ELIAHU. I'm telling you this, Your Excellency, so that you know I'm not softhearted like some people here, and I ask you not to listen to them, sir, when they try to deter you from the war. I can show you in all the writings of the prophets that we must have no fear. Because the Almighty himself will be at our side in person in any war, and we will win it, as it is written in the Book of Zachariah, chapter 13, verse 8...

BINDER. *(loses his patience)* The minister of defense isn't here. He won't be here. There's war going on outside and he's got to run it. He won't trouble himself for us. He's long forgotten that we ever existed...

ELIAHU. *(points at the member of the audience he thought was the minister)* That isn't the minister?

BINDER. No!

ELIAHU. *(to the member of the audience)* My dear sir, I beg you to tell me the truth...

BINDER. *(screams)* He isn't the minister! *(sits despairingly on one of the beds)*

NATAN. My ears are ringing again, Lola...

LOLA. *(moves over to ELIAHU)* Eliahu, please. Calm down…

ELIAHU. *(continues)* Because I've told you the truth, sir, the whole truth… *(to the audience)* And I'll tell you the truth, too…. Yes. We will be victorious in this war. We will strike them with a great and powerful blow. We will annihilate and destroy and devastate them all…

LOLA. You should stop while you still can…

ELIAHU. *(hysterical)* And after this war, men and women and old and young will die intact in their own beds. And all I will have to do is wash and purify them, wrap them in a shroud, dig them a grave, bury them, pray for the elevation of their souls…. O God in Heaven… after this war the Messiah will come and the dead will be resurrected, without a wound and without a bruise, without a scratch and without a burn, and they will have all their limbs…. O God in Heaven… *(He is trembling with excitement. LOLA drags him off. Music.)*

Scene 4

> *BINDER enters the office of the Head of the Council of Torah Sages. MENDEL and AVI, who play the RABBI's ASSISTANTS, are waiting for him. Throughout, AVI is holding his suitcase.*

BINDER. *(to the audience)* Ladies and gentlemen, we regret the disruption. Some of us have suffered so much that their desire for redemption has driven them mad and they think they know how to save the world… *(announces)* **The office of the Council of Torah Sages…**

> *MENDEL and AVI put a yarmulke on BINDER's head and examine his clothing.*

ASST. A. Welcome, Mr. Prime Minister…

ASST. B. When you see the Rabbi, sir, you must wear a yarmulke…

ASST. A. And don't forget to give it back when you leave, sir.

ASST. B. Is your honour sure that his jacket is kosher?

BINDER. Kosher?

ASST. B. *(explains)* That it does not contain, Heaven forbid, a mixture of wool and flax. Where did you buy it?

BINDER. My wife bought it.

ASST. B. Here, in the Holy City?

BINDER. Yes.

ASST. B. Well, so be it. There isn't a single clothing store here today that isn't inspected…

ASST. A. And about your wife. You should wash your hands. Maybe she hasn't cleansed herself in the ritual bath this month…

> *BINDER washes his hands. SHULAMIT suddenly addresses the audience.*

SHULAMIT. Why isn't there a ritual bath here? Ever since I came I've been begging the administration. God wants me pure…

BINDER. Not now, Shulamit… *(She gives up.)*

ASST. A. What about the blessing, sir?

BINDER. What blessing?

ASST. A. "Blessed art thou, O Lord our God, King of the Universe, who hast sanctified us by thy commandments, and hast commanded us concerning the washing of the hands…"

> *BINDER mutters the blessing after him. The assistants say "Amen".*

ASST. B. You're not, God forbid, a communist?

BINDER. No.

ASST. B. Lucky for you, because if you were he wouldn't talk to you.

ASST. A. I trust that you're not by any chance, Heaven forbid, a socialist?

BINDER. No.

ASST. A. Very good. He doesn't talk to socialists either. And don't forget to return the yarmulke before you leave.

> *BINDER accidentally touches AVI's suitcase. He rebukes him angrily.*

AVI. Don't touch it! Don't touch it!

BINDER. I'm sorry…

> *Enter the RABBI, played by YUDA, who has stuck a beard and side-locks onto his face. He is holding a page of text.*

RABBI. Welcome, Isaacle [1]… *(to the audience)* I'm replacing our friend Eliahu, whose cup of suffering, as you have seen, has run over with all the electric shocks they give him here…

BINDER. Peace unto you, Honoured Rabbi…

RABBI. *(reading from the page)* Nu, I see you're wasting no time and putting the "piss" [2] at the top of our agenda. "He who maketh 'piss' in his high places, may he make 'piss' for us and for all Israel."

BINDER. Amen. I'm glad to hear that your honour also seeks peace.

RABBI. "Piss"? We live in "piss" all the time.

---

[1] The Yiddish diminutive of "Isaac", pronounced "icicle".
[2] This is the Rabbi's Yiddish-accented pronunciation of the word "peace".

BINDER. Yes, absolutely. But the country also needs peace…

RABBI. *Nu, nu,* not exactly, Isaacle. It's the pork-eaters who need "piss."

BINDER. Your blood is also spilt in this war sometimes, sir. If bloodshed can be prevented, then should we not prevent it?

RABBI. *Nu,* of course. But how can we prevent bloodshed? By praying to the Almighty, blessed be He…

BINDER. Honoured Rabbi, you have to help me save this country of ours. You have to support the agreement I have reached…

> *ELIAHU, who has recovered backstage and heard YUDA speaking his lines, hurries onto the stage and addresses BINDER as the RABBI.*

RABBI. You come to us to save this country? To us, who have been warning you for a hundred years that even contemplating a country is a great sin? And our warnings have fallen on deaf ears. Six million Jews died just because you couldn't wait for the Messiah and established this accursed state yourselves. And now you too are going to be punished for it. Not for nothing has the Almighty gathered another six million Jews in this Holy Land. Not to save you, Heaven forbid. Not to redeem you. These wars that he condemns you to, are intended to visit your sins upon you and destroy you. All of you. Men, women, the aged, and the young. You will all die.

BINDER. He sent six million to their deaths and now he wants to kill another six million? Why?

RABBI. Because you have interfered with his plans, Isaacle…

BINDER. What is so important in his plans that justifies killing another six million people? Did those men, women, old people and children stand in his way from redeeming the world?

RABBI. Man is a small and insignificant creature, Isaacle. He cannot know God's plans…

BINDER. If man cannot know God's plans, Honoured Rabbi, how can he know that his intentions are good? Can you, Honoured Rabbi, give me a single piece of historical proof of his good intentions? Perhaps they're evil? Perhaps they're even monstrous? Perhaps this God is nothing but a brutal murderer thirsty for human blood? There is ample proof of that in history. And if this God, Honoured Rabbi, is a bloodthirsty murderer, then why worship him? Why fulfill his wishes?

RABBI. You cast doubt on the grace of God? You doubt his goodness, his mercy, his redemption? Those who doubt God's grace are unworthy of it. They are unworthy of his mercy. They are unworthy of his redemption! *(He spits at BINDER.)*

BINDER. *(wiping off the spittle)* The next time you speak to him, Honoured Rabbi, please tell him that I'll manage without his grace and mercy. Or his redemption… *(exits)*

ASST. A. *(calls after BINDER)* The yarmulke... the yarmulke...

RABBI. *(to his assistants)* The day will come when this state will be destroyed, and instead of the Jewish state, a Gentile state will arise. Arabs, Turks, English. And they will enact laws for themselves, and make an army for themselves, and fight their wars, and make their "piss." And they will profane the Sabbath, and sell pork, and commit adultery. What do we care for them? And we, we will build our holy communities here, with *yeshivas* and synagogues and ritual baths. And we will have our own courts. And we will worship the Lord, blessed be he, "each under his own vine and fig tree" forever and ever, until the end of time.

> *The two ASSISTANTS say "Amen" and applaud. ELIAHU is embarrassed by what he has said and addresses the "minister."*

ELIAHU. Mr. Minister, I hope you have not misunderstood what I said. The Almighty does not annihilate without warning. He sends his warnings in intimations in the Holy Scriptures. Only if you do not heed him, there will be great destruction... *(stops, to BINDER)* Is he the minister or isn't he?

BINDER. He isn't!

> *BORIS gets up from his chair and grips his baton. Silence. TALIA suddenly addresses the audience. She speaks quietly but because of the silence she is heard clearly.*

TALIA. Now I know how I want to die. I don't ask for an easy death. Here people usually die with a loud noise. Screaming in agony. But the agony is the easy part. Even when death surprises you with fire or a thunderbolt, you always manage to see it coming and then you're attacked by this terrible fear.... I want to die without that fear. I want to go to the train station and lie down on the track, breathe deeply and hear the announcement through the loudspeakers that the train is about to depart in one minute...

NATAN. *(shouting)* Somebody shut her up!

> *LOLA hurries to TALIA and embraces her. BORIS sits down. YUDA sees AVI about to exit. He quickly grabs his shirt.*

YUDA. Where do you think you're going?

AVI. I'll be right back.

BINDER. Yuda, please...

YUDA. When I tell you to stay, you stay. And when I tell you to talk, you talk...

LOLA. Yuda!

MENDEL. Quiet! I want quiet...

> *YUDA is still holding AVI. BORIS gets up again.*

AVI. *(with difficulty)* The news is coming on now. I wanted to hear the names of the dead.... Perhaps my brother hasn't come because someone from our family has...

YUDA. *(interrupts him)* You know full well why your brother hasn't come to see you. Why he will never come…

MENDEL. I'm a colonel. When I say "quiet," there's quiet…

> *YUDA lets go of AVI. BINDER signals the orchestra to play.*

Scene 5

> *The orchestra plays. YUDA and AVI return to the play. The characters on stage become mourners at a soldier's funeral. YIGAL is lying on a stretcher as the dead soldier.*

TALIA. *(sings)* The Prime Minister has come to the funeral to give the family some support, but his pain is so great that he has no words of comfort…

ELIAHU. *(recites from a prayer book)* "He is the Rock, his work is perfect: a God of truth and without iniquity, just and right is He…" *(murmurs, and then aloud)* The Lord gave, and the Lord hath taken away; blessed be the name of the Lord…"

BINDER. *(interrupting)* It wasn't the Lord who took him away. It was a man. A soldier who shot him…

ELIAHU. Shhhh… *(continues)* "Magnified and sanctified be his great name in the world which he hath created according to his will…" *(murmurs and then aloud)* "He who maketh peace in his high places, may he make peace for us and for all Israel; and say ye, Amen."

BINDER. He won't make peace. There will only be peace if *we* make it…

ELIAHU. Shhh… *(continues)* "May God comfort you among all the other mourners of Zion and Jerusalem…"

BINDER. He won't comfort anybody. We will all mourn until the end of our days. Unless we accept the peace agreement I have brought you…

YUDA. *(to BINDER)* Pardon me, Mr. Prime Minister, but exactly what peace are you talking about?

MENDEL. What exactly would we gain from it?

SHULAMIT. How exactly would we benefit from it?

AVI. Why should we give anything up for it?

ELIAHU. *(angrily)* Shhh… *(continues)* "O God, who art full of compassion, who dwellest on high, grant perfect rest beneath the shadow of thy divine presence…"

YUDA. If you were to propose making peace with the Americans or the British—even with the Germans—we would understand. But with the Arabs?

AVI. With poor, primitive villagers?

MENDEL. Have you ever been in their villages? Have you seen the filth? The sewage in the streets? Their illiterate children running wild in the alleys?

ELIAHU. *(as he prays)* Shhh... "In the exalted places among the holy and pure, who shine as the brightness of the firmament, shelter for evermore under the cover of thy wings..."

SHULAMIT. Arabs have no culture. They don't wash. They stink... *(laughs)*

MENDEL. They fuck camels. Sheep. Murder is nothing to them. They simply slaughter people with knives, axes, whatever they can lay their hands on.

AVI. Do you believe them, the Arabs?

SHULAMIT. They're liars, thieves, they're flatterers... *(laughs)*

ELIAHU. *(as he prays)* Shhh... "Shelter his soul for evermore. The Lord is his portion. May he rest in peace..." *(announces)* Thank you. The next funeral will be held in one hour...

MENDEL. Tell us. Without any hypocrisy. Do you really like Arabs?

AVI. If you like *hummus*, do you have to like the cook?

MENDEL. If you like goat's cheese, do you have to like the goat?

YUDA. Do you see a single Jew who can put his hand on his heart and say that he likes Arabs?

SHULAMIT. Do you see a single Arab who can put his hand on his heart and say that he likes Jews?

BINDER. *(finally manages to get a word in)* Hatred is not a decree of fate. There's no God who commands us to hate. There's no God who commands them to hate. Their hatred will be cured if we stop hating...

Enraged, YIGAL sits up on the stretcher.

YIGAL. There is a God! Blessed be he... and he did command us to hate. To hate and take revenge... blessed be his name... *("shoots" BINDER three times)*

BINDER. *(startled)* No! *(flees to the edge of the stage)*

NATAN. *(despairingly)* Take the gun from him! Take the gun from him!

LOLA. It's nothing, Binder. He forgot again. You know how he is. When he hears "Hello" he pulls out a gun...

BINDER. I'm a sick man. I'll never get out of here. I expect some consideration from you... *(angrily)* They sent him to shoot me so I'll die of fright!... *(sits down on bed and addresses LOLA)* Are you sure you checked everybody at the entrance? And their bags too?

LOLA. Yes... *(to YIGAL)* Why do you keep running after him with that stupid gun? Give it to me...

YIGAL. You keep away!

LOLA. Do you want me to give you an injection?

YIGAL. You keep away from me...

YUDA. He won't do it again. I'll take care of him…

LOLA. Give me the gun before I tell Boris to restrain you…

YIGAL. I'm afraid of Boris? Have you ever seen me afraid of anyone? *(to the audience)* When a car bomb exploded right next to me and my friends were ripped to shreds, the Holy One himself plucked me from the flames…

LOLA. I don't want you sitting on your bed later and crying…

YIGAL. Now you're pitying me? You, who walks around here all day seeking pity… *(mockingly mimics her)* "My sons… my brave sons… my glorious sons… they both fell in the war…"

> *YUDA clamps a hand over his mouth. LOLA is deeply wounded. She turns to the audience.*

LOLA. Yes. I talk about my sons all the time. About both of them. For twenty-five years. Ever since that war that killed them. First the younger one and then his older brother. You only talk about them on Remembrance Day… *(insisting)* If you care about the living, talk about the dead before you go to war… *(silence)* I'm a simple woman. I know only about human pain. And ever since that war I've asked myself: Do we have to suffer such pain in order to live here? *(silence)* After the war hundreds came to console us. We sat in silence. We couldn't talk. We didn't cry either. But a few months later the government signed a peace agreement. We saw it and we were shocked. This agreement had been negotiated well before the war. The very same agreement. Suddenly we realized that we'd sacrificed the children for nothing… that we'd wasted their lives for nothing… that they were slaughtered for nothing… for nothing…

BINDER. *(quietly, to the orchestra)* Music…

Scene 6

> *TALIA brings on blind NATAN who plays the HEAD OF THE SECURITY SERVICES, and she addresses BINDER, singing.*

TALIA. Dear Mr. Prime Minister
The Head of the Security Services is here on a mission most sinister
Your life is undoubtedly in great danger…

> *She begins her striptease. YUDA follows it with visible enjoyment.*

HSS. Mr. Prime Minister. The settlers have decided to fight you with every means at their disposal…

BINDER. I'm sure the security services know how to protect me. Thank you very much. *(ends the conversation)*

HSS. *(feels with his cane and finds BINDER)* The writing is already on the wall, sir. They have been living in the occupied territories as conquerors for a whole generation. Power has made them brutal, arrogant, and violent. After subjecting the Arabs to pogroms, they will easily pull the trigger against Jews. Now, as they fear you'll evacuate them, they'll use any weapon against you.

BINDER. *(angrily)* My dear sir, you are the head of the security services. It is your job to protect me, not frighten me. Thank you very much. *(gestures to TALIA to lead him away)*

HSS. *(despairingly)* Just a moment, sir. You have eyes to see.

> *He feels his way and turns over a bed, revealing AVI who plays SETTLER A. He cocks his rifle and aims at BINDER.*

SETTLER A. *(to BINDER)* I'm a settler from Judea. Tonight my wife and I will be returning home from a wedding. On a bend in the road they'll open fire. She'll be hit instantly. In the head. I'll try to accelerate, but another burst will shatter the windscreen. I'll lose my grip on the wheel, the car will spin out of control and burst into flames…

AVNER. Enough, enough…

SETTLER A. And I'll still be able to see the flames coming closer to me…

> *The HEAD OF THE SECURITY SERVICES turns over another bed revealing MENDEL who plays SETTLER B who also cocks a rifle and aims it at BINDER.*

SETTLER B. *(to BINDER)* I'm a settler from Samaria. Soon I'll be taking the sheep out to graze near the settlement. When I enter the *wadi*, from the corner of my eye I'll see three young men armed with axes. Before I manage to scream, they'll split my head open with a single blow…

AVNER. Enough, enough…

SETTLER B. And my mouth will fill up with blood…

> *The HEAD OF THE SECURITY SERVICES turns over another bed revealing SHULAMIT who plays a SETTLER and is also carrying a rifle, which she aims at BINDER.*

SETTLER. *(to BINDER)* It's nighttime. The children are already in bed. A masked man will be bursting into the house soon. He'll shoot my husband and the two sleeping children. The children won't even know they're dying…

> *The HEAD OF THE SECURITY SERVICES raps his cane and the SETTLERS exit. AVNER, who has been doing his utmost to control himself, can do so no longer and turns weeping to YUDA.*

AVNER. Do me a favour, get me out of here. Please. I can't listen to any more of this…

YUDA. You've heard it all before…

AVNER. *(continues)* Take me to my room. I need my medicine. Please. I'll clean your room for you. I'll give you my cigarettes…

YUDA. Shut up already! *(drapes the Attorney General's robe over him)*

AVNER. I'll do anything for you… *(sobs)*

BINDER. *(to TALIA, who is amusing herself with her striptease)* And you! Get dressed! The only thing you haven't shown them is the fillings in your teeth… *(TALIA is hurt and turns to exit. BINDER relents.)* I'm sorry. Don't go. Show them. Show them everything…

> She halts, turns to the audience and reveals the deep scar running across her belly. Silence. She takes blind NATAN's hand and runs it along the scar.

TALIA. *(to her mother in the audience)* It's just a scar, Mother. It doesn't hurt. The skin's a bit rough, a bit hard. You can touch it. You can stroke it. You don't have to keep running away, telling me you can't bear my pain… *(laughs)*

BINDER. *(to TALIA, gently)* Now you have to sing…

TALIA. *(She leads AVNER to centre stage and turns to the audience, singing.)*
The Attorney General is here
He has something for us to hear
So what do you have to say, mister?
How can we save the Prime Minister…?

BINDER. *(to AVNER)* Mr. Attorney General, what are you going to do about these people? How can we stop them? *(AVNER has difficulty in replying.)* I'm waiting for an answer…

ATTORNEY. *(recites with difficulty)* The judicial system is a tool in the hands of the regime, but not in the hands of the prime minister…

BINDER. These people are not only endangering me, they're also endangering the regime…

ATTORNEY. The judicial system must have evidence…

BINDER. Isn't what you've seen enough?

ATTORNEY. Evidence is… *(bursts into tears)*

TALIA. *(prompts him)* "Evidence is a proven fact…"

BINDER. Can't they be stopped according to the Emergency Laws?

ATTORNEY. The use of the Emergency Laws is…

TALIA. The use of the Emergency Laws is not constitutional…

BINDER. Does the constitution protect the murderer more than me?

> AVNER goes on weeping. TALIA again addresses the audience in song.

TALIA. The Attorney General was here
His words we did hear

But he didn't tell us, mister
How we can save the Prime Minister... *(She leads AVNER off.)*

BINDER. *(to the HSS)* What do you suggest we do?

HSS. Bug the settlements, plant agents in the *yeshivas*, install cameras in the synagogues...

BINDER. The synagogues?

HSS. Sir, democracy cannot show mercy to those who seek to destroy it...

BINDER. Democracy has to protect itself without harming the freedom of speech.

HSS. If they kill you, sir, there'll be no democracy here...

BINDER. And freedom of speech is put to the test precisely when someone expresses a dangerous opinion. The truth we need so much is sometimes hidden in the very opinion that is considered dangerous...

HSS. If they kill you, sir, the war will go on...

BINDER. If people are robbed of their freedom, they'll become a herd and be ready to fight in far more terrible wars...

> *YUDA loses his patience and addresses somebody in the audience.*

YUDA. What are you so happy about? That it sounds good? That it's nice to hear? That it's clever? *(grabs a pillow from one of the beds, and lights a cigarette lighter next to it)* If I set fire to this the whole place will go up in flames.

NATAN. What's happened?

YUDA. The moment you see the fire you'll run for the doors. You'll shove and scream and hit one another, you'll trample one another. Nobody will give freedom of speech to anyone else. Nobody will give freedom of life to anyone else. Not to his wife. Not to his children. Not to his friends. At that moment you will see who you really are...

NATAN. *(worried)* What's happening now?

> *A moment of tension. BORIS picks up a fire extinguisher and moves towards YUDA. BINDER gestures to him to stop.*

(hysterically to TALIA) I want to know what's happening...

BINDER. You can burn us, Yuda. Burn us and prove to us who you think we are... *(YUDA hesitates)* But perhaps we can do something so you won't want to kill us. Then we won't have to flee and we'll all remain human...

YUDA. The need to kill is the need to live, Binder. You don't have to apologize for it... *(to the audience)* He'll soon apologize for the people he's killed. In fifty years he hasn't missed a single opportunity to weep over them...

BINDER. What's so terrible about being human, Yuda? *(YUDA remains silent.)* Why do you despise it?

YUDA. I do not despise it. I'm trying to show you what it means. Look at me. This is what it is to be human... *(He falls silent.)*

> *BINDER takes the lighter from him and puts it out. YUDA does not resist.*

NATAN. The fire's out. I can see it's out. Not with my eyes, but I can see.

BINDER. Thank you, Boris... *(gives him the lighter)*

NATAN. See what a nice place it is? People are not allowed to set others on fire here... *(laughs)* No other rules. Not from Heaven. Not from Earth. Not from Hell.... Except for one rule. Once a month they bring us ladies... *(laughs)*

BINDER. Thank you, Natan... *(to the audience)* Ladies and gentlemen, we will now hear a very special song. Shulamit's song. She wrote it herself, words and music...

> *Music. SHULAMIT, AVI and MENDEL are wearing orthodox-Jewish women's head covering, plastic breasts on their chests and their aprons have a groin design at the front. SHULAMIT sings accompanied by the other two.*

SHULAMIT. I'm a nice Jewish girl at a college
For nice Jewish girls who think right
And like all my friends at the college
I'll stay a virgin till my wedding night.
Ay, ay, ay.... Ay, ay, ay.

On the wall of my room at the college
Hang pictures of our holy rabbis so fine
But under my bed there's a picture
Of the great Killer Doctor of Hebron
Ay, ay, ay.... Ay, ay, ay.

Night after night after prayers
Under my blankets I lie
Hoping that God is busy punishing Leftists
I take my picture of him from its hide
Ay, ay, ay.... Ay, ay, ay.

Kissing the face of my hero
His eyes, his ears and his lips
Curling his beard in my fingers
I play with myself as I pray
Ay, ay, ay.... Ay, ay, ay.

At midnight, the witching hour
My redemption finally comes
My hero fires and fires
Into the crowd with his giant gun...
Ay, ay, ay.... Ay, ay, ay.

I count every Arab that's fallen
Passion mounting with each one
At the height of salvation I keep counting
And at twenty-nine corpses I come...
Ay, ay, ay.... Ay, ay, ay.

> *The three take a bow. AVI and MENDEL take off the breasts and skirts.*

BINDER. *(applauds)* Thank you.... Thank you very much...

> *Hesitantly, AVI addresses the audience.*

AVI. I also killed twenty-nine people. In a POW camp in Lebanon. They were rioting and I opened fire. They fell. Twenty-eight didn't get up. Next day the sergeant major gave me a day's leave. I went home and there I killed the twenty-ninth. My father. When the war broke out I had hidden at home. A few days later the military police came looking for me, and he sent them down to the basement... *(He falls silent. LOLA takes his arm.)*

Scene 7

> *BINDER regains his composure and signals the orchestra to play.*
> *A moment later he signals MENDEL to begin.*

MENDEL. *(announces)* The Leader of the Opposition has come to visit the head of the settlers in Judea, Samaria and Gaza...

> *YUDA turns to SHULAMIT who plays a Settler's Leader. His attention is focused on her plastic breasts, that he calls "Judea and Samaria," and her groin, which he terms "Gaza."*

YUDA. My dear lady. I have come to ask for your support in the elections. As you know, I am a proud man and if you vote for me I will be a proud prime minister, and when I become a proud prime minister we will become a proud nation. And if we become a proud nation, we won't have to withdraw. Not from Judea and Samaria *(gestures at her breasts)* and especially not from Gaza. *(gestures at her groin)*

SHULAMIT. Proud? We've already seen proud prime ministers, and they all collapsed and withdrew...

YUDA. I'll collapse? I'll withdraw? *(laughs)* But we have an alliance, Shulamit. An alliance of love of our homeland. Although you may view this homeland as an expression of the hand of God, and I see it as a creation of Man, we are both prepared to kill and be killed for it. What is Man without a homeland? A fish out of water. A bird without wings. He is a believer with no god. He has no past. He has no future. He lives without meaning and content, without depth...

SHULAMIT. I've had enough of promises, proud sir. I want proof...

YUDA. What proof?

SHULAMIT. His head... *(indicating BINDER)*

YUDA. *(aside)* I see that breasts aren't enough to be a politician. *(to SHULAMIT)* There are cleverer ways of getting rid of him, madam. Words, for instance, are accepted weapons in a democracy. And words contain ideas. Ideas that can be dangerous, that can whistle like bullets, that can hit, that can wound...

SHULAMIT. Ideas aren't enough. Not for Samaria or Judea *(indicating her breasts)* Nor for Gaza... *(indicating her groin)*

YUDA. There are also ideas that can kill, madam...

> She shakes her head. Enter MENDEL and AVI who play YUDA's aides.

MENDEL. Good evening Mr. Leader of the Opposition...

YUDA. I'm busy. Come back tomorrow.

MENDEL. All our people are abandoning us, Sir...

AVI. The prime minister is offering peace and they're following him...

YUDA. Nobody's following him... *(goes back to SHULAMIT)* Madam...

AVI. Until yesterday we all believed you, that human beings are beasts of prey. Now all of a sudden everybody believes him, that people are innocent lambs...

YUDA. Don't worry. Tomorrow a bomb will go off in some square and they'll all go back to believing that human beings are beasts of prey... *(goes back to SHULAMIT)* My dear lady...

MENDEL. We've also been having some doubts recently. Perhaps Man isn't actually that bad...

AVI. Maybe there really is something in the Prime Minister's ideas...

MENDEL. Perhaps we should go and hear him in the square this evening...

AVI. And maybe we'll bring a few friends with us...

MENDEL. Goodbye...

YUDA. Wait... *(They stop.)* You're right. Some of our people are being carried away by the Prime Minister. They have somehow become convinced that war is a calamity and peace is life. We must get them back on track. If we tell them how much blood will be spilt because of this peace, they won't believe us. So we shall propose peace as well.

MENDEL. We'll propose peace?

YUDA. You don't have to declare war for war to break out. We can propose peace to our enemies and provoke them until *they* declare war... *(tempting SHULAMIT)* and then we'll fight, and win, and conquer and rule...

SHULAMIT. Judea and Samaria are yours. And Gaza too... *(embraces him)*

YUDA seizes the opportunity and slips his hand into her plastic bosom. She slaps him.

Don't you touch me! I put this outfit on for His truth. Not for your cock... *(to the audience)* I would even kill for His truth... *(to YUDA)* And if you try getting into my room again, I'll kill you too...

YUDA. *(angrily)* Shut the fuck up...

Angrily, she throws down her cabaret costume. MENDEL turns to YUDA in rage.

MENDEL. I don't want this war to conquer or rule. I want it because for the last twenty-five years I've been sitting in my room all day. When I hear a knock on the door I hide under the bed. I don't go out, not even to buy a paper...

YUDA. Mendel, stop it...

MENDEL. Because they could come at any moment. Soldiers in camouflage. Speeding through our streets. Spraying the houses with flames. Anyone in the street will be massacred. Even people standing outside reading papers...

YUDA. Mendel, I told you to stop it...

MENDEL. *(to the audience)* We must finish them off once and for all. We must shoot them. Burn them. Expel them. They'll pay for everything they did to me in prison, for the beatings, the electric shocks, for the teeth they broke, the fingernails they pulled out, for the toes they cut off... *(takes off his shoe and shows his foot)*

YUDA. *(angrily)* One more word and I'll pull your tongue out too...

MENDEL. *(ignoring him)* They'll all die, all of them.... Every last one... Tatatatata.... Tatatatata.... And then there will be quiet. Only then will there be quiet... *(calms down)*

YUDA. *(to BINDER)* What are you waiting for?

Scene 8

Music. BINDER gets onto the bed that is his stage. LOLA is at his side.

TALIA. *(sings)* The Prime Minister has come to the square
Fear deep in his bones
He saw the crowds waiting, aware
That their lives depend on him alone...

BINDER. *(to the audience)* My dear friends. You all know why we have gathered here this evening. To choose between life and death. The agreement I have reached assures you of life. If you support me, I'll...

YUDA. *(interrupts him)* Just a minute...

BINDER. What do you want?

YUDA. I concede. You've won. The people are behind you. We are a small and defeated minority...

BINDER. What do you want?

YUDA. To speak on behalf of this defeated minority that wants its voice to be heard. You yourself have said that very often the truth is concealed in the voice of the defeated minority. You surely wouldn't want us to feel that you're gagging us...

NATAN. *(to BINDER)* Don't let him speak, sir. You know he's a demagogue...

BINDER. The truth is stronger than any demagoguery. *(to YUDA)* Go ahead...

NATAN. *(anxiously)* Not everyone here knows the difference between the truth and demagoguery...

BINDER. *(to YUDA)* You can speak. After me.

YUDA. After you? I am the lesser man so I should speak before you. It's your audience, sir. I just want to make a few opening remarks... *(to the audience)* When you're being shot at in the trenches and you have nowhere to hide, you discover the truth pretty quickly. They had this bastard there with a flamethrower. Spewed flames ten metres...

BINDER. *(to Yuda)* Go ahead, speak...

NATAN. Take care, sir...

YUDA gets onto one of the beds and addresses the rally.

YUDA. I'd like to thank the Prime Minister who has most generously given me the floor. Indeed he is a generous man, our prime minister. But where does his generosity stem from? It stems from his ability to give. From his power to give. The secret of his generosity is in his power.

AVI. Very true...

YUDA. So let us become more powerful so that we can become more generous. And if anybody thinks that power only means generosity, he's wrong. Power also means order. The planets revolve around the sun in perfect order only because of its power...

SHULAMIT. Long live order...

YUDA. And order endows power with another wonderful attribute. We all know that chaos is ugly and order is beautiful. So power is beauty!

MENDEL. Long live beauty...

AVI. Long live...

YUDA. So why be ashamed of power? Why apologize for it? Power assures us of life. The weak are trampled. The weak are destroyed. Crushed. Annihilated. Who wants to be weak?

MENDEL. Nobody...

AVI. Nobody...

SHULAMIT. Nobody...

YUDA. We shall be weak no longer... (*He deviates from the text.*) Anyone who thinks that the war has ended is an idiot. It will never end. All their talk is nothing but a trick. They're just waiting to catch us sleeping on guard... (*He returns to the text.*) We shall no longer live by charity. We shall live by right. The right of power. Unlimited power. Power that will defeat. Power that will deter. A power so generous. A power so proud. A power so cruel that will assure us peace...

ALL. Hurray! *(applause)*

> YUDA *signals the orchestra to begin playing. From under the mattresses his supporters take out long poles to which bleeding doves are nailed. They raise the poles and sing.*

CHOIR. This is the dove sent from the ark
To see if the waters had receded,
It brought an olive branch in its beak,
And we slit its throat in the dark.
And then the war broke out, Oh, what a good war
A beloved war...

BINDER. Quiet! This man is deceiving you. He's misleading you. Power is an illusion. It is built on quicksand. Yes. If there's another war, we will win it. But this victory will be the beginning of our destruction, In order to keep its fruits we will have to continue living by the sword. And in the coming wars we will no longer be able to win. We will not win because we'll discover that winning is not worthwhile. That fighting is not worthwhile. We'll discover that life loses its meaning in wars...

CHOIR. This is another dove sent from the ark
To see if the waters had receded,
It brought an olive branch in its beak,
And we slit its throat in the dark.

BINDER. (*to YUDA*) Shut them up! (*YUDA does nothing. BINDER turns to the audience.*) If you think we'll prevent these wars by amassing power, you are wrong. If we amass power, we only encourage our enemies to amass more power. Power more destructive. Power more reckless. If you want to prevent war you should abolish the reasons for war...

CHOIR. And then the war broke out, Oh, what a good war
A beloved war...

BINDER. I am not insane. It's not possible that someone who believes in Man is hallucinating. Man can abolish the reasons for war. He can put an end to oppression and exploitation. He can put an end to cruelty and fanaticism. This is our only hope.... Only reform of Man will prevent war. Only justice...

CHOIR. This is another dove, and this is another.
And this is another dove, and this is another,
Until a vulture comes from afar
With carrion in its beak,
Then we shall all blow the horns
And the world will be redeemed...

BINDER. *(breaks down)* In the war stands a youth, still wet behind the ears, and he is clutching a rifle and shooting at the enemy. The enemy that hides in the village houses. He shoots a man who peeks over the roof. And another in a window. And another in a second window. And then an old man appears in the doorway. And he shoots him too. And the woman behind him, and the child behind her, and the child behind him. And he can't stop...

> *YIGAL suddenly appears and "fires" three shots at BINDER. BINDER is shocked and stunned and bursts into tears. LOLA hurries to him.*

YUDA. Lights! Lights! Close the curtain! Close the curtain!

> *Before the curtain closes AVNER screams. He raises his arms and slashes his wrists. LOLA leaves BINDER and rushes to him. The curtain comes down. Music. Darkness.*

> *End of Act One.*

ACT TWO
Scene 9

The curtain is open. The house lights are still on. The stage is empty. Blind NATAN bursts onto the stage, cane in hand. He stumbles, falls, gets up, loses his sense of direction and addresses the audience with his back to them.

NATAN. ...I'll tell everything. Everything. What they don't want you to hear is most important of all... *(He carries on talking in the wrong direction.)* Ladies and gentlemen, Binder was frightened by the story of his murders in the war, so he chased me all through intermission to cut out my lines. I came here this evening to talk...

TALIA. *(enters after him)* If you want to talk, then talk!

> *She leads him towards the audience but remains at his side, starting her striptease.*

NATAN. *(angrily)* Binder didn't have to tell me he's a murderer. Only a murderer is that frightened that somebody will come and kill him any minute...

TALIA. *(revealing a thigh)* See, Mother? I've had three operations here...

NATAN. I saw it on the day I arrived here. I see everything ...

BINDER. *(enters after NATAN)* We're not cancelling your speech, Natan. We're just postponing it...

NATAN. I'm not postponing anything. If I'd said it before the war maybe I wouldn't be here... *(to the audience)* Man isn't a lump of meat on the state's butcher block. The state can't knead him with its bloodstained hands as if he were a chunk of clay. The state was created for Man. It can't wipe its filthy ass with him and then bury him in the ground.

BINDER. I promise that you'll have a chance to say that...

TALIA. *(reveals her back)* I had three operations here too. One wasn't all that successful...

NATAN. Man is the heart of the matter. Not the state. The state can't rob Man of his life... his conscience... his dignity...

BINDER. What you have to say is very important, Natan. We shouldn't waste it on interjection...

NATAN. Man has the right to live according to his will. According to his conscience. And we here have waived that right. Because we were cowards. We were fools. We were blind...

BINDER. *(angrily)* If you go on talking they won't come onstage...

TALIA. *(points at her face)* I had nine operations here, Mother. I'm having another two next month...

NATAN. And if this country can't assure Man that he won't kill and be killed, if it can't assure him of his life, his sanity, his sight, then it does not deserve to exist…

TALIA. *(reveals her belly)* These are the scars from the last surgery…

YUDA. *(enters, to NATAN)* We asked you not to say that… *(to the audience)* They've just announced that another seven soldiers have been killed… and another twenty-two have been wounded…

NATAN. No one has the right to demand that another person die for him. Or go crazy for him…. Neither a father from his child nor a child from his father… And certainly not this bloody country…

YUDA. Shut your mouth! *(clamps a hand over his mouth)*

NATAN. *(with his last strength)* We can live without a state…. We don't have to be so afraid to live without it…

> *YUDA takes him off. BINDER to the audience.*

BINDER. I'm sorry that those things were said. He didn't mean to say that we should all pick up our suitcases today and go back to wandering the earth. He thinks that one day, when the world is no longer divided into states, we will be able to give up this state too. I apologize for the delay. The noise of the helicopters bringing the wounded to the hospital, flooded some of us with painful memories…

> *He turns to exit. TALIA, who is almost naked, addresses the audience.*

TALIA. This isn't so nice to look at, is it? You'd rather see something more appealing, more tempting? *(laughs)* But this is ugly isn't it? It's very troubling, it raises questions. Why did it happen? Why me? Who's to blame? It is very easy to blame the bastard who blew himself up right next to me. But why did he blow himself up? None of you were part of it? You're all innocent? *(laughs)*

> *BINDER comes back and addresses her angrily.*

BINDER. Get dressed right now! Can't you see we have a problem here that's more important than your ass?

TALIA. There's nothing more important than my ass!

BINDER. Do you want us to talk about it right now?

TALIA. My nose and cheeks were made out of this ass. And my lips too, Binder. So nothing is more important to me than my ass. *(to the audience)* Think about that when the next sonofabitch blows up right next to you. When everything shatters. When everything is on fire. Not about friends or family. Or the prime minister. Not even about God. Just think of your ass…

> *She laughs, and then removes her wig revealing a bald scalp. BINDER hurries over to her and leads her out. Music. The curtain opens. LOLA conducts the choir.*

CHOIR. From the hills blood flows deep
Washing down the slopes
In the houses children weep
While in the squares mothers mope
And the earth was without form, and void;
And darkness on the face of the deep.

In the cities open graves lay
Funerals make their way
Weeping mourners trudge in the
Thunderous silence of their cries
And the earth was without form, and void;
And darkness on the face of the deep.

Amputees limp through the streets
Burned faces wearing their masks
The blind feel their way in the dark
And the shell-shocked hide their faces
And the earth was without form, and void;
And darkness on the face of the deep.

But on the day they'll all be there
The bereaved, orphans and widows
The wounded, beyond repair,
All will stand in line at the polls.

And blinded by their amnesia
Forgetting what war is about
They'll cast their votes one by one
And elect a new government,*
The government that will declare the next war.

And the earth was without form, and void;
And darkness on the face of the deep,
And God saw that it was good.

> *Applause. The actors bow. MENDEL turns to the doctor in the audience.*

MENDEL. I was looking for you during the intermission, doctor. I can't find my house key. How can I get in without a key? I want somebody to come with me to the neighbours tomorrow...

BINDER. Don't worry, Mendel...

MENDEL. And I want my full uniform. The neighbours won't recognize me like this...

LOLA. I'll bring it to you, Mendel...

> *BINDER leads him to his place and signals the orchestra to play.*

Scene 10

Music. The funeral of a youth who was murdered in a terrorist attack. YIGAL is lying on a stretcher as the dead youth. ELIAHU says the prayer for the dead. BINDER and LOLA are among the mourners.

ELIAHU. He is the Rock, his work is perfect: a God of truth and without iniquity, just and right is He... *(murmurs)*

Enter TALIA wheeling AVNER. His wrists are bandaged.

The Lord gave and the Lord hath taken away; blessed be the name of the Lord... *(murmurs)*

TALIA. *(sings)* The Prime Minister has come in dread
To the funeral of a young man shot dead...

ELIAHU. *(aloud)* "He who maketh peace in his high places may he make peace for us and for all Israel; and say ye, Amen."

ALL. Amen...

TALIA. Stand up, Avner. You did it yesterday... *(to the audience)* He's afraid that if he gets out of the chair they'll send him back to the army. *(to AVNER)* If you stand up, so will he... *(indicating his groin)*

ELIAHU. Shhh... *(continues)* "May God comfort you among all the other mourners of Zion and Jerusalem..."

TALIA. *(sings)* Soldier boy, soldier boy, guard your cock well, if you come home without it, you can go straight to hell...

ELIAHU. Shhh.... O God, who art full of compassion, who dwellest on high, *(murmurs and then aloud)* The Lord is his portion. May he rest in peace...

TALIA supports AVNER who manages to stand up. Now he plays the bereaved brother.

SHULAMIT. *(to the audience)* I got a nurse to stitch him up during the intermission. The doctors were all drinking tea in the kitchen... *(laughs)*

BINDER. *(to those present)* Dear friends. Death has struck us once more and once more the pain is unbearable...

AVNER. *(with difficulty)* Mr. Prime Minister, get out of here...

BINDER. I have come to lament your brother, my friend...

AVNER. *(with difficulty)* He was murdered because of you. Go. Let us mourn him...

BINDER. I mourn him as if he were my son...

AVNER. I curse the day I believed you... *(He is suddenly standing without TALIA's support.)* I curse the day I followed you... *(collapses into his wheelchair, weeping)*

MENDEL. *(to BINDER)* Go!

AVI. Go!

SHULAMIT. Go!

TALIA. *(as the murdered youth's girlfriend)* Mr. Prime Minister. I loved him and he loved me. Now he's dead. And our love is dead too. Hatred has grown in its place. I hate everything that lives because he is no longer living. I hate everyone who loves, because I no longer love. I hate everyone who hopes because I have no hope. But more than anything I hate you, sir, because you blinded us with the hope that hatred can be abated...

MENDEL. *(to BINDER)* Go!

AVI. Go!

SHULAMIT. Go!

> *YIGAL sits up on the stretcher, the cocked pistol in his hand. He suddenly hesitates and addresses BINDER.*

YIGAL. Now? Should I fire now?

BINDER. No!

YIGAL. Not even aim?

BINDER. No!

YIGAL. *(apologetically)* I was only asking. *(lies back down)*

> *BINDER and LOLA, who were turned away from the ceremony, move to the apron.*

LOLA. They're not the only ones who've abandoned you, Isaac...

BINDER. We should not judge them in their grief...

LOLA. They've abandoned you because you're asking too much of them...

BINDER. Too much?

LOLA. A person who has always seen the other as an enemy can't see him as a friend overnight...

BINDER. If he doesn't see him as a friend, then the other will continue seeing him as an enemy too...

LOLA. They need time...

BINDER. And until that time comes, we'll just go on burying the dead?

LOLA. If you pressure them, they'll...

BINDER. Are you trying to scare me?

LOLA. I'm trying to save you. You're racing forward without looking to see who's behind you. Which of them has fallen. Which of them is exhausted. Which of them has despaired. Even if you get to where you're going, you'll find yourself alone there...

BINDER. Alone?

NATAN moves towards him.

NATAN. Mr. Prime Minister, leave right away. One of them is about to murder you…

BINDER. How do you know?

NATAN. I saw the murderer. He's already cocked his gun…

BINDER. You saw him?

NATAN. In my mind's eye I can see into hearts and minds, Sir. I can hear whispers softer than the wind…

YIGAL sits up on the stretcher and interrupts him.

YIGAL. He's not a murderer. He's a martyr. He's a divine messenger…

LOLA. Not now…

YIGAL. A person who kills an enemy is not a murderer. Whether the enemy is an Arab or a Jew…

BINDER. Lie back down!

ELIAHU. *(bursts out)* A Jew who kills an Arab is never a murderer…

AVI. Right!

BINDER. Eliahu… please…

ELIAHU. If you had studied the Torah, Binder, you'd know that the Almighty himself permits the killing of Arabs…

BINDER. *(angrily)* Eliahu!

ELIAHU. *(to the audience)* The Almighty built the entire world by degrees. There are inferior creatures and inferior people. The cat is not like the lion. "Thou Shalt Not Kill" does not apply to Arabs, just as it doesn't apply to lambs and calves. And a Jew who needs a heart transplant is permitted to kill an Arab in order to use his heart …

SHULAMIT. That's right…

BINDER. *(to ELIAHU)* That was the one thing I asked you not to say…

LOLA. *(to YUDA)* Grab him!

YUDA grabs ELIAHU and claps a hand over his mouth.

TALIA. *(to her mother)* You're not leaving, Mother!

NATAN. *(to the audience)* Man is the heart of the matter, not the state…

BINDER. Where does this insanity come from? In which of our wanderings in the world did we become infected with it?

YUDA. Stop it, Binder!

BINDER. Is it possible that we were always like this? Could it be that only because we did not have sufficient power, we didn't dare think like this and didn't dare speak like this?

YUDA. *(threatening)* If you go on chattering, Binder, I'll let him *(indicating ELIAHU)* talk too...

BINDER. *(furiously)* I wasn't born a murderer. I wasn't born to become a murderer...

> *BINDER quells his anger and signals the orchestra to play.*

Scene 11

> *Music. Enter AVI who plays a SETTLER Leader.*

MENDEL. *(announces)* The settler leader has come to meet the Prime Minister...

SETTLER. ...But still, Mr. Prime Minister, before we vote for you, we want to be sure that this agreement of yours will not uproot us from our land...

BINDER. My dear friend, you know me. You know I am a man of my word...

SETTLER. Thank you very much, sir. *(shakes his hand and turns to leave)*

BINDER. I hope that this handshake means that you'll support the peace agreement I have reached...

SETTLER. What peace agreement? It's a European peace. It's not a Jewish peace.

BINDER. What's a Jewish peace? Isn't "Nation shall not lift up sword against nation, neither shall they learn war anymore," a Jewish peace?

SETTLER. The Prophet Isaiah is very specific about what must happen so that "Nation shall not lift up sword against nation, neither shall they learn war anymore."

BINDER. What must happen?

SETTLER. Listen. *(takes a Bible from his briefcase)* "And it shall come to pass in the last days, that the Lord's house shall be established in the top of the mountains." In other words, first we must build the Temple. "And all nations shall flow unto it." That is, all the nations will recognize the house of the Lord. "And He will teach us of his ways, and we will walk in his paths." This means that all these nations will obey the commandments of the holy Torah of Israel. "And He shall judge among the nations, and shall rebuke many people," means that the kingdom of Israel will be a power. "And they shall beat their swords into plowshares." Who will beat their swords into plowshares? The many nations! Not us! All the nations must lay down their arms, and only then, says Isaiah, only then will "Nation not lift up sword against nation, neither shall they learn war anymore."

BINDER. That's a Jewish peace?

SHULAMIT. *(to the audience)* Yes... *(laughs)*

SETTLER. Yes. *(turns to exit)*

BINDER. *(after him)* One more word, my friend. When I look at the world, I see it is no longer possible to resolve conflicts by force. Conflicts that have not ended with compromise have not been resolved...

SETTLER. Perhaps countries cannot settle conflicts by force. But the Almighty can.

BINDER. But my dear friend, if the Almighty does not resolve our conflict immediately, a war will break out here and our little country will not survive it...

SETTLER. So it won't survive. What makes it worthy of survival? A few million assimilated Jews? Jews who eat pork, who profane the Sabbath, who are ignorant, hedonistic adulterers? This pitiful state is nothing more than a first step. The Almighty chose you to establish it for us, and now you can go. And when you are gone the true Messiah will appear in a storm, and fight for us and destroy all our enemies. And then there will be peace... *(exits)*

BINDER. *(after him)* The Messiah will destroy all our enemies? I've got a better suggestion for him. He should try conciliation with them first... *(The SETTLER has gone. He speaks to the audience.)* This is Judaism? What's happened to it? Even the words of the prophets sound like the voice of the Devil. Fear of God and love of Man can't dwell together?

He suddenly realizes something. He looks around and turns to leave.

LOLA. *(stops him)* Where are you going?

BINDER. *(confused)* Where am I going?

LOLA. We're continuing...

BINDER. *(confused)* I have to leave. There are some reasonable people in this country. I must talk to them...

LOLA. *(indicates the audience)* They are already listening to you...

BINDER. I should have seen it long ago. The settlers are sure that a Messiah will come and fight for them. That's why they're dragging us into this war. If they realize there's no Messiah on their side, they'll stop the fighting...

LOLA. You want us to go on without you?

BINDER. There are people out there, who can still be saved... *(turns to exit)*

NATAN. *(worried)* My ears are ringing, Lola...

AVNER. *(mockingly)* Bye, bye, Binder...

BINDER. If the truth has no emissary, I must be that emissary.

LOLA. Please, Binder. You've been doing so well. I'm begging you...

BORIS stands up, but TALIA quickly grabs BINDER's cane. He falls down.

TALIA. If you can save someone out there, then save me first. The Messiah can burn in Hell. I don't want to rot here until I crumble. Where shall I go? Show my scars in a circus? What can I do with myself except lie down on the tracks?

> *YUDA and his friends laugh. LOLA goes to TALIA and calms her down. She takes BINDER's cane and returns it to him. She takes out a tissue and wipes his nose. BINDER regains his composure, grasps the rail of one of the beds and stands up. BORIS sits down.*

BINDER. Did you check everybody at the entrance? And their bags?

LOLA. Yes... *(to TALIA)* Get him some water!

BINDER. Are the doors locked? Are the guards outside?

LOLA. Yes... *(to the orchestra)* Play...

> *Music. SHULAMIT plays a SETTLER. She is no longer wearing the plastic breasts and the apron depicting her groin. She still refers to her own breasts as "Judea and Samaria" and her groin as "Gaza." YIGAL mimes trying to kiss her. She mimes pushing him away. The music stops.*

SHULAMIT. First kill him.

YIGAL. I've already bought a gun. I've got a plan.

SHULAMIT. Judea and Samaria are holy sites. Entrance is forbidden to a Jew who has not killed.

YIGAL. But I've fired rubber bullets at hundreds of Arabs.

SHULAMIT. That's not enough.

YIGAL. I'm sure I shot out the eye of one of the children...

SHULAMIT. What's shooting out the eye of a child?

YIGAL. All right. Let's go down to the Nablus road tonight and you'll see me shoot at cars. With live ammunition.

SHULAMIT. That's just kid's stuff, too.

YIGAL. I'm willing to plant a roadside bomb for a bus in Ramallah.

SHULAMIT. Any Hezbollah maniac can do that.

YIGAL. So what do you want me to do?

SHULAMIT. To kill him. *(points at BINDER)*

YIGAL. I'll kill him. I'll kill him, I swear. I've already got a silencer...

SHULAMIT. *(excited)* Just the opposite. With a big bang. Just as Phineas the priest killed a fellow Jew for fucking a non-Jewish woman. And just as Mattathias the priest did to a Hellenistic Jew who sacrificed a pig. They both killed Jews in full public view. Without rabbis. Without courts. But with faith, heroism and devotion. And they attained sanctity and dignity. If you kill him, you will conquer both Judea and Samaria, and you'll invade Gaza as well... *(falls into YIGAL's arms but immediately regains her composure, pushes him away and addresses the audience)* He had to be killed. My husband said so every day.

He came home after the war in Lebanon. But only his body returned. His soul remained in the mountains near Beirut. For ten years he'd wake up screaming at night, cowering in a corner and crying with fear, thinking I was a Shi'ite with a bazooka. Ever since that man *(BINDER)* brought his "agreement," he didn't leave the house. During the day he would scrape the walls with his fingernails. That night, when that murderer came into the house, he went towards him empty-handed, he wanted to die so much… *(mustering all her strength)* The two children died too. But their death was not in vain. The Almighty, blessed be He, took them to Him to put me to a test. And I'm meeting that test. I won't stop believing in Him and I won't stop obeying Him. And if one day He asks me for my two other children, I'll give them to Him. I'll give them to Him in faith… *(Her voice breaks.)*

> *BINDER gets up, goes to her and takes her hand. YUDA hurries to push him away.*

YUDA. Don't touch her! *(to SHULAMIT)* Don't cry. We'll get out of here. Both of us. Whoever shut me up in here is afraid that I'll ruin his dream that the world is a Paradise and that people are angels, and that one day tanks will plow the fields and fighter planes will carry flowers. Only crazy people have dreams like that. I speak the truth. That's why I'm here. *(to the audience)* I'm not crazy. In all our wars I was always the first. In my whole life I've never run away. In the battle for Jerusalem I caught a burst in the stomach. My intestines were hanging out. That's why I didn't charge. Look! *(shows his stomach)* After the war I begged them: Take me back. Let me be a driver. Let me be a mechanic. Let me be a clerk. Nobody listened. For thirty years they've shut me up in here for nothing! Nothing!

SHULAMIT. *(crying)* I've wet myself…

> *YUDA takes SHULAMIT's hand, sits her down on a bed and sits next to her.*

Scene 12

> *Music. BINDER, NATAN and AVNER take their places for the next scene. NATAN plays the HEAD OF THE SECRET SERVICES (HSS) and AVNER the ATTORNEY GENERAL.*

BINDER. *(despairingly)* Mr. Head of the Security Services. The murderer is approaching. Maybe he's one of my aides. Maybe he's one of my advisors, maybe he's the barber, maybe the cook. Maybe he's even one of my guards… *(points at YIGAL)* Maybe he's a settler with a gun in his pocket…

LOLA. *(to NATAN)* You've got to find him and arrest him…

HSS. We've detained a number of settlers, sir, but they cover up for one another. The court released them. Insufficient evidence... *(to the audience)* You need more than eyes to see evidence. You need a heart...

BINDER. So why didn't you bring enough evidence?

HSS. I did everything possible within the borders of the law...

BINDER. *(angrily)* Bring me the Attorney General...

NATAN. *(to the audience)* The law is blind. Like these eyes. If it allows the state to wage so many stupid wars, we should shit on the law and whoever made it...

TALIA. *(sings)* The Attorney General is here
He has something for us to hear
So what do you have to say, mister?
How can we save the Prime Minister...?

NATAN. And if I have to stay here to be able to shit on the law, I'll stay here all my life...

BINDER. *(to AVNER)* Sir? Sir? *(AVNER opens his eyes.)* Mr. Attorney General, the murderer is already breathing down my neck. Is there no way to save my life?

LOLA. First you should arrest the rabbis who sent him...

AVNER. That's not possible...

BINDER. Not possible?! Doesn't this country have a law against murdering a prime minister?

AVNER. We can only arrest the rabbis when... *(sinks back into a doze in his chair)*

BINDER. Only when I'm murdered?

AVNER. *(opens his eyes)* Only when we can prove...

BINDER. Prove what? *(AVNER is silent.)* Prove what?

TALIA. That they actually sent somebody to murder you...

BINDER. But I want to prevent them from sending a murderer...

AVNER. *(with difficulty)* The judicial system cannot prevent.... It can only... *(He is unable to continue.)*

TALIA. It can only judge a suspect when there is evidence against him...

BINDER. The rabbis talk about murdering me every day. They incite against me in every synagogue...

AVNER. So far... *(He is unable to continue.)*

TALIA. So far the law hasn't found any connection between incitement and murder...

BINDER. All the wisdom in your books is not enough to see that incitement might convince someone to murder?!

AVNER. And so... and so it is impossible to... *(bursts into tears)*

TALIA. *(sings)* The Attorney General was here
His words we did hear

But he didn't tell us, mister
How we can save the Prime Minister...

BINDER. *(to NATAN)* So what shall I do? Wait until somebody finds the connection between incitement and murder? Run away? Hide? *(to AVNER)* Surrender to him? If I surrender to fear, then those who rule through fear will rule the lives of us all...

> *YUDA, who has been sitting angrily on the bed with SHULAMIT, turns towards BINDER.*

YUDA. Nobody is ruling here through fear. You're afraid because you're a coward, because you die every time a car passes, a window opens, a match is struck, a door is slammed, or a plate smashes. When you hear a leaf fall on the ground, you hide under your bed...

BINDER. *(insistently)* Please, let us continue...

YUDA. Nobody's trying to kill you. Nobody's even interested in you. You'll die of old age, of feebleness, of stupidity. And you'll be buried in some hole, without a name, without a headstone. As if you'd never lived...

BINDER. *(forcefully)* Please, Yuda, let us continue!

LOLA. I don't think I have to explain to you what fear is, Yuda. It's deep in your bones too...

YUDA. You're going to tell me what fear is? *(contemptuously)* Have you ever known fear in your life?

LOLA. I don't know what fear is?

YUDA. *(to the audience)* Her biggest fear is of the secretary's poodle...

BINDER. You're right, I am afraid. But I don't surrender to the fear. I don't obey it. I haven't become cruel and evil like you because of it...

LOLA. *(to the audience)* I don't know what fear is. It was two days after Gadi was killed in Sinai. He was twenty years old. Burned in his tank. There was nothing left to bury. We were sitting at home. Towards evening. The window was open. On the table there was a letter from Ze'evik who was fighting on the Golan Heights. We could see the gate from the window. The sun hadn't yet gone down. Suddenly, we saw a car approach and then another one. And I didn't understand. A woman officer got out of the first car, and then a civilian, maybe a doctor. And from the second car came a social worker and a psychologist. And even then I didn't understand.... They hesitated for a moment by the gate, as if they were frightened to open it.... I told myself that this couldn't possibly be. They'd already told us that Gadi had been killed... what else was there to say? And Ze'evik's letter was lying on the table. Perhaps it was our neighbour's son. I prayed that it was the neighbour's son. Then the girl rang the bell... and then I knew fear ... *(falls silent)*

> *BINDER goes to her. She avoids him and signals the orchestra to play. She sings to the audience.*

Death walks through the streets
Like a Siren tempting with song
And our boys awaken, afire
With the desire to ravish it

It walks through the streets
Playing love songs on its pipe
And our boys follow its beat
Without question, without thought

We watch from our windows in wonder
Captured, like them, by the sound
We don't stop the boys who don't question
Because answers have yet to be found

When the time comes he'll be there for the funeral
And choking he'll voice a cliché
He'll pat us on our slumped shoulder
Then get into his car and go away

We'll beg him: stay and tell us
How our boy charged forward
How he ran, how he fell, how hellish it was
Tell us his final words.

Wait, stay, tell us more
Of his bravery, how he fought back
You must remove the blame from us
For we voted for you and your pack

SHULAMIT. *(to LOLA)* You're so afraid of death because you only know the pitiful, momentary life in this world. When it's over, everything is over for you. *(to the audience)* We who believe know that death is only the beginning… *(laughs)*

Scene 13

A house of mourning. The occupants are sitting shiva for a victim of a terror attack. ELIAHU and AVI are wearing prayer shawls.

MENDEL. The Leader of the Opposition has come to console the bereaved family… *(puts on a prayer shawl)*

YUDA. *(to those present)* I have come to you in your darkest hour not just to console you in your bereavement. There is no consolation when young people's lives have been cut off prematurely. I have come to assure you that your pain is ours too, and we'll obey this pain until all his murderers are murdered. In every house, in every cellar, in every cave. We'll pursue them and annihilate them. Them and their families. Them and those who send them out. Them and those who assist them. All of them...

AVI. Thank you, Sir...

The mourners shake his hand.

YUDA. I thank you. I came to fortify you and I leave fortified myself. *(to AVNER in his wheelchair)* I have one small request from you...

AVNER. *(with difficulty)* Yes, sir...

YUDA. You are an influential poet. An intellectual...

AVNER. Yes, sir.

YUDA. You must surely understand that in order to kill these murderers, we must train the best of our young men for it. We are better than our enemies in everything, and we can also be better murderers. We can murder more cleverly, more cunningly, more cruelly than them.

AVNER. I see...

YUDA. You must also see that it's no simple matter to establish this army of murderers. There are writers and poets who are likely to oppose the whole idea...

AVNER. *(with difficulty)* How can I help?

YUDA. I have to admit that there's no one in my camp to respond to them. I've never had much to do with writers and poets. I'd appreciate it if you would write something about the situation. About the lack of choice, about the necessity. Write about it so that we won't be misunderstood. What is more moral? To bare your neck to the murderer, or kill him?

AVNER. Yes, sir.... No...

BINDER sees that AVNER is incapable of saying what he is supposed to, and he answers in his place.

BINDER. At least, sir, we must make sure that whoever we have decided to kill is indeed a murderer. Perhaps we should put them on trial before we kill them...

YUDA. You are certainly right, sir. When we can put them on trial, we'll try them. You're a great poet. You can describe how difficult it is to decide to kill somebody...

AVNER. Of course...

YUDA. By the way, I read your latest book. Very touching. It's a pity it didn't sell all that well. But I believe in you and I'll write the introduction to your new book. It will surely sell much better...

AVNER. Excellent, Sir... morphine... morphine... shut up... calm down...

YUDA. And you should stress that we're fighting for our lives...

AVNER. You're right, sir... morphine... give me a little morphine...

BINDER. You're right, sir. When we are fighting for our lives, killing is permissible. But are we truly fighting for our lives? Perhaps we are fighting for entirely different purposes—telling ourselves that we're fighting for our lives, only to justify the killing?

AVNER. The men.... Where's the men? Morphine.... My legs... my legs...

YUDA. Your doubts are the doubts of us all, my friend. I'll put that into the introduction to the book...

> *YUDA extends his hand to AVNER. AVNER cannot control his flow of fragmented sentences and weeping.*

AVNER. Morphine... morphine... no... there's no morphine for the men... get water... get bandages... bite down... bite down... morphine... morphine... there's no morphine... no morphine...

YUDA. *(blocks his ears and shouts)* Stop whining! Stop screaming! Stop it!

AVNER. My legs... take me home... my legs... take me home... my legs...

> *TALIA bends over him, kisses him on the lips and shuts him up. YUDA sits despairingly on one of the beds further away. As AVNER calms down, TALIA turns to the audience:*

TALIA. He'll be quiet now. He doesn't want to see, or hear, or even think. He doesn't believe in anyone anymore. Me neither. Not in a man. Not in a woman. Not in a child just born... *(to her mother)* Don't worry, Mother, I'm not receiving guests in my room. Nobody here comes near me. Even I don't come near myself...

> *She falls silent, buttons her blouse and straightens her skirt. At the same time ELIAHU, MENDEL and AVI light black candles and conduct the "Black Lightning" ceremony in front of BINDER. BINDER takes the curses in silence.*

RABBIS. We, the rabbis of Israel, shepherds of His holy flock, cast the Curse of the Black Lightning upon Isaac, son of Rosa, who has given parts of the land of our fathers to the Gentiles. We hereby enjoin you, angels of heaven, in the name of the Almighty and the name of this congregation, on this holy scroll of the Law, in the name of the Lord God of Hosts, God of Israel. Cursed is he by the twelve angels charged with the months of the year. Cursed is he by the seven angels charged with the days of the week. Cursed is he by the four angels charged with the four seasons of the year. Cursed is he by the great, mighty and revered God. Destroy and annihilate him. Angels of destruction wound him. Cursed be he in all his actions. May his soul flee affrighted. And let us say Amen...

> *The music reaches a climax. Silence. AVI takes his suitcase and turns to leave, but the case opens and dozens of cans of peanuts fall out.*

MENDEL. What's this? Why so many peanuts?

AVI. They're for my father...

MENDEL. Your father? But your father's...

AVI. *(stubbornly)* My father likes peanuts...

MENDEL. But he's...

AVI. And what will I do if the resurrection of the dead starts without warning? Go shopping?

> *AVI turns to collect his cans. ELIAHU bursts in and addresses the audience.*

ELIAHU. Thus spake the Lord of hosts. Go to the children of Israel and say unto them: The day is not far off when a great war will engulf you. And in this war tens of thousands will fall and many tens of thousands will be wounded...

LOLA. Enough, Eliahu... *(She moves towards him.)*

ELIAHU. *(He evades her.)* And after that terrible war all the faint-hearted pork-eaters will flee from the Land and be dispersed to the four corners of the earth. The day is not far off when there will no longer be pork-eaters in this Land. Only the valiant who follow my laws and commandments will remain in it. The day is not far off when all the Jews of the Land will wear yarmulkes and prayer shawls, and whoever does not wear a little prayer shawl beneath his shirt will be jailed. And whoever profanes the Sabbath will be stoned. And whoever sells non-kosher meat will be burnt...

LOLA. *(to ELIAHU)* I said enough!

> *LOLA tries to chase him, but ELIAHU manages to evade her.*

ELIAHU. The day is coming, and after the next war rabbis will sit in judgment in the courts. And all your schools will become religious. The universities will be turned into *yeshivas* and the swimming pools into ritual baths. The theatres will become synagogues and the sports stadiums cemeteries...

BINDER. *(to YUDA)* Please, catch him...

> *But YUDA remains on the bed, sulking. LOLA, who is short of breath, cannot go on chasing after ELIAHU.*

LOLA. *(to BORIS)* Catch him, Boris...

> *BORIS catches ELIAHU, but allows him to continue.*

ELIAHU. *(panting)* And so I command you not to support any peace. On the contrary, the next war will be a Holy War. And after that Holy War your Land will be the Holy Land once more. And you will live in it according to the Holy Torah, and your lives in it will be holy.... Holy, holy, the Lord of Hosts, holy, holy, the Lord of Hosts...

ELIAHU kneels. BORIS takes him by the arm and sits him on one of the beds.

Scene 14

BINDER addresses the audience. He is fuming over ELIAHU's outburst.

BINDER. Please, forget what you have just heard. He simply lost his mind. With all his devotion to his God he forgets that there are people here. Another few years and that crazy God of his will devour us all… *(to behind the scenes)* Yigal! *(to YUDA)* Where is he? *(to the audience)* Just when you need him he's gone… *(to behind the scenes)* Where are you?

YIGAL. *(enters)* Here I am…

BINDER. You don't shoot now.

YIGAL. Okay. I don't shoot. *(But he holds the gun. He speaks to BINDER.)* Hello, sir…

BINDER. *("doesn't recognize him")* Hello.

YIGAL. I'm Yigal. Your murderer. *(He plays with the gun.)*

BINDER. *(concerned)* What do you say? My murderer? Are you sure?

YIGAL. No, I'm not. That's why I've come to talk to you.

BINDER. To me?

YIGAL. Well after all, it's your life.

BINDER. You want me to tell you whether or not to kill me?

YIGAL. Not exactly. You see I'm no ordinary observant Jew. I'm a believer. And I have a certain feeling that the Almighty has chosen me. That he's speaking to me. That his words are echoing inside me. That he is commanding me to kill you…

BINDER. *(cautiously)* You think that you hear the word of God?

YIGAL. That's a big question. How can anyone be sure that God is speaking to him? Look, since the destruction of the Temple, prophecy has been the domain of fools. So I'm trying to be logical. First, there can clearly be no contradiction between the word of God and our Holy Law. Right?

BINDER. Let's say so.

YIGAL. Second, God's interest must fit the words of the prophets as they appear in the Scriptures. Right?

BINDER. Let's say so.

YIGAL. And third, it's perfectly natural for the Almighty to choose me to kill you, because he, like me, has a vested interest in killing you.

BINDER. The Almighty has a vested interest in killing me?

YIGAL. Haven't you realized yet that the Almighty is opposed to peace?

BINDER. The Almighty is opposed to peace? But the Talmud says that the world stands on three things: the law, the truth and peace...

YIGAL. The Almighty, blessed be he, opposes peace because war is the beginning of redemption. He wants to redeem us through it. So all the believers have to want war in order to help him redeem them...

BINDER. Mortals have to help the Creator?

YIGAL. Of course.

BINDER. *(cautiously)* So if you have been commanded to kill me in accordance with Jewish law, in accordance with all the prophesies and God's will, then what's the problem?

YIGAL. The problem is that the Lord moves in mysterious ways. And just as he tested Abraham with the sacrifice of his son Isaac on Mount Moriah, then perhaps he's testing me with you. And don't forget that you're an Isaac too...

BINDER. I think I might be able to help you solve your problem.

YIGAL. *(surprised)* That's not what you're supposed to say now, Binder...

BINDER. *(impatiently)* That's what I should have said long ago. There is no God, Yigal. There's no such thing, and he doesn't want to kill me and he doesn't want war at all. The God of war is the invention of men who want to kill in wars.

YIGAL. *(scornfully)* There's no God?

BINDER. No. You are sovereign. You are the one who thinks, feels, decides and kills. You and no one but you. Not an angel and not a seraph and not an emissary...

YIGAL. There's no God?

BINDER. No, and he didn't command you to kill me...

YIGAL. But he pulled me from the flames himself. Without him you wouldn't be alive either. *(to the audience)* None of you would be alive. If he doesn't fight for you, they'll drag you out of your homes. They'll stand you in rows. They'll slaughter you, and burn you, and smash your children's skulls. If he doesn't fight for you, they'll destroy and kill and annihilate you all... *(turns to exit)*

BINDER. *(blocks his way)* People have become such monstrous murderers either because they made themselves bloodthirsty gods, or because they believed in bloodthirsty gods...

YIGAL. I'll kill you. I swear to God I'll kill you... *(exits)*

LOLA. *(enters)* What are you doing here? Come back to bed. It'll soon be morning...

BINDER. I couldn't sleep...

LOLA. What's the matter? Was somebody here? Who? Why are you so pale? You're trembling...

BINDER. I must go. *(turns to leave)*

LOLA. Where to? Without bodyguards? You're not going...

BINDER. I have to...

LOLA. I'm coming with you.

BINDER. There's no need...

LOLA. You're not leaving this house alone... *(exits after him)*

Scene 15

Night. BINDER searches for YUDA among his people. LOLA is with him.

BINDER. I've come to talk to you. *(YUDA signals his people to leave them alone.)* You know that the murderer is already aiming a gun at my head...

YUDA. I don't know anything...

BINDER. He won't be satisfied with just me. After he kills me, he'll go on killing. He is likely to get to you as well...

YUDA. I told you I don't know what you're talking about...

BINDER. To incite him against me you flooded the country with fear of destruction, until we lost our power of reasoning. We won't be able to live in such fear...

YUDA. I'm doing exactly the same as you. To incite against me you flooded the whole country with fear of war...

BINDER. Do I need to arouse the fear of war? Isn't war terrifying enough?

YUDA. We are not terrified by it. We're a healthy people. We understand that our destiny has always been determined by wars.

BINDER. But that doesn't mean we can't determine our destiny otherwise. Human beings have suffered enough to understand that they can manage their affairs with common sense.

YUDA. Human beings are bloodthirsty. Man is a beast of prey. He zealously protects his tribe, his people and his race. He will not flinch from slaughtering millions for their sake. He will not flinch from spilling his own blood. And whoever does not fight will not live.

BINDER. Yes, there are bloodthirsty people. Some are worse than beasts of prey. But is there no remedy for them?

YUDA. There isn't and there never will be. People kill for the sake of killing. They sometimes justify it with God. Sometimes with land. Sometimes with "justice." But the reason is always the same. The lust for blood. *(to the audience)* When I was crawling in that trench, my gun jammed. I raised my arms in surrender. Yes, I did... I did raise my arms... I did surrender.... That shit didn't have to shoot. But then I saw this lust in his eyes, a lust that whole rivers of blood could not cool down...

BINDER. What do you mean "killing for the sake of killing"? When you kill a man, he dies. A moment earlier he was alive and breathing and blood flowed in his veins, and he loved and was loved, and now he's a corpse lying in a field...

YUDA. Don't lecture me about death. You are afraid of it. I use it. You flee from it. I toy with it. Death is power... *(to the audience)* When he squeezed the trigger, even before I heard the shots, even before the lead ripped into me, even then I could see its power. If I have this power I'll live...

BINDER. How can you say these lines? Look at what has become of us because we have lived with this power...

YUDA. What's become of us?

BINDER. Don't you see?

YUDA. What's there to see?

BINDER. I've imprisoned myself here for life so that I won't be forced to go on killing...

YUDA. You have imprisoned yourself here because you are afraid that you'll go on killing willingly...

> *BINDER gives up and signals the orchestra to play. Music.*

Scene 16

> *BINDER and LOLA. BINDER is preparing to leave for his speech at the rally. LOLA tries to stop him.*

LOLA. He's right.

BINDER. How is he right?

LOLA. The time is not yet ripe.

BINDER. What else has to happen for it to be ripe?

LOLA. Far too many among us are still beasts of prey...

BINDER. They're not. They're human beings capable of thinking...

LOLA. They know only one way to survive. War and another war and yet another. That's how they've survived to this day...

BINDER. That's not true.

LOLA. They're willing to spill a lot more blood before they start thinking...

BINDER. I have no choice. I have to fight for their lives too.

LOLA. And what about your life?

BINDER. I've got people who are responsible for my life. *(turns to exit)*

LOLA. *(stops him)* Just a minute. Aren't you wearing the vest?

BINDER. There's no need.

LOLA. Please.

BINDER. There's no need.

LOLA. Put it on.

BINDER. It's too bulky.

LOLA. You're going to the rally to die there, aren't you?

BINDER. If the war is being waged in the town squares, that's where I have to be.

LOLA. You think that if you're murdered, the whole country will be shaken and people will open their eyes and see…

BINDER. That's not true.

LOLA. Your death is unnecessary. You won't redeem anybody with it.

BINDER. I don't want to die…

LOLA. Wait. Please. Wait…

BINDER. How long must we wait?

LOLA. Until we suffer the most awful blow. Until every family suffers death. Until mourners weep in every home. Only then will people open their eyes… *(to the audience)* Mine only opened after weeping for my two sons…

BINDER. I won't wait for that day to come…

LOLA. And if we pray for that day to come soon…

BINDER. I won't pray for it… *(turns to exit)*

LOLA. *(shouts after him)* I won't come to watch you die!

> *But BINDER has left. Enter YIGAL wrapped in a prayer shawl, his gun in his hand, and turns his eyes heavenward in prayer.*

YIGAL. O Lord of the Universe, who sits on high, please give me a sign to kill him, may his name be erased. For even if I stand before him with my gun drawn, I will be unable to end his life unless I know that I am fulfilling your will. I know that you will not be revealed to me in a burning bush as you were revealed to the Father of the Prophets. You haven't even sent me an ordinary dream lately. Please, Lord of the Universe, give me a sign. Maybe a little earthquake. Perhaps a partial eclipse of the moon. A tree falling in the wind. A chirping bird. A sign, Lord of the Universe, give me a sign. The moment I shoot him, his bodyguards will kill me. Tell me it is your holy will that I die for you. That I die for your land, and then I will shoot him and die without fear. Lord of the Universe, give me a sign. Just one sign… *(regains his composure)* You know what, Lord of the Universe, I've got a suggestion for a sign. A little sign. When I aim the gun, make sure his bodyguards don't hide him from me. Make sure that I don't have to kill anyone except him. That will be the sign...

Scene 17

BINDER is addressing the rally. His bodyguards, TALIA, AVNER and NATAN, are in front of him. LOLA watches from a distance. YUDA, AVI and MENDEL are watching BINDER from their corner. ELIAHU, wrapped in his prayer shawl, murmurs a prayer.

BINDER. ...I do not want to delude any of you. I promise you peace, but it is not an absolute peace. It is not an eternal peace. But even if this peace is partial, even if it is flimsy, it will save us a lot of bloodshed and tears... *(He deviates from the text.)* I opened the paper this morning and on the front page I saw the smiling faces of young soldiers. They're not smiling anymore. Their bodies buried in the ground have begun to rot. Only those who have seen rotting bodies know what a horrific sight it is. You take your comrade's hand and it falls to pieces in yours.... And the busy maggots hurry to find another piece of meat.... And the gaping eyes are empty.... What really justifies such death? What is so much bigger than our life that's worth dying for like this?

Enter YIGAL, his gun drawn. He sees a space between TALIA and NATAN.

YIGAL. O Lord of the Universe. This is the sign. There is no one standing between me and him, may his name and memory be erased...

BINDER. *(pleading in fear and despair)* Shoot me! Shoot! What are you waiting for?

YIGAL. Blessed art thou, O Lord our God, who wreaks our vengeance...

LOLA. *(trying to block him off)* No, don't shoot!

But YIGAL shoots him. BINDER falls. YUDA and MENDEL capture YIGAL and lead him away. LOLA kneels beside BINDER.

CHOIR. In the square three shots rang out
A man fell, his blood poured out.
A great hope failed
A vision ended, a dream curtailed.

LOLA. Damn you! All of you. May you be damned to your dying day. I will never have peace again, but neither will you. I will walk among you mourning. I will not dress the wounds. I will not heal the scars. You will see the bleeding wounds and the gaping scars and you will know it was you who spilled this blood... *(She deviates from the text.)* Just as you spilt the blood of my children. Their blood was also drunk by this bloodthirsty land... I should never have given birth to them... I should never have raised them on it...

Meanwhile, two yeshiva students played by AVI and MENDEL, have brought in BINDER's "grave" and place it at centre stage. BINDER "wakes up" and protests.

BINDER. Just a minute. We agreed not to do this scene.

MENDEL. We didn't...

AVI. The truth is more important than any agreement....

BINDER. Let us end with the hope that it is possible to live here.

SHULAMIT. They'll perform what they want to perform.

ELIAHU. And in the way they want to perform it.

BINDER. They'll perform what we agreed to perform! *(to the choir)* Sing! Sing! Why have you stopped?

YUDA gags BINDER and allows the yeshiva *STUDENTS to go on.*

LOLA. Boris!

BORIS draws his baton.

STUDENT A. *(to the audience)* Ladies and gentlemen, we are students from a well-known Jerusalem *yeshiva*.

STUDENT B. It is now midnight. A few hours ago your prime minister was buried here.

STUDENT A. May his name and memory be erased.

STUDENT B. And we have broken in to found a new Jewish tradition: the tradition of pissing on the grave...

STUDENT A. And now, in secret, away from prying eyes, we stand on the grave, open our flies, take out the redeemer from its underwear, and observe the commandment...

BOTH. Blessed art Thou, O Lord our God, King of the Universe, who has kept us in life, and hast preserved us, and enabled us to reach this day...

The students urinate on the grave using big phalluses hanging from their hips. LOLA rushes to YUDA and slaps his face. He is shocked and releases BINDER.

BINDER. *(to the chorus)* Sing! Sing the finale! Sing!

YUDA. We'll end the play with the national anthem. I ask the audience to please stand!

LOLA, NATAN, TALIA and AVNER begin the song.

CHOIR. We are the living dead
Showing you our faces,
Faces that cannot hide the scars...

But NATAN loses his patience. He rushes towards MENDEL and AVI brandishing his cane. Despite his blindness he manages to hit them.

NATAN. Bastards. Bloody murderers.... We are not dead yet. We could have gone out of here... all of us... I still want to live. I want my eyes back. I want to get rid of the shrapnel in my brain...

AVI, MENDEL and SHULAMIT hit NATAN forcefully. He keeps struggling.

I don't want to live among the dead any more... I don't want to hear any more wounded... no more tears... no more blood... no more shame.... No more fear...

MENDEL and AVI knock him down. LOLA rushes to rescue him. AVNER tries to scream but can't utter a sound.

LOLA. Let go of him.... Let go...

TALIA can't bear the violence and she turns to her mother in the audience.

TALIA. Take me home, Mother.... Take me home...

Meanwhile YUDA tries to restore order according to his plans.

YUDA. *(to the audience)* Please, stand up. Start singing...

LOLA. *(to MENDEL and AVI)* Leave him alone...

BINDER. *(in deep despair)* I told you to continue with the finale... *(to the orchestra)* Play! Play!

YUDA. Sing! Sing!

TALIA. Take me home, Mother.... Take me home...

BORIS tries to rescue NATAN from MENDEL and AVI. BINDER limps to YUDA.

BINDER. What more do you want of me? I was prepared to die. You saw how I welcomed this cursed death. What else? Do you want to punish me too? For what dream? For what hope? I've already paid the price for the people I killed. I've paid it all my life. I've died here every day of my life.... Isn't that enough for you?

Suddenly, YIGAL goes to BORIS, snatches the gun from his belt and rushes to BINDER.

YIGAL. There *is* a God in heaven. You won't say there isn't. You won't be saying anything anymore...

He manages to fire three real shots into BINDER before BORIS overpowers him. BINDER falls, tries to get up, but falls to the ground.

LOLA rushes to him and discovers he is dead. Shock. AVNER suddenly manages to stand on his feet.

YIGAL. Blessed art thou, O Lord our God, King of the Universe, who wreaks our vengeance…

Silence. Only YIGAL's laugh echoes around the hall. Darkness.

Curtain.

The Trials of John Demjanjuk
A Holocaust Cabaret

Jonathan Garfinkel

• Jonathan Garfinkel •

Jonathan Garfinkel is a poet and playwright. He is the author of the book of poetry *Glass Psalms* (Turnstone Press 2005), and the plays *Walking to Russia* (Playwrights Guild of Canada 2002) and *The Trials of John Demjanjuk: A Holocaust Cabaret* (Playwrights Canada Press 2005). He lives in Toronto.

• Playwright's Notes •

This work blurs the boundaries between fiction and non-fiction. I have remained faithful to actual courtroom events, compressing them to fit the temporal needs of the theatre. The prosecution and defense scenes contain direct quotes from trial transcripts. Scene 15 contains direct quotes taken from the testimony of the survivor Czarny. The line, "There's no business like Shoah business" was originally coined by Abba Eban, former Israeli foreign minister. All flashbacks, interactions between John and Ivan, and scenes outside the court of law are from the author's imagination.

• Acknowledgements •

I would like to thank Adam Sol, who read the poem version of this and said it was wanting to be a play. Thanks also to John Murrell, Alex Poch-Goldin, Gadi Roll, Jason Sherman, Paul Thompson and Kelly Thornton for their invaluable insights at various stages of the play's development. Thanks to The Banff playRites Colony, Lise Anne Johnson and the NAC, Marc Glassman, Mitch Smolkin and the Ashkenaz Festival, and Buddies in Bad Times Theatre. Thanks to all of the actors in all the workshops and productions, whose feedback and enthusiasm helped push this play past its original skin. To Christine Brubaker, Dmitry Chepovetsky and Clinton Walker for their commitment to *The Trials* over the years, and to Christine for scoring the music.

Many thanks to Jennifer Herszman Capraru, who suggested the Brechtian cabaret style with scene titles, who gave birth to the character of Fraülein, and submitted this when it was still a poem to the Rhubarb! Festival. Thanks to the drunken singing of JHC, Josh Dolgin and Tobaran Waxman, which inspired the possibility of song.

• Note on the Music •

The score for the original music by Allen Cole and Christine Brubaker is available in the single title version published by Playwrights Canada Press.

"*Two souls, alas, reside within my breast*
And each withdraws from and repels its brother."
—*Goethe*

• Production History •

The Trials of John Demjanjuk received its world premiere at the Chutzpah Festival, Vancouver, produced by Theatre Asylum, Toronto in February 2004, with the following company:

John Demjanjuk	Frank Moore
Ivan the Terrible	Dmitry Chepovetsky
Fraülein/Mama	Christine Brubaker
Rosie/The Survivor/Mordecai	Clinton Walker
Shaked/Nazi 1/Sher	Michael Rubenfeld
Sheftel/Nazi 2/Russek	Dov Mickelson

Directed and dramaturged by Jennifer H. Capraru
Lighting by Sandra Marcroft
Set and Costumes by Andjelija Djuric
Sound design by E.C. Woodley
Stage manager: Andrew Dollar

• • •

For a full production history, please see the single title version published by Playwrights Canada Press.

• **Characters** •

DAS FRAÜLEIN - Accordion-playing German cabaret narrator and temptress
ROSIE - Fraülein's sidekick
YORAM SHEFTEL - Defense Attorney, late 30s
MICHAEL SHAKED - Prosecuting Attorney, early 30s
MR. RUSSEK - Head of Israeli War Crimes Unit
MR. SHER - Head of Office of Special Investigations
JOHN JR. - John's 12-year-old son
JOHN DEMJANJUK - 67, Ukrainian
IVAN THE TERRIBLE - Mid 20s, Ukrainian
THE SURVIVOR - 60s
MAMA - John's mother
MORDECAI - Communist Jew, 20s
NAZI 1 & 2 - Two cartoonish dimwits of any age

•The Trials of John Demjanjuk: A Holocaust Cabaret •

Prologue

"The Ballad of John Demjanjuk"

FRAÜLEIN. There once was a man
    named John Demjanjuk
    They said he was Ivan
    that terrible prep-line cook

    Who sent off the Jews
    to bake and to rise
    And smeared their black breath
    in the blue Polish skies

    The place was Treblinka
    where the summers were hot
    Kurt Franz and Stangl
    were the big shots

    They had dreams of a golf course,
    a garden, a zoo
    And they employed Germans,
    Ukrainians and Jews

    It was there they made lampshades
    and the gold supply grew
    They served near one million
    before the first year was through

    And though the skies were still hungry
    there were no more Jews

ROSIE. Except for the fifty
    who escaped through the fields

    Now I know about Ivan
    his scar and his scowl
    The lead pipe he carried
    made the kids howl

    He ran the gas chambers
    vodka his muse
    And his face was that
    of a young Demjanjuk

FRAÜLEIN. In an Israeli courtroom
    two lawyers stand grim

It's 1987
and the prosecution wants him

SHAKED. John Demjanjuk
must be punished and tried
It's justice we want
we say he must die

SHEFTEL. My name is Yoram Sheftel
and I drive a white Porsche
I'm Israel's top
defending lawyer of course

And the people ask why
I rose to defend
I'm an Israeli
and I'll fight to the end

SHAKED. What has happened to John

SHEFTEL. shows what can go wrong

ROSIE. when a people are angry

ALL. and want their revenge

FRAÜLEIN. These are the trials of John Demjanjuk.
(*speaking*) Welcome. To our Cabaret of Life

ROSIE. and Death.

FRAÜLEIN. Tonight is a night of nightmares

ROSIE. and paperclips.

FRAÜLEIN. Secrets spoken.
Shocking revelations revealed.
The horrors of the human condition exposed.

ROSIE. Thrills and chills,

FRAÜLEIN. Truth—

ROSIE. and lies.

FRAÜLEIN. Tonight we present our Holocaust Cabaret.
So you came for some fun, *naja? (a beat)*
Why don't Jewish cannibals eat Germans?

ROSIE. Because it gives them gas.

FRAÜLEIN. So you came to laugh.
Or not.
To forget your problems.
To watch the torments of another man.

Thank God it is not me, you will say.
Thank God it is a monster.

This is not my story.
This is not me.

ROSIE. *Eins—*

FRAÜLEIN. How can one of the nicest men you'd ever want to meet also be a sadistic murderer?

ROSIE. *Zwei—*

FRAÜLEIN. Is he in fact a sadistic murderer?

ROSIE. *Drei—*

FRAÜLEIN. Or is this just… a show-trial?

Scene 1

FRAÜLEIN. Washington. 1976. Voices behind closed doors.

ROSIE. Sunglasses.

FRAÜLEIN. Trenchcoats!
Mr. Russek:

ROSIE. a bold moustache.

FRAÜLEIN. A Russian nose. The head of war crimes in Israel—*(points to RUSSEK)* visits Mr. Sher:

ROSIE. A very crafty

FRAÜLEIN. intelligent American

ROSIE. Head of the OSI—

FRAÜLEIN. Office of Special Investigations—

TOGETHER. the American Nazi hunters— *(points to SHER)*

>*SHEFTEL plays RUSSEK, SHAKED plays SHER. They speak spy-ishly.*

RUSSEK. We need to talk.

SHER. *(motions to walls, whispers)* We must talk quietly.

RUSSEK. *(whisper)* I have come a long way for your help.

SHER. I know. We need your help too.

RUSSEK. I need… *(whisper)* a *donut.*

SHER. A what?

RUSSEK. Last time, we had a braided vanilla… *(short pause) donut.* Hmm? The Germanic cruller type.

SHER. Uh-huh.

RUSSEK. But we don't want to have to kidnap this… *donut.*

SHER. I'm sorry Mr. RUSSEK. We're not familiar with this code in Washington.

RUSSEK. We. The War Crimes Unit of Israel. Have not had... a good... *DONUT* in twenty years. *(motions a Seig Heil several times)*

SHER. Ahhhh. I see.

RUSSEK. Your country has let dozens go through its hands uneaten.

SHER. We need survivors, witnesses, evidence. Be patient.

RUSSEK. Patience leads to... *donuts* running away to Argentina or the Bahamas.

SHER. What are you implying?

RUSSEK. If you give us one, I will ensure it gets eaten in Jerusalem.

SHER. Really.

RUSSEK. But it has to be... clear cut. Open and shut.

SHER. Like Eichmann—

RUSSEK. Shhhhh! Now, we're hungry for a... *donut*, but we have to be sure it's a murderous *donut*.

SHER. Which... *donut*... do you have in mind?

RUSSEK. Good, Mr. Sher, very good. I hear they make excellent donuts in Cleveland. A soft—

SHER. Ukrainian—

TOGETHER. jelly donut.

Scene 2

FRAÜLEIN. Meanwhile, at the very same moment in Cleveland—

ROSIE. fifty-thousand screaming fans!

FRAÜLEIN. Hot dogs!

ROSIE. Popcorn!

FRAÜLEIN. A baseball game. A father. A son.

JOHN JR. *(to game)* Catfish, you're a bum!

JOHN. Are we still losing?

JOHN JR. Yes, Dad. Just look at the scoreboard. *(groans)* That's ten strikeouts. They're gonna cream us.

JOHN. You take it so seriously.

JOHN JR. It's do or die, Dad. The Indians haven't been in the Series since '54.

JOHN. Why does the pitcher always scratch himself like this? Is it part of the game?

JOHN JR. Yes.

JOHN. Does he get a point for scratching himself?

JOHN JR. No. It's just the way they do things. Shut up and watch the game.

JOHN. Look at the way the man holds his bat. Such strength. You see, Junior? To succeed, you have to be strong.

JOHN JR. Do you always have to talk like everything is some kind of lesson? *(to game)* Come on, ya bum. Keep your eye on the ball! Strike one. You can do it! Strike two. The pitch. A hit. He hit it!

JOHN. Hard.

JOHN JR. It could go.

JOHN. It's going—

JOHN JR. It's going—

JOHN. It's gone.

JOHN JR. Home run, Dad. Off Catfish Hunter!

JOHN. He did it.

JOHN JR. It was impossible.

JOHN. No son. It's not impossible. It's America.

Scene 3

"John was a Regular Fella"

FRAÜLEIN. *(singing)* It was a bright and sunny
    Cleveland day
    The elm trees sighed,
    life was gay

    John was tired
    needed to rest his feet
    His work was over
    Goodbye to the week

       Neighbours' VOICES: a chorus.

VOICES. John was a regular fella
    He worked in his garden
    He played with the kids
    He liked to get his hands dirty
    He fit in well with our
    Ohio digs

FRAÜLEIN. John did not believe
    the noises he heard
    His quiet home
    had become a circus of the absurd

A camera flash
click click and dash
What's going on
to poor old John?

> *The sound of cameras. JOHN is bombarded by reporters speaking.*

REPORTER 1. Mr. Demjanjuk, what do you have to say about the accusations?

REPORTER 2. Is your wife upset?

REPORTER 3. Did you really enjoy gassing Jews?

CHORUS. John was a regular fella
He worked in the garden
He played with the kids
He liked to get his hands dirty
He fits in well with our
Ohio digs

> *Speaking.*

REPORTER 1. Is it true you were a POW?

REPORTER 2. Do you have a criminal record?

REPORTER 3. Did you know that the OSI has been tracking you for three years?

REPORTER 1. What do you have to say to the public?

REPORTER 2. Your neighbours

REPORTER 3. your children

REPORTER 1. your church

REPORTER 2. your mother

FRAÜLEIN. your wife?
(singing) John says nothing
What's there to say?
Vera faints in his arms
and she's carried away

JOHN. *(speaking)* My poor Vera.
Frail, white Vera.
These are my tears
on your neck.

What are they doing to us?

Scene 4

FRAÜLEIN. Jerusalem is a passionate place.
Prime Minister Shamir has just promised to crush the Palestinians like grasshoppers.
The first Intifadah has begun.

ROSIE. That's not what we're talking about tonight.

FRAÜLEIN. I smell blood.

ROSIE. Fresh blood.

FRAÜLEIN. John is nervous.

ROSIE. Terrified.

FRAÜLEIN. Life

ROSIE. or death. (*They laugh somewhat hysterically.*)

FRAÜLEIN. 1976.

ROSIE. Survivors identify Demjanjuk as Ivan of Treblinka.

FRAÜLEIN. 1978.

ROSIE. John's family goes on a hunger strike

FRAÜLEIN. 1981.

ROSIE. John's American citizenship is revoked.

FRAÜLEIN. 1985.

ROSIE. John is thrown into a Cleveland jail.

FRAÜLEIN. 1986.

ROSIE. John is deported to Israel.

FRAÜLEIN. The long-awaited trial...
Begins NOW.
The star of our show.
Alone in the Promised Land

ROSIE. They promised us the trial would be short.

FRAÜLEIN. But it wasn't.
John sits in the court and watches.

ROSIE. The audience watches him.

FRAÜLEIN. The accused takes the stand!

JOHN. In 1952
I entered the United States
And though I left out a few irrelevant details about my past
I received my certificate of Naturalisation
I have the number
to prove it

It was different in those days
Fighting in Ukraine in the war
Who knew what we were doing

When the Nazis caught me
I walked through it all in a fever
In 1942-43
I was a POW in Chelm
Mourning for my dead father

I never lied
except during the first immigration hearing
When I said I was a farmer in Sobibor
it was to protect my wife
I didn't know it was a death camp
Never heard of the place
Saw it once on a map

As for the tattoo
under my armpit
the SS put it there
In the Displaced Persons camp
I rubbed it out with a stone
I thought it might be taken
the wrong way

      Various voices whisper/echo JOHN.

JOHN. I was starved

ROSIE. *starved*

JOHN. beaten

ROSIE. *beaten*

JOHN. I forgot everything
I was dead to myself
Only the dust in my throat
reminded me I had breath

ROSIE. *Breath*

JOHN. But I'm innocent

EVERYONE. *innocent*

JOHN. I am not Ivan of Treblinka.
I know it.
My hands
they're twitching
with the truth

EVERYONE. *truth*

Scene 5

FRAÜLEIN. There is fear in this theatre.
People are fainting.
Loved ones are crying.

ROSIE. Everyone is afraid to remember.

FRAÜLEIN. But who is telling the truth?

Our young *ünd* dashing prosecutor, Michael Shaked, wants to see the defendant dead. All rise in the court of law!

SHAKED. We are the children of Auschwitz. Majdanek. And Treblinka. Our country has been born from the smoke of such terrible fathers and mothers.

Eleven years ago, survivors in Tel Aviv and New York were shown a series of photographs, a "photospread." Without being prompted, several of these eyewitnesses positively identified John Demjanjuk as Ivan the Terrible of Treblinka. How is this possible? The horror which marked the lives of the survivors will never allow them to forget. No matter how many years pass, their memories remain clear and precise.

The central evidence for our case is the Travniki identity card. This ID card will prove, beyond a shadow of a doubt, that John Demjanjuk voluntarily trained at Travniki camp to become an SS guard, an expert in torture and extermination techniques.

In this trial, we will prove that Mr. Demjanjuk's alibi is based on lies. That he willfully participated in the murder of nearly one million people at Treblinka death camp. That he committed atrocities such as slicing open the bellies of pregnant women with a machète. This man, who insists on his innocence, is the embodiment of evil itself. I beg the judges to consider the evidence very carefully, and judge Demjanjuk guilty, before this court, before our nation, and before God.

Scene 6

FRAÜLEIN. Alone in his cell… John tries his best not to be afraid.

JOHN in his cell doing pushups.

JOHN. One hundred and ten. One hundred and eleven. One hundred and twelve. *(stops)* Strong body. Strong mind. Strong spirit. They think they're going to defeat me? They think I am weak?

ROSIE. *(whisper)* Monster

SHAKED. *(whisper)* Murderer.

TOGETHER. *(whisper) Death to Ivan of Treblinka*

JOHN. Isolated. Humiliated. Video surveillance. Not a second goes by without people watching me. I saw my son cry in the courtroom today. My wife Vera sends me packages that are opened before I get them. I miss conversations with her, in the middle of the night, when one of us can't sleep. Ordinary people. And below our bedroom, the ordinary streets of Seven Hills, Ohio.

VOICE 1. *Never late*

VOICE 2. *Never called in sick*

VOICE 3. *Never talked about the war*

VOICE 4. *If he's guilty they made him do it*

ALL. *And his perogies are absolutely the best!*

       JOHN gets down on his knees.

JOHN. Mama
Look at your boy. I'm sixty-seven years old.
Don't let them destroy me.
I never hurt a soul.
Pray for me, Mama.

Tonight the full moon will rise. I know this because the Jews do. Their calendar tells them so. I've begun to study their language. *Ani naki. Ani eesh shalom.* I am innocent. I am a man of peace.

Scene 7

       JOHN falls asleep. IVAN the Terrible appears. He sings.

"The Myth of Ivan the Terrible"

IVAN. I'm Ivan the Terrible
God, what a name
I put the devil
and his angels to shame
I am here to bring out the darkness in men

If your water's too pure
Your garden too green
If your body is soft
and your mind is too clean
I'll be sure to muck it and maim it again

Oh the moon has a nice look tonight
But it's only reflection
It is not its own light

If your conscience seems a little too quiet
I have come to inspire it
To remember some things that you'd probably rather forget

Treblinka was grand
But since that great war
There's been lots to do
Thank God life's no bore
And I have many an SS to thank
Yes the moon has a nice look tonight
But it's only reflection
It is not its own light
If your conscience seems a little too quiet
I have come to inspire it
To remember some things that I'm sure that you'll never forget

Scene 8

JOHN wakes up suddenly. He is frozen with fear.

IVAN. *Achtung!* Good. You're standing at attention.
You're still a soldier.

JOHN. What do you want?

IVAN. To help you.

JOHN. I don't want your help.

IVAN. You didn't fare too well up on the stand today. Very nervous.

JOHN. Wouldn't you be?

IVAN. I'm grateful to you. For bringing me into the spotlight again. I enjoy the attention.

JOHN. I don't.

IVAN. No. You always were a shy boy. Even during the famine, when your mother found you the meat. You didn't tell a soul. *(pause)*

There's an old Ukrainian saying:
Speak your mind,
the truth is your gift.

JOHN. I can't remember everything.

IVAN. Just tell them the truth, John.

JOHN. There were many details. It was very long ago.

IVAN. You know who you are.
You know where you come from.

Scene 9

FRAÜLEIN. *(whispers)* John has a flashback, just like in the movies. The hamlet of Duboviye Makharyntsy, Ukraine 1933. It's the Great Famine, compliments of Comrade Stalin. John is thirteen years old.

MAMA. Vanichka! Come and eat.

JOHN. Where did you get this meat? *(Silence. JOHN is eating.)* It tastes like heaven, Mama.

MAMA. We are harvesting the will of the Lord. He has willed that you survive.

JOHN. The meat is so tender.

MAMA. The Lord provideth.

JOHN. I feel strong already, Mama. I could go back to work in the fields, right now. *(searching, whistling)* Here, Pisha, Pisha. Hey. Where's Pisha?

MAMA. Eat. You need your food. You're a growing boy.

JOHN. I love you Mama…. Wait. Where did this meat come from? *(pause)* Mama?

MAMA. Pisha is giving you strength, John.

JOHN. What?

MAMA. There was nothing to feed him.

JOHN. You…

MAMA. Don't you dare waste it.

JOHN. Pisha is our dog. You gave him to me ten years ago.

MAMA. Your father is not to know of this. It will only make him jealous.

JOHN. Oh God.

MAMA. Do you want to be like the neighbours? Eating their dead?

JOHN. *(a beat)* Thank you, Mama. *(resumes eating)*

MAMA. Tomorrow you're going to work for Vladimir.

JOHN. Yes, Mama.

MAMA. Say grace with me. "Thank thee, O Lord, for providing us this…"

JOHN. *(aside)* Smell of bodies
rotting on the banks
Eyes of my dog
stare
wherever I turn

Scene 10

"The Ballad of John the Good"

FRAÜLEIN. Now Johnny was a good boy
   he worked in the Ukrainian fields
   In the year of 1933
   Stalin took all their yields

ROSIE. And the Ukrainian people starved to death
   In fact seven million did die
   In the empty fields where the food once grew
   that's where the bodies did lie

TOGETHER. Johnny moved to a farm
   where he drove a big truck
   He liked to fix engines
   he had the good luck

ROSIE. To be skilled as a driver
   was a rare and very good thing

FRAÜLEIN. And though our Johnny he wasn't a genius

TOGETHER. The bastard could fix anything

Scene 11

FRAÜLEIN. Yoram Sheftel, that famous defence attorney, visits John in his cell.

JOHN. How much is my family paying you?

SHEFTEL. You're getting a bargain, John.

JOHN. But how can they afford it?

SHEFTEL. I'll admit, I'm not the cheapest lawyer in the business. But let's face it: without me, you don't stand a chance in hell.

JOHN. I know.

SHEFTEL. And I know what you Ukrainians did to us during the war. My grandmother told me all about it. But I've chosen to defend you anyway.

JOHN. Because we pay you a lot.

SHEFTEL. No. I don't need your money. I'm defending you because I don't trust this country. They won't give you a fair trial.

JOHN. What does this mean?

SHEFTEL. You're going to hang.

JOHN. Then what the hell are you defending me for?

SHEFTEL. Don't get excited.

JOHN. Don't you believe I'm innocent?

SHEFTEL. Of course I do.

JOHN. This is about having your name in the newspaper.

SHEFTEL. No, John. This is about you.

JOHN. *(unsure)* Uh-huh.

SHEFTEL. I'm going to do my best to save your skin. But I need your help. I need you to tell me what you really did during the war.

JOHN. I have. I told it in court. I'm an honest man.

SHEFTEL. *(a beat)* Good. Talk about your family more. We need to appeal to their sense of humanity.

Scene 12

FRAÜLEIN. A white Porsche.

ROSIE. *Kapo.*

FRAÜLEIN. Love beads.

ROSIE. *Self-hating Jew.*

FRAÜLEIN. Got the gangster Meyer Lansky off the hook.
Won the Billion Shekel Robbery.
Ladies and gentlemen, bachelor #2, Yoram Sheftel,
Defence attorney, begins his... Crusade for Truth.

SHEFTEL. My dear Judges. All the questions in this case can be reduced to one: Do we want justice, or do we want retribution?

We, the Jewish people, have spent two thousand years demanding justice. We abhor those, like the Nazi state, who set up separate laws against us. But are we doing anything different to this man?

My client has already been denied the basic tenets of international law. He is guilty, waiting to be proven innocent. In this case, I will prove that the KGB forged the "Travniki identity card." And that the photos of suspected Nazis were biased. Through the haze of forty-five years, the survivors chose the man whose photo was the largest. Why? Because they want an answer. And we need an answer.

But this former theatre is proof you did not come to give John Demjanjuk a fair trial. You came to watch the performance of vengeance. You bow to the TV camera, to the press, and have decided that this man is Ivan the Terrible of Treblinka.

We all live next door to neighbours. This man who sits before you is your neighbour. He works hard and lives an honest life. You know his kids. You've seen him at Church or Synagogue. Because of people like him, the world is a good place. Take a good look at this man. And before you send him to the gallows, be sure. This is not the face of evil.

Scene 13

FRAÜLEIN. What's the difference between a carp and a lawyer?

ROSIE. One's a bottom-feeding, scum-eating animal...

FRAÜLEIN. ...the other makes great gefilte fish.

(announces) **"The Dueling Lawyers' Duet"**

SHAKED. To defend the person before you
    is to reject history's trial
    The defence's primary funder
    is a Holocaust denier

    Justice is implicit in this courtroom
    This is a righteous prosecution
    Demjanjuk's crime of genocide
    grants his guilt and execution

SHEFTEL. If it's the defence's funder you condemn
    then will you please invite him to the stand
    If it's truth and wisdom you condone
    then a fair trial I demand

SHAKED. I'll fight for the memory

SHEFTEL. I'll fight for the truth

SHAKED. I'll fight your damn ego

SHEFTEL. I'll find all the proof

SHAKED. I'll fight you until the end

SHEFTEL. I'm sharpening my claws

SHAKED. We'll meet up in this courtroom

TOGETHER. We'll see who knows the laws

SHEFTEL. Do you hear how the state beckons
    with the vengeance of the ages
    Israel listens not to reason
    and puts liberty in cages

My dear client is a victim
of the whims of the state
The OSI wants to indict him
and hang him for their mistakes

SHAKED. If it's truth and wisdom you condone
then please invite your client to the stand
If it's Israel that you condemn
your blindness I reprimand

SHEFTEL. I'll fight for the underdog

SHAKED. I'll fight for the truth

SHEFTEL. I'll fight this damned government

SHAKED. I'll find all the proof

SHEFTEL. I'll fight you until the end

SHAKED. I'm sharpening my claws

SHEFTEL. We'll meet up in this courtroom

SHAKED. We'll see who knows the laws

SHEFTEL. I am a proud Israeli

SHAKED. You're a Judas of Jews

SHEFTEL. Here in this televised courtroom

SHAKED. The world is watching us

SHEFTEL. We'll see which one of us

TOGETHER. We'll see which one of us will lose!

Scene 14

FRAÜLEIN. John's cell. An Invitation.

   JOHN alone.

JOHN. I saw Junior.
   He's too thin.
   I liked Vera's blue hat.

   IVAN appears.

IVAN. Sentimental crap.
   I watched the survivors. Their stories make me sound like a god.

JOHN. Their faces were dripping with tears.

IVAN. I wanted to kill them all.

JOHN. How can you say that?

IVAN. It's us or them, John.
Soon the court will bring the survivors to the stand.

JOHN. What will they say?

IVAN. Whatever the prosecution wants.

JOHN. What do they want?

IVAN. You.
So. Do you want my help yet?

Scene 15

FRAÜLEIN. The defence calls to the stand
The Survivor
from Treblinka death camp

ROSIE becomes the SURVIVOR.

THE SURVIVOR. In Warsaw I studied the Bible and Dostoevsky
My dream was to be a scholar
When home became a ghetto
I became the breadwinner
scavenged Dluka Street for food

The last time I saw my mother I was seventeen
On the train to Treblinka
she gave me her wedding ring
I traded the gold for bread

SHEFTEL. In 1976 you were shown a photo spread. You identified John Demjanjuk as Ivan the Terrible.

THE SURVIVOR. Yes.

SHEFTEL. Do you remember the size of the photograph of Mr. Demjanjuk?

THE SURVIVOR. Not exactly.

SHEFTEL. Allow me to help you remember. The picture of Mr. Demjanjuk was twice as large as any of the others. Did you ever think this might help influence your identification of John Demjanjuk?

THE SURVIVOR. Certainly not. I remember what Ivan looked like.

SHEFTEL. What do you remember from Treblinka?

THE SURVIVOR. A dog, named Bari. He belonged to the commander Kurt Franz, whom we called Lalka.

SHEFTEL. Lalka?

THE SURVIVOR. It means doll. Lalka used to set his dog Bari against us. He was trained to attack a Jew's genitals. Lalka would say to Bari, "Man, bite dog!" And the dog would attack. The man would be running with blood between his legs—

SHEFTEL. I'm sure that was a terrible thing to have witnessed.

THE SURVIVOR. You cannot imagine.

SHEFTEL. Unfortunately, this has nothing to do with our case from a legal standpoint. Sir, I need you to tell the court about the process of identifying Ivan the Terrible—

THE SURVIVOR. There he is, sitting in front of me.

SHEFTEL. How do you know?

THE SURVIVOR. Three times a day we used to pray to Jerusalem. That was our hope. Now I am in Jerusalem. But I am still in Treblinka.

SHEFTEL. We need you to be sure—

THE SURVIVOR. This man sitting before you pushed children into gas chambers with an iron pipe and a bayonet.

SHEFTEL. Sir I—

THE SURVIVOR. I never wanted my children to hear this. Do you know if my daughter is here?

SHEFTEL. Did the survivors get together in Florida to discuss this case?

THE SURVIVOR. No.

SHEFTEL. Did you discuss this case with any of the survivors before you came to court?

THE SURVIVOR. We're friends. Do you think I don't talk to these people?

SHEFTEL. Did you discuss the photo spreads?

THE SURVIVOR. Not in any way that would seem inappropriate.

SHEFTEL. So there was a group discussion?

THE SURVIVOR. We often get together. We need to talk about our experiences.

SHEFTEL. Thank you. No further questions, your honour.

Scene 16

In the cell. JOHN is practicing for the case.

FRAÜLEIN. Lessons for Survival.

JOHN. Your honour, I worked on the Ford Assembly Line for twenty-five years.

IVAN. Louder.

JOHN. YOUR HONOUR, I WORKED ON THE FORD ASSEMBLY LINE FOR TWENTY-FIVE YEARS.

IVAN. More dignified.

JOHN. I'm a retired mechanic from the Ford Company. I worked there for twenty-five years, *sir*.

IVAN. Better. Then tell them about the engines. You were a *great* mechanic.

JOHN. I was a decent mechanic.

IVAN. You *love* engines.

JOHN. No, I like engines. When I open the hood of my truck, I look inside, I feel there's an order to things, the world can be understood.

IVAN. Good. So what does your truck run on?

JOHN. Diesel.

IVAN. Why?

JOHN. Cheaper fuel.

IVAN. More efficient.

JOHN. Diesel doesn't break down as much.

IVAN. The fuel injector of a diesel engine is beautiful.

JOHN. No. Reliable.

IVAN. A work of genius.

JOHN. Practical. The fuel injector can withstand incredible amounts of heat and still deliver fuel in a fine mist. And it's not exposed like the internal combustion engine.

IVAN. But diesel's more expensive.

JOHN. Not in the long run.

IVAN. You save on gas.

JOHN. And maintenance.

IVAN. Diesel has less horsepower.

JOHN. Higher torque.

IVAN. It's slower.

JOHN. Who needs to rush? Life is a marathon—

IVAN. not a sprint. You love your diesel truck.

JOHN. I love my wife.

IVAN. You appreciate it.

JOHN. I like to fix the problems. To get in there, and work with my hands. It brings me peace.

IVAN. Me too, Vanichka. Now. Let's start again.

Scene 17

In the court.

FRAÜLEIN. Today in court, Shaked is wearing a very tight suit. The prosecution sharpens its claws.

JOHN. I'm a retired auto mechanic from the Ford company. I worked there for twenty-five years, *sir.*

SHAKED. When did you learn how to drive a truck?

JOHN. 1947.

SHAKED. Your visa states you drove for the US Army at a DP camp starting from 1945.

JOHN. It's not true.

SHAKED. So you lied on your entry form?

JOHN. They must have misunderstood me. I told them I only knew how to drive a tractor.

SHAKED. And fix it?

JOHN. Yes. But to drive a truck one needed seven grades schooling, and I only had four.

SHAKED. Mr. Fedorenko was a truck driver during the war.

SHEFTEL. Objection! My client is not Fedorenko.

FRAÜLEIN. Overruled.

SHAKED. As a prisoner at Chelm, Mr. Fedorenko's life was saved because of his skills, and he became a driver at Treblinka.

JOHN. I am not Fedorenko.

SHAKED. No. But with only three years schooling he was a driver. *(pause)* At Chelm, the Germans asked all drivers to step forward. You volunteered to do so and you saved your life.

JOHN. I knew nothing about trucks.

SHAKED. You did. This is why your driver's license in 1948 said: Skilled Driver. You were a mechanic and driver during the war.

JOHN. Never.

SHAKED. Mr. Demjanjuk, you are accused of operating the gas chambers in Treblinka. Do you know that Jews were gassed in Treblinka not with Zyklon B, but by carbon monoxide from running a diesel engine?

JOHN. Yes.

SHAKED. And Ivan's duty was to maintain the diesel engine?

JOHN. Yes.

SHAKED. You admit that you knew how to fix engines before the war. The Trawniki ID card says you were trained as an SS guard—

SHEFTEL. Objection! The Trawniki card has not been proven authentic.

FRAÜLEIN. Sustained.

SHAKED. Yes, the Trawniki card which would allow a mechanic to operate the engine that killed two thousand Jews daily in Treblinka has not been proven authentic. I agree.

JOHN. The gas chamber was diesel. A tractor runs on gasoline.

SHAKED. And this court is supposed to believe that you did not learn how to operate a diesel engine until two years after the war?

JOHN. It's the truth.

SHAKED. Have you ever killed a man Mr. Demjanjuk?

JOHN. No. I could not even kill a chicken. My wife did it.

SHAKED. But you fought in the Red Army. You never shot anyone?

JOHN. NO. The very idea made me sick.

Scene 18

FRAÜLEIN. John has another flashback. 1941.

ROSIE. Not a very good year to be a German, eh, Fraülein?

FRAÜLEIN. Shut up.

ROSIE. How do you bake a German chocolate cake?

FRAÜLEIN. Not now.

ROSIE. First you occupy ze kitchen. Ha! In the trenches. Desperation! Darkness! Flashes of light! The Soviets—

FRAÜLEIN. are pushed back by the Nazis. John and his comrade Mordecai are the only ones left in their unit...

MORDECAI. Look at it. The hills are crawling with Krauts. I can feel them crawling in my skin. I'd shoot myself if it wouldn't kill me. *(They laugh.)*

JOHN. All you talk about is shooting. I'm hungry.

MORDECAI. Well, we've got a quarter loaf of mouldy bread—

JOHN. Ssssh! I think I hear someone.

MORDECAI. Let 'em hear. Maybe they'll have something for us to eat. Maybe we'll shoot 'em and roast 'em. Human flesh. Tastes like pork but it's kosher.

JOHN. Quiet.... Mordecai, you're not right in the head.

MORDECAI. This is it, John. There's no rules. It might be a war, but we can do whatever the hell we want. *(hinting)* There were a couple of hungry 16-year-old girls in the village back there.

JOHN. I liked the redhead.

MORDECAI. Oh. You're not such a mama's boy after all. Here. Take my gun.

JOHN. What am I shooting?

MORDECAI. Me.

JOHN. I don't want to kill you.

MORDECAI. You're not gonna kill me. *(puts bread on his head)* Target practice.

JOHN. You know I'm not a good shot.

MORDECAI. So you better practice up.

JOHN. What if I kill you?

MORDECAI. What's another dead Jew?

JOHN. Oh stop. We've known each other since we were kids.

MORDECAI. Yeah. And you're an anti-Semite. Like all Ukes.

JOHN. Look, it's not my fault you killed Christ.

MORDECAI. I didn't kill Christ. My uncle Lazer did it. *(They laugh.)*

JOHN. The priest once said you use Christian blood to make matzoh.

MORDECAI. It's true. Those little Christian boys make the best matzoh. *(MORDECAI puts the bread back on his head.)* Come on. Shoot me. This is your chance to get even. Stupid peasant.

> *JOHN shoots. Gun is empty. They laugh.*

Scene 19

> *Enter NAZI 1 and NAZI 2.*

NAZI 1. *Halts maul!* Drop ze gun!

NAZI 2. DON'T MOVE!

NAZI 1. We've been listening.

NAZI 2. We couldn't see you.

NAZI 1. Idiots.

NAZI 2. Fools.

NAZI 1 & NAZI 2. Ha ha ha ha ha!

NAZI 2. Shut up.

NAZI 1. Shut up.

NAZI 2. Shut up!

NAZI 1 & NAZI 2. Ha ha ha ha ha!

NAZI 1. I want to kill them.

NAZI 2. I want to squeeze them.

NAZI 1. Little Russian Teddy bears.

NAZI 2. Little bears.

NAZI 1. Kill them.

NAZI 2. Can't.

NAZI 1. Kill them!

NAZI 2. CAN'T. Remember our orders.

NAZI 1. Remember Nietzsche. Or Goethe.

NAZI 2. Or Sven, the great herring merchant from Bremen:

NAZI 1. Everything German is Great!

NAZI 1 & NAZI 2. *Sieg heil!*

NAZI 2. Okay. We kill one. Keep the other.

NAZI 1. *Jah.* Which one of you was talking about roasting krauts?

> *A beat. No one says anything. NAZI 1 and NAZI 2 become menacing.*

NAZI 2. Is no one

NAZI 1. Talking?

NAZI 2. Are you two

NAZI 1. Friends?

> *Pause.*

JOHN. He was, sir.

> *NAZI 1 kills MORDECAI.*

NAZI 2. Oh. *Gott im Himmel.* Maybe that was the wrong one.

NAZI 1 & NAZI 2. Hahahahahaha!

NAZI 1. Shut up!

NAZI 2. Shut up!

NAZI 1. Shut up!

JOHN. If it pleases you, sir, he was a Jew.

NAZI 1 & NAZI 2. Jew?

JOHN. Yessirs.

NAZI 2. Well. Then justice has clearly been done.

NAZI 1. Once again, Divine Providence is *mit ze* German people.

NAZI 2. *Heil* Hitler!

NAZI 1. *Deutschland über alles!* (*a beat*)

NAZI 2. You're fairly strong, I see.

NAZI 1. Well-built.

NAZI 2. You have blue eyes—

JOHN. They're green, actually—

NAZI 1 & NAZI 2. Blue!

NAZI 2. There's something very

NAZI 1. Aryan about you.

NAZI 2. Can you drive a truck?

JOHN. Yes.

NAZI 2. Good *mit* engines?

JOHN. Yes.

NAZI 1. *Sehr gut.* (*a beat*)

NAZI 2. Why don't you join our club?

JOHN. No.

NAZI 1. Well there is another way out, you know.

NAZI 2. Yes, through the chimney.

NAZI 1 & NAZI 2. Hahahahahahaha.

NAZI 1. Membership you will find

NAZI 2. Has its privileges…

NAZI 2 imprints tattoo under JOHN's arm.

Scene 20

FRAÜLEIN. Back in court, Shaked further tightens his grip. John begins to *shvitz*.

SHAKED. Why did you remove your tattoo in 1945?

JOHN. Because I found out it identified me as an SS soldier.

SHAKED. So you were SS?

JOHN. No. The tattoo indicated my blood type.

SHAKED. Then why remove it?

JOHN. I was afraid it might be taken the wrong way.

SHAKED. And how did you come by your tattoo?

JOHN. At a certain point as a prisoner I was made to be a soldier.

SHAKED. What year?

JOHN. 1944.

SHAKED. By the Nazis?

JOHN. Yes. A Ukranian auxiliary. Vlassov's army. We were all given tattoos but different from those of the SS.

SHAKED. You just said they were the same.

JOHN. They were similar.

SHAKED. What did you do in this auxiliary?

JOHN. I guarded military personnel.

SHAKED. Did you choose to be a soldier for the Nazis?

JOHN. No, I was ordered to.

SHAKED. The years 1942-43 you claim you were a POW in Chelm.

JOHN. Yes.

SHAKED. Describe to the court what it was like.

JOHN. The Nazis would beat us constantly. I was starving. I would've done anything for a piece of bread.

SHAKED. Really? How long were you in Chelm for?

JOHN. Eighteen months.

SHAKED. Can you tell me any of the names of the other prisoners?

JOHN. No. But their faces are clear to me.

SHAKED. Mr. Demjanjuk, you claim you spent most of the Second World War as a POW in Chelm.

JOHN. Yes.

SHAKED. And it was an atrocity you can't forget, just as you can't forget the famine in Ukraine.

JOHN. These are atrocities that I want to forget, but can't, just as anyone who survived the Holocaust.

SHAKED. So when you were first indicted in 1978 these details were still fresh in your mind?

JOHN. Yes.

SHAKED. But in 1978 you never mentioned Chelm.

JOHN. Because it didn't come to mind then.

SHAKED. You spent a year and a half in Chelm.

JOHN. I can't help what I forget.

SHAKED. Your alibi is Chelm, Mr. Demjanjuk. Do you understand what that means?

JOHN. Yes.

SHAKED. And yet there is not a single witness to support this claim. And your testimony is vague and contradictory.

JOHN. I am answering in this manner because no one prepared me the way they prepare witnesses in Israel to give replies.

SHAKED. Mr. Demjanjuk—

JOHN. My only mistake is I can't think properly and I don't know how to answer accordingly.

SHAKED. You don't need to be prepared to tell the truth.

Scene 21

In the cell. JOHN is alone.

JOHN. But I was in Chelm.
So what if I can't remember their names?
I don't even remember the names of people I met last week.

I live in America.
I work, eat, spend time with my family.
I sleep well.
I'm a good man.

IVAN appears.

IVAN. As remarkable as a diesel engine.

JOHN. No. Practical.

IVAN. 1941.

JOHN. I was starving in the mud flats of the Steppe.

IVAN. 1942.

JOHN. I was a ghost in the forests of Poland.

IVAN. 1943.

JOHN. I… don't remember.

IVAN. Really? How is it you haven't broken? Do you put your memories in a compartment and just forget? I can't. Killing was so easy back then. The hard part was how to dispose of the bodies. *(pause)*

At first we just threw them into ditches with some lime. But after a few months the smell was unbearable. Sometimes the earth would breathe. Geysers erupted when we walked the camp. Someone had the idea to burn them. But how does one burn one hundred thousand bodies? First you put the women on the bottom. Then the children. Then you attach the railroad ties. The men go on next. And then you light your match.

JOHN. Please.

IVAN. The motor of a tractor that sows the land that grows the crops
The motor of a tractor that runs and runs and never stops
The gasps the wails
The songs and tales
O, I can never forget those

Diesel. Thank God we switched to diesel. *(pause)* The worst was when the engine would break down, and the room was still full.... The wails human beings can emit. Like dogs. Only worse.

JOHN. I was never near a gas chamber.

IVAN. Well let's go. Every man should see it. At least once.

ROSIE. Or twice.

IVAN. Fraülein, *musik, bitteschön!*

Scene 22

Ukrainian music.

FRAÜLEIN. Step right up, step right up. Welcome to the Treblinka Death Camp! Men, women, children. Everyone is welcome. Admission is free.

IVAN. *(singing)* Can you hear the music
the prisoners play?
It's got a good reprise
today's a good day

I like their jazz
their kick and their swing
Here in Treblinka
they've got everything

There's vodka to drink
and whores in the village
So many benefits
who needs to rape and pillage

Ah, it's a good day for work
isn't it
isn't it

It's a good day to work
yes it is
Oh how I like it very much
running my engine in the sun

> *IVAN continues to take JOHN on a tour through the camp. IVAN and THE SURVIVOR play a sadistic game.*

IVAN. Main Exports, 1943

IVAN.	**THE SURVIVOR.**
suitcases	372 freight cars
bedding, down quilts, feathers	260 freight cars
men's suits	248 freight cars
religious artifacts	122 freight cars
hair compressed in bales	25 freight cars
miscellaneous items	400 freight cars

IVAN trips up THE SURVIVOR.

IVAN. A strong body. A strong mind. A strong spirit.

An artist must always
push himself.
I understood those children.
Their tears, like my art,
longed for the great audience.

I don't know why I asked
to have them thrown into the air.
Did Goethe control the words
that flew from his hands?

It was a mother's rain.
You should have seen
the waxed glint
on the babies' heads.

My blade
    blazing
beneath the lights

Achtung! How would you say life is here?

THE SURVIVOR. Well the guards are very hospitable. They let us eat, for starters. Not much mind you, but they let us eat.

IVAN. How do you spend your days?

THE SURVIVOR. If I'm not hauling corpses, I'm playing in Arthur Gold's orchestra getting the prisoners excited for their imminent deaths.

IVAN. Isn't there any off time?

THE SURVIVOR. Certainly. The officers encourage us to fuck and fall in love. It seems to amuse them, the possibility of love. And on Yom Kippur they bring us succulent roast pig and Belgian endive salad.

IVAN. I like Belgian endive salad. Do you?

JOHN. *No.*

IVAN. *(aside)* A mahogany pipe,
a gift from my dead father.

Smoke reflected
in my sword's blade.

Too distant to hear.

The shower of bodies falling,
night swallowing day.

Almost silence.

The ashes, the light,
these small bones.

I smoke my pipe.
Wanting peace.

Scene 23

"The Ballad of John Demjanjuk Part II"

FRAÜLEIN. Now the years went by
    and the war was long past
    John raised a family
    in Cleveland at last

    He had what he wanted
    the American dream
    A job at Ford factory

SHEFTEL. Is that so obscene?

THE SURVIVOR. 1976
    the place was New York
    We the survivors
    read the report

SHAKED. They looked at his picture
    they were sure it was him
    The man who had tortured them
    at every whim

SHEFTEL. The photos were biased
    the survivors confused
    No wonder they all said
    he's the gasser of Jews!

Scene 24

FRAÜLEIN. Now to the stand, the prosecution calls the survivor from Treblinka
death camp—

THE SURVIVOR. I used to carry the bodies from the showers
Sometimes I'd hide and
nap beneath the incinerators
The fumes left me with
a bad eye and throat

When Ivan made me lie with a corpse
I had no choice
I knew what he wanted me to do
Nobody ordered him to do that

You wonder how I can remember this man so well?

(to JOHN) The night of the rebellion
I made off with your eyes
Stitched them into the wallet
of my skin
Forty-four years I've carried
this ashen currency

A thousand curses
unto you, Ivan of Treblinka

May you hang from the olive tree and weep

Scene 25

FRAÜLEIN. Isn't barbed wire pretty?
The way sunset
can turn a fence
to purple and gold?

The end of the war! A Displaced Persons camp in Southern Germany. Behold
the ruins that remain. And the love that grows from them.

"Love in the DP Camp"

(singing) The barbed wire was sparkling
and the angels were calling
That was the night John and Vera consummated their love

ROSIE. A new alibi John was trying
So on the forms he kept lying
John was afraid of being sent back to the Soviets

FRAÜLEIN. Now John wasn't alone
The lovers longed for a home

ROSIE. They dreamed of a place in the States

FRAÜLEIN. He worked hard in the camp
It was cold it was damp

ROSIE. He gave Vera the food on his plate

FRAÜLEIN. Yes the barbed wire was sparkling

ROSIE. And the angels were calling

CHORUS. That's when he popped that old question
And married her

JOHN. Under the fence

Scene 26

IVAN and JOHN in the cell.

IVAN. Are you lonely?

JOHN. I've been alone for two years in this cell.

IVAN. So you're happy we're together.

JOHN. No.

IVAN. That's right. Vanichka doesn't get happy. Always working. Trying to make the American dream. Only now there's no work to do. So what does he do to pass the time?

JOHN. I write letters to my family. To Vera.

IVAN. Nice. I'm curious. How do you two like to fuck?

JOHN. Shut up.

IVAN. I prefer it from behind. Like a dog.

JOHN. Kurva.

IVAN. You like to talk while you do it?
Are you tender?
Or do you like to throw her against the wall—

JOHN. You're disgusting.

IVAN. Don't be so innocent. You used to talk like this with the boys when you were in Vlassov's army.

JOHN. I never talked about my wife in this way.

IVAN. Poles, Jews, Germans. All those women. They didn't even have time to say yes or no, did they? Sluts.

JOHN. I never raped.

IVAN. Oh no. The best thing about war crimes is when you're doing them they're not crimes. Words like "rape" don't enter your mind. You're just "making love." The hard part is afterwards.

JOHN. I raised a family.

IVAN. So did I.

JOHN. I live for my family.

IVAN. You say that as though you could be sure of who you are.

JOHN. I am.

    IVAN nods to FRAÜLEIN.

Scene 27

"Two Faces are Better than One"

FRAÜLEIN. Oh yes it's true
 a good possibility
 That a man is a man
 with many personalities
 But can two faces
 be one?

 Well you know two faces
 are better than one

 You take your chances
 you play your hand
 The cards are shuffled
 where do you stand?

 You take your chances
 You have your fun
 But are two faces
 just one?

 It's not so easy
 we all know
 Being more than one person
 can be very hard on the soul

 A man is a killer
 A man loves a lot

Is this the same man
what proof do we got?

Friedrich Nietzsche
did he have it right?
Are we doomed to our past
no matter how hard we're gonna fight?

People change
so some experts say
A man can forget
what he did yesterday

A face is different
or stays the same
Is it the same man
if a photo's all that remains?

So from your past John
you cannot run

If two faces
are one

Scene 28

FRAÜLEIN. The Travniki card
Is an SS card
It has a photo of John

The Travniki card
Is it an authentic card?
Sheftel prays that it is wrong

    In chambers.

SHEFTEL. The Travniki document is a forgery.

SHAKED. Prove it.

SHEFTEL. The signature is completely unlike that of my client's.

SHAKED. Then why did John admit it was "the way he wrote his name"?

SHEFTEL. The card says he was at Sobibor.

SHAKED. And Sobibor is 130 km from Treblinka.

SHEFTEL. The KGB supplied the card to this court.

SHAKED. They have the documents—

SHEFTEL. and they want John dead.

SHAKED. John himself admitted the picture resembles him.

SHEFTEL. He was confused by the question. I know this card's a forgery.

SHAKED. Such a good forgery nobody can tell that it's fake?

SHEFTEL. You're a self-righteous, Talmudic hair-splitting asshole.

SHAKED. You're an opportunistic *mamzer*, feeding off the desperation of the Ukrainian community.

SHEFTEL. I am going to demolish, shred this document to pieces, until there is nothing left.

FRAÜLEIN. *Bitte.* I hope he leaves us a little for the trial.

SHAKED. *(to the court)* The prosecution would like to submit as evidence a 1942 paperclip. On this ID card there are rust marks left by a paperclip. If the rust mark is authentic, the card must be too. And John trained to be an SS guard at Travniki.

SHEFTEL. Is this card forged?

SHAKED. Or is it real?

FRAÜLEIN. The court must decide.

> Item #2641.
> John's life held
> by a paperclip

SHAKED. FRAÜLEIN. *Bitte.*

> *FRAÜLEIN becomes the paperclip.*

THE PAPERCLIP. I am the paperclip
> That might have held
> the picture
> of John to this card

> I am really a 1942 German
> paperclip
> Yes, evidence is
> getting hard

> If I turn rusty
> then the card
> is true
> the evidence in my lips

> But no one's sure
> if there was rust on
> German-made
> paperclips

> So submit me for evidence
> Hand me past the weak defence
> I will make John hang
> or set him free

His life is a paperclip
Trying to keep things
in one place

Oh, but it's loose
Things don't hold
Order turns to disgrace…

Scene 29

Voices whisper:

VOICE 1. *Never cursed*

VOICE 2. *Never angry*

VOICE 3. *Never talked about the war*

VOICE 4. *He's the kinda guy who'd fix your bike*

IVAN. *even if you didn't really know him*

ALL. *And his perogies were…*

JOHN JR. Dad?

JOHN. Junior.

JOHN JR. What did you do during the war?

JOHN. Nothing.

JOHN JR. Is that why you never talked about it?

> *JOHN moves toward JOHN JR. They start to bring their hands together. Just before they touch, the lights go out on JOHN JR.*

Scene 30

IVAN. I have a gift for you.
A field. It was dark.
The earth was hard.
The moonlight fell on this in a particular way.
As though the moon were pointing, *here you are, here you are…*
Sleep, old friend. Sleep.

Scene 31

"Time Passes Slowly"

> *While singing, IVAN reveals a baby shoe and puts it in the pocket of JOHN, who is sleeping.*

ROSIE. Time passes slowly
 with the drip drip drabble
 Listening to the holy
 cell wall rabble

IVAN. Let the dark
 leave its mark

 Twelve years waiting
 while the world is spinning

 memories forgotten,
 now reappear

ROSIE. Time passes slowly
 with the drip drip drabble
 He's listening to the holy
 cell wall rabble

Scene 32

FRAÜLEIN. Trial day three-hundred and ninety-five. What goes on in the boys' room? Our two handsome lawyers, Shaked and Sheftel, get close and personal at the urinals.

SHAKED. Sheffie.

SHEFTEL. Mickey.

> *An awkward piss.*

SHAKED. Report's back. There was rust on the paperclip.

SHEFTEL. Of course. You forge that too? *(a beat)* I saw Mike Wallace up in the balcony.

SHAKED. "Sixty Minutes" is doing a special.

SHEFTEL. There's no business like Shoah business.

SHAKED. Tell that to the survivors.

SHEFTEL. Sentimental prick.

SHAKED. I can't wait to see you lose in front of the entire world.

SHEFTEL. I don't lose anything I take on.

SHAKED. Your client's not doing too well out there.

SHEFTEL. My client's a stupid goy. He's too dumb to have killed a million people.

SHAKED. Glad to see you respect your client.

SHEFTEL. I want you to know: I've got a lead that could destroy you.

SHAKED. You're bluffing.

SHEFTEL. Am I? I don't want a plea bargain. Even if you offered it to me.

SHAKED. What's this lead?

SHEFTEL. You think I'm gonna tell you?

SHAKED. What you know could be in both our interests. That is, if you actually care about the truth.

SHEFTEL. Whose truth? I'm the only person in this damned country who wants to find out what this man actually did during the war.

Scene 33

FRAÜLEIN. Trial records page eight thousand and sixty-five. Back in court, the defense calls the Survivor from Treblinka death camp to the stand. Again.

SHEFTEL. *(places a book down on the stand)* Sir, is this your handwriting?

THE SURVIVOR. Yes.

SHEFTEL. Do you remember when you wrote this?

THE SURVIVOR. 1945.

SHEFTEL. Would you say that what you wrote was a true account of life in Treblinka?

THE SURVIVOR. Yes.

SHEFTEL. Is it true that the night of the Treblinka uprising you saw Ivan the Terrible killed in the gas chamber?

THE SURVIVOR. No.

SHEFTEL. But you wrote it in your account.

THE SURVIVOR. I wrote what I was told.

SHEFTEL. You wrote that you saw him killed.

THE SURVIVOR. It was the others who told me.

SHEFTEL. You wrote, right here, that you saw Ivan the Terrible killed with a shovel.

THE SURVIVOR. I wanted to believe that. That was our dream.

SHEFTEL. Then why did you not point out the difference between what you wrote and what you saw?

THE SURVIVOR. I wish I had been there. *(pointing to John)* If I had been there, he would not be sitting across from me. Wipe that grin from your face!

> *JOHN starts to laugh. THE SURVIVOR walks over to JOHN. JOHN rises.*

JOHN. *Atah Shakran!*

THE SURVIVOR. Don't you call me a liar.

Scene 34

> *Courtroom freezes.*

JOHN. Did you see that? The Survivor's made a fool of himself.

IVAN. This is Israel. They're going to hang you. Even if you're not Ivan.

JOHN. I AM NOT IVAN. You were killed.

IVAN. Maybe I was. Maybe I wasn't.

JOHN. I will not die for something I didn't do.

IVAN. And what did you do, John?

JOHN. I don't remember the details.

IVAN. You don't want to remember.

JOHN. I thought you were going to help me.

IVAN. I already have.

JOHN. Where are you going?

IVAN. To the Western Wall. I like to watch the Jews pray. Their songs bring me a certain peace.

> *IVAN whispers into THE SURVIVOR's ear, "Atah Shakran."*

Scene 35

> *Unfreeze.*

THE SURVIVOR. Don't you call me a liar…

FRAÜLEIN. Order in the court! Order in the court!

SHEFTEL. Your Honour, I need a short recess. John? What the hell was that about?

JOHN. I can't do it.

SHEFTEL. Just take a deep breath. Everything will be fine. We're winning. It's your final statement. Relax.

JOHN. I can't think straight—

SHEFTEL. John, grab a hold of yourself.

JOHN. Not guilty. Guilty.

SHEFTEL. Jesus, John.

JOHN. What if I was a guard.

SHEFTEL. What?

JOHN. *(pause)* At a camp.

SHEFTEL. *(A beat. SHEFTEL is taken aback. He recovers.)* That's not what you're on trial for. The rules were different during the war. Maybe you did some wrong things back then. But not genocide.

JOHN. Yoram. Am I a good man?

SHEFTEL. You're a survivor, John.

JOHN. Yes. I am.

SHEFTEL. Now get up there and make your final statement. I will not lose this case.

Scene 36

Back in court.

JOHN. I'm a simple man
with a simple mind.
I have no knowledge of
systems and laws.

I live in America
with my family.
I have a vegetable garden.
When I sink my hands into the earth
I feel peace,
moist and soft,
something to grab onto.

You've been watching me for twelve years now.
You're watching to see
what I have seen.
It's these hands that have seen a lot.
Motors and children
harvests and perogies.
These hands have seen the ocean,

embraced love,
filled out forms—

People of Israel, I need you
to understand. I am not Ivan of Treblinka.
I learned the order of the engine
so I could survive.

I breathed
hot metal,
the sparks from a torch,
bodies of automobiles
cooling on the line.
Ten hours a day
five days a week
for twenty-five years...
Thank God for America,
I remind myself each day.
Thank God for America.

Scene 37

FRAÜLEIN. April, 1988. The day of the Verdict has arrived. The doors to the courtroom open at eight a.m., but the first spectators have lined up since midnight. When the police van arrives at the court, John refuses to get out. A sound emits from his mouth, a high-pitched whimper, like a dog. He must be carried into court by four guards. Kicking and screaming and crying.

The Court of Israel finds John Demjanjuk... guilty!

JOHN. *(speaking)* My Vera faints.
Junior weeps. The Jewish students chant.

VOICES. *Am Yisrael Chai, Am Yisrael Chai!*

JOHN. An eye for an eye.
A tooth for a tooth.

Scene 38

IVAN. Soon they'll put that noose around your neck
and you'll be sweating
and the people chanting
blood, blood, we have his blood—

JOHN. I'm not dead yet.

IVAN. No.

JOHN. I still have hope.

IVAN. Really. Why?

JOHN. I don't know. Maybe that's how I survive.

Scene 39

FRAÜLEIN. So you think it's over for John?

ROSIE. Yes!

FRAÜLEIN. No way. Sheftel's appeal races forward like a white Porsche on the Autobahn.

ROSIE. John sits on death row for four years.

FRAÜLEIN. Sheftel is persistent

ROSIE. Sheftel won't quit.

SHEFTEL. I would like to submit as evidence, a telegram from the KGB to the OSI.

Dear Sirs: Your request to identify John Demjanjuk as Ivan the Terrible has turned out negative.
Eighty accounts from thirty former Treblinka guards name Marchenko as Ivan. John Demjanjuk never at Treblinka.
Date of telegram:
April, 1978.

Ladies and gentlemen. Fifteen years ago today there was evidence that would have acquitted my client in any standard court of law. Why the U.S. and Israeli governments chose to suppress this information we can only imagine.

Scene 40

FRAÜLEIN. All rise in the court of law!
The Supreme Court of Israel rules
that John Demjanjuk
is not Ivan of Treblinka.

The verdict overturned. The appeal won.

JOHN. *(singing)* Tonight I dream of home in Ohio
The lawn smells like the sun
and the trees
shush golden in the breeze

Cries of children
ice cream trucks
and my face
full of sun
Summer on my skin
at last

FRAÜLEIN. John returns to his loving family in America. But at a Cleveland Indians' baseball game…

JOHN. It's all over now.

IVAN. Over? They picket on your lawn.

ROSIE. *Murderer.*

IVAN. Wear gold stars.

ROSIE. *Ivan the Terrible.*

IVAN. But you got away with it.

JOHN. Justice was served.

IVAN. Congratulations. Let's have a hot dog.

JOHN. I don't want a hot dog. I'd like to just enjoy the game.

IVAN. Who's winning?

JOHN. We are.

IVAN. The U.S. is reopening your naturalisation file, Vanishka. Your trials aren't over.

Scene 41

IVAN. 1941.

VOICES. *1941*

JOHN. I was starving in the mud flats of the Steppe.

IVAN. 1942.

VOICES. *1942*

JOHN. I was a ghost in the forests of Poland.

IVAN. 1943…

VOICES. *1943*

> *Flashback, 1943.*

JOHN. I'm in the field.

IVAN. The sky is black.

JOHN. The trees are listening.

IVAN. There's only a few of them.

JOHN. And I don't even have to dig their grave.

IVAN. All you have to do is pull the trigger.

JOHN. All they have to do is gather themselves and kill me.

IVAN. They won't.

JOHN. There's a girl in a white skirt.

IVAN. That's the girl I'm gonna have.

JOHN. There's a man praying.
His passion rises toward me.

IVAN. His passion is mine.

JOHN. Life

IVAN. or death.

JOHN. I wish I could drop my gun and run.

IVAN. The choice is yours.

JOHN. I wish that one didn't look like my mother.
I want to run back to Ukraine.

IVAN. Not even the moon is innocent.

JOHN. A woman breastfeeds her child.
The child wipes its mouth,
there's too much milk,
the skin is so white

IVAN. I want to drink it!

JOHN pulls out the baby shoe from his pocket.

JOHN. The child drops its shoe.

IVAN. No bigger than my finger.

JOHN. Criminals?

IVAN. We were gods.

JOHN looks at the shoe, then the gun in IVAN's hands. Blackout.

Epilogue

Out of the black, the survivor enters. He sings.

The Survivor. This is the end
of our story tonight

But when I go to sleep
will things be all right?

What once was Treblinka
is now farm and grass
There are lupines and elm trees
where the slow train rolls past

But what's dead's not done
what's gone comes again
Good night my children,
my judges, my friends

    Fin.

Hand in Hand

Simon Block

• Simon Block •

Simon Block was born in North London, where he still lives. He was educated in London, and then Southampton and Cambridge Universities. His theatre credits include *Not a Game for Boys* (Royal Court Theatre, 1995); *Chimps* and *No Exp. Req'd* (both Hampstead Theatre, 1997 and 1999 respectively) and *A Place at the Table* (Bush Theatre, 2000). His writing for television includes "Attachments" (BBC-2, 2001/2002); "North Square" (Channel Four, 2000) and "Safe as Houses" (ITV, 2000). He is married with two sons.

• **Playwright's Notes** •

Loaded with the myth of Israel received at his parent's knee as a child, Ronnie—a North London Jew—went out to undertake postgraduate study at an Israeli university, discovering a country so at odds with his parents' fables that he returns to London in a state of moral confusion. He attempts to secure his old room at the flat of his best friend, only to discover the room—earmarked for a baby's nursery—no longer available. Desperate to escape the disappointment and anger of his parents to whom he's forced to move back, Ronnie embarks on a campaign to undermine the relationship between his best friend and his sister, which has sprung up in his absence. Only then, Ronnie, concludes, will he get back what is rightfully his—his old room. In sticking zealously to his task, Ronnie puts both family and friends under unbearable pressure.

By insisting on everyone around him seeing the terrible truth of the world as he sees it, Ronnie terrifies his parents and alienates his immediate circle; who ultimately just want to live in relative ignorance and peace. Ronnie is driven to despair—the more he screams about what is happening in the occupied territories the less anyone wants to hear. He finds himself increasingly isolated.

A sub-plot of the play focuses on the nature of modern relationships, and the act of faith required for two people to form a partnership and move forward. The poster for the play was of two hands shaking—which was in fact a close-up of the hands of Arafat and Rabin at the White House in 1993.

The action of the play takes place in two locations: in Act One, on Hampstead Heath overlooking the City of London; in Act Two, on the rooftop patio of Ronnie's friend's flat, on the eve of the last total eclipse of the sun, on 11 August 1999.

• **Production History** •

Hand in Hand was first staged in February 2002 at Hampstead Theatre, London, with the following company:

DAN	Guy Lankester
RONNIE	Ben Miles
CASS	Rebecca Egan
LOU	Tilly Blackwood
DOUGLAS	Simon Coates
HELEN	Sarah Alexander

Directed by Gemma Bodinetz
Designed by Soutra Gilmour
Lighting Designed by Tim Mitchell

• Characters •

DAN
RONNIE
CASS
LOU
DOUGLAS
HELEN

• *Hand in Hand* •

Act One

The top of Parliament Hill, overlooking the City of London spreading into the distance.

Late afternoon in early summer, 1999. Two park benches. A lamp post.

A large, beaten up old holdall sits on a bench, wearing fresh travelling tags.

RONNIE stands on the bench looking at the view. He wears loose, crumpled clothes for travelling rough, and sandals, also past their best. He slowly scans the horizon. After a while he places one hand over one eye, looks at the view, and then removes the hand. He looks at the view, and then replaces the hand over his eye. He looks at the view and removes the hand, as DAN approaches from the left and stops a little way away, watching this hand choreography.

Pause.

DAN. Let me guess.

RONNIE. *(without turning)* Money says you won't.

DAN. A very small animal just flew into your face. Probably not furry.

RONNIE. Make it *a lot* of money.

DAN. You just suffered a discrete stroke.

RONNIE. Not even close.

DAN. I give up.

RONNIE. You'll owe me a lot of money.

DAN. You know where I live—when I get a lot of money, it's yours.

RONNIE. *(beat)* I'm trying to remember how the horizon was before I went away.

DAN. Don't waste your time. In a few months they'll put up the Millennium wheel and it'll all look completely different again.

RONNIE. I don't want it to all look completely different.

> *RONNIE regards the view. Pause.*

The view from up here's still the best.

DAN. They say the view from the wheel's going to be even better.

RONNIE. If that's true it will only be because when you're on it, you won't actually be able to *see* it.

DAN. From what I've seen so far, I like it.

RONNIE. *(turning to face DAN for the first time)* 'Course you do, Dan. You kept hamsters.

> *RONNIE gets off the bench and faces his old friend. Pause. DAN smiles.*

DAN. How was the flight?

RONNIE. You're looking at a man who got bumped up.

DAN. You got bumped up?

RONNIE. Club class.

DAN. No!

RONNIE. Oh yes!

DAN. Between lessons I sometimes stare out of the window at passing airplanes, and fantasize about paying economy but flying Club. What did you do?

RONNIE. What did I do?

DAN. You must've *done* something.

RONNIE. To what end?

DAN. To catch their eye. What was that eye-catching thing? Your trick?

RONNIE. No trick.

DAN. But I once read there's a knack for selection. For being singled out. To increase one's chances. What was yours?

RONNIE. During the flight I sat next to an erudite orthodox couple from Manhattan wearing matching velvet loafers. I thought they would be very dull, but they were completely the opposite. I think we had a very fascinating discussion over champagne as we crossed the Med.

DAN. You *think*?

RONNIE. My attention was distracted by how much better free food tastes when people in the next seat paid through both nostrils for theirs.

DAN. I thought you had to at least look smart to get bumped up. Did you look smarter before? Did you change in the plane? Or when you landed?

RONNIE. This is how I looked when I got bumped up.

DAN. I find that very difficult to swallow.

RONNIE. I swear.

DAN. It flies in the face of everything I respect.

RONNIE. I was standing in Ben Gurion waiting to check in, when a woman from the airline walked over, took my ticket, and handed me a better one.

DAN. Then you must've been standing differently. Show me how were you standing?

RONNIE. I wasn't standing differently.

DAN. You were standing like somebody special. Do it.

RONNIE. Do it?

DAN. Do how you were standing.

RONNIE. I stood like I'm standing now. Can you believe I slept like a rock over the Alps?

DAN. French or Swiss?

RONNIE. The plane flew between both.

DAN. You slept with Alps on either side?

RONNIE. Full stretch. Pillow. Blanket. Eye patch. Ear plugs. Air socks. Little basket of *petit fours*.

DAN. Air socks?

RONNIE. In a sterilized polythene bag.

DAN. You slipped them on?

RONNIE. In Club Class it's *de rigueur*.

DAN. What were they like to fly in? Comfy? Snug?

RONNIE. From today I refuse to fly in anything else.

DAN. You always did land on your feet.

RONNIE. I'm taking it as an omen.

DAN. An omen?

RONNIE. For my return.

The two men look at one another. Pause.

DAN. Pinched myself when I heard your voice from Heathrow. Got other people to pinch me. You didn't give any hint you were coming home.

RONNIE. I only made up my mind a week ago. I would've come back immediately. But it's coming into the busy season, so I had to wait for a flight.

DAN. After so long, why the big hurry to leave?

RONNIE. Because there's nothing for me there, Dan.

DAN. What do you mean?

RONNIE. I mean… there's nothing for me there.

Pause. They regard one another.

DAN. I have an overwhelming urge to hug you.

RONNIE. It's been a long time.

RONNIE opens his arms wide for embracing. Pause.

DAN. What, you want me to come over there?

RONNIE. I'm flexible.

DAN. You're the one who's come home. You're the one who rang from the airport asking to meet before you've even spoken to your parents.

RONNIE. For a very good reason.

DAN. Nevertheless.

RONNIE. You expressed the urge to hug, Dan.

DAN. I don't want to rush over like a dick. I'm feeling a torrent of emotion right now, which is fine because you're my oldest friend and I haven't seen you in four years. But I'm not going to fall at your feet like an idiot.

> *RONNIE regards DAN for a few moments.*

RONNIE. Have you changed?

DAN. Well…

RONNIE. Put on a little weight, perhaps? Lost some hair?

DAN. Hair's not important.

RONNIE. But how we hug is?

DAN. I always used to be the second one. Ronnie and Danny. Starsky and Hutch— never Hutch and Starsky. Only I'm not a kid anymore. I'm thirty-five, with a kid of my own.

RONNIE. I know that.

DAN. I think it's important to state. If you're back for good, it's important to start as we mean to continue.

RONNIE. Okay.

DAN. I'm over the moon you're home, but it's important to recognize how things are.

RONNIE. *(beat)* And I recognize that by coming over to you?

DAN. Better yet, would be moving towards one another simultaneously.

> *DAN opens his arms. RONNIE opens his. The two men face one another with their arms outstretched. Pause.*

RONNIE. Who's going to make the first step?

DAN. I suggest a count of three.

> *DAN counts down with his fingers. They slowly walk towards one another and embrace affectionately. They hold each other tightly in silence for several moments.*

God, it's good to see you…

RONNIE. You too, Dan. I can't tell you…

DAN. The twat who took your season ticket's a tosser.

RONNIE. Why I called from the airport—

DAN. Thinks he's at the clock end—jumps on his seat when the game goes quiet and tries to get us all to chant. Doesn't understand that's why we sit where we're sitting.

RONNIE. Dan?

DAN. That we've passed through the "leaping about and chanting like a tosser" phase, and are now in the "sitting down and actually watching the game" phase.

RONNIE. Dan, I need a place to stay.

DAN. Tonight? Have the sofabed, no problem.

RONNIE. Not just tonight.

DAN. Not just tonight?

> *Beat.*

Okay…

> *They break away. RONNIE takes out a packet of cigarettes and lights one. DAN watches him.*

RONNIE. *(casually)* You remember the night before I left?

DAN. Of course. We got hammered and urinated off the roof.

RONNIE. The night before I left, before we got hammered and urinated off the roof, you made me a promise. I didn't ask you to. It was a spontaneous gesture on your part.

DAN. If it's about keeping in regular touch, you've always known I'm a lousy correspondent.

RONNIE. It wasn't a promise about keeping in regular touch, Dan.

DAN. Okay.

RONNIE. The night before I left you promised that my room in the flat would always be here for me.

DAN. Your room in the flat?

RONNIE. Would always be here for me. That was your promise. That was what you promised me. *Unsolicited.*

DAN. That was a long time ago. And made—if not entirely under the influence— pretty close to it.

RONNIE. As you say, a long time ago. Four years, one month, and twenty-six days.

DAN. During which time I've been married and divorced.

RONNIE. I know.

DAN. Become a father.

RONNIE. If you're worried about rent—

DAN. Rent doesn't come into it.

RONNIE. I'll put an envelope on the kitchen table at the end of each month. Or if you'd prefer, we could set up something more formal.

DAN. It's not a question of *letting* the room.

RONNIE. If it's because you're seeing Cass, I give you my word. I'll be less than a fly on the wall.

DAN. You don't understand.

RONNIE. Believe me, the last thing I'd want is to be present when the two of you.... My oldest friend and my sister? No offence, but just thinking of the two of you locked together turns my stomach.

DAN. *(beat)* It's my boy's room now.

RONNIE. Your boy's room?

DAN. It's Oscar's room now.

RONNIE. *(beat)* But you told me he lives with your ex. I distinctly remember reading an email—

DAN. And when he comes to stay, he stays in his room.

RONNIE. You mean my room.

DAN. Now it's his. Gunners curtains. Denis Bergkamp duvet. Ray Parlour pillowcase. I sleep there myself sometimes, when the weather... sometimes in a storm. Or if my day has been particularly shit.

RONNIE. May I refer you back to your promise...

DAN. Made in a universe without Oscar.

RONNIE. Move Oscar into the studio.

> *Pause.*

DAN. Why won't you—

RONNIE. You haven't made a film in years. Gut your studio and move Oscar's stuff in there. He's three years old, Dan. He won't even notice.

DAN. *(beat)* Gut my studio?

RONNIE. Do you good. Scorched earth, with nothing left to torture yourself over what might have been.

DAN. I'm not tortured over what might have been.

RONNIE. Nevertheless, problems solved all round.

DAN. *(beat)* Okay.

> *Beat.*

Look.

> *Beat.*

Right.

> *Beat.*

Even if I did that.

RONNIE. If you did, it would be the right thing to do—believe me.

DAN. Even if I *did* move Oscar into the studio.

RONNIE. Which, for the purposes of this conversation, I feel we should now call "Oscar's cosy new bedroom."

DAN. Even if I moved him across, you can't come back.

RONNIE. But my point, Dan, is that I could. More to the point, I sort of came home on the back of that promise.

DAN. But you should have checked first. Surely you understand this.

RONNIE. I just assumed you'd keep your word.

DAN. *(starting to lose his patience for the first time)* I'm sorry, Ronnie. But I need the flat clear.

RONNIE. Need?

> *Beat.*

DAN. For me and Cass.

RONNIE. Like I *said*, when she's round—

DAN. But my hope is that in the not-too-distant future Cass will *always* be round.

> *Pause.*

RONNIE. I didn't realize things had become that serious.

DAN. I know what you're thinking.

RONNIE. I'm not thinking anything.

DAN. You're thinking, "oh the irony."

RONNIE. I wasn't thinking "oh the irony," Dan.

DAN. How could a misdirected email from you cause your best friend and your sister to get together?

RONNIE. I wasn't thinking that.

DAN. Well, we got together, Ron. More to the point, I'm entertaining the serious hope that we're going to stay together.

> *RONNIE takes out his packet of cigarettes and lights another.*

I see you smoke now.

RONNIE. *(more insistent)* You made a promise, Dan. I don't want to put you on the spot. But a promise is a promise or else *it's* a lie, and *you're* a liar.

DAN. Like I said a few minutes ago—

RONNIE. *(more insistent)* If a promise is to have *any* value it has to override temporary changes in circumstances. The country I've just flown from would never have got off the ground if some rather extraordinary people hadn't held fast to a two-thousand-year-old covenant—it's what sustained them until willpower and tragedy forced Israel onto the map. It's what's sustaining some of them *still*—even as they're told on a daily basis that the doctrine of all or nothing is unacceptable.

DAN. Hang on—

RONNIE. A *true* promise between people who mean what they say is a powerful thing, Dan. It's simplicity is its strength.

DAN. Jesus, Ron. When did you get this emphatic?

RONNIE. If we remain unchanged by travel why leave the comfort of the sofa?

DAN. Ask me for anything else.

RONNIE. I don't *need* anything else. It's either the flat or back to my parents.

DAN. So go back to your parents.

RONNIE. I can't.

DAN. Why not?

RONNIE. I'm thirty-six years old.

DAN. You always used to say that in their eyes you never stopped being twelve.

RONNIE. Exactly.

> *He takes a deep drag and then drops the cigarette on the floor—crushing it underfoot.*

So I'm going to ask you one more time.

DAN. Four years ago I would have ummed and aahed and given in. But not now. I no longer um and aah and I'm not giving in. I'm sorry.

RONNIE. I don't wanna have to beg.

DAN. I'd do anything for you. You know that.

RONNIE. So I can come back to the flat?

> *RONNIE picks up his holdall and slings it over his shoulder.*

DAN. Anything but that.

> *They regard one another for several moments, before DAN exits stage right.*
>
> *RONNIE slowly sits on the bench facing front, sharp daylight blending into dusk over the city. He pulls his jacket close around him, turning up the collar against the cool evening air. He looks straight ahead, smoking the cigarette, watched by CASS, who has appeared stage left.*

CASS. That's new.

RONNIE. *(standing)* If we only ever did what we've only ever done we'd still be squatting in caves, wiping our arses with moss.

> *RONNIE stubs out the cigarette on the arm of the bench, and stands.*

You look very well.

CASS crosses into the scene proper.

CASS. You mean *older*.

RONNIE. Older doesn't suit everyone. You it suits.

CASS. You've started to go grey.

RONNIE. In Israel, grey is the new light black this season.

They smile and embrace.

CASS. You sounded a little tense on the phone. How is it at Mum and Dad's?

They pull apart.

RONNIE. You have to ask?

CASS. I meant… how *bad*?

RONNIE. *(sitting)* Well… I'm tending not to get up until I hear Dad leave for work. And Mum's been slipping me a fiver for dinner before he gets back. I'll either sit in a burger bar ingesting the carcinogenic fog of vaporized animal fat, or come up here 'til it's past his bedtime.

CASS. It's only been a few days, Ronnie. Give him time.

RONNIE. Time? Yesterday I made the mistake of going home too early. I heard him through their bedroom door telling Mum he wished either he or I was dead.

CASS. You must've expected a certain level of disappointment. They put a lot of eggs in you.

RONNIE. Well… all smashed now as far as they're concerned.

CASS. Don't be so melodramatic.

RONNIE. Our father wishes I was *dead*, Cass—I think we've inched ever so slightly beyond melodrama, don't you?

CASS. There was a time when Dad's penchant for talking like a character out of Sophocles had you in stitches.

RONNIE. This time there was no playing to the gallery. This time he meant it.

CASS. I'm sure you think—

RONNIE. *(adamant)* This time he meant it.

Pause. CASS regards her brother as he takes out the packet of cigarettes to light another, and takes a deep drag.

CASS. What happened with the doctorate?

RONNIE. It wasn't for me.

CASS. *(taking a deep breath)* Why didn't you tell me you'd dropped out over a year ago? Do you know what it felt like to find out yesterday?

RONNIE. When I told Dad he told me not to tell you, in case Mum found out.

CASS. Good old fashioned Jewish patriarchy—don't you just love it? So between dropping out and coming home you did *what* out there?

RONNIE. A lot of things.

CASS. Such as?

RONNIE. All sorts.

CASS. Anything specific you're bursting to elaborate about?

RONNIE. Not really.

CASS. Okay. So why come home now? Run out of money?

RONNIE. No.

CASS. Luck?

RONNIE. No.

CASS. Arrested? Thrown out for doing a Vanunu? Your emails dried up ages ago—give me some kind of clue. Did you just get bored?

RONNIE. Anyone who can get bored in Israel is clinically dead.

CASS. So why?

RONNIE. The situation became impossible.

CASS. The situation? But everyone's saying Barak's going to be better than Netanyahu. Best chance of a breakthrough in years, I read.

RONNIE. Look—can't we just leave it that I couldn't stay.

CASS. Jesus, Ronnie, but *why* couldn't you?!

RONNIE. *(standing)* Let me ask you a question.

CASS. No, but hang on—

RONNIE. *(turning on her)* Dan.

CASS. Dan?

RONNIE. Dan.

CASS. What about Dan?

RONNIE. You like him?

CASS. Obviously.

RONNIE. Love?

CASS. While you were away I discovered there's considerably more to Daniel than meets the eye. I've developed the view that you were a bad influence.

RONNIE. Oh really. Well, I could tell *you* some salty stories about Danny.

CASS. No need. He already told me the really disgusting ones.

RONNIE. And you still like him?

CASS. You know how much of a sucker I am for reformed bad lads.

RONNIE. And Malcolm and Josie?

CASS. Malcolm and Josie?

RONNIE. They like Dan?

CASS. You've been taking him to their house for years. You know they've always liked him.

RONNIE. When he was with me he wasn't a horny Gentile *schtupping* one of their children.

CASS. When we've been round on a Friday night I don't think Mum and Dad were gazing into their soup picturing Dan doing me over the table. I may be wrong. Oh shit...

RONNIE. What?

CASS. That's what I'm going to be thinking Malcolm and Josie are thinking every time we go round. That won't erase. Great present on your return, though a face-pack from En Gedi would've been sufficient.

RONNIE. But the Jewish thing?

CASS. What Jewish thing?

RONNIE. I just wouldn't want you thinking something's not a problem when it possibly is.

CASS. What?

RONNIE. A problem.

CASS. The Jewish thing?

RONNIE. The Jewish thing.

CASS. Yes, but what are you actually talking about?

RONNIE. Surely it's better to be wide-eyed than blind to the possibility.

CASS. If I knew what possibility you're referring to I'd be better placed to agree.

RONNIE. I'm not saying I'm insensitive to the anxieties surrounding the issue.

CASS. Which issue?

RONNIE. I'm simply saying let's not pretend they don't exist.

CASS. Mum and Dad and Dan?

RONNIE. I'm only saying.

CASS. Well you don't have to. Because even if there was a problem, which there isn't, but even if there was, Dan took care of it.

RONNIE. He took care of it?

CASS. Dan's Arsenal. Dad's Tottenham. Dan plays *goy* to Dad's *yid*. Since we started seeing one another Dan's used the difference as their common ground.

RONNIE. Dan did that?

CASS. Perky banter about who's higher than who in the table. I don't know what the hell they're talking about but they get on fine.

RONNIE. And that works with Mum?

CASS. She asks as subtle as a sledgehammer if we've "talked about the future." I tell her our generation finds it difficult to even *think* about the future let alone talk about it. But with my track record, she's so relieved I'm with someone who changes his pants and doesn't dribble, she won't push it.

RONNIE. And you?

CASS. What do you mean?

RONNIE. We both know how deep it goes, even if we don't think it does.

CASS. You're not suggesting *I* have a problem with Dan not being Jewish?

RONNIE. I don't think you *think* you have. But if you had it would hardly be a failure on your part.

CASS. Are you serious?

RONNIE. It wouldn't be seen as some lapse in decency. It's what's been done to you. How you've been indoctrinated.

CASS. *Indoctrinated?*

RONNIE. Indoctrination. Heritage. Call it what you will. Either way it's beyond your control.

CASS. *(bridling at the suggestion)* Have I *ever* expressed a problem with Dan not being Jewish before?

RONNIE. You weren't going out with him before.

CASS. I'm finding it difficult to believe I'm actually hearing this.

RONNIE. I ask only because on the day I came back I came straight from the airport and met him up here.

CASS. I know.

RONNIE. I asked if I could move back—

CASS. —into the flat. Yes, Ronnie. I know.

RONNIE. And he said I couldn't, because he was keeping the flat clear.

CASS. For Oscar. I *know.* Contrary to what you might wish to believe, your best friend and I enjoy a pretty full-blown relationship—with all the open lines of communication that entails.

RONNIE. Except Dan isn't just keeping the flat clear for Oscar, is he?

CASS. *(beat)* What do you mean, not just for Oscar?

RONNIE. You haven't discussed moving in together?

CASS. *(beat)* What?

RONNIE. You've not even *considered* the possibility?

CASS. Wait a second—

RONNIE. You see, this is what I find interesting. Because Dan *has.*

> CASS stares at RONNIE, wrong-footed. DAN strolls up the hill and onto the scene holding a remote-controlled car control unit (box with an aerial coming out of the top) and looking back in the direction from which he's just come.

DAN. Has it run out already?!

> *RONNIE leans forward and gently kisses the top of his sister's head, before walking away.*
>
> *CASS looks up and watches him go as DAN fiddles with the controls.*

I've been using it for all of what—ten minutes? How can I give him this?

CASS. Be honest. It was never really a present for Oscar anyway.

DAN. Of course it was.

CASS. How many three-year-olds do you see with remote control cars?

DAN. *(walking off to collect the car)* Perhaps the batteries hold up better on flat ground.

> *CASS watches as DAN returns holding a shiny plastic, fairly cheap-looking remote-controlled car.*

This was going to be a major part of my attempt to get him outdoors. His mother's big on videos, but since when was *watching* the same as *doing*? No one's saying she's a bad mother. Just a lazy one.

CASS. A little rich considering you don't have him full-time.

DAN. Just because my contact can't be full-time needn't mean my concern isn't.

CASS. Come here.

DAN. *(crossing to CASS)* What?

CASS. *(pulling him closer by his lapels)* I know how your mind works, Dan.

DAN. You couldn't possibly. I'm an enigma.

CASS. As a child you always hankered after a radio-controlled car, but your parents never had the excess wherewithal to waste on anything so pointless. But now *you* have, you're at an age where prowling round your local rec area in dim, solitary pursuit of a miniaturized vehicle would be a sad comment on you and your kind. So you buy the toy under the guise of buying it for your three-year-old—a little boy, lest we forget, with insufficient strength in his arms to snap a wet match, let alone wield a radio control unit.

DAN. *(smiling, beat)* I was going to whip up a leather harness.

CASS. A leather harness?

DAN. Toddler *Leiderhosen*, with attachments.

CASS. Toddler *Leiderhosen*?

DAN. With any leftover leather I was planning to knock you up a pair.

CASS. Oh really.

DAN. Slim-fitting. Cut high on the—

> *CASS puts a finger on his mouth, stopping him. They regard one another for a few moments.*

(with CASS's finger still on his mouth) I lub do.

CASS. Don't say that.

DAN. *(removing her finger)* But I do.

CASS. Say it after I've been jogging and I've got a roasted potato face and a sweaty arse.

> *DAN adjusts himself.*

What?

DAN. You're bending my antenna.

CASS. Dan, I need to talk to you.

DAN. You are talking to me.

CASS. Seriously.

DAN. That sounds serious.

CASS. About us.

DAN. Should I sit down?

CASS. Are your legs tired?

> *CASS moves off a little and turns to face DAN, holding the car.*

Ronnie told me not to tell you, but I get the impression he hasn't grasped the shift in loyalties since you and I started seeing each other.

DAN. Ronnie told you not to tell me what?

CASS. That he told me something you told him.

DAN. I didn't tell him anything.

CASS. About us.

DAN. Us?

> *Pause.*

CASS. That you hoped I'd move in with you one day.

DAN. *(beat)* I see.

CASS. And I just wanted to make something absolutely clear.

DAN. Is the hope unfounded?

CASS. I just wanted to make it absolutely clear that the reason I've never voiced a similar hope has nothing to do with the fact that you're not Jewish.

DAN. What?

CASS. In case you were thinking it might have.

DAN. It never occurred to me.

CASS. No?

DAN. Not for a single, solitary second.

They regard one another, as LOU pushes a pram to the top of the hill and takes a breather.

Long pause.

CASS gets up from the bench and moves away, looking out over the view.

LOU. A single, solitary second?

CASS. *(still looking at DAN)* That's what he said.

LOU. And this is a problem because?

CASS. *(still looking at DAN)* Because when I thought about it... I thought perhaps he should have.

LOU. Uhuh.

CASS. I mean, if he's as serious about me as he so often professes it's an issue he should at least be alive to. If not from his own point of view, then from mine.

DAN crosses to CASS and kisses her.

DAN. *(tenderly)* Love you, Cassie.

He walks out of the scene.

LOU. Isn't it enough to hold people accountable for the things they *do* think?

CASS. It just flagged another little question, that's all.

LOU. Another little question? Or yet another little question *mark*?

CASS. You don't think it's a legitimate concern?

LOU. Is Daniel a long-term prospect, yes or no? You want to come to a conclusion you won't regret, of *course* I can understand that.

CASS. But your problem is?

LOU. My problem is less with your need to come to the right conclusion, than the agonizing you're going through to reach it.

CASS. I've been burned too many times.

LOU. You've a predilection for arseholes, free-loaders, and man-boys. You're hardly alone.

CASS. My emotional skin is a veritable lattice of shiny scars on shiny scars.

LOU. It's not helped by the fact that it's getting easier and easier for a bit of old chaff to pass himself off as wheat. You have to fan hard to expose the dross. *But—*

CASS. If I fanned any harder I'd take off.

LOU. But fan *too* hard and you could be left with nothing. Just you, in a field, empty-handed.

CASS. *(not sure what LOU actually thinks)* So... you *don't* think I should be concerned by Dan not being concerned about the Jewish thing?

LOU. What I think is… what do *you* think?

CASS. My brother suggested I'm reluctant to admit an innate aversion to the idea of a permanent relationship with a non-Jew.

LOU. The question is, is he right?

CASS. The question is, if he *is* right, what does that make me?

LOU. A traditionalist.

CASS. Or some kind of a racist?

LOU. Well, that all depends how you look at it.

CASS. I'm doing my best to look at it as honestly as possible. I don't know, Lou. The greatest bigot I ever knew? Guess.

LOU. In real life?

CASS. My grandmother.

LOU. On whose side?

CASS. Mum's. One minute she was a lovely old woman in pressure stockings, shouting at minor celebrities on TV to get their hair cut. And next she was a wrinkled ball of malevolence, screeching venom at Blacks, Asians, Catholics— you name it, and if it wasn't Jewish she hated it.

LOU. Jesus.

CASS. I can't help but wonder if a little bit of that managed to wheedle its way onto my chromosomes.

LOU. You haven't got a bigoted bone in your body.

CASS. Not that I know of. We like to think that our past means we've cornered the market in racial tolerance. But Nana alone kicks that little bit of self-aggrandizement into touch.

LOU. Maybe, but nothing wrong with sticking to your own kind in principle.

CASS. You didn't.

LOU. I said there's nothing wrong with it. I didn't say you had to turn it into a fetish. Anyway, Doug's vague Methodism hardly posed the greatest hurdle for a Catholic in guilt and reverence for ceremony only.

CASS. I've gone out with non-Jewish guys before. I've certainly slept with them. Lots of them. Very nice they were too.

LOU. You've slept with them, but have you ever thought about moving in with any of them?

CASS. I've come close.

LOU. You've come close but never completed. What does that tell you?

CASS. That I'm a sexually predatory hypocrite?

LOU. It's a possibility. But only one of several.

CASS. Yet taken as a whole, Lou. My unease about Dan being married when we started seeing each other. My concerns about becoming a fixture in his son's life, and the trauma that could result from a break-up. The Jew non-Jew thing, and the revelation that he's not given it a single solitary second of thought. And don't forget, these are all in addition to the litany of more general anxieties— such as my chances of finding someone else *as good* if not better. Compatibility. Reliability. How we raise any children we might have? To circumcise or not in the event we had a boy? The possible friction arising from the fact that I earn twice as much as Dan. Dan's capacity for violence, mental or physical.

LOU. Physical? You mean, Dan—

CASS. No of course not. But I've noticed if we ever watch a documentary about the African savannah, he always roots for the cheetah, never the gazelle.

LOU. *(beat)* Right…

CASS. And then there are my parents to consider.

LOU. Malcolm and Josie?

CASS. Though I've never said as much to Dan, I've consciously been keeping our relationship uncomplicated in their eyes.

LOU. How uncomplicated?

CASS. Very much on a day-to-day basis, with little or no emphasis on what may or may not develop.

LOU. I see.

CASS. In many ways it was so much easier for them. I don't mean economically, but their choices were so much more straightforward for being limited. On a simple geographical level, my parents rarely mixed socially beyond their Jewish circle, so the chances of going out with a non-Jew—let alone marrying one—were so much slighter.

LOU. But you're not talking about marrying, Dan.

CASS. I'm only talking about the possibility of *moving in* with him. But the resonance is never far away. As are the overriding fears, which are perhaps more real to them than they seem to me.

LOU. The overriding fears?

CASS. For the gradual disintegration of the community.

LOU. Never a fear with us Catholics—abstract or concrete.

CASS. And yet.

LOU. And yet?

> *DOUGLAS, LOU's husband, comes up the path from the left, holding a serious-looking stunt kite and rewinding the twine back on its spool. He stops within hearing range of CASS and LOU, though they don't see him. He listens as he spools the twine.*

CASS. And yet, whether I set out to or not, I seem to have fallen for Danny boy. So taken as a whole—

LOU. Is it possible to take all this as a whole?

CASS. Taken as a whole, what do you think I should do?

LOU. *(beat)* No, Cass. Don't do that.

CASS. Don't do what?

LOU. Don't lead yourself up the garden path and then ask me to knock on the door for you.

CASS. Is that what I was doing?

LOU. Your brother's really stirred your porridge, hasn't he.

DOUGLAS. *(advancing a few steps and pointing into the distance)* You see that couple beside that tree under that blanket...

> *CASS and LOU look over.*

CASS. There ought to be a law.

DOUGLAS. Or failing a law, a mounted short-range telescope for interested voyeurs.

LOU. *(hinting broadly)* Douglas. Why don't you carry on flying your kite. You know. Somewhere else.

DOUGLAS. You may not have noticed, but what wind there was has dropped like a stone.

LOU. Only, Cass and I were talking.

DOUGLAS. Oh? About anything interesting?

LOU. I doubt to you.

CASS. My brother thinks I might be an unconscious religious fanatic with a fascistic libido.

LOU. He's somehow managed to plant the idea that the reason Cass hasn't been *actively* thinking about Dan in the long-term might be rooted in their religious differences.

DOUGLAS. I didn't think you were religious, Cass.

CASS. I'm not.

DOUGLAS. I didn't think Dan was either.

CASS. He isn't.

DOUGLAS. I'm so relieved you cleared that up.

CASS. It's easy for you. You don't really believe in anything.

DOUGLAS. Not easy at all. It takes a lot of effort not to believe in anything.

LOU. And anyway that's not true. He does.

DOUGLAS. No I don't.

LOU. Equality, justice, freedom with opportunity. All that stuff.

DOUGLAS. Oh, all that stuff's a given. You have to understand how all that stuff works, but it's too obviously right to require concerted *belief.*

LOU. It's what makes him the only ideological taxman in the Inland Revenue.

DOUGLAS. Well, you want the good life, pay for it.

LOU. Yes, Doug. We know.

DOUGLAS. Don't want to pay taxes? Fine. Buy yourself a large gun, turn out the lights, and wait for them to come for what's yours.

LOU. Please, Doug.

DOUGLAS. Doesn't take a genius. Everything has a price. Only question worth asking: are you prepared to pay for what you want, or not?

LOU. He's only telling you all this because I stopped listening years ago.

CASS. *(sotto)* I'm not really listening. Just giving the appearance.

LOU. I find occasional little grunts convey interest where none exists.

DOUGLAS. And there was I hoping the feminist struggle amounted to a little more than taking the piss.

LOU. Also, tilting your head to one side in mock fascination.

CASS. A simple question often keeps Dan chauntering on indefinitely, without requiring any response this side of actually falling asleep.

> *DOUGLAS has been rewinding the twine on the kite as the two women talk.*

DOUGLAS. What Lou and I have *really* been wondering about you and Dan, Cass…

> *LOU and CASS suddenly turn to DOUGLAS. Beat.*

Oh. Listening?

LOU. *(trying to head him off at the pass)* Doug.

CASS. No. Go on.

DOUGLAS. Why he hasn't asked you to move in with him before now?

LOU. Now is neither the time—

CASS. No, Doug's a friend. I'd be interested in a male perspective.

LOU. Then Douglas isn't your man.

DOUGLAS. *(ignoring his wife)* Dan's been married before, so he's obviously not opposed to cohabitation in one form or another.

LOU. Did it ever occur to you that he's perhaps once bitten twice shy.

DOUGLAS. It's a nice expression but hardly holds up. It's the equivalent of flipping a coin, getting tails, and then believing you've got more or less chance of getting heads with the next flip. Surely, regardless what happened before, either Cass is or isn't the woman for him now.

CASS. He has been *thinking* about asking me to move in.

DOUGLAS. Unfortunately, the fact that he's been thinking about it without discussing it—that he's only come clean because your brother blew the gaff. Well. I'm sorry, Cass. But speaking as a *male* and a *friend*, it almost makes the situation worse.

LOU. *(to CASS)* Excuse us for a moment.

> LOU takes DOUGLAS by the elbow and leads him firmly away from CASS.

DOUGLAS. I know what you're going to say.

LOU. The question of why Dan hasn't yet asked Cass to move in arose as part of a private conversation between *us*.

DOUGLAS. Rather than you and I gossiping among ourselves about what Dan may or may not be thinking, I thought it might be more pertinent to ask—if not the horse's mouth—then at least the person who kisses it.

LOU. You have no idea what's happening inside her head right now.

DOUGLAS. It's always been my understanding that complicated issues become progressively *less* complicated when you actually talk about them—the key syllables in that sentence being *pro* and *gress*.

LOU. You really don't understand what's going on here, so I would greatly appreciate it if you would, please, not speak.

> LOU turns to walk back to CASS, but DOUGLAS grabs her arm and pulls her back.

DOUGLAS. Whenever you tell me "I don't understand" all you mean is I don't happen to agree with you. As though disagreement in itself is a form of betrayal. It's a cheap way of silencing an opposing view, but if that's ultimately your aim it would at least be more honest if you simply punched me in the mouth.

LOU. Don't tempt me.

DOUGLAS. Take your best shot.

LOU. *(on the attack)* Dan is a lovely, lovely man!

DOUGLAS. *(matching her)* Who doesn't know what he wants!

LOU. That's not true! He seems to be wanting to live with Cass.

DOUGLAS. *Seems* to be. At some point in the near or distant future. For some period of time, hitherto unspecified. I'm very fond of Cass—I don't want to see her hurt any more than you do!

CASS. Um. You do know I can hear you.

> LOU and DOUGLAS freeze. Pause.

I didn't think it was fair to let you carry on thinking I couldn't.

LOU. You heard what we've just been saying?

CASS. I just don't think you're very good at being discreet.

LOU. I think we must be out of practise around grown-ups. Around Claire we don't need to be anymore discreet than we would if we were talking in front of a small cat, or a log.

CASS. *(to DOUGLAS)* Do you really think Dan might not actually know what he wants?

LOU. Don't ask him, he doesn't even know how to park straight.

DOUGLAS. Untrue. I just choose not to.

LOU. *(to DOUGLAS)* Why don't you take chummy back to the car? The sun's gone in.

DOUGLAS. She's wrapped up like an immersion heater.

LOU. *(firmly)* Douglas, it wasn't a request.

    LOU regards DOUGLAS firmly. Beat.

DOUGLAS. *(taking a deep breath, repeating as rote)* Why don't I take chummy back to the car. It's getting cold.

    DOUGLAS crosses to CASS and kisses her on the cheek.

Listen to Lou, Cass. I mean it. Everything will be fine. You're lovely. Dan's lovely. We're all lovely, lovely people in a lovely, lovely world.

    DOUGLAS peers for a moment into the pram and then wheels it back down the hill. LOU and CASS watch him go.

LOU. Dan's what, thirty-four?

CASS. Thirty-five.

LOU. His failed marriage aside, would it be any wonder if he was proceeding with due caution?

CASS. Douglas didn't say "due caution." Douglas said "uncertainty."

LOU. Isn't it around their mid-thirties that men of Dan's age face the realisation that they're never going to slide the winner past Brazil in the world cup final? Row the Atlantic. Or in Dan's case, win the best original short category at the Sundance Film Festival.

CASS. I think Dan came to terms with that one a while ago.

LOU. But don't we see them on the tube every morning? Showered, bleary-eyed, wondering how in God's name they ended up with a silk noose round their neck, comedy socks, a low sperm count, and an annually renewable travelcard.

CASS. If we have to be realistically aware of the clock why can't they?

LOU. I'm merely suggesting that Dan's prudence might be all the more authentic for being measured.

CASS. We started exchanging emails three-and-a-half years into his failing marriage, and when that broke up we started seeing each other. From her to me. Before her, someone else, and before someone else, if you examine the chronology, someone else again. I saw it all from the vantage point of Ronnie's sister, don't forget. Turns out, when you put all Dan's dates together, there's scarcely three months between one woman and the next.

LOU. Not wanting to be lonely is hardly a crime, Cass.

CASS. But if he's really not sure about me, how sure can I be about him?

LOU regards her friend for a few moments.

LOU. Please don't do this.

CASS. Don't do what?

LOU. Don't talk yourself out of being happy.

LOU sets off after DOUGLAS, leaving CASS standing alone for a few moments.

Pause.

The light darkens to late night, the bench illuminated by a pool of orange sodium. City lights sparkle in the distance.

CASS pulls her coat around her and turns the collar up. She looks at her watch impatiently.

After a few moments RONNIE slowly walks onto the scene behind her, holding a white plastic carrier bag. He silently lowers the bag to the floor and stealthily advances on CASS from behind, grabbing her, and putting his hand over her mouth.

RONNIE. One sound and I'll slit your throat…

CASS's eyes widen in terror, but she instinctively raises her arm and drives her elbow hard into RONNIE's side.

Fuck!

RONNIE immediately releases his sister who turns round and sees who it is.

CASS. You stupid fucking cunt! Do you know precisely *how* unfunny that was?!

RONNIE sinks to his knees in agony. He is unable to speak, just moans, quietly.

We're not kids anymore, you *prick*!

RONNIE. *(severely winded)* It was meant to be a joke…

CASS. *(the anger focusing)* You were *meant* to be here three quarters of an hour ago! Where the fuck have you been?!

RONNIE. *(vaguely pointing in the direction of the carrier bag on the floor, still winded)* Felafel van by the Royal Free…

CASS. *(furious)* Do you know how many invitations to *rape* I've had to decline while you were stuffing your face?!

RONNIE. *(winded)* I was hungry.

CASS. *(beat)* You were *what?*

> *Pause.*

RONNIE. *(low, winded)* Sorry.

CASS. Too fucking late.

RONNIE. *(beat, winded)* Need to… sit.

> *RONNIE offers his hand so CASS can help him to his feet. She doesn't move.*

CASS. *(ignoring him)* The bench is over there.

> *CASS doesn't move to help him—just watches RONNIE struggle to the bench. He sits, and breathes in a controlled rhythm. Pause. Finally he sits up, and lets out a deep breath.*

(the anger subsiding, but leaving her feeling assertive) Mum says you're now avoiding all meals at home.

RONNIE. It's easier.

CASS. So why don't you leave altogether?

RONNIE. With what? To where?

CASS. I could lend you some rent money until you got a job.

RONNIE. A job?

CASS. What tedious little people like me do.

RONNIE. I'm qualified to sit in academic libraries and read. Hardly puts me in a prime spot in the marketplace.

CASS. What about Dad?

RONNIE. What about him?

CASS. Maybe there's something around the office you could do?

RONNIE. Be serious.

CASS. I am being serious.

RONNIE. What happened the last time I worked for him?

CASS. He gave you the sack after twenty-five minutes. But that was different. Now you know not to get his seventy-eight-year-old cutter mashed on cannabis. Though, she's not seventy-eight anymore, of course. She's dead. Nevertheless—

RONNIE. Anyway. I can't leave the house. Not yet.

CASS. Decide to leave and then leave. The rest takes care of itself.

RONNIE. Staying at Mum and Dad's isn't about not having to pay rent, Cass.

CASS. No—it's about being thirty-six and still not taking responsibility for yourself.

RONNIE. Oh please...

CASS. Oh please *nothing*—that's what it is.

RONNIE. You don't believe things could actually be ever so slightly more complex?

CASS. Israel was a flop, you can sniff forty on the breeze, with no clue where next to turn. No, I'm sorry, I really don't think it is any more complex than that.

RONNIE. *Think* about it—

CASS. Here we go.

RONNIE. Not "here we go." I came back with nothing. All that money, for what? He won't even talk to me.

CASS. Maybe it's gonna take him longer to cool down than you originally thought.

RONNIE. And maybe he never will. You know what he's like with a *broigus*.* He's got twenty-year-old feuds with cousins whose names he can no longer remember. And others he rings just to slam the phone down when they pick up. Am I exaggerating?

CASS. So he lives in black and white.

RONNIE. So if I walk away with the situation unresolved Dad and I are probably finished. *Finished*, Cass. No-show at his funeral. *Over*. Which has—if you only care to look—profound repercussions for everyone. Because if Dad and I stop talking, Mum and I stop talking—at least, until he dies.

CASS. I didn't ask you up here to listen to this.

RONNIE. *(continuing his theory)* After he's dead—assuming he goes first— whatever feeling Mum has left for me will be crippled by loyalty to his memory. Until she goes herself, angry and bitter.

CASS. If this is the sort of stuff you're thinking over there, the sooner you get out the better.

RONNIE. *(concluding)* Inevitably you'll be drawn in and made to take sides. Which you'll refuse to do, or will be unable to resist—either way expanding the rifts already there in one direction or another—until it all caves in.

> *Beat.*

For everyone's sake, I can't leave yet.

> *CASS regards him. Pause.*

CASS. Did you know Mum thinks you've been brainwashed?

---

* *broigus* – quarrel, feud.

RONNIE. In Israel…?

CASS. She's no other way to account for something you said in response to an enquiry about whether you'd come across any nice Jewish girls.

RONNIE. Oh that. I merely said some of them would've seemed a lot nicer if they weren't so vitriolic about their Arab counterparts.

CASS. Perhaps they had a lot to be vitriolic about.

RONNIE. You have to hear some of the things that get said to believe them. Ordinary, decent people, spouting extraordinarily vile garbage.

CASS. Look, I'm not trying to defend people I've never met, in a situation I know relatively little about—

RONNIE. Good.

CASS. —I'm just trying to relate how worried Mum is about you since you got back.

RONNIE. Mum goes to sleep worrying about the sunrise. If they severed her head from her neck she'd worry which bit most needed her scarf.

CASS. She rang me at work this morning.

RONNIE. So she's got your work number.

CASS. She told me they don't see the same Ronnie they drove to the airport four and a half years ago.

RONNIE. It would be an indictment of foreign travel if they did.

CASS. But her implication was you're not *any* kind of Ronnie they can relate to.

RONNIE. Then what kind of Ronnie am I?

CASS. That's the problem. They don't *know*.

RONNIE. What do *you* think?

CASS. I can't say.

RONNIE. Look at me.

CASS. I'm looking.

RONNIE. Who am I?

CASS. You're Ronnie Stoll.

RONNIE. To *you*. Who am I to you?

CASS. You're my brother.

RONNIE. Looking at me, does that feel strange to say in any way?

CASS. *(beat)* No.

RONNIE. You hesitated.

CASS. There's a different quality about your eyes.

RONNIE. In what way?

CASS. More sombre than I remember.

RONNIE. Yeah, well. It's dark.

> *RONNIE stands and walks a little ways away. He takes out a pack of cigarettes and lights one. He takes a deep drag.*

CASS. *(watching)* Can I ask something?

RONNIE. I could never stop you in the past.

CASS. I've always wondered what effect living off Mum and Dad for most of your adult life must have had on you?

> *Beat.*

RONNIE. You think I'm some kind of *leech*?

CASS. I imagined it couldn't be entirely healthy, that's all.

RONNIE. Cass, let's get one thing straight. I never took anything they didn't insist I take.

CASS. I wasn't implying—

RONNIE. Every penny was linked in one way or another to education. You know Dad.

CASS. You're not listening to what I'm saying.

RONNIE. If you hit him for a few hundred for an old banger he'd ask "there's something wrong with the bus?"

CASS. Ronnie—

RONNIE. But go to him for a few thousand for a Masters—his hand was a fucking blur he couldn't write a cheque fast enough.

CASS. The way you say that makes it sound like a bad thing.

RONNIE. Beyond a point there was a certain recklessness to it, certainly. I grew to regard them like a pair of speculators blindly pumping money into a potentially hot—yet ultimately flawed—proposition.

CASS. I wish they'd been a little more reckless with their chequebook towards me over the years.

RONNIE. For as long as I can remember I was cultivated to be the family brain.

CASS. You make it sound like we lived in the Hammer House of Horror.

RONNIE. You know what I mean. The scholarship boy. The school-prize winner. It was an image of me they were only too keen to sustain. All that reflected glory they could bask in. All that *naches*.* I'm not blaming them.

CASS. Maybe not right at this very moment—but I think I can hear the gears of blame *cranking* up.

RONNIE. I know it sounds like blame, but it isn't. It's just that somewhere along the road I ceased to be a sound investment. Trouble is, they never stopped investing.

---

* *naches* – joy.

I thought perhaps they couldn't. Like inveterate gamblers putting their shirt on one last punt after another in the hope that one would come good. Over the last couple of years I've realized it was much more desperate than that.

CASS. What're you talking about?

RONNIE. I'll give an illustration. Just over a year ago, when I contacted Dad to let him know my PhD had collapsed, I assumed my subsidy would stop immediately, with an instruction to return home forthwith.

CASS. It didn't?

RONNIE. The call to come back never came. And in fact the subsidy *increased*.

CASS. Increased?

RONNIE. Think about what that signals.

CASS. I don't understand.

RONNIE. It signalled that as long as I remained *out there* he was more than happy to keep me afloat.

CASS. I still don't understand.

RONNIE. Because PhD or no PhD, at least I was still in *Israel*—and no matter how hopeless and bloody the country gets, simply being in Israel still counts for something back here among the folks who aren't. In Israel he could still pass me off as a success to friends and family.

CASS. You think that's what it signalled?

RONNIE. Until that moment I never realized what a God-sent opportunity September the 13ᵗʰ, 1993 must've seemed to them.

CASS. September 13ᵗʰ—?

RONNIE. 1993. A few weeks before my thirtieth birthday. I'd been driving a bus for a couple of months, remember?

CASS. I remember how pompous you looked in the *optional* cap you *chose* to wear.

RONNIE. Finsbury Park to Battersea. Battersea to Finsbury Park. Backwards and forwards trying to decide what to do with the rest of my life.

CASS. So?

RONNIE. Mum and Dad were aware I was going through some kind of crisis. Though there's no way of knowing for certain that I was invited over *deliberately*, the spread laid on for the occasion should've warned me.

CASS. What occasion?

RONNIE. *(impatiently)* September the 13ᵗʰ, 1993.

CASS. The more you say it like I'm stupid for not knowing what you're talking about, the more I want to rupture your other kidney.

RONNIE. On September 13ᵗʰ, 1993 the Israelis and Palestinians signed the Declaration of Principles on the White House lawn, and the Middle East peace process moved into a new and stupendously optimistic phase.

CASS. Oh. That.

RONNIE. The Oslo Accords—otherwise known as "oh that." Mum and Dad asked me over to watch the signing ceremony with them. Share a little bit of history. Peace at last. The light unto nations was aglow once more. Or so we were led to believe at the time.

CASS. Was that '93? Thought it was longer for some reason.

RONNIE. Tell it to the Palestinians in the Occupied Territories…

CASS. I would, only I don't go into them quite as often as I'd like. Now if they could set up a Palestinian camp in the car park at Brent Cross, I swear, you'd have to beat me back with tear gas.

RONNIE. (his humour dropping) Anyone who'd spent even two minutes at an Israeli checkpoint would never make such a crass remark.

CASS. Christ, Ronnie. It was meant to be a joke.

RONNIE. Yeah. Only it's not. Is it?

> *Pause. RONNIE takes a hard draw on his cigarette.*

CASS. So why would Mum and Dad "deliberately" ask you over that day? What are you getting at?

RONNIE. The suggestion that I up sticks and actually go out there to study came the evening of the signing, or shortly after.

CASS. Is that so odd? You were looking for direction. Israel's always been a place for people in search of some kind of permanence. They were crudely matchmaking. They'd never have suggested going during the Intifada because of safety fears. But when Arafat and Rabin shook hands maybe they just thought—in their rather sweet naiveté—that it would also be the fresh start you needed.

RONNIE. Exactly. Studying in Israel. And if the study doesn't work out, there's always Israel itself. Like I said. A godsend.

> *Beat.*

Until, that is, I decide to come home. With nothing. Not even a tan.

CASS. (cautiously) Mum thinks all it would take for Dad to start talking to you is a simple apology.

RONNIE. So that's why you wanted to see me. I was beginning to wonder.

CASS. That's not why I wanted to see you.

RONNIE. Obviously Mum couldn't ask me directly. Even though she sleeps the other side of my bedroom wall, far better chance of a result by sending an influential envoy.

CASS. Mum didn't ask me to come up here.

RONNIE. Quite the shuttle diplomat, aren't we?

CASS. I came to ask you about Dan.

RONNIE. *(incredulous)* An apology for what? Fuck's sake, Cass—when we were kids how many nights were we put to bed with the story of the Zionist pioneers who turned an empty desert into a garden?

CASS. *(trying to keep up)* Sorry—where's this coming from?

RONNIE. Or the Jews' miraculous triumph over the Brits in '47 and the Arabs in '48?

CASS. I don't see what any of this has got to do with what we've just been talking about?

RONNIE. *(rolling over her)* Or the prowess of her pilots in '67? The villainy of '72?

CASS. One person firing dates at another person isn't the same as an actual *conversation*, Ronnie. What's your *point*?

RONNIE. Or '73? Or Entebbe? *Apologize*?!

CASS. Are you saying none of that's true?

RONNIE. It's *all* true, but that's not the same as it being the *whole* truth. We were deliberately fed the edited highlights. They sent me out on half the story, and when I discovered the other half for myself, everything fell apart. *Apologize*?

CASS. They had a full-time clothing business to run. Maybe edited highlights were all they had time for. Perhaps they assumed we'd fill in the background for ourselves. We were smart enough, perhaps we should have.

RONNIE. We were children. Jews were the cowboys, Arabs the Indians. That's how basic the level of programming.

CASS. *Programming*? Ronnie, they're not historians. They've never been political. They make cheap, snazzy outfits for large, snazzy women. *Programming*? Give me a fucking break.

RONNIE. They had a duty as parents to make us informed.

CASS. Oh now that's just absurd. Their duty as far as they were concerned was to keep us fed, happy, and in broad agreement with their view of the world as gleaned from the *Daily Express*, the *Mail on Sunday*, and the *Jewish Chronicle*. Anything extra was down to us. They'd lay down their lives for me and you, Ronnie—you know they would.

RONNIE. Don't dive into sentiment to avoid my point!

CASS. I'm not avoiding your point—I just think you're rather shamefully manufacturing a position from which you can accuse Mum and Dad of deliberately abetting your dissolution. All so you won't have to *abase* yourself with an apology for screwing up an opportunity they underwrote with a *completely* open hand!

RONNIE. *(adamant—his bottom line)* I don't believe that. I'm sorry. Not completely open. If they don't like what happened to me over there, so be it. But whether they like it or not they had more than a "completely open" hand in it. So as far as I'm concerned, I have *nothing* to apologize to them about.

CASS. In their mind it would seem you do, but maybe you're right. Maybe you don't. It doesn't matter.

RONNIE. It matters to me.

CASS. It doesn't matter because the real question is: how much will it actually cost you to do the big thing and just settle this?

RONNIE. It's not about being big, Cass.

CASS. Isn't it?

RONNIE. It's not about *settling* something.

CASS. What is it about?

RONNIE. It's about being *right*.

> *CASS cannot move this further. She stands, tired from the fray. Pause.*

CASS. *(quieter—a different tack)* You always enjoyed arguing more than I did, and I really didn't ask you up here for an argument.

> *Beat.*

I asked you to meet me to talk about Dan…

RONNIE. I don't wanna talk about Dan.

CASS. You and Danny have always talked about each other's girlfriends.

RONNIE. Not for years. I'm tired.

CASS. You've known him longer than anyone. And now I'm the girlfriend.

RONNIE. Tell Mum to expect nothing. I'll call you.

> *RONNIE starts to walk away.*

CASS. *(her anxiety suddenly exploding)* Please, Ronnie! It's a simple question.

> *RONNIE stops.*

(getting herself under control) I just need to know I'm the one.

> *Beat.*

Am I the one, Ronnie? Or am I merely Dan's *next* one?

> *CASS looks at RONNIE's back. Pause. RONNIE walks off.*

> *After a few moments, night turns to muted morning sunlight, as DAN walks onto the scene holding a spindle of twine which disappears into the sky. DAN looks up at his kite. CASS watches DAN for a few moments, then stands and slowly exits.*

DAN. The next one in the range was so big that Cass had visions of Oscar being lifted off the ground.

> *RONNIE walks on behind him in shirtsleeves.*

RONNIE. It's certainly more appropriate than the car. But do you know he actually *likes* kites?

DAN. Not sure he's ever seen one. But Cass got the idea from a friend's husband, who's apparently a big enthusiast.

RONNIE. And what do you think about that?

DAN. What do I think about what?

RONNIE. Well... that she's getting increasingly involved with Oscar.

DAN. She's given him a kite, Ronnie. Not a scoop of bone marrow.

RONNIE. Even so. I know the extent of her involvement with Oscar is one of Cass's concerns. Perhaps buying the kite is a signal she's coming to terms with the idea.

DAN. I'm taking the fact that she's thinking about him at all as a positive sign.

RONNIE. Sure. Though.

> *Beat.*

No.

DAN. What?

RONNIE. I don't want to be negative. Only, isn't it also possible you're clutching at straws in the absence of anything more concrete?

DAN. *(looking up at the sky)* Go on.

RONNIE. Well, she now knows you've been thinking ahead to a time when she might move in with you.

> *Beat.*

And yet she still hasn't expressed the desire to make that a reality from her end.

DAN. I get a sense she's thinking things through.

RONNIE. Well... of course, she's had a lot of failed relationships. As you know.

DAN. *(looking at the kite)* Uhuh.

RONNIE. So I've started to wonder if my sister's actually cut out for the long haul at all. We used to joke about it, remember?

DAN. When we were kids.

RONNIE. And when we weren't.

DAN. *(looking at RONNIE)* What're you getting at?

RONNIE. You know how Cass likes to examine every decision from every angle. In her heart I'm convinced she thinks she's looking for reassurance about a relationship's viability. But in her head I've begun to wonder if she's not actually looking for an escape hatch, should the need arise.

> *RONNIE lights up a cigarette and takes a drag. DAN looks at RONNIE. Beat.*

DAN. Escape?

RONNIE. She told me last week I should move out of my parents'.

DAN. She told me too. I agree.

RONNIE. I told her I couldn't until me and the old man had resolved some fundamental differences.

DAN. She's really worried your attempt at resolution could blow up in everyone's face.

RONNIE. Did Cass mention that three days after our conversation up here she left a message for me to call her at work?

DAN. *(looking back up at the kite)* She might've.

RONNIE. Seems her boss has been talking on and off for a while about developing some kind of documentary series around episodes of mass hysteria.

DAN. I suppose it's 1999 and all that. Total eclipse of the sun in a couple of months. Millennium and the possible end of the world at the end of the year. Her boss apparently likes things with a topical edge.

RONNIE. They thought they'd probably missed the boat, but then Cass showed this woman—

DAN. Her boss's name is Helen.

RONNIE. Until Cass showed this Helen a tiny section of my unfinished thesis, where I talk a little bit about a phenomenon called the Jerusalem Syndrome.

DAN. *(not really paying attention)* Right…

RONNIE. When I rang the office, Cass told me she'd persuaded this Helen person that—late in the day as it might be—having me have a crack at a research treatment might be worth a punt.

DAN. Congratulations mate. Great.

RONNIE. Great and more to the point… money in my pocket.

DAN. More to the point?

RONNIE. At the moment I have no money, so it's relatively easy to stay at the parents. If this proposal secures me some sort of advance, well. Then I'll have the means to find and fund my own accommodation, and no reason to stay at Mum and Dad's. I'll have to leave—and sooner rather than later. Bingo.

DAN. Bingo?

RONNIE. Cass's concern about the family imploding is avoided. Which brings us to you.

DAN. Me? How does all that bring us on to me?

RONNIE. We all think Cass is deciding about the future, but perhaps—and this is just a thought—but perhaps she's actually already decided.

DAN. Has she said something?

RONNIE. No, but that doesn't mean anything.

DAN. She would've told me.

RONNIE. How do you tell someone you really care about that perhaps you don't care about them quite as much as you thought?

DAN. But.

RONNIE. Or indeed… quite as much as you need if you're to fully commit?

DAN. *(beat)* Hang on.

RONNIE. If you're about to ask when is she planning to come clean with you, I can't help you.

DAN. I wasn't.

RONNIE. All I know is a state of protracted hiatus—by definition—can't be dragged out forever. Though it can be spun out until the right time.

DAN. Which would be when exactly?

RONNIE. When the impact of her "thanks but no thanks" to moving in could be softened by something that would lessen both the blow for you, and the guilt for her.

DAN. You what?

RONNIE. A time when—for example—and this is just theory. This is pure conjecture. But until such time as I might be in a physical and *financial* position to move back into my old room at the flat.

> *Pause. RONNIE waits for this to sink in.*

DAN. You're suggesting.

> *Beat.*

You're suggesting.

> *Pause.*

You're suggesting Cass is—

RONNIE. Not "is," Dan. Not "is." "Might be." Pure conjecture, remember.

DAN. You're suggesting your sister *might be* holding off telling me we're finished until she's engineered you out of your parents' and back into the flat.

RONNIE. The mind of *Woman*, Daniel. If they could equal our strength and cruelty I firmly believe they would have us in stalls, like pigs, milking our nuts, like cows.

> *Long pause.*

DAN. Hang on.

RONNIE. Think about it. I'm liberated from my parents. She's liberated herself from you. You're liberated from uncertainty. In one light it almost assumes the appearance of a grand humanitarian gesture.

DAN. I said *hang on.*

RONNIE. Perhaps you'd like me to run through the analysis again?

DAN. If Cassie's biding her time to let me down gently, why would she give me this at the weekend?

> *With his free hand he takes a silver fountain pen from his inside jacket pocket and holds it up.*
>
> *Beat.*

RONNIE. A fountain pen.

DAN. The inscription *on* the pen.

RONNIE. Inscription?

DAN. "With love always, Cass."

> *RONNIE stares at the pen as CASS and HELEN walk to a standstill around the park benches, leaning on them for support. Their faces flushed and sweaty.*

RONNIE. *(beat)* So the pen would be a sop to buy the time she needs to manoeuvre all the pieces into alignment. *With love always.* What does that actually mean? I'll always love Django Reinhardt, but that doesn't mean I'm never going to buy someone else's records. You can love *always* with passion like a lover. Or in fond regret, like an *ex.*

> *The two women just about regain their breath when LOU limps onto the scene—her jogging bottoms soaking wet, and very muddy.*

LOU. Whose idea was it to jump that fucking stream?!

CASS. I chose the route, if that's what you mean.

LOU. There isn't enough *terra firma* out here you had to seek out vast rivers to leap over?

HELEN. It was hardly a *vast* river. Barely more than a trickle.

LOU. But with embankments of mud in which you could stage *Journey's* Fucking End.

HELEN. Cassie and I jumped it.

LOU. *(beat, pointing at CASS)* Next time *you* run at the rear.

> *LOU sits at a bench and takes out a mobile phone.*

CASS. What're you doing?

LOU. What any sane woman would do in this situation—ringing my husband to pick me up.

> *LOU stands and crosses upstage to make the call. DAN and RONNIE regard each other as before.*

DAN. *(calm, measured, icily certain)* Listen to me very carefully. You're not getting your old room back. If your sister rules out any possibility of moving in with me... you're not getting your old room back. If my teaching contract is torn up tomorrow and I'm suddenly desperate for a tenant... you're not getting your old room back. Four years ago you upped and left to be a part of modern history. You did what you felt you had to do. It was bloody difficult for me, but now I'm glad, because it forced me to step out of the glorified playground of our twenties and find a life. I stopped kidding myself I was Fellini, and got a job. I found someone. Married her. Had a kid with her. And even though we eventually broke up, I learned how to maintain relations with her for the sake of my son. In short, your departure was the making of me, and now I have Cass I have no intention of becoming unmade again by you, or anyone else.

HELEN. For what it's worth, Cassie... I think your route was fine.

CASS. Thanks.

HELEN. Nicely varied. Plenty of up as well as down. Just the right degree of flat.

DAN. And before I forget. I'm not your fucking sorting office.

> *DAN takes out a blue airmail letter and tosses it at RONNIE's feet.*

RONNIE. I gave your address because—

DAN. I know why you gave my address. Your mistake.

> *LOU returns to the other two women, putting her mobile away.*

LOU. He's on his way.

> *CASS looks out over the view of the city. HELEN regards her.*

HELEN. *(to* CASS*)* Is it working?

CASS. Sorry?

HELEN. Jogging. Is it having the desired effect?

CASS. It's too early to say.

LOU. If the desired effect is to convince me to exercise in a luxury gym before a large, noisy telly, then categorically, *yes*.

HELEN. I suggested jogging would help clear her mind.

LOU. Of what?

CASS. Helen thought it might help clarify my thoughts about Danny and Ronnie. The open parkland. Fresh air.

DAN. Why did you come back, Ron?

HELEN. Cassie told me what's been going on between her, Dan, and brother Ronnie. And that she didn't know what to make of it all. So I said "jog."

CASS. Helen believes my various anxieties are different expressions of the same thing.

HELEN. An elemental crisis.

DAN. Why didn't you just stay out there?

LOU. An elemental crisis?

HELEN. Of trust, which jogging could help bring into focus.

LOU. An elemental crisis of trust solved by *jogging*?

HELEN. Unlike room-based exercise, jogging forces us to become creatures of environment once more. Out in the open the self-serving rationalisations of the cosmopolitan metropolitan give way to more primary desires and anxieties.

LOU. And Cass is a cosmopolitan metropolitan, is she?

HELEN. What do I *want*? What do I *need*? That sort of thing.

LOU. (*sarcastically*) Cool.

CASS. Helen produced an extremely well-received series scrutinizing contemporary relationships.

LOU. Is that right?

CASS. Award-winning.

LOU. Congratulations.

HELEN. Thank you.

RONNIE. Dan, let me just say one thing—

DAN. (*cutting him off, quiet, resolved*) I don't think so. My days of listening to you are over. I'm going to take what's written on Cass's pen at face value, and then I'm going to carry on and hope for the best.

RONNIE. Hope for the best?

DAN. Who was it who said when you lose hope you die.

RONNIE. That would be Martin Luther King.

DAN. Well then.

RONNIE. He also said freedom is never voluntarily given by the oppressor, it must be demanded by the oppressed. For which he—like several other men of peace—was rewarded with a Nobel Prize and a bullet in the chest.

DAN. I'll take my chances.

CASS. All I want to know is, am I the one?

RONNIE. You're living in a dream, Daniel.

CASS. Am I the one? Or am I merely his next one?

DAN. If anyone's living in a dream, it's you.

> *The kite now packed away, DAN pockets CASS's pen, and walks offstage.*

> *RONNIE hesitates for a moment, then picks up the airmail letter. He slips the letter into a pocket, and walks away down the hill in the opposite direction.*

LOU waves at DOUGLAS offstage and exits in his general direction, while CASS remains on a bench as HELEN stretches, limbering up.

The sound of London rises—the background growl of traffic; airplanes overhead; trains rolling past; birds; mopeds; children. Comforting everyday noise of contemporary London.

Slow fade to black.

Act Two

A roof garden in inner-city London, overlooking tightly-packed housing of the area.

The morning of August 11th, 1999. A sturdy tripod stands in the centre of the roof. At its base lies a relatively small cardboard box. Around the perimeter of the area lies the remote-controlled car on its side, the kite, with its twine unravelled and dumped in a heap on top, and a deflated leather Arsenal football—in addition to a host of forgotten and broken toys discarded by Oscar.

After a few moments, DAN carefully reverses onto the roof with DOUGLAS, each holding an end of the tubular body of an astronomical telescope, which they carry carefully over to the tripod—and then just as carefully lower it to the floor beside it.

DOUGLAS. The beauty of a kite, of course, is its portability.

DAN. Portability wasn't his mother's issue. His mother's issue was a three-year-old standing around in a cold wind holding a piece of string.

DOUGLAS. Goes with the territory, I'm afraid.

DAN. I was up for it. And I think Oscar was, in the way they'll go along with anything at that age.

DOUGLAS. Mother's prerogative to worry about her child, Dan.

DAN. Within reason worry is more than reasonable.

DOUGLAS. Within reason?

DAN. First it was the cold, then the wind chill factor, then exposure to rain, and then sun. *Then* the possibility of permanent damage to his neck from looking up too much. And finally, an all-consuming anxiety that the thing could plummet from a hundred feet, point down, directly onto his still-hardening skull.

DOUGLAS. I've only seen that happen once in twenty years of kite-flying.

DAN. I told her if it happened every day they'd ban it.

DOUGLAS. The girl was back on her feet within… I'm not exactly sure… a week, two tops. Minimal indentation. Slight permanent hair loss along the line of impact. But nothing that wouldn't become the basis for an amusing party anecdote later in life.

DAN. I told her the chance of Oscar being impaled on his own kite was like, very, very small to minute. But when she delivered the ultimatum that he either goes to the park in a crash helmet or not at all I thought, you know… fuckit. Life is for living, even at three-and-a-half.

DOUGLAS. Especially at three-and-a-half.

DAN. If it was up to her she'd swathe him in bubble wrap and embed him in concrete for ten years.

DOUGLAS. *(beat)* Astronomy's an interesting compromise.

DAN. Too many people on the planet with an outlook no further than the nearest switch. I want to ensure my boy grows up at least aware of "outside."

DOUGLAS. *(apropos the telescope)* A lot of outside to be aware of with this.

DAN. That's the beauty. An interest for life.

DOUGLAS. For sure.

DAN. Had the idea when I took him to the Planetarium over Easter. Didn't really have a clue what was going on, of course, except he twigged when it went on outside. So I start him off with something big and obvious like the Moon, and gradually expand his horizon as he gets older.

DOUGLAS. Oscar's a lucky boy.

DAN. Don't know about that.

DOUGLAS. Shame he couldn't be here for the eclipse.

DAN. His mother suddenly produced pre-booked tickets for some cartoon shite at the pictures. Deliberate. Terrified he'll blind himself by accident, so she makes sure he can't by hiding him in a windowless black box when it all goes down. Or up.

DOUGLAS. Or across.

DAN. Exactly.

DOUGLAS. Perhaps he'll catch the next one.

DAN. If he still has his sight when he's ninety-five.

> *DAN crouches and opens the cardboard box and unpacks a small array of smaller boxes. DOUGLAS watches.*

So where is little chummy? Cass was rather hoping you'd bring her over.

DOUGLAS. We left her at home with a box of matches and a large bottle of lighter fluid.

DAN. *(not paying attention)* Right…

> *He stops unpacking the small boxes, and freezes for a moment.*

DOUGLAS. *(beat)* When she keeps me up for more than three nights my paternal instinct turns murderous. No—chummy's with my mother. Hands like oven mitts, eyes like an endoscope, mind like a health and safety manual.

> *DAN rolls the body of the telescope over, and pulls the tripod down to attach it.*

DAN. Could you…? *(indicating DOUGLAS should hold the tripod steady upside down—which he does)* Between you and me I think Cass was hoping a baby's presence would take her mind off it.

DOUGLAS. *(helping DAN attach the telescope to the tripod)* Off what?

DAN. This little gathering.

DOUGLAS. But it's just friends on the roof going "ooh" in awe.

DAN. Didn't Louise tell you?

DOUGLAS. That depends. Lou keeps me informed about things on a don't-need-to-know basis.

> *The telescope is now screwed onto the tripod. DAN stands and bends to pick it up.*

DAN. So you don't know.

> *DOUGLAS helps set the tripod and telescope on its legs.*

DOUGLAS. I work for the Inland Revenue, Dan. I'm really not very good at elliptical.

DAN. About me finally asking Cass to move in.

DOUGLAS. Oh that.

DAN. So you *do* know?

DOUGLAS. Lou must have let something slip in her sleep.

> *DAN unpacks a couple of viewfinders (coarse and crosshair) from the smaller of the boxes and carefully fits them to the telescope.*

I'm still in the dark why Cass would be nervous about having a few people over?

DAN. *(looking into the eyepiece and making an adjustment)* We've never entertained here as a couple before.

DOUGLAS. Hardly entertaining. No offence, but these are clothes I wear for gardening.

DAN. The point is—it's like Cass and I on show in the flat for the first time. At least I'm guessing that's it. She won't talk about it, but she's been jittery all morning. Hardly slept. I didn't want to push it, because pushing edgy women usually makes things worse.

DOUGLAS. *(from experience)* Oh yes.

DAN. But I think it's like, this is it. Grownup time. People coming over. Can we manage? Are we the real McCoy as a couple?

DOUGLAS. But I'm assuming it's all people she knows.

DAN. You and Lou. Ronnie and Helen.

DOUGLAS. Helen?

DAN. Cass's boss.

DOUGLAS. I met her when she was jogging with Lou and Cass on the heath. Lou had spectacularly failed to hurdle a small puddle and I was summoned to salvage the wreckage. You've met her?

DAN. Spoken to on the phone once or twice but not met. Very smart producer according to Cass. Very sharp.

DOUGLAS. I couldn't say. I only saw her in skin-tight leggings and a figure-hugging crop top.

DAN. And?

> *DOUGLAS smiles.*

I hear you.

DOUGLAS. I'm a married man with a young child, Dan. You hear *nothing*.

> *LOU comes onto the roof, followed by CASS, holding two glasses of white wine—which she hands to DOUGLAS and DAN.*

LOU. Is that a telescope on your roof, or are you just pleased to see me?

DOUGLAS. It's a telescope on the roof.

CASS. Dan. Helen's here.

LOU. *(in DOUGLAS's ear)* A tad over-dressed for a solar eclipse in my opinion. But then I don't work in television—where every gathering of two or more people is a potential career move.

> *HELEN comes onto the roof, watched by the others. She is very smartly dressed—powerful but chic. She crosses directly to DAN, extending her hand.*

CASS. Dan this is Helen. Helen this is Dan.

HELEN. Hello, Danny.

DAN. *(shaking her hand)* Nice to finally put a face to the name.

HELEN. *(shaking it back)* You too.

LOU. *(to HELEN)* My husband—

DOUGLAS. Douglas.

LOU. *(to HELEN)* —you've met.

> *HELEN regards DOUGLAS for a moment, unsure when and where.*

HELEN. Um…?

DOUGLAS. *(extending his hand)* On the heath. My wife tripped over a leaf, and I airlifted her to a large bar of chocolate.

LOU. Douglas is the Inland Revenue's leading stand-up comedian. His wit has a small but loyal following within tax officialdom, but we're not sure how it translates beyond the world of the un-dead.

HELEN. *(shaking his hand)* Good to see you again, Douglas.

DOUGLAS. Call me Doug.

LOU. He thinks it makes him sound vaguely antipodean.

DOUGLAS. *(to HELEN)* It's simply less of a mouthful.

LOU. Helen's mouth looks suitably wide, Douglas. I'm sure she can manage.

DAN. *(to CASS)*. No sign of Ronnie?

CASS. My brother knows what time the eclipse starts, like everyone else in the hemisphere.

DAN. I don't know why you asked him.

CASS. I asked him because I want to speak to him.

LOU. How is Ronnie? The last you told me he'd been commissioned to put together some kind of document based on his travels.

HELEN. Just a small paper about the Jerusalem Syndrome.

DOUGLAS. *(his ears pricking up)* The Jerusalem Syndrome?

HELEN. You did tell him a page and a half would be enough to begin with didn't you, Cassie?

CASS. Of course.

LOU. What's the Jerusalem Syndrome when it's at home? Though I'm guessing its home is Jerusalem.

HELEN. I'll be in a better position to inform you once I've read Ronnie's paper.

DOUGLAS. The Jerusalem Syndrome is a phenomenon often—though not exclusively—associated with the end of millennia.

LOU. Yes, thank you, Douglas, but I was asking Helen.

DOUGLAS. Devout Christians in Jerusalem occasionally experience a disparity between their mental image of the ancient city, and the realities of a modern metropolis.

LOU. I said I was asking Helen.

DOUGLAS. I know what you said. In addition, particularly religious Jews with the syndrome may believe that the building of the Third Temple is imminent, that the ancient animal sacrifices will be restored, and that their own Messiah will arrive shortly. It's a delusive condition whose origins date back as far as 1033.

> *Beat.*

I heard a feature on Radio Four.

> *DOUGLAS smiles at LOU and takes a sip of wine. LOU fumes. Pause.*

HELEN. If we can submit a proposal before the next commissioning round, we could be greenlit by Christmas.

LOU. That sounds painful.

DAN. I'm going downstairs for a refill, before the light fades and the birds go berserk.

LOU. I'm sure we'll stay perfectly calm.

DOUGLAS. *(indicating the sky)* I think Dan is referring to the period when the moon passes in front of the sun, and the birds will—

LOU. —think it's dusk and bed down for the night. Yes, Douglas. I *know*.

DOUGLAS. Good for you.

DAN. Anyone's glass need refreshing?

DOUGLAS. I wouldn't mind.

DAN. Follow me.

> *DAN and DOUGLAS go inside. Beat.*

CASS. *(to LOU)* You two are on form.

LOU. *(to HELEN)* Some marriages are built on romantic slush—we've chosen mouth-to-mouth combat as our stimulant of choice.

HELEN. Right. Cassie, could I have a word. *(to LOU)* Excuse us.

LOU. She didn't say "yes."

HELEN. I'm her boss—the question was rhetorical.

> *HELEN leads CASS a little away from LOU.*

He will deliver, won't he? It's been four weeks. I'm not exactly asking for *The Ascent of Man*.

CASS. He gave his word.

HELEN. It would be a shame if he took the money and ran, because I really think that we could be in with a shot with it.

CASS. I've explained to him what a terrific opportunity it would be to get things back on track.

HELEN. Things?

CASS. His life.

HELEN. We're a television production company, Cassie, not Battersea Dog's Home.

CASS. I know.

HELEN. I hate to see ideas of real potential taken away from the people who bring them in. But you know I will if I have to.

CASS. What do you think of Dan?

HELEN. Nicer than you described.

CASS. I didn't want to overdo the lavish description in case it unduly affected your line of approach. What's your first impression?

HELEN. I would. Definitely. If I did men anymore. Which I don't.

CASS. I meant of his, of you.

HELEN. It's difficult to be precise about these things. But dilated pupils, moist, parted lips, strong handshake, subliminal self-grooming during open conversation—I'd say it was a solid start.

CASS. I don't know. I'm not sure this is such a good idea.

HELEN. Relax, Cassie. All things come to those who—

LOU. (her eye at the telescope) Oh my word...!

> CASS and HELEN turn to LOU, who is looking through the telescope, now pointed out front.

CASS. (looking into the sky, shielding her eyes) Has it started?

LOU. Flats over there. About ten floors up. Old geezer on balcony. *Completely starkers!*

CASS. (peering into the middle distance) Where?

HELEN. (also peering, entirely matter of fact) Oh yes.

LOU. You can't possibly see unaided.

HELEN. (peering) Uncircumcised.

> LOU looks into the eyepiece. Beat.

LOU. That's *incredible*. Was your mother by any chance fertilized by a hawk?

HELEN. I've always been long-sighted. Show me a ten inch penis three feet away and all I'll register is an unfeasibly long blur. But at distance, everything comes out clear as crystal.

CASS. I can barely see the block of flats let alone his block and tackle.

> HELEN moves behind CASS, and takes her head in both hands and redirects her line of sight.

HELEN. There.

CASS. Without my glasses everything beyond the edge of this roof is basically a blur.

HELEN. (still holding CASS's head in her hands) I didn't know that.

CASS. Ronnie's the same.

LOU. If he doesn't turn up soon he'll miss it. From here, at least.

CASS. He's probably tied up at Mum and Dad's.

LOU. What's the situation there at the moment?

CASS. Not good.

LOU. No?

CASS. After the big freeze came the little thaw, followed shortly after by the enormous heated argument.

LOU. Doesn't sound very promising.

CASS. What began as an encouragingly well-behaved opening dialogue about Ronnie's conduct in Israel, rapidly degenerated into a slanging match about Israel itself—with Dad insisting on its right to do whatever it needs, to protect itself, and Ronnie insisting that the only real threat comes from Israel's treatment of the Palestinians, and increasing numbers of settlements in the Occupied Territories.

HELEN. Whenever that issue comes up on the news I tend to switch over. I just find it too...

> Long pause, while CASS and LOU wait for HELEN to find the appropriate word. They wait for what seems like an age.

...boring, I suppose.

CASS. *(beat)* They've been going at it hammer and tongs, according to Mum.

HELEN. Not to mention depressing.

LOU. *(trying to ignore HELEN)* Josie's caught in the middle?

CASS. She generally follows Dad's line, but I think she just wants them to stop fighting.

LOU. Of course.

CASS. It seems Ronnie dropped out of his PhD after falling in with some young radicals, apparently only too pleased to befriend an impressionable young Jew from the West. Claiming to be disaffected with the leadership of both sides—

LOU. *Claiming* to be?

CASS. I'm giving you my parents' take on what happened.

LOU. Right. Sorry. Go on.

CASS. So claiming to be disaffected with both Israeli and Palestinian leaders, they seemed to have convinced my brother that winning over foreign opinion was central to their objective of highlighting human rights abuses. Dad's guessing they took Ronnie under their wing, showed him lots of emotive photographs of shot children, pumped him full of propaganda, and sent him home to spread the word.

LOU. Going by what I've read in the papers their word is pretty compelling.

CASS. That rather depends on *which* journalists in *which* papers.

LOU. I suppose.

CASS. Anyway, they came across a letter sent to Ronnie by the brother of some young Palestinian woman from the West Bank—who Dad's rather feverishly decided was used as some kind of sexual lure.

HELEN. How exciting!

CASS. It's all become horribly messy. With Ronnie regurgitating all manner of horror stories about the Territories, and Dad trying to shout him down.

LOU. What I know of your father, I'm assuming his views on that area are pretty solid.

CASS. He's supported Israel from before the beginning.

LOU. Sure.

CASS. Why should he take lectures from Ronnie?

LOU. No, of course. But having a view on the occupied territories is hardly the same as attacking the foundations of Zionism, Cass. I mean, I know I'm not Jewish, but—

CASS. Not *Occupied* Territories.

LOU. Sorry?

CASS. *Disputed.* A change in status effectively conceded by Yasser Arafat at Oslo, as part of a deal accepting *partial* as opposed to *complete* withdrawal of Israel from the West Bank and Gaza, as specified by United Nations resolution 242 of November 22nd, 1967.

LOU. Right.

CASS. I've been boning up.

LOU. *(beat)* I know I know virtually nothing. But all I meant before in regard to the Occupied—sorry, *disputed* territories—

HELEN. I'd drop it if I were you.

LOU. Sorry?

HELEN. Fucking minefield.

LOU. But I'm allowed to have an opinion.

HELEN. Are you Jewish?

LOU. I think I already said I wasn't.

HELEN. Are you Palestinian?

LOU. Patently not.

HELEN. Then what would your opinion actually be *worth*?

LOU. *(bridling)* I beg your pardon?

CASS. Helen's right, Lou. It is a fucking minefield. Now's probably not the time.

> LOU looks at CASS, who smiles. Pause.

LOU. I think I'll go and let Doug's mother know we arrived safely.

CASS. The phone's on the wall in the front room.

LOU. It's okay. Doug's got his mobile.

CASS. *(looking at her watch, calling after her)* Tell them it's not long to go. *Minutes*, Lou!

> LOU goes inside. Pause. HELEN crosses to the telescope and looks through the eyepiece. CASS seems edgier than before.

I'm having massive second thoughts.

HELEN. Don't. Every woman featured in the series had exactly the same anxiety as you're now experiencing. But when they received the result. For those whose fears *were* founded and those whose fears *weren't*… the relief of *knowing* was overwhelming.

CASS. But they had more reason to doubt than I have. You just said yourself how very nice Dan seems.

HELEN. The days of skipping hand in hand to the Promised Land with a partner for life are over, Cassie. We no longer have to subject ourselves to leaps of faith about the people we spend our lives with. Some see this as a problem. Not me. I say let's be modern and judge the world by what we see—not by what we might wish to see. It's been a long road, but if women are finally learning better than to take men on trust, so be it. Isn't that why those poor cows on the documentary put themselves through the ordeal?

CASS. Yes, but—

HELEN. Isn't this why your eyes widened like saucers when I gave you the tape to watch? It's not how nice they *seem*. It's how trustworthy they *are*.

CASS. It feels like entrapment.

HELEN. Who was it who said he has the profile of a serial monogamist? Not me.

CASS. I just need to know I'm—

HELEN. —the one, and not just the next one. And why not? And this is how. It's not exact, but it will give you a robust pointer to help you make up your mind about Dan once and for all.

> *HELEN crosses to CASS and stands a couple of feet from her. She puts a hand reassuringly on her arm.*

I like you, Cassie. You should be happy. I can see in your eyes that you're worried about the duplicity. Don't be. It's in Danny's interest as well as yours. It protects all parties.

CASS. Except you.

HELEN. Some women do this for a living. The peace of mind of a good friend is the only reward I seek.

CASS. But are you *sure* you can do this?

HELEN. *(smiling)* You think I've never done this before?

> *Long pause. HELEN holds out her empty glass.*

Send Danny up with a pair of safety specs. Tell him in my excitement I'm threatening to stare at the sun unprotected.

> *Pause. CASS regards HELEN, who regards her back.*

(gently) It isn't about the man you know, Cass. It's about the man you don't.

> *Beat. CASS regards HELEN for a moment longer and then takes her glass. She then returns inside. HELEN watches her, and then takes a compact from her jacket and refreshes her lipstick and make-up. HELEN puts her compact away, shades her eyes with her hand and looks up at the sky.*

The sky almost imperceptibly starts to darken. A few city lights far and near automatically flicker on, as DAN appears on the roof holding a pair of black safety specs used for looking at the eclipse.

Pause.

DAN. Cass said you wanted to get a head start on the rest of us.

HELEN doesn't turn, but stands with her back to DAN, shading her eyes.

HELEN. *(pointing)* Were you aware that you are overlooked by an old-age exhibitionist. 1, 2, 3, 4, 5, 6… 12 floors up over there.

DAN. *(looking)* Mm. It's Raoul. *(waving)* Raoul! See—he's waving back.

HELEN. Raoul?

DAN. When he used to live here, Cass's brother decided after a bit of a session that the old flasher was Raoul Wallenberg. And don't think the nudity's a summer thing. That's what Raoul wants you to think, so you'll find him endearing and look longer. Summer, autumn, winter, spring. It's all out, all the time.

HELEN regards DAN with mild mystification.

As Secretary to the Swedish Legation in Budapest, Wallenberg saved a ton of Jews from the Nazis. Non-Jews who helped Jews used to rank among Ronnie's favourite people.

HELEN. And Ronnie thinks that's him?

DAN. No more than I think it's Glen Miller. Raoul was arrested by the Soviets after the war and disappeared. With enough lager down your throat the old perv could also pass for Lord Lucan, Captain Oates, Elvis, and God. In fact… just about anyone who vanished without trace a long time ago.

Beat.

Your specs.

HELEN takes the glasses. Beat.

HELEN. I like your telescope.

DAN. Thank you. Strictly speaking I bought it for my son as a crude way of spending lots of time together. I was planning to surprise him with it when he comes over tomorrow. But since it was here I thought we may as well make use of it this once-in-a-lifetime time.

HELEN. Won't it be dangerous?.

DAN. Special filters—super-dark.

HELEN. *(beat)* Cassie tells me you're a filmmaker, Danny.

DAN. She didn't.

HELEN. Um. Yes. She did.

DAN. I gave up telling people that years ago. I teach media studies. I teach film. I don't make it.

HELEN. But you have done.

DAN. I indulged a fantasy of myself that reality significantly failed to live up to. Cass shouldn't have told you that. Really. Because it's not true.

HELEN. *(beat)* I liked "Doors Without Keys" very much.

    Pause.

DAN. I'm sorry?

HELEN. I thought you packed into a quarter of an hour what many celebrated filmmakers scarcely manage in their entire careers.

DAN. I'm sorry, but how—

    Pause. HELEN smiles at DAN.

HELEN. Don't be angry at her, Danny. She only had your interest at heart.

DAN. That chapter of my life is officially closed. It's more than officially closed. It's dead.

HELEN. Perhaps Cassie doesn't think it should be.

DAN. She knows I'm perfectly content with the way my life has panned out.

HELEN. Content? Content is the coward's word for "resigned."

DAN. Okay. Listen. I have no ambitions. No illusions. I don't feel the need to compete with anyone. I'm just me. Slightly less stupid than the stupid people I teach. Happy telling them where to look up what I don't know. I have a nice little flat. A reliable little car. An adorable little boy, and I pay all my *little* bills on time.

HELEN. And?

DAN. There is no and. That's it. Why does there always have to be an and?

HELEN. With people of real talent there's always an *and*, Danny. I know how hard it is to find people who'll back an idea. I know how soul-destroying it is to go cap in hand to Philistine Row for what to them is meter-money. The best ones, the real artists, they walk away. While people like me—the blockheads who don't know any better—just keep banging away until the walls of resistance finally crack.

DAN. Cass had no right to give you my tape.

HELEN. She's proud of your work. She had *every* right.

DAN. *(floundering a little)* I feel like I'm being disinterred here…

HELEN. She knows I can help you.

    Pause.

DAN. You can help me—what? Reintroduce failure as the major theme of my life? No offence but no thanks.

HELEN. Whatever you earn as a teacher I could quadruple overnight. After two years double that. Within four you could buy out the other residents of this building, and knock it into your own. How's that for lemons?

DAN. Look. I already told you—

HELEN. *(affecting losing patience)* I know what you already told me, Danny. And I'm telling you I think you've embalmed yourself in mediocrity by way of consolation that things didn't take off as soon as you expected. I'm also telling you I can make what I just said—all I just said and more—happen for you. Not as some favour to Cassie. Not out of the goodness of my heart. Because you've *got* something, and so few people have.

> *Pause. They regard one another. HELEN puts on her dark safety specs.*

DAN. *(quiet, nervous now)* What are you doing?

HELEN. I'm protecting my eyes from your dazzle.

> *Pause.*

DAN. You've seen one film. A single, fifteen-minute film. That's all.

HELEN. There are two more. I know. Cass wanted to bring them to me, but I said uh-uh. I said, Danny has to bring them to me or there's really no point.

> *HELEN slowly crosses to DAN. She stands in front of him.*

Will you bring them to me, Danny?

> *Beat.*

Shall we meet one evening, and you can introduce them to me before we watch? You could come to the office.

DAN. I don't think—

HELEN. Everyone leaves by seven. I know how self-conscious you'll be. I know how to handle talent, Danny. Believe me. I can be very supportive.

DAN. *(beat)* So. Um. Let Cass know when you're free and—

HELEN. You tell me. You. Not little Cassie.

DAN. Not little Cassie?

HELEN. Let's give the researcher the night off.

> *Pause. DAN regards HELEN. After a few moments CASS appears on the roof, and regards HELEN and DAN—unseen by both. CASS comes slowly onto the roof proper.*

CASS. Everyone's coming up for totality.

> *LOU and DOUGLAS come onto the roof.*

DOUGLAS. You are aware it's not complete totality in London, just—

LOU. —ninety-five per cent. Yes, Doug. We are.

DOUGLAS. I just wouldn't want you to be disappointed.

DAN and HELEN separate and take up places downstage at the opposite ends of the roof.

DAN. No sign of Ronnie?

LOU. Actually he just buzzed up.

DAN. *(close to CASS)* I really don't know why you invited him.

CASS. *(close to DAN)* I told you why I invited him. I invited him because I need to speak to him.

DAN. *(pulling CASS to one side)* Don't you think you've done enough *speaking* to people?

CASS. What's that supposed to mean?

DAN. Your boss has just been telling me about your conversation concerning my history as a maker of films nobody wanted to see.

CASS. Not now, Dan.

DAN. Not now?

HELEN. Look! It's starting!

Everyone turns to the front and looks up.

Almost as one they put on their black safety specs and look up at the sun, as the light gradually dims from crepuscular to almost black, to complete darkness. The twittering birds slowly fall silent.

Pause.

DOUGLAS. There it is… the first diamond ring…

CASS. It's…

DAN. *(beat)* Isn't it just.

Pause. In the darkness RONNIE comes onto the roof.

RONNIE. Sorry I'm late. Something—

DAN. Sssh.

LOU. I still don't understand how it fits over the sun so completely.

DOUGLAS. Most of the time it doesn't. That's why most of the time we don't get totality. Two minutes of relatively complete occlusion every seventy or so years. Not much when you think of it in those terms.

LOU. Saying I don't understand how it fits completely over the sun is not the same as inviting you to explain how it does.

DOUGLAS. I was attempting to illuminate your darkness.

LOU. When I need my darkness illuminating, I'll buy a torch.

DOUGLAS. I'll come with you. We can pick one out together.

DAN. Sssh!

They all continue to look up at the eclipse. RONNIE joins them, already wearing his black safety specs. He also looks up.

Pause.

HELEN. It's quite extraordinary.

DAN. Right now, I feel about yea small.

CASS. Just think, all over the world, right now, whatever people were doing two minutes ago, they've stopped.

Beat.

Working. Eating. Driving.

HELEN. Shagging. Dancing. Singing. Swimming.

DAN. Punching. Shooting. Stabbing. Killing.

LOU. If we agree it's basically all the verbs, can we say that we don't *actually* need to list each and every one?

HELEN. Just imagine, at this very moment, because torturers and murderers are also watching this—fewer people are being tortured or murdered during these two minutes than possibly during any two minutes for seventy-two years.

DOUGLAS. Your assertion needs a little modification, Helen.

HELEN. Does it?

DOUGLAS. Only along the lines of limiting what you've just described to the actual path of the eclipse across Northern Europe, the Balkans, etcetera. But in principle, it's a nice thought.

LOU. It was until you modified it to its knees. Occasionally. Just occasionally, Douglas, it would be nice to live in an unqualified moment.

DAN. Look! The corona!

CASS. Oh my word…!

They all look in wonder at the corona.

HELEN. That is just gorgeous!

CASS. Gorgeous doesn't even come close.

Pause. They look.

RONNIE. *(beat)* Last night I found myself in an internet cafe. As you do.

DAN. Yeah—only we're all looking at this now.

RONNIE. So I log on. As you do.

DAN. Ronnie…

RONNIE. And I came across this website which had a poem about the eclipse by a ten-year-old girl. As they do.

DOUGLAS. Quite wonderful.

RONNIE. The girl lives in Ramallah. As she does.

CASS. *(suddenly turning)* Ramallah?

RONNIE. And her poem compares what we're watching right now to the light of her people being slowly extinguished—

CASS. Ronnie, shut up!

RONNIE. —by the relentless construction of settlements across—

CASS. *(urgent) Ronnie!*

RONNIE. —Palestinian territory. Of course, like anything on the net it could've been penned by a trucker from Wigan. But then again. Perhaps not.

> *Long pause.*

DAN. *(pissed off)* Thanks, Ronnie…

> *DAN takes off his safety specs and breaks away from the line, crossing upstage. CASS stares at RONNIE, still wearing her glasses.*

CASS. *(looking directly at RONNIE)* You selfish shit.

DOUGLAS. *(still looking up)* Baily's beads!

> *The light starts to rise, quicker than it dimmed, but not immediately to full daylight. DAN stands upstage looking at RONNIE from behind.*

CASS. *(looking directly at RONNIE)* I don't believe you. Not only do you turn up late. But when you do eventually grace us with your presence, you simply can't resist ruining what for most of us would probably have been one of the most memorable moments of our lives.

DAN. It's not worth it.

CASS. *(deeply angry)* No, Dan, it fucking is! You don't know what's going on so don't tell me it's not worth it.

RONNIE. I'm so sorry a little bit of unpalatable despair tainted your magic moment everyone. But there really is a limit to the amount of infantile horseshit those of us on *planet Earth* can bear!

CASS. Planet Earth? You?

DAN. What—do you mean I don't know what's going on?

CASS. Please, take our guests downstairs.

DOUGLAS. *(the only one still looking and pointing up)* The second diamond ring!

LOU. Doug, it's *over*.

RONNIE. "Oh look, the sun's gone out—the world's a better place for thirty seconds. Doesn't it just make you *wonder*?" Couldn't possibly occur to you that your torturers and your murderers would actually take the opportunity to stick the boot in all the harder for being *unseen*? That they operate at their peak efficiency with the blinds drawn and the lights off!

CASS. Dan!

DAN. Now?

CASS. It can't wait.

> *HELEN crosses to DAN.*

HELEN. *(gently)* Why don't we watch the coverage downstairs?

DAN. What's going on, Cass?

HELEN. I hear people are chasing the eclipse in Concorde. Why don't we go and see how the other half blows its cash?

> *HELEN gently starts to lead a reluctant DAN towards the entrance.*

DAN. *(to RONNIE)* I told her you'd spoil it. I told her not to ask you. You've become a spoiler, Ronnie.

RONNIE. Whatever I've become, I'd rather be anything than you!

DAN. *(beat)* You see enjoyment. You take out your dick. And you piss all over it.

HELEN. Come on...

> *HELEN leads DAN down.*

LOU. *(standing where she was, but talking low)* Douglas?

DOUGLAS. *(low)* But we came to watch the eclipse.

LOU. *(low but firm)* And now the eclipse is over—

DOUGLAS. *(low)* No—*totality's* over. The end of the eclipse *proper* still has a way to go.

CASS. Please, Doug.

> *DOUGLAS regards CASS. Beat.*

DOUGLAS. When I reached a certain age, and it was time to choose the way I would pass what little time I got to myself, it never entered my head that looking up at sky could get so fucking complicated.

> *LOU and DOUGLAS also cross to the entrance. With a glance behind them at CASS and RONNIE, LOU and DOUGLAS go downstairs.*

CASS. *(to RONNIE)* Have you gone completely insane?

RONNIE. In twenty-four hours you're the second person to ask me that.

CASS. Who was the first?

RONNIE. Dad. Immediately after giving me this.

> *RONNIE takes off his specs, and reveals a dark new bruise over his left eye.*

I know he goes to the gym twice a week, but I assumed it was purely aesthetic. You have to hand it to the *alte kacker*.* Full fist to the socket. No messing. Boom.

CASS. What did you say to him?

RONNIE. What did I say?

CASS. God knows he's no angel, but he would sooner cut off his hands than lay a finger on either of us. You said something to provoke him.

RONNIE. I see. So as long the wrong thing is *said* extreme violence is justified, is it?

> *Pause.*

CASS. Israel.

RONNIE. Extreme violence followed by expulsion.

CASS. Wasn't it?

RONNIE. Mum bawling in the background. I tell him it's five-and-twenty past midnight. I've nowhere to go. Apparently, that's no longer his concern.

CASS. Where did you sleep?

RONNIE. On the heath—why, is there a room here I could have had?

> *Beat.*

Think I'll join the party downstairs. I need a drink.

> *RONNIE starts to cross to the entrance.*

CASS. (*a controlled shout*) I didn't ask you here to party! I asked you here to tell you I *know* what you're doing, and it's going to stop!

> *RONNIE stops and turns.*

RONNIE. (*beat*) "It"?

CASS. First you sow a seed of doubt in my mind about Dan. Then you sow a seed of doubt in Dan's mind about me. And when that failed to break us up and see you back in your room, you turn plain nasty and start goading Mum and Dad.

RONNIE. Goading?

CASS. About Israel. Not resolving your issues. The exact opposite.

RONNIE. Not goading. Opening the mind of.

CASS. Dad's mind has been blissfully ajar for most of our lives. Prising it any more open against his will could only succeed in scaring him shitless. He's a simple, essentially decent man looking for a quiet life. But attack him where it matters and he'll dig a trench and take up the position. As well you knew.

RONNIE. As well I knew?

CASS. When you set out to destroy my relationship with your best friend.

---

* *alte kacker* – old shitter.

RONNIE. *Now* who's insane?

CASS. You couldn't manage it directly, so you set about trying to dismantle the context in which we exist as a couple. Where better to start than the home of my parents?

RONNIE. What?!

CASS. Don't play the dumb innocent with me!

RONNIE. Let's get the others up here. I think they'd love to hear paranoia this riotous…

CASS. Israel is central to the parents' sense of themselves. They lived the death of European Jewry and the birth of Israel *first hand*. It was real life to them, not an hour on the History Channel. A real sanctuary. A real haven. A real miracle built on—and by—blood and guts.

RONNIE. Necessary myth-making aside. Have I *ever* said I didn't respect the moral imperative behind the establishment of the State?

CASS. I don't know what you think anymore. You seem to have come back more messed up than you went—which is something of an achievement in itself.

RONNIE. Every realistic Palestinian I spoke to has moved on from that. Nobody likes to be on the losing side of history. What they don't understand is why they have to lose quite this badly for quite this long.

CASS. All I know is by haranguing Mum and Dad you make them feel threatened at their core. Which gets manifested as a heightened sensitivity towards phenomena they were already struggling to get to grips with.

RONNIE. *Phenomena?*

CASS. Such as seeing their daughter in a serious mixed relationship.

RONNIE. Let me get this straight—

CASS. You know the effect it has. You must! What other reason would you have for creating it?

> *DAN appears at the entrance.*

DAN. I heard shouting.

CASS. Go downstairs, Dan.

DAN. Please don't tell me where to go in my own flat.

CASS. *(looking at* RONNIE*)* This is what you want, isn't it? Divide and conquer.

RONNIE. I don't know what you're talking about.

CASS. Up until four days ago Mum had always been nothing but affable towards Dan.

DAN. What happened four days ago?

CASS. I wasn't going to tell you. But four days ago Mum rang me at work. And in the course of a general discussion about nothing in particular, she asked when

was I going to stop messing about with you, and make a serious effort to find—
her words—"one of your own."

DAN. Josie actually said that?

CASS. I could hear Dad in the background, so I was in no doubt she was speaking for both of them.

RONNIE. I don't believe you.

CASS. Don't blame her, Dan. *He* did it.

RONNIE. If that's true, you should both be grateful I flushed it out sooner rather than later.

CASS. *If* that's true?

DAN. *(to RONNIE)* Why would you do that?

CASS. Because you wouldn't let him crawl back to his old room. Because you wouldn't let him turn back the clock to a time when his life was less poisoned by abject failure.

RONNIE. No offence, but you should see a psychiatrist.

CASS. No offence but you should see a whole fucking clinic. Coming back to England with your eyewitness accounts and your shocking reports.

RONNIE. I came back with the *Truth*.

CASS. The "truth"? I've been reading up since your return.

RONNIE. *(mocking)* Oh? You've been *reading*?

CASS. I wanted to find out what had turned my brother into a sour mouthpiece. Precisely which *truth* did you bring back exactly, Ronnie? There are literally hundreds. Shall we start with some Palestinian truths?

DAN. Cass—

CASS. *(not to be stopped)* Which perspective would you like? The Palestinian people's? The Palestinian Authority's? The Palestinian National Council's? The Palestinian Legislative Council's? The Palestinian intellectuals'? The Palestinian MPs'? The Palestinian unions'? The Palestinian Diaspora's? The PLO's? Or just Fatah's? Or the PFLP's? The DFLP's? Hamas? Islamic Jihad's? The Muslim Brotherhood's? Or shall we try someone else's truth now?

RONNIE. What I've been describing to Mum and Dad are things I saw with my own eyes.

CASS. It's not even *what* you're describing. It's *why* you are.

RONNIE. The White House handshake simply allows them sovereignty over their own misery.

CASS. It's what you seek to achieve by describing it.

RONNIE. A mockery of sovereignty for which they have to police their own dissidents—

CASS. *Dissidents*?!

RONNIE. —build settlements for American Zionists, have no right of return for refugees, and watch their unelected and corrupt representatives negotiate the Palestinian "*State*" into a series of smashed up, disconnected encampments, where freedom is relative, and cardinal resources like water, power and access are outside their control. This is actually happening.

CASS. Fanatics who blow themselves up in shopping centres aren't dissidents, Ronnie.

RONNIE. I'm talking about political dissidents. Lawyers. Academics. Doctors—not just fanatics.

CASS. They pack the bombs with nails so that if they don't kill outright they at least disfigure for life.

RONNIE. Repulsive and abhorrent, of course. But just like Dad, you'll focus on the outrage of individual incidents rather than the broader reality of repression and resistance to repression going hand in hand. That each atrocity from whichever side is yet another step on the spiral of terror and counter-terror. That the spiral is downwards, into an ever-deepening pool of innocent blood—Jewish and Palestinian, pouring into each other until the distinction is no longer apparent, and it's all just thick, red, sickening blood.

CASS. Are you quoting from memory, or did you just make that up? No wonder Dad got physical. Anything to stop you spouting like a badly-written pamphlet.

RONNIE. Dad hit me because I called him an anti-Semite.

CASS. *(beat)* You called him what?

DAN. I think I've heard enough. I think you'd better leave.

RONNIE. He called me a self-hating Arab lover, so I called him a blinkered anti-Semite.

CASS. You called your own father an anti-Semite? Dad would never have told you to your face, but the day you boarded the plane for Tel Aviv was the proudest day of his life!

RONNIE. Mine too! Mine too! But I came to realize that anyone who supports the denial of basic human rights to the Palestinians is endorsing a situation whose outcome is always going to be more murdered Jews. It's not classical anti-Semitism, but in terms of the end result it may as well be. Millions of Israelis understand this—why not him?

CASS. Do you resent Dan and I so much you'll say just about *anything* to undermine us?

RONNIE. How self-obsessed are you? What's passing between me and them has nothing to do with you and Dan!

CASS. Don't insult my intelligence.

RONNIE. A letter from the West Bank was sent here. Dan passed it on to me. *(to DAN)* Yes?

DAN. Yes.

CASS. After everything he's been trying to do to us, you're on his side now?

DAN. It's not about sides—it's about not losing the capacity to recognize something for what it actually is.

CASS. Oh I see what's happening. Ronnie and Danny ride again!

RONNIE. Dan gave me the letter. Mum found it cleaning my room. Showed it to Dad. He claimed he wanted to understand. I started to explain. But when he heard *what* I was explaining, boy did he not want to know. Start of rumpus, end of story. It's not about you. You're so crippled by your own inability to be definitive about a man you've only known for twenty years why would you need me to interfere?

DAN. But you did.

RONNIE. When I came back it seemed you two didn't know what you wanted from one another so yes, I thought maybe you needed a... a *catalyst* to force you together or put you out of your misery—I don't know.

DAN. So you could move back to your room.

RONNIE. Maybe moving back to my room was mixed up in it somewhere—I was straight off the plane from one war zone into another. Everything I was expecting to be the same had changed. I was looking around for some solid ground and I couldn't find a single patch.

CASS. Who was the letter from?

RONNIE. Letter?

CASS. From the West Bank.

RONNIE. From the brother of a woman I...

> *Pause.*

CASS. You...?

RONNIE. She doesn't fit into your awesome web of intrigue so it really doesn't matter.

CASS. A Palestinian woman?

RONNIE. No, the letter was written outside the Territories but posted inside for the novelty postmark. What do you think?

CASS. *(beat)* What's her name?

RONNIE. What do you care, Cass?

CASS. You had feelings for her?

RONNIE. What do you care?

CASS. You loved her?

RONNIE. Answer my question.

CASS. What's her name?

RONNIE. *(beat)* Her name is. Her name *was*... Zahra.

CASS. Zara?

RONNIE. Za*h*ra.

CASS. Where did you meet?

RONNIE. What's the point?

CASS. I'm interested.

RONNIE. *(beat)* She worked in a youth hostel I stayed at. We had a thing for about nine months, after which time I asked her to come back to the U.K. with me. Happy?

CASS. She didn't want to?

RONNIE. She couldn't leave her family. So I said I would stay with her— a suggestion she openly laughed at.

DAN. Why?

RONNIE. It made no sense to her that someone with the freedom to pursue his wildest ambitions would willingly consign himself to a life under occupation. But I insisted I was serious, until one morning she came to me and sat me down. She took my hands and told me to look into her eyes. And then in her most serious voice, she told me she was pregnant with my child.

DAN. Pregnant?

RONNIE. She wasn't. She knew it even as she said it.

DAN. Then why say it?

RONNIE. To read the eyes of her Jewish lover at the moment of truth. Empty promises litter the streets over there. She needed to test the veracity of mine.

CASS. And what did she read in your eyes?

RONNIE. What does it matter what she read?

CASS. It may be the last time the real you was spotted.

RONNIE. The real me?

CASS. What did Zahra read in your eyes at the moment of truth?

RONNIE. *(beat) Maafee farah. Khawf faqat.*

DAN. In English?

RONNIE. *(beat).* No joy. Only fear.

> *Pause.*

CASS. And then what?

RONNIE. And then what?

CASS. And then what?

DAN. *(beat)* There is no *and then what.* Isn't that right, Ronnie? Just Ben Gurion airport. Getting bumped up to Club Class. And home.

> *Pause.*

CASS. How could you use people like that?

RONNIE. Use her? We had an affair. It didn't work out. It happens all the time.

CASS. I meant, when you came back. But possibly while you were there as well. Dear God…

RONNIE. What're you talking about?

CASS. Appropriating their struggle.

RONNIE. Appropriating?

CASS. Seeking association with the spirit of the underdog in the absence of any defining spirit of your own. Adopting the mantle of the aggrieved to avoid having to face that your own life has been without grief. Without pain. Without injustice. Without—in fact—any reason for its failure other than your own failings as a human being.

DAN. *(gently)* Cassie…

RONNIE. *(quiet)* The Palestinians have been shafted by everyone for more than thirty years. They stand and watch as their land is clawed away from under their noses, while their leaders are either bought off, humiliated, held responsible for acts they have no way of stopping, or simply executed.

CASS. As Lou might say… yes, Ronnie, we *know*. But that's their struggle. Before we can be of any use to that, we have to sort out our own.

> *RONNIE stands silently.*
>
> *Pause.*
>
> *CASS slowly crosses to him, and puts her arms around her brother, and holds him. DAN watches.*
>
> *After a few moments, HELEN comes out onto the roof, holding a lighted cigarillo.*

HELEN. Um. I thought I'd better come up and let you know that Douglas and Louise are talking about going. I've tried persuading them to stay, but the coverage quickly boiled down to lots of excited people in cagoules pointing at the sky. I'm afraid there's a very real sense that the party's literally moved on.

DAN. I'll go down.

> *DAN crosses to the entrance and goes downstairs. HELEN watches DAN exit. RONNIE breaks away from CASS and sits alone, upstage, watched by CASS.*
>
> *Pause. HELEN approaches CASS.*

HELEN. *(glancing at RONNIE, his head now in his hands)* Everything okay?

CASS. *(looking at RONNIE)* I don't think he knows who he is anymore.

HELEN. And you?

206 • Modern Jewish Plays

CASS. *(snapping out of it)* Thanks anyway.

HELEN. Thanks anyway?

CASS. Obviously if I'd've known Ronnie was going to come in like he did.

> *Beat.*

Bit of a disaster all round. But perhaps it's for the best you weren't able to... you know.

HELEN. But I was.

CASS. When?

HELEN. When you sent him up with my glasses.

CASS. But you scarcely had time.

HELEN. You know what I'm like working to a deadline, Cassie. Given the circumstances I'd've been more than a little taken aback if his response had been immediate.

CASS. Of course.

HELEN. So you can imagine my surprise when I went for my cigarillos just now, and found this in my coat pocket.

> *HELEN offers CASS a folded piece of notepaper. Beat.*

> *CASS stares at the piece of paper.*

CASS. What is it?

> *Pause.*

I suddenly feel extremely sick.

HELEN. In the documentary at this point—I don't know if you remember, Cassie. At this point the clients were offered two choices. Not all of them did this, but the practitioner we shadowed offered two choices in recognition of the fact that some women—even when faced with overwhelming evidence of their partner's capacity for infidelity—some women will nevertheless choose to turn a blind eye.

CASS. *(a wave of fear comes over her)* Oh Christ, Helen...

HELEN. She offered these choices to leave control with the client.

CASS. What's choice number one?

HELEN. Choice number one is I destroy this immediately and we pretend it never happened. The key word I'll emphasize is *pretend*.

CASS. Let me see it.

HELEN. Letting you see it is choice number two.

CASS. Give me the paper.

> *CASS holds out her hand. After a moment HELEN steps forward and places the piece of paper in CASS's hand.*

HELEN. He must have slipped it into my pocket while I was begging some free tax advice from Douglas. Mind you. I did lay it on pretty thick. Sexual favours for complete career resurrection, so possibly not so difficult to resist for a thirty-five-year-old duffer going nowhere.

> *CASS opens the note and stares at it.*

CASS. *(beat)* This isn't Dan's handwriting.

HELEN. *(beat)* What?

CASS. This isn't Dan's handwriting.

HELEN. It must be.

CASS. This isn't the number of his mobile.

> *LOU comes out onto the roof, wearing her coat.*

LOU. Dan's very sweetly trying to get us to stay—

CASS. It's Doug's number.

> *LOU stops in her tracks. CASS looks up from the piece of paper.*

LOU. *(beat)* What did you just say?

> *CASS instinctively screws up the piece of notepaper.*

What's that in your hand?

CASS. Nothing.

LOU. *(beat)* Cass. In the twelve years we've known each other, have I ever previously struck you as a total fucking moron?

CASS. No.

LOU. So show me what's in your hand.

CASS. *(beat)* No.

LOU. Show me what's in your hand.

> *CASS shakes her head. They regard one another. Long pause.*

What the fuck's going on here?

HELEN. I offered to screw little Danny to determine if Cassie could completely trust him.

CASS. Helen…

HELEN. I just went for a cigarillo and discovered a piece of paper in my coat pocket, inscribed with a mobile number and the message, "let's meet."

CASS. Helen, don't!

HELEN. I assumed it was Dan, inviting me to call to arrange a rendezvous.

LOU. Cass?

HELEN. I assumed wrong.

> *DAN now enters.*

DAN. I tried bribing Doug with unlimited access to the telescope, but he seems pretty set on—

> *DAN picks up the atmosphere on the roof and stops talking. He regards the three women on the roof. After a moment DOUGLAS comes onto the roof in his jacket.*

DOUGLAS. I told him we couldn't be so easily bought.

> *DOUGLAS crosses to LOU and gently kisses the nape of her neck. She doesn't respond, looking directly at CASS all the time.*

We should be making a move.

> *DOUGLAS is suddenly aware of the atmosphere on the roof. LOU stands frozen, facing CASS.*

> *Long pause.*

LOU. After what you've just seen. Do you trust yours any more, or any less? You think he's one thing, Cass. And he is. But he's also other things. Do you think this is the first time?

CASS. But you and Douglas are... you're Lou and Douglas.

LOU. Unfortunately my husband has a weakness for fuckable stupidity. We try not to broadcast it.

HELEN. Hey! *Bitch!*

LOU. Being married is no guarantee, Cass. Having children is no guarantee. There are no guarantees. *(pointing at HELEN)* So if this vacuous fake has sold you one, I'd ask for your money back.

HELEN. *(offended)* How fucking dare you? No-one's being paid here.

LOU. *(facing HELEN)* You mean... you do this for *free?*

DAN. I'm sorry, but did I miss something when it all went dark?

DOUGLAS. *(beat, subdued)* I'm... I'll go down to the car.

LOU. Do that.

DOUGLAS. *(pathetically brave face)* It's taking longer to start every time.

DAN. *(trying to help him out)* Have you checked the battery?

DOUGLAS. In summer?

DAN. Average lifespan is approximately three years, regardless.

DOUGLAS. I didn't know that.

DAN. Most die in winter because usage is that much heavier.

DOUGLAS. Of course. Heaters, demisters, wipers, headlights, starting up from frozen—

LOU. *(sharp, not looking at him)* Douglas.

DOUGLAS stops his litany. Beat.

DAN. Bring chummy over one night when I've got Oscar round. Point them at the sky. Blow two tiny minds for the price of one.

DOUGLAS. I'd like that. Well.

Beat.

Thanks, Cass.

CASS. Doug.

DAN. I'll see you to the door.

DOUGLAS. *(to LOU)* I'll wait for you downstairs.

LOU. Yes.

DOUGLAS hesitates for a moment.

DOUGLAS. Lou—

LOU. *(cutting him off)* Not here.

DOUGLAS. *(beat)* No.

DOUGLAS makes a wide berth of HELEN and goes back downstairs, followed by DAN. Beat.

CASS. I'm so sorry.

LOU. Stop asking how is it all going to end before it's even begun. Stop living in uncertainty, start living *with* it. My relationship with Douglas is an open-ended condition. I accept that because the alternative is unacceptable.

HELEN. I'm sorry but that is such bollocks.

LOU. *(pointing again at HELEN)* The alternative is to become a lethal little zealot like your boss here. Cynically squinting at the world from inside her Prada bunker. Be brave, Cass. Build on the past, don't be a slave to it. Move forward. *(kissing CASS on the cheek)* God bless.

LOU exits downstairs. Pause.

HELEN. If my self-esteem ever sank that low I hope I'd at least have the dignity to drown myself.

CASS. *(beat)* I'll see you at the office in the morning.

HELEN. *(looking at RONNIE)* I'm not going to get the treatment, am I?

CASS. I don't think so, no.

HELEN. Whatever he's been paid, *I want back.*

Beat.

See myself out.

> *CASS lets out a long, deep breath, the tension finally leaving her. DAN comes onto the roof.*

DAN. I know you think the sun shines out of that woman's—

CASS. Hold me.

> *DAN stops, hesitates for a moment, and crosses over to CASS, taking her in his arms. They hold one another, clinging on for dear life.*

> *Pause.*

I'm so sorry.

DAN. I'm burning my films.

CASS. I am so so sorry.

DAN. I can't offer you more than you're holding right now. You have to decide if that's enough.

> *CASS pulls him tighter to her. The telephone rings downstairs.*

CASS. *(beat)* I'll go.

DAN. *I'll* go. The answerphone picks up after six rings.

CASS. *(crossing to the entrance)* Then I'd better get used to it.

> *CASS goes downstairs. DAN watches her.*

> *Pause.*

> *After a moment he turns to RONNIE.*

DAN. The letter, Ronnie. What did it say?

RONNIE. It asked me that whatever happened, not to forget them.

DAN. *(beat)* If I receive any more, where shall I send them?

RONNIE. *(beat)* I don't know.

> *Long pause.*

What now, Dan? What now?

DAN. Ask Raoul. He was never short of a plan.

RONNIE. *(looking up)* Raoul's gone.

DAN. Well, then. I guess you're on your own.

> *DAN and RONNIE regard one another as CASS appears at the entrance to the roof.*

> *DAN slowly turns away from RONNIE, and faces CASS.*

CASS. It was Mum. Asking if I'd heard from Ronnie.

DAN. What did you tell her?

CASS. I said he *was* here. But then he went.

> *CASS holds out her hand. DAN crosses to the entrance and takes it. She kisses his hand and leads him downstairs.*
>
> *RONNIE looks ahead as the sounds of London rise. After a moment the sounds of Hebron rise in competition—a muezzin* calling the faithful to prayer, and the thok-thok of a helicopter gunship overhead. The noise rises in volume, as RONNIE covers his ears with his hands.*
>
> *Slow fade to black.*
>
> *End.*

---

* *muezzin* – the official of a mosque responsible for calling the faithful to prayer.

Shooting Magda

(The Palestinian Girl)

Joshua Sobol

translated from the Hebrew by Miriam Shlesinger

• Joshua Sobol •

Joshua Sobol, born in Tel Mond, Israel, was active as a young man in the socialist Hashomer Hatzair youth movement and was a member of a kibbutz from 1957 to 1965. He then studied Philosophy at the Sorbonne. A leading Hebrew playwright, he taught Esthetics and directed workshops at Tel Aviv University, the Kibbutz Teacher Seminary and the Beit Zvi Drama School. From 1985 to 1988, he served as the artistic director of the Haifa Municipal Theater. Many of his plays have been staged in Europe and the USA to great critical acclaim. One of his plays, *Soul of a Jew*, was performed at the Edinburgh, Berlin and Chicago Festivals, while another play, *Ghetto*, was named Britain's "Play of the Year" in 1989, and has been staged in Vienna, Cologne, Toronto, Oslo, Paris, Los Angeles, Berlin and Washington.

• Setting •

The plot is set in a television studio, where the television film, "Magda" is being shot. The plot of the film becomes a part of the play. The set is that of the television play, "Magda," surrounded by the typical paraphernalia of a television production, such as video cameras and recording equipment.

The plot takes place over a single 24-hour period, during which the play is shot from start to finish on a shoestring budget.

The circumstances: time is short and the filming must be completed by the following morning, since the budget does not allow for more than one day of shooting, and the studio must be vacated within 24 hours.

• Production History •

Shooting Magda (The Palestinian Girl) had its world premiere at Haifa Municipal Theatre, Israel, in October 1985, with the following company:

Dahlia, Magda	Leora Rivlin
Samira	Salwa Nakara
Benesh, Rodney	Roberto Polak
Fahed, Adnan	Makram Khuri
David, Udi	Yiftah Katsor
Ada, Miriam	Shosh Shlam
Itzhak, Efraim	Yosef Bashi
Havkin, Herbert	Kay Lotman
Jonas, Avi	Gideon Shirin
Singer	Tami Alon
Barry, Cameraman	Erez Shafrir

Directed by Gedalia Besser
Set by Adrian Vaux
Costumes by Edna Sobol
Lighting by Yehiel Orgal

• **Characters** •

BENESH - a director. Together with Samira, Benesh wrote the film script of
"Magda," based on Samira's own story. Besides being director of the film, he
also plays the role of Rodney, a British playwright, who was Samira's lover.
Benesh is forty-eight and married. For the past three years he has been having
an affair with Dahlia.

DAHLIA - an actress, forty years old. Plays the role of Magda, the dramatic
persona representing Samira. Magda is twenty-three, the same age as Samira
when the story takes place.

SAMIRA - a young Arab actress, twenty-five years old. The co-author, with Benesh,
of the film script "Magda". In the film she is the one who reads the lead-in texts,
in which she tells her story. These texts serve to introduce the scenes.

UDI - an actor, about thirty. He plays the role of David, who is twenty-five in
the film script. David is a law student and a member of an ultra-rightwing
organization. Udi himself holds radical leftwing ideas.

YITZHAK - a thirty-year-old actor who plays Ephraim, a fifty-year-old colonel
(Reserves) and David's father. Yitzhak is an expert at buffoonery, which is why
he was chosen to play Ephraim, who appears in the film dressed as a clown,
having just returned from a Purim masquerade party.

ADA - Udi's real-life mother, who plays David's mother Miriam in the film. Ada
teaches creative drama classes, as does Miriam. She was cast as Miriam both
because of the film's limited budget and because of her suitability for the part.

FAHED - an Arab actor, forty-two years old. He plays Adnan, Magda's boyfriend in
the film, a twenty-five-year-old drama student.

YONAH - a thirty-five-year-old filmmaker. A good friend of Benesh's. In the film,
he plays Barry, a student, originally from the States, and a member of an ultra-
rightwing group.

PAUL - the production's musician and pianist. He also plays the part of Avi,
member of the rightwing group and Barry's accomplice in his hooliganistic
activities.

HAVKIN- a onetime small-parts actor and a dancing teacher who barely makes ends
meet by teaching dancing at acting schools. He is an old man, without family
and utterly alone. In Vienna in the thirties, he was an Ausdruck-Tanz
(Expression-Dance) dancer. In the film, he plays the part of Herbert,
a former dancing teacher in whose studio Magda supposedly re-lives the
story of the film.

SINGER - she scats vocalisations of the music played by the pianist.

• Characters in the Film-Within-the-Play •

RODNEY *played by Benesh*
MAGDA *played by Dahlia*
DAVID *played by Udi*
EPHRAIM *played by Yitzhak*
MIRIAM *played by Ada*
ADNAN *played by Fahed*
BARRY *played by Yonah*
AVI *played by Paul*
HERBERT *played by Havkin*

• *Shooting Magda (The Palestinian Girl)* •

ACT ONE
Scene I

Outdoors. Nighttime. On the lawn.

Commotion. Yelling. Swearing in Hebrew and Arabic by everyone around the set. The participants are not yet visible.

Just when the racket has reached its peak, a sheep is hurled onto the stage. This is MAGDA, covered from head to toe in a sheepskin. She falls on the lawn, screaming:

MAGDA. Adnan! Adnan! Help! Leave me alone! Help!

Enter three toughs: DAVID, BARRY, AVI. They are screaming.

DAVID. Traitor.

BARRY. Terrorist.

AVI. Stinking leftist.

DAVID beats MAGDA, who is trying to get up off the floor. He is yelling.

DAVID. I'll show you "Nuernberg Corner of Auschwitz".

Kicks her. She screams.

MAGDA. Help! They're killing me! Help!

DAVID. *(still kicking her)* You Jewish traitor. Whoring with Arabs, you filthy bitch! I'll show you "Nuernberg Corner of Auschwitz".

MAGDA. *(under the barrage of their attacks)* I'm not an Arab! I'm a Jew. I'm a Jew!

BENESH. *(shouting)* Cut!

The action stops. They all step out of their parts. Work lights go on.

DAHLIA. *(Pushing her head out of the sheepskin, she turns to DAVID.)* Can't you control yourself? Do you know you're really hurting me?

UDI. Complaints—to the director.

DAHLIA. *(to BENESH)* I don't have to take any more of this. He's really killing me.

BENESH. And you're killing me. How many more times are we going to have to take this lousy scene until we're lucky enough to hear the text the way it should be?

DAHLIA. Wasn't I coming across?

BENESH. What were you saying? Do you know what you were saying?

DAHLIA. When?

BENESH. Before I said to cut. What was the last sentence you said?

DAHLIA. "I'm not a Jew, I'm an Arab. I'm an Arab."

BENESH. You wish! You said the exact opposite.

DAHLIA. I did not.

BENESH. Samira, what did she say?

SAMIRA. *(to DAHLIA)* You said: "I'm not an Arab, I'm a Jew. I'm a Jew."

DAHLIA. *(to BENESH)* Just a minute. Don't I know what I said?

BENESH. You know what you think you said.

ADA. What's the point of bickering? Why don't we just listen to the recording.

BENESH. That's all we need now—to spend time on playbacks.

ADA. It'll take less time than this shouting match, believe me. *(to the recording TECHNICIAN)* Let's hear the recording.

> As the technician runs the tape back.

UDI. Mother, you don't have to be in the middle of everything.

ADA. Udi, my love, I know what I'm doing.

BENESH. We're very short of time. We've got to finish shooting by tomorrow morning. We've been through every scene a thousand times. Every step. Now that we've reached the shooting stage, everyone keeps getting mixed up.

ADA. Benesh, you're working with people, not computers. And even computers make mistakes.

BENESH. What am I asking, for heaven's sakes: just concentrate.

HAVKIN. It's getting late. So concentrate.

TECHNICIAN. Can I play you the recording?

ADA. Go ahead.

RECORDING. *(MAGDA screaming)* I'm not an Arab! I'm a Jew! I'm a Jew! *(BENESH shouting)* Cut!

> The TECHNICIAN stops the tape. Silence.

BENESH. All right. Back to your places. We're shooting the scene from the top.

DAHLIA. *(stepping out of the sheepskin)* I can't do it.

BENESH. Dahlia.

DAHLIA. I just can't go through that scene again. I can't.

ADA. Weren't you going to call a break?

BENESH. We'll run through the scene once more properly. Then we'll take a break.

DAHLIA. *(to herself)* I can't stand it. I can't.

ADA. *(to BENESH)* You've been working four hours straight. There's no point in putting the pressure on when people are exhausted. It'll just make things worse.

YONAH. *(to BENESH)* Give us a break. Everyone's starving.

BENESH. *(glancing at his watch)* Okay. Time out. But don't start preparing any gourmet dinners.

ADA. *(announces)* Listen, everybody: there are box lunches ready in the canteen. Sandwiches with Bulgarian cheese and vegetables. There's coffee in the black thermos, tea in the red one.

BENESH. You're all back here in fifteen minutes. We'll go straight into the Independence Day Ball scene.

They all leave, except for DAHLIA, and ADA who lingers behind.

DAHLIA. *(to BENESH)* Can I talk to you for a minute?

BENESH. Let's go get some sandwiches. I'm famished too.

ADA. I'll have them bring you some sandwiches.

ADA leaves. DAHLIA and BENESH are left to themselves.

Scene 2

DAHLIA and BENESH on the set.

DAHLIA. Good thing we have a personal attendant. Otherwise I'd never get to talk to you.

BENESH. She's okay, that woman.

DAHLIA. Sure. Everyone's okay except me.

BENESH. Poor Dahlia. Is that the game we're playing? Fine, I'm all yours.

DAHLIA. Thanks a lot. Go ahead and eat with whoever you feel like.

BENESH. Good timing is an important quality not only in acting; in life too. Good timing shows that you're with it, that you're tuned into people, not just busy with yourself.

DAHLIA. I know I'm complicated, and that I've got a sick personality.

BENESH. You simply refuse to accept responsibility.

DAHLIA. Responsibility, responsibility. You've got one answer to everything: responsibility. I can't accept responsibility when I've got that one sitting there, staring at me all the time.

BENESH. Who's "that one"?

DAHLIA. You know perfectly well.

BENESH. She has a name, doesn't she?

DAHLIA. Samira, all right?

BENESH. No, it's not all right.

DAHLIA. So it's not all right.

BENESH. Why do you call her "that one"?

DAHLIA. Are you picking a fight?

BENESH. First you say "all right." I say it's not all right. So "It's not all right." Just what's the matter with you?

DAHLIA. I've got a headache and I'm not up to explaining every word I say.

BENESH. First you want to talk to me. The next minute you tell me to go ahead and eat with whoever I feel like.

DAHLIA. You were getting on my nerves.

BENESH. Do you have a headache or was I getting on your nerves?

DAHLIA. What do you want?

BENESH. You're hiding.

DAHLIA. You're very open.

BENESH. I think I am.

DAHLIA. Really? Then, get rid of her.

BENESH. I beg your pardon.

DAHLIA. I can't do the part with her looking at me.

BENESH. Everyone's looking at you. Why is she the only one who bothers you?

DAHLIA. I'm not playing everyone. I'm playing her. When she looks at me, whatever I do doesn't feel right.

BENESH. That means you're not really concentrating on the "job."

DAHLIA. I certainly am concentrating on the "job."

BENESH. What are you talking about?

DAHLIA. Benesh, do me a favour. Not a personal one. I'm asking you as an actor of yours: keep her away from here, at least while we're shooting.

BENESH. I can't. It's her story. She wrote the script.

DAHLIA. She doesn't have to be here the whole time.

BENESH. I need her for the lead-ins.

DAHLIA. You can shoot those separately.

BENESH. It won't turn out the way I want. You've seen how she works. She reacts to the scenes, she adlibs the text. It comes out natural, spontaneous. If I record her part in isolation, it'll be dead. It's impossible.

DAHLIA. She makes me freeze. I keep feeling unnatural.

> SAMIRA appears in the distance, carrying a couple of box lunches and two bottles of beer. They don't notice her.

BENESH. Dahlia, between us, you're a creature of the stage. Why should she be giving us a hard time?

DAHLIA. Is it so hard for you to give her up for a while?

BENESH. Impossible. Besides, she'd be terribly hurt.

DAHLIA. If she were a Jew you wouldn't think twice.

BENESH. She isn't a Jew.

SAMIRA. *(from a distance)* I've brought you something to eat.

> *The two of them fall silent. SAMIRA hands DAHLIA the box lunch and the beer.*

DAHLIA. Thanks.

> *Takes the food and walks away, but stays within earshot.*

SAMIRA. *(handing the food and the beer to BENESH)* I've got to take a few hours off.

BENESH. What happened?

SAMIRA. I've got a problem with my apartment. I'll be back this evening.

> *She walks over to her corner, packs her text and a few belongings in a knapsack. Meanwhile, HAVKIN appears and corners BENESH.*

HAVKIN. Forgive me for butting in. I've still got a problem with the last scene. I don't understand...

BENESH. *(His mind is on SAMIRA, who is busy gathering her things.)* What don't you understand? It's Christmas Eve, you hear someone crying, you go in, you see a lonely girl, you invite her over to your place.

HAVKIN. But what do we actually do in the scene?

BENESH. You meet.

HAVKIN. But I don't understand. Don't I remember inviting her, or am I just pretending? It's only been one day; am I senile? There's something unclear about the character.

BENESH. That's right. Something unclear about the character.

HAVKIN. Something confused...

BENESH. That's right. Confused.

HAVKIN. What should I do about it?

BENESH. Go along with it.

> *Calls SAMIRA, who is on her way out.*

Samira! Samira!

> *She exits.*

Scene 3

HAVKIN looks around him, at a loss, and notices DAHLIA.

HAVKIN. I don't get it. Did I say anything to upset him? I don't get it.

DAHLIA. What don't you get? Samira has some problems with her apartment.

HAVKIN. That much I know. Her lover, that no-good English playwright stood her up on Christmas Eve. She's sitting in her room, crying and I go in there and invite her over to my studio.

DAHLIA. That's right.

HAVKIN. But the following morning, I come into the studio, I see you, and I don't even recognize you?

DAHLIA. Believe me, Havkin, I wish I had your part. Just let the text lead you along, and it'll be smooth sailing.

HAVKIN. The text is a problem in itself... I don't understand: am I senile?

PAUL enters, finishing a sandwich.

PAUL. Are we rehearsing the scene?

DAHLIA. Give us the accompaniment. We'll run though it.

PAUL sits down at the piano and starts playing the waltz. DAHLIA assumes the role of MAGDA. HAVKIN becomes HERBERT. MAGDA starts dancing.

HERBERT. One-two-three, one-two-three.

HAVKIN. Help me with the text, if I forget.

HERBERT. One-two-and, one-two-good.... In a big circle, nice and wide, use up the space, all of it. Free and easy. Throw your weight back. Leave it behind you. All of it. That's the way. Relaxed and easy.

HAVKIN. What comes next?

DAHLIA. *(still dancing in the role of MAGDA)* "Life happens from one minute to the next!"

HERBERT. Life happens from one minute to the next!

DAHLIA. "And burns out from one minute to the next."

HAVKIN. I remember. That line is certainly philosophical.

HERBERT. That's fine, that's fine.

HAVKIN. Life really does burn out from one minute to the next.

HERBERT. That's fine. Nice big circles, use up the space, that's right. One-two-three, one-two-three.... A big circle, nice and big. Let yourself go. Majestic movements. You're a princess now. A queen. The world is yours. You cross over borders. You sweep over ice. Over water. Air. You're a solitary bird. All alone in the sky.

HAVKIN. That's rather poetic, actually.

HERBERT. Way, way up. The wind is with you. Take to the wind. Spread your wings. Wide. Nice and open. Glide. Float. Forward. Forward. You're creating space. Work your way into it.

HAVKIN. Real Ausdruck-Tanz...

HERBERT. Behind you there's a fire raging. A landslide. Destruction. Roads, buildings turning to dust. Forward, forward. Up and away.

HAVKIN. I can't help myself...

He joins in the dance, completely carried away.

HERBERT. Living is getting away. From one minute to the next. That's good. Excellent. Excellent!

HAVKIN. I remember the whole monologue.

DAHLIA. Go on with the text.

HERBERT. Where did you learn to dance like that?

MAGDA. From you.

HERBERT. You were a student of mine?

MAGDA. Yes.

HERBERT. Hello, Student.

MAGDA. Hello, Teacher.

HAVKIN. He's not senile.

DAHLIA. Of course not.

HAVKIN. He's just an old devil with a sense of humour.

DAHLIA. You said it!

HAVKIN. How does it go after that?

DAHLIA. "Were you a student of mine in Vienna."

HAVKIN. What?... Ah!...

HERBERT. You were a student of mine in Vienna?

MAGDA. No, here. In London.

HERBERT. Just when did you study with me?

MAGDA. Yesterday.

HERBERT. What's your name?

MAGDA. Magda.

HERBERT. Hello, Magda.

MAGDA. Hello, Herbert.

HERBERT. Where do we know each other from?

MAGDA. From the staircase.

HERBERT. You're the girl in the staircase.

MAGDA. I'm your neighbour on this floor. I live right across the hall from you.

HERBERT. Hi, Neighbour.

MAGDA. Hi, Neighbour.

HERBERT. Who told you my name?

MAGDA. You did.

HERBERT. When?

MAGDA. Last night.

HERBERT. Was I stoned?

MAGDA. It was Christmas Eve.

HERBERT. I was stoned.

MAGDA. And I was crying.

HERBERT. Why?

HAVKIN. What a naïve question. Maybe he really is naïve?

DAHLIA. If it works for you, use it.

HAVKIN. If it works for me... I'll be dead soon. It works for me.

DAHLIA. We'll all be dead soon.

HERBERT. Where were you fifty years ago?

MAGDA. I wasn't born yet.

HERBERT. Have you got a place to sleep?

MAGDA. At your place.

HERBERT. Since when?

MAGDA. Since last night.

HERBERT. Did you sleep well?

MAGDA. I hope I didn't yell in my sleep.

HERBERT. You're the girl who yelled last night.

MAGDA. I'm sorry.

HAVKIN. I always forget the line after that.

DAHLIA. "The fight you'll keep losing..."

HAVKIN. Yes!

> Enter SAMIRA. She returns to her usual place, puts down her bag and takes out the things she packed earlier. She is behaving as if she decided to come back. DAHLIA notices her, but doesn't react directly.

HERBERT. The fight you'll keep losing is the one against yourself.

HAVKIN. (pondering that line) How does that tie in?

MAGDA. I'm not fighting against myself. I spend my whole life fighting against what they're trying to make of me.

DAHLIA. *(addressing her remarks to SAMIRA)* Declarations, declarations. I can't believe the things that I'm saying.

HERBERT. That battle is doomed too. If you don't know what you want to be, you'll wind up having others call the tune.

MAGDA. I want to be Magda.

DAHLIA. That's another line I hate.

> SAMIRA *lights up a cigarette and stares at DAHLIA without saying a word.*

HERBERT. What is Magda?

MAGDA. Magda is something that nothing sticks to. No label. Magda is the kind of stuff that can't be frozen in any form. Magda isn't the result. She isn't the continuation. Magda is what happens from one minute to the next. Magda is something that doesn't belong, something that'll never belong to anyone…

> She stops and goes back to being herself.

DAHLIA. I can't go on with that monologue. I can't say it. *(turns to SAMIRA)* Is that really the way you feel about yourself?

SAMIRA. Look… *(hesitant, then resolute)* I wrote the script together with Benesh.

DAHLIA. But it's about you. It's your story.

SAMIRA. It's based on my story.

DAHLIA. That monologue is by Benesh.

SAMIRA. That's right.

DAHLIA. Naturally, as if I didn't recognize him? It's just what Benesh enjoys thinking about himself.

HAVKIN. Shouldn't we get on with the scene?

DAHLIA. I can't. I don't know how to go on at all.

> BENESH *enters holding a cup of coffee and a cigarette. He sees that they are immersed in their work, and sits down on the side. He listens. But does not interfere.*

You know, Havkin, I'm in a much lousier position that you are. The part of Magda is so contrived. It's such patchwork…

> She expects a reaction from BENESH, but he keeps silent.

If I acted on my instincts, I'd quit the production right now.

HAVKIN. What's the matter with you? What are you talking about? You'll do the part beautifully!

DAHLIA. How can I? The way the character is written is so shallow. Making declarations about herself. She doesn't develop at all. I don't understand her, and I told you: I don't believe a word she says.

HAVKIN. And what about you? Are you so understanding? Do you really believe every word you say? Take me. Here I am, a man of sixty-eight. Yes, that's right. And what do I know about myself? Very little.

To be precise, only the biographical details and the few things I don't keep from myself. But what do I keep from myself—do I know? And I'm no slouch. I'm not coarse or thick-skulled either. I'm a gentle and sensitive person. I like to dance. I like music, art, books. I like to observe people. This morning, for instance, I went outside and stood in the bus-stop. Two girls walked by, still fresh from a good night's sleep. One of them was sort of plump. Sensual. And they were singing some song. Suddenly this boy came towards them in the opposite direction. Not much of a man. Skinny, with glasses. But a male. And suddenly the girl was singing that song differently. Something inside her came alive, something got into her body. And it was perfectly timed. You know what I mean...

And it wasn't that way with the other one. You could tell right away which of the females had caught the male. All because of that timing of hers. What do you called it—synchronisation?

BENESH. "Timing" will do.

HAVKIN. And you could see a human being in the mainstream of life. And what does she know? Instincts. It's all instincts. No really. I'm a man who's seen a thing or two in life. Married three times. Divorced once, widowed once, and now taking care of a wife who is sick... senile... not to mention my share of affairs. And what do I know about myself as far as morality is concerned? Do I know how I'll behave if I fall in love again? Take me, for instance. I'm a shallow person too, making declarations about himself. And what do you mean about a character developing? Who develops anyhow? What I am today is what I was at twenty. Believe me. Nothing really changes. Except for the face, which keeps getting older. Character development is the concoction of theoreticians. Back then, I used to lose my head when I'd fall in love, and I could still do the same today. God have pity on anyone who develops out of that. *(to BENESH)* I'm sorry to be using up production time.

BENESH. You're not using up time. It's part of the production.

DAHLIA. Why did you say earlier that you'll be dead soon?

HAVKIN. I haven't got anyone left to offer my love.

SAMIRA. Maybe you don't want to?

HAVKIN. Who wants what I have to offer?

PAUL. *(from his seat at the piano)* Is that any reason to die?

HAVKIN. Do you know any better reason?

PAUL. I'm not in love with anyone and I'm not about to die on account of it.

HAVKIN. Oh, well, with you it's just temporary.

PAUL. No it isn't. I haven't been in love for years.

DAHLIA. Me either. I'm careful not to fall in love.

SAMIRA. How can you play Samira then?

DAHLIA. Do you think I don't do your part well too?

SAMIRA. Magda isn't exactly me.

DAHLIA. I don't introduce my personal life into my work either.

SAMIRA. That's not the problem.

DAHLIA. Then what is?

SAMIRA. Maybe I shouldn't tell you. I'm liable to spoil things.

DAHLIA. On the contrary. If you tell me, you might do me some good.

SAMIRA. You stay out of it. Nothing happens to you. Nothing hurts you.

DAHLIA. I really think the best thing for the production would be for me to call it quits. No harm would be done. On the contrary. You're here anyway. You're an actress. You know your text. I'm sure you understand it better than I do. Why don't you do the part yourself?

SAMIRA. I can't play myself. I won't believe my lines. And I want you to play me.

DAHLIA. Why? Why is it so important to you that I do the part?

SAMIRA. I want a Jew to play Magda, and if you think about it, you'll know why. I'm sure you can do a very good job too, especially after hearing you earlier.

DAHLIA. What did you hear?

SAMIRA. I think you've got a problem of truth and falsehood. I think you've got to come to grips with some ethical questions and ask yourself if every word you utter is true or if you're not just making all sorts of empty declarations about your feelings and your views while your behaviour keeps exposing something entirely different.

DAHLIA. I know. I'm completely empty and I don't have anything to give people.

SAMIRA. That's an easy way of avoiding the truth. And it's another mask that you've got to tear off yourself if you really want to know who you are.

DAHLIA. Mind being more specific?

SAMIRA. When we met, you declared that you're against the Occupation, against having one people rule over another and a whole list of lofty declarations.

DAHLIA. I stand behind everything I said.

SAMIRA. How do you intend to set things right and to free society of lies and depravity if you're just as depraved?

DAHLIA. I beg your pardon?

SAMIRA. I get in your way when you're playing me. You'd like me not to be here. Why don't you have the guts to tell me so straight to my face? Why do you try to work it out behind my back, with Benesh?

DAHLIA. You're right.

SAMIRA. I overheard you. Don't start explaining. If I were a Jew, it would have been much easier for you. For me too. Sorry, I'm not a Jew. No, don't apologize. Words don't mean anything. Only deeds. You're not a politician and I don't expect you to remake the world. But you're an actress and could do Magda the way she is. Warts and all. With whatever problems she has. Or you can cop out. But then at least you'll know what you're doing and who you are.

DAHLIA. I've got plenty to say to that, but we'll carry on with this argument some other time. *(to BENESH)* I'm ready. Go ahead and roll.

BENESH. To your places, everyone.

As they all return to their positions, he turns to SAMIRA:

I'd like to include that conversation in your last scene with Rodney, before you and he say goodbye for good.

SAMIRA. It's more or less what I really told him.

BENESH. Why didn't you tell me about it when we were writing the script?

SAMIRA. I forgot.

BENESH. Sit down and write it.

SAMIRA. Now?

BENESH. Just a minute. *(to everyone)* Listen, everybody: we're starting with Samira's story. We go straight into the scene with the dance caller, and don't forget to make plenty of noise. *(to YITZHAK)* Haka'leh, you lead the scene through to "Etz Ha-Rimon" and if all goes well we move right into my scene with Dahlia. Yonah… where's Yonah?

YONAH. Right here.

BENESH. When I come in as Rodney, you take over the set.

YONAH. Aye, aye, sir.

BENESH. Is Samira ready?

SAMIRA. I'm adlibbing.

BENESH. Tell the story in the simplest possible words. Just the way it happened. Sound rolling?

TECHNICIAN. Rolling. 10, 9, 8, 7, 6, 5, 4, 3, 2, 1. Go.

BENESH. Now get this: we don't stop until I say so. Let's go.

Scene 4

SAMIRA is telling her story. A close-up of her face appears at the same time on a giant video screen.

SAMIRA. It was the eve of Independence Day. They were having a big party on campus. Adnan and I were preparing a small number.

BENESH signals to YITZHAK, who steps onto the set in the role of a DANCE CALLER, holding a microphone. A well-known folkdance tune ("Hey Harmonica") is blaring on the P.A. system. A singer enters. She's holding a wireless microphone and scatting to the music. Meanwhile, SAMIRA walks over to her corner, to write out the dialogue between herself and RODNEY.

DANCE CALLER. Where's your holiday spirit folks? Where's the good mood? Did you leave it back in the reserves? Back on the Beirut-Damascus road? I see a whole bunch of you just sitting there near the cafeteria. Are you from the chronic-care ward? Or the Society for the Handicapped? What is this, folks? A nursing home or a university? Everyone, without exception, come join the dancing.

He gets off the stage and starts to sing Naomi Shemer's "Shir Ha-Shuk" ("Song of the Marketplace"). The singer joins him and the two of them move off the set as though heading to liven up the celebration at some other end of the lawn. The actors keep passing back and forth in front of the camera, to create the effect of a large crowd of dancers. On the gigantic video screen, meanwhile, there appears a documentary sequence of large crowds of dancers. Now the DANCE CALLER returns and announces, on camera:

And now—the men all turn to the right, the girls to the left. Everybody takes a partner, and let's all form couples for "Etz Ha-Rimon".

The singer preforms the song "Etz Ha-Rimon" with the DANCE CALLER humming along. The music and the singing fade out. Meanwhile, BENESH has changed clothes and gone over to DAHLIA. The cameras follow them as they head for a different corner of the set, dancing. BENESH is playing RODNEY and DAHLIA is MAGDA. They go on dancing. RODNEY leads MAGDA to the front of the stage.

Scene 5

RODNEY and MAGDA are dancing. Far off, the melody of "Etz Ha-Rimon" continues playing softly.

MAGDA. Where are you leading me?

RODNEY. To London.

MAGDA. Watch out, I might just take you seriously.

RODNEY. I've been following you all evening.

MAGDA. This party has much more interesting subjects than me, if you're from the Secret Service.

RODNEY. You don't know everything there is to know about yourself.

MAGDA. Go ahead and tell me something I don't know.

RODNEY. How long will you give me?

MAGDA. Thirty seconds.

RODNEY. You get exactly two questions.

MAGDA. Who are you anyway?

RODNEY. Rodney Lawson.

MAGDA. What are you doing here?

RODNEY. Looking for material for a BBC series I'm doing.

MAGDA. You a playwright?

RODNEY. We agreed on two questions. That's the third.

MAGDA. Never mind that. I'm an actress.

RODNEY. You don't say! Why do you think I've been watching you?

MAGDA. What, you knew?

RODNEY. I've got an eye for that sort of thing. I can smell an actress from miles off. *(pulls out a flask)* Do you drink?

MAGDA. Thanks, perfect timing. I'm on in a few minutes and I'm going to need all the courage I can get. *(She takes a sip, hands back the bottle. He takes a sip.)* Well, then. Are you here to find a theme for a play?

RODNEY. Yes. I've got the writer's blues, as they say. I sit down at the typewriter and I just can't get started. *(smiles)* I'm in trouble. I can't churn out any more of those idiotic dramas about marital woes and cheating spouses. It's all too close to my own life for me to be able to see the point. *(takes another sip)*

MAGDA. Why? Do you think your life is pointless?

RODNEY. I don't think so, I know so. You have no idea just how empty life can become. Here in Israel, you people live a life that's tense, dangerous, full of contradictions. Almost everything you do has some meaning—political, moral, existential...

MAGDA. What do you want to write about?

RODNEY. A love story between a nationalist Arab girl and a nationalist Jewish boy.

MAGDA. Couldn't you find anything more complicated to write about? In any event, you're going to have to make it all up. In real life it could never happen.

RODNEY. Why not? Couldn't you see yourself falling in love with an Arab?

MAGDA. I'm not good for your story. I am in love with an Arab.

RODNEY. Is that so?!... Would you be willing to tell me your story?

MAGDA. What made you choose this party at the university tonight?

RODNEY. A friend of mine. A British journalist who lives in Israel. He told me there's going to be a fight between Jews and Arabs here tonight.

MAGDA. What'll it be about?

RODNEY. The Arab students have prepared some number that's going to break up the party.

MAGDA. What?!

RODNEY. Would you mind introducing me to your boyfriend, the Arab?

MAGDA. There he is.

> *ADNAN appears, carrying some furs over his arm.*

Adnan, there's a British playwright here who'd like to meet you.

RODNEY. *(holds out his hand)* Rodney Lawson.

ADNAN. Adnan.

RODNEY. Why don't we go sit down somewhere quiet.

ADNAN. I'm sorry, maybe later if that's okay with you. We're very busy right now. We've got a performance in a few minutes.

RODNEY. After the performance then, here?

ADNAN. Fine. See you later.

> *RODNEY leaves. BENESH steps out of his role as RODNEY and replaces YONAH as director. FAHED abandons the role of ADNAN for a minute and turns to BENESH:*

FAHED. Should we go ahead?

BENESH. As long as you've stopped, wait just a minute. Dahlia, wait a while before you put on the fur, to make it clear that you're scared.

DAHLIA. Did you notice the changes I made?

BENESH. Yes, yes. It was excellent. Keep on along the same lines. Can we go ahead?

TECHNICIAN. Sound rolling.

BENESH. Let's get going everyone. It's going fine. Don't stop until I say so. Roll 'em.

Scene 6

ADNAN puts down the furs. They are in the shape of a sheepskin and a wolf's fur. Both are made as an all-in-one outfit, including the animal heads.

ADNAN. *(inspecting the furs)* I've been looking all over for you. I thought you'd run away. Then I find you here with that British guy.

MAGDA. Adnan, I'm scared.

ADNAN. You seem to be having a pretty good time actually—dancing, laughing, drinking. From what I can see, you're really enjoying the whole business.

MAGDA. That Englishman knows everything, do you know that?

ADNAN. Great. You should be ashamed of yourself.

MAGDA. You idiot. I wasn't the one who told him. He told me. He heard it from one of the journalists. If they know, then the fascists know too for sure...

ADNAN. *(handing her the sheepskin and climbing into the wolf outfit)* Take it easy. Our people invited the foreign press.

MAGDA. I thought you and I were the only ones who knew...

ADNAN. I'm not ashamed of our performance. Put on the fur.

MAGDA. Why didn't you tell me you were spreading the word?

ADNAN. I didn't tell them everything. Get into your costume.

MAGDA. Adnan, I don't like it when you do that sort of thing, without asking anyone, and hide it even from me...

ADNAN. I know what I'm doing. Hurry up and get dressed.

MAGDA. There's going to be bloodshed...

ADNAN. By the time they realize what's happening, the show will be over. They won't catch on until later. Don't worry.

Scene 7

The DANCE CALLER appears, holding a microphone. As he announces the next number, ADNAN and MAGDA finish putting on the furs. They are now completely covered, as a sheep and wolf.

DANCE CALLER. Ladies and Gentlemen, Students and Hoi Polloi: I'd now like to call upon the members of our theatre group who have prepared a special performance for the Independence Day Ball. Let's have a big round of applause, ladies and gentlemen!

He applauds. All of the others in the production also applaud and try to make as much noise as possible, for the effect of a large gathering.

Actors, the stage is yours!

The applause continues. A SHEEP climbs onto the stage and dances a debka to the tune of "La-Ma'ayan Bah Gedi Katan" ("A Small White Kid Approaches the Stream"). The SHEEP walks to the riverbank and drinks. The WOLF appears.

WOLF. Oh, it's so hot in this country. I'm so thirsty. Is there any water around here? Where is there some water? *(spots the river)* Oh, a river. *(The WOLF walks down to the river. He is about to start drinking when he spots the SHEEP and stops.)* What are you doing here?

SHEEP. Drinking.

WOLF. Why here of all places?

SHEEP. This is the river that I've been drinking from since the day I was born. My father and his father and his father before him all drank from this river too.

WOLF. Why does it have to be upstream? You're deliberately contaminating the water that I use for drinking. You want me to eat you up?

SHEEP. God forbid, no... I'm sorry... I'll go drink downstream.

The SHEEP passes the WOLF and goes on to drink downstream.

WOLF. I told you you're contaminating my water and you still persist. I'll have no choice except to eat you up.

SHEEP. How can I contaminate the water you drink upstream when I only drink downstream? You have no reason to eat me up.

WOLF. You dare to argue with me? There's another reason for eating you up. I'm hungry—there's a second reason for eating you up. I'm strong—there's a third reason. And if that's not enough, we wolves get a craving for skewered mutton on our holidays. When I see a sheep like you... *(starts singing to the tune of "Heigh-ho")*

Heigh-ho. Heigh-ho.
This lamb has got to go.
No matter why.
He'll leave or die.
Heigh-ho. Heigh-ho.

Everyone in the audience starts screaming.

AUDIENCE. Stop them! Get them off! Kill them!

All hell breaks loose. Catcalls and whistling. SAMIRA faces the camera and tells her story. A close-up of her face appears on the giant screen.

SAMIRA. What went on after that was unbelievable. The lawn became a battlefield. Bottles and glasses went flying in all directions. I tried to run away but I tripped over my fur. I tried to get it off but the zipper was stuck. I didn't see anything after that. All I knew was that they were hitting me all over. *(DAVID, BARRY and AVI surround MAGDA and drag her to the front of the stage.)* I felt myself being pushed and dragged. I called out to Adnan but he didn't answer.

MAGDA. Adnan! Adnan!

BARRY. *(echoing her)* Adnan! Adnan!

DAVID. You Arab-whoring slut!

MAGDA. Leave me alone. What do you want from me?

DAVID. Who was that Arab son-of-a-bitch?

MAGDA. If you know his mother...

DAVID. Every Arab is a stinking son-of-a-bitch.

MAGDA. They used to say that about the Jews once. You know who?

DAVID. Shut up, or we'll set you on fire right inside that fur!

AVI. Give us the name and address of that Arab motherfucker you've been shacking up with.

MAGDA. *(still in the sheepskin)* Nuernberg Avenue Corner of Auschwitz.

DAVID. What?! *(kicks at the fur)* I'll show you Nuernberg! You no-good Jewish traitor! Whoring with Arabs. You filthy bitch. *(bashes the fur)*

SAMIRA. *(in a flash on the screen)* Suddenly I realized they were taking me for a Jew. I screamed as loud as I could:

MAGDA. *(from within the sheepskin)* I'm not a Jew! I'm not a Jew! I'm an Arab! *(sticking her hand out of the fur, holding up her ID card)* Here's my ID card!

BENESH. *(Meanwhile, BENESH—who has become RODNEY again for his next scene—shouts in his capacity as director.)* Why don't you get out of that fur?

DAHLIA. I can't! It's tangled. I can't find the zipper. My head. I haven't got any air... damn it.... What's wrong with it? What's going on...

> She takes a step, collapses and lies motionless.

BENESH. Cut!

UDI. *(forsaking the part of DAVID)* Someone get some water.

BENESH. Never mind the water. Get a knife. We've got to cut through the costume.

ADA. *(running up to them)* Here are the scissors.

> BENESH takes the scissors, slits the fur lengthwise, helps DAHLIA to sit up, shakes her and slaps her cheek. DAHLIA comes to.

DAHLIA. Where am I! What happened!

BENESH. Are you all right?

DAHLIA. What?...

YONAH rushes over to the cameraman.

YONAH. *(whispers an order to the cameraman)* Roll'em! Action! Keep rolling! *(signalling to the sound TECHNICIAN)* Sound! Roll it!

TECHNICIAN. It's rolling!

ADA. Udi, stop dreaming. Hurry up and get an ambulance!

DAHLIA. No, no…. Not an ambulance…

YONAH. *(from a distance, ordering everyone)* Move back, move back. Give her some air!

> *They obey without realizing that he's filming. They move back. Only BENESH, dressed as RODNEY, and DAHLIA dressed as MAGDA, remain in the focus.*

BENESH. *(busy tending to DAHLIA, rubbing her temples, opening her blouse)* Let me do it. Don't get in the way.

DAHLIA. What are you stripping me for?

BENESH. To give you some air.

DAHLIA. My head is spinning.

BENESH. Should I get a doctor?

DAHLIA. No. I'll be all right in a minute. I'm okay.

BENESH. Sure you're okay…. You fainted!

DAHLIA. I'm sorry… how did it come out?

BENESH. Great. You were terrific.

DAHLIA. I'm glad….Water…. My mouth is dry…

YONAH. Samira!

> *Signals her to introduce a piece of narrative.*

SAMIRA. *(Blending in as the camera angles in on her. She recounts.)* Rodney took me home in a cab, to my apartment. He helped me up the stairs. He was very gentle. He helped me undress and put me into bed. He brought me some water. *(ADA brings BENESH a glass of water, which he brings to DAHLIA.)* He made me some coffee, lit me a cigarette… *(BENESH gradually enters the role of RODNEY. He lights up a cigarette for DAHLIA. SAMIRA continues.)* He asked me what else he could do for me. I told him: "Get me citizenship papers and a British passport." "Sorry," he said. He didn't understand. I told him: "I'm a Palestinian." "You're not Jewish?" "No, I'm really sorry. I'm a Palestinian Arab." Then he said; "Why that's wonderful!" "What is?" "That you're a Palestinian. I'm really glad."

YONAH. *(waving his hands to DAHLIA and BENESH and whispering:)* Go on! Go on!

> *DAHLIA grasps the situation. She realizes that YONAH is seizing on the opportunity to film a scene of* cinéma vérité. *She bursts out laughing and is too weak to control herself. SAMIRA stops talking. YONAH, exasperated, waves his hands at BENESH and prods him from a distance:*

Keep going! Keep going!

> *BENESH has made the complete transition to RODNEY and DAHLIA has become MAGDA.*

RODNEY. Why are you laughing?

MAGDA. *(An improvisation of DAHLIA's.)* I can't help laughing... I can't help laughing at how happy it makes you...

> *She notices how happy YONAH is and laughs even harder.*

RODNEY. *(an improvisation of BENESH's)* What's so funny about my being happy?

MAGDA. Because I'm not exactly thrilled to be a Palestinian...

RODNEY. I want you to know how I feel about your problem... I'm convinced the Israelis are making a terrible mistake.

MAGDA. Sure, a terrible mistake. They beat me up as a Jew.

RODNEY. They're behaving towards you the way the anti-Semites behaved towards the Jews.

MAGDA. Is that so? Are you an anti-Semite?

RODNEY. God forbid. I"m a socialist. Of course, I'm an anti-Zionist, and a staunch supporter of the Palestinian cause.

MAGDA. Really? Then will you marry me?

RODNEY. What!? We hardly know each other...

MAGDA. We don't actually have to live together. All I want is a passport and citizenship. People get married for a lot less, don't they? You'll be able to divorce me as soon as you want. I promise.

RODNEY. *(whom BENESH is using to get his own ideas across)* Are you sure you're all right?

MAGDA. You're a regular escape artist. I see... I've never been more clear-headed than right now. You're really prepared to do anything for me.

RODNEY. *(Here BENESH is conducting a direct dialogue with DAHLIA.)* Look... I'm in the process of separating right now...

MAGDA. *(also conducting a direct dialogue with BENESH)* "Process of separating..." Don't bother with that line. I'm not going to sit around and wait. Me you can tell the truth to.

RODNEY. I love you.

MAGDA. Liar.

RODNEY. As an actress. Finish studying, come to London and I'll take care of you.

MAGDA. *(This time she really is DAHLIA speaking directly to BENESH.)* I love you too, as a director.

RODNEY. *(reminding her)* A playwright…

MAGDA. Sure, sure. You're one of those people who only love themselves. Just my luck, I always wind up with that kind of man… the kind that can twist my feelings just like that…

BENESH. *(forsaking the character of RODNEY completely, and stopping the scene)* Okay, Dahlia, let's hold it right there…

YONAH. Cut! *(to BENESH)* You've got a piece of *cinéma vérité*. I should be so lucky in my film!

BENESH. *(Hugging DAHLIA, there's warmth between them)* Now you really can take some time off. You've earned it.

DAHLIA. Why? I could have gone, you know, but you had to cop out, as usual…

BENESH. All right, lay off…

ADA. Come on, Dahlia, let's get you something hot to drink.

> As she walks out, *DAHLIA passes SAMIRA.*

SAMIRA. *(to DAHLIA.)* The two of you got a pretty good improvisation going there.

DAHLIA. You did something to me. Touched some spot in me…

HAVKIN. There's supposed to be a dance at this point. *(cornering BENESH)* No really, I mean it. If I'd known this is all I'd have, I wouldn't have taken the part. *(makes them all his audience and talks about BENESH for all to hear)* The whole play, he tells me, is set in your dance studio in London. So I sign on! I take the text, I go home, I sit down to read it… *(starts laughing a strange kind of laughter, mingled with near-crying)* From one page to the next, I kept getting more and more upset. One dance at the beginning, one dance at the end, and that's my whole part.

UDI. You've got that scene in the middle, too.

HAVKIN. With no dancing.

UDI. A dramatic scene.

HAVKIN. With no dancing.

YITZAK. Where do you want to fit in more dancing? This isn't a musical.

HAVKIN. What do you mean where? If you ask me, I'd finish the fight scene with a dance.

YITZAK. This time you're really going too far.

HAVKIN. Now you listen here.

YITZAK. How can a fight scene end with a dance? Just who's going to do the dancing?

HAVKIN. The three thugs, that's who! Do you know what Ausdruck-Tanz is all about? Expression-Dance! Couldn't you find the music for that? You took this Viennese dance instructor, this Herbert, from the twenties… I'm sure he must have been an Ausdruck-Tanz dancer. You take those three thugs, give them the right kind of music, and you bring out the whole character. *(to PAUL)* Couldn't you find the music for that?

PAUL. Why not? Here it goes.

> *PAUL sits down at the piano and starts playing a wild, violent rendition of "Joshua Fit the Battle of Jericho" (traditional). The singer scats along. HAVKIN starts swaying to the beat of the music. UDI joins in. The two of them drag YONAH into the dance. The others form a kind of improvised band, banging on whatever they happen to find. Someone takes over the lighting and creates a nightmare effect. HAVKIN becomes HERBERT and calls out the steps, as he continues to dance and lead the others.*

HERBERT. Sharp movements—*eins zwei drei!*
Head high—*eins zwei drei!*
Back straight—*eins ünd zwei!*
Stomach in—*eins ünd zwei!*
Eyes ahead—*eins zwei drei!*

> *The dance develops into a real Ausdruck-Tanz number in which the three dancers externalize a character and psyche which draw upon the feelings of weakness, fears, self-hatred, the availability of a vulnerable victim (at this point, DAHLIA may join in the dance, personifying the weak victim), brutality against one's victim, a feeling of strength that fills the attackers, the togetherness of a gang united behind its leader. The dance now engulfs the others, who join in, one by one, as the group grows into a drove-on-the-rampage, tightly packed, unvarying, steeped in repressed violence.*

ACT TWO

Scene I

The scene opens with the sound of knocking on the door. The set is dark.
The light is on SAMIRA who is facing the camera.

SAMIRA. The following morning I woke up and my whole body ached.
Someone was knocking on the door. I got out of bed and put on a robe.
Then I realized that I could hardly stand up. I felt a strong pain in my back,
on the lower right hand side. I dragged myself to the door.

The light on the set goes on. MAGDA walks to the door. Knocking again.

MAGDA. Who is it? Rodney? I'm coming.

VOICE. *(A sheep bleating.)* BAH...

MAGDA opens the door. Enter a SHEEP—i.e. someone wearing the sheep
costume that MAGDA wore the night before. The SHEEP launches into
a ridiculous dance and sings in an oriental accent. The song is a well-
known oriental style ditty about a little white kid.

SHEEP. "El ha-ma'ayan / Ba gedi katan / ba gadi lavan..."

MAGDA. Adnan? You sure know how to make a quick getaway! Where's the foreign
press? We'll give them a show that really breaks up the party.... What's this
I see? Heigh-ho, heigh-ho...

Stepping out of the sheepskin is DAVID. He is laughing.

(recoiling) What are you doing here?

DAVID. Appearing. *(holds out his hand)* I'm David.

MAGDA. I don't want to know you.

DAVID. Why not? Know thine enemy.

MAGDA. Get out.

DAVID. Is that your oriental hospitality? Not very impressive.

MAGDA. Very funny.

DAVID. With the law to defend us
No barb will offend us.

MAGDA. I don't find your barbs very amusing.

DAVID. You're pretty when you're mad.

MAGDA. You're not.

DAVID. Sorry. What can I do? A guy can't be held responsible for his face.

MAGDA. That's where you're wrong. A person is responsible for his face.

DAVID. Maybe. Let's not get into any philosophical arguments.

MAGDA. Why not? Aren't you responsible for the words you use either?

DAVID. What's the matter with you? Don't you have any sense of humour?

MAGDA. I have enough sense to know that you're not even responsible for your own arms and legs, or your head either for that matter.

DAVID. Listen, today is Independence Day. I'm in no mood to fight. All I came for was to apologize for the mistake we made when we beat you up, and to give you back this fur and your ID card.

He pulls her ID card out of his pocket and gives it to her.

MAGDA. You could have mailed it back, or just thrown it away. An Arab's ID card doesn't mean a thing to you anyway, right?

DAVID. Wrong. I'm treating you with respect. I only beat you up because I thought you were a Jew. One of those bleeding-heart leftists from the Theatre Department. Remember—as soon as I found out you were an Arab I stopped. Didn't I? Listen, an Arab with sound nationalist views I can definitely understand and appreciate. If I were an Arab, I'd behave the same as you. I think there's a good reason for mutual respect between us—the kind you find between two honourable enemies.

MAGDA. You're wrong.

DAVID. Why? We're enemies on the political plane, but personally I've got nothing against Arabs. Especially not against nationalist Arabs.

MAGDA. I'm not a nationalist.

DAVID. What do you mean? Then why did you put on that show last night?

MAGDA. Because it was a parable that gave a true picture of the situation.

DAVID. Oh, come on! There's truth and there's truth.

MAGDA. That may be your way of seeing your own life. There can only be one truth.

DAVID. Sorry, what you call your truth is no more than the outward expression of your own nationalist feelings.

MAGDA. I don't know what you're talking about.

DAVID. What do you mean? Don't you have any nationalist feelings?

MAGDA. Do you?

DAVID. Of course I do. What do you mean…

MAGDA. I feel sorry for you.

DAVID. Why's that?

MAGDA. Apparently, you don't even know what feeling means.

DAVID. Just a minute. I want to get this straight: don't you love your own people?

MAGDA. Do you love yours?

DAVID. Of course I do!

MAGDA. Then I guess you don't even know what love is.

DAVID. Is that so?

MAGDA. If you love three million people and you've got three million loves then you don't really have a single love. I can't love more than one person, and when I do, I don't have any love left over.

DAVID. With me it's just the other way around. I love wine, I love women, I love chickens, I love fish on the grill...

MAGDA. You love to babble away without thinking. You're a naïve kid.

DAVID. Lady, I'm not a kid, and I'm not naïve. I'm twenty-five already.

MAGDA. And you don't know who you are.

DAVID. I know exactly...

MAGDA. If you knew you you were, you wouldn't let people with the conscience of a pimp use you for unethical purposes and turn you into human trash.

DAVID. How's that again?

MAGDA. You can hit me, if you want, and finish the job.

DAVID. I didn't come here to hit you. I'm rather enjoying our conversation actually.

MAGDA. Well I'm not. I don't have the patience for your kind of humour. My whole body aches and I don't have anything more to say to you.

DAVID. I told you I was sorry about the beating. I really am. I didn't sleep all night.

MAGDA. My heart bleeds. You want me to feel sorry for you. Do me a favour and go.

DAVID. Do you think it was easy for me to come here?

MAGDA. I'm not interested.

DAVID. doesn't my coming here prove anything?

MAGDA. I find it suspicious.

DAVID. Somehow or other, I feel guilty towards you.

MAGDA. So go and nurse your guilt feelings somewhere else.

DAVID. Listen, I'm talking to you like one human being to another. Why do you answer me like that?

MAGDA. You're sitting across from me now, with your face all soft and gentle. But how can I forget the other face that you had. The meanness and the evil. And the beating you gave me. I don't like people who have a double standard. First they hit you, then they feel guilty and start whimpering.

DAVID. I really do feel guilty.

MAGDA. Your feelings are your own problem. Besides, you needn't feel guilty. You really are guilty.

DAVID. I know.

MAGDA. No, you don't. I'm not just speaking in general terms. I'm referring to something very specific that you have no way of knowing about.

DAVID. What exactly?

MAGDA. None of your business.

DAVID. Tell me please. I'm asking you. I'd like to know.

MAGDA. Why not actually? You should know. I have a kidney problem. My left kidney doesn't work properly. And now, thanks to your kicking, I've got strong pains in my right kidney.

DAVID. Are you sure it's the kidney?

MAGDA. I know my body well enough. I'm scared you might have wrecked it.

DAVID. I don't know what to say.

MAGDA. Then just shut up. *(She gets up.)* Now you really can go, and celebrate with your friends.

DAVID. *(gets up too, paces the room)* What do you mean I can go…. What do you mean I can go…. I'm not about to go now…. I couldn't…. What do you…. What am I…. I'm not human trash yet…. I'm…. I did something to you, now I've got to take the consequences…. Listen, you're getting dressed and coming with me right now.

MAGDA. Where to, where to?

DAVID. What do you mean where to? To the hospital, that's where to…

MAGDA. I don't have health insurance. I haven't paid for six months.

DAVID. What?… I'll pay whatever it costs.

MAGDA. Leave me alone. You can keep your money.

DAVID. What do you mean "leave me alone." Forget it. Just stop telling me to leave you alone and to keep my money and to go celebrate with my friends. What am I, a piece of shit? What am I, some kind of rat? You can't throw me out now. I'm not moving, got that? I'm not moving until you get dressed and come with me straight to the hospital. Oh, God, what did I do? Oh God. Hurry up and get dressed. What are you waiting for? Come on! Get dressed already! God…. What are you looking at me for? Do you know you've got no sense of responsibility? You know what it means to get kicked in the kidneys?

> *DAHLIA walks off the set. ADA and UDI rush over to her, take off her robe and quickly help her dress for the next scene. Meanwhile SAMIRA is talking to the camera and FAHED is pacing in the wings preparing for his scene with MAGDA.*

SAMIRA. *(to the camera)* David was on the verge of hysteria. He was pacing the room like a wild animal. I'd never seen anyone in such a state. I have to admit I was pretty scared. David's concern was contagious. He almost forced me into getting dressed. We took his car, an old Renault 4 that he sold to pay my hospital bills. I spent a week in the hospital. David didn't budge from my bedside the whole time. He brought me a transistor radio. He bought me a Walkman and cassettes. He bought me a chess set and taught me how to play. I must admit the time really went by quickly. When it turned out my kidney wasn't damaged, he was happy as a child. He kept buying me presents. A few days after I left the hospital, I met Adnan.

BENESH. Is Dahlia ready?

DAHLIA. Ready.

BENESH. Roll it. Move straight into the next scene. *(to YONAH)* Smooth as can be. At this rate, we'll be through on time.

YONAH. Knock on wood.

Scene 2

BENESH. Roll VTR.

YONAH. VTR rolling. 4, 3, 2, 1, 0.

DAHLIA. It's so empty here without you. I woke up last night and looked for you everywhere. Even in the bathroom. Then I suddenly remembered that you're in Lebanon. How are you? Hello…. Hello… damn it, the line's gone dead.

Enter FAHED as ADNAN. He meets MAGDA.

Adnan?! Look who's come back from the cold…

ADNAN. You were in the hospital, I hear.

MAGDA. It's you they were after, but you disappeared. Someone had to take their beating.

ADNAN. Who beat you?

MAGDA. Someone who was in love with his people, like you.

ADNAN. Could you identify him?

MAGDA. What for? You want to get beat up too?

ADNAN. Tell us who it is. We'll finish him off.

MAGDA. Haven't enough people been hurt already? Do you have to drag even more victims into it?

ADNAN. I can't just ignore the fact that a Jew beat you up.

MAGDA. Pretend it was an Arab. Where we come from, men do still raise a hand on women sometimes.

ADNAN. He hit you as an Arab.

MAGDA. You're wrong. He hit me precisely because he took me for a Jew. When he found out that I was an Arab, he actually stopped.

ADNAN. Why are you trying to cover for him?

MAGDA. What's eating you? Your sense of honour?

ADNAN. You don't know what that means, do you?

MAGDA. Of course not. After all, I'm a woman…

FAHED stops acting, abandons the characterisation of ADNAN.

BENESH. Cut! What's the matter, Fahed? I thought we'd overcome the problems with the text already.

FAHED. It isn't the text. There's something about the character that doesn't seem right to me.

BENESH. Now you tell me?

FAHED. One actor quit the production already because of that character. Now you're blaming me for agreeing to pinch-hit at the last moment?

BENESH. Rassan didn't leave because of the character.

FAHED. I've spoken to him.

BENESH. I don't know what he told you.

FAHED. Let's not talk about Rassan now. I don't want to get into politics. *(to SAMIRA)* Was Adnan your boyfriend?

SAMIRA. He was in love with me. But we were no more than friends.

FAHED. He heard you were in the hospital and he didn't go to see you?

SAMIRA. He was hiding. He was afraid the police were after him.

FAHED. Why doesn't he say so?

SAMIRA. He didn't say so because he was embarassed. By the time I met him, he already knew the police hadn't been looking for him at all. I found out about it but it wasn't until much later that I understood.

FAHED. Couldn't you find some way of working that into the scene?

BENESH. I don't want to show him as a coward.

FAHED. A coward? Do you know how the police behave towards Arabs they pick up?

DAHLIA. She told you the police weren't looking for him.

FAHED. How was he supposed to know they weren't?

DAHLIA. How was he supposed to know they were?

UDI. Have you ever lived as a second-class citizen? Have you ever lived like a minority that's regarded as a fifth column and an enemy of society?

ADA. Have you?

UDI. Oh, Mother, I can imagine what it's like.

ADA. Imagine, can you?

FAHED. He's right. That's just the way it is. You live in a constant feeling of insecurity. As soon as you see a police roadblock you get that empty feeling in the pit of your stomach. Anyone who's been involved in something like that

Independence Day party prank has good reason to stay out of sight. *(to BENESH)* I don't understand why you didn't include it in the scene. Why doesn't he bring it up? To begin with, it's the truth and you get to show what the political situation does to people. Besides, it would make him stronger.

YONAH. On the contrary. The fact that he manages to hide both his fear and his shame makes him much stronger. From the dramatic standpoint. He has negative feelings about himself. They block his relationship with Magda and make him almost violent towards her.

FAHED. How will the audience know all of these lovely things? Are you going to just tell them?

YONAH. Act it out.

FAHED. You "act it out." No, buster. That message is too complex and intricate to act out. The audience will see that Adnan is angry, that he's got a problem. That much I can work in, but how are people going to know the guy is angry with himself because he's been hiding, because he was afraid of the police and that he's ashamed to admit it because he discovered that it was unfounded fear stemming from his predicament as an Arab? How do you want all that information to get through simply by acting it out?

BENESH. It's not the information that counts here.

FAHED. And how the information counts! Forgive me, Benesh, when you decide to present an Arab, you've got a problem. You don't treat him as an equal.

BENESH. I don't treat the Arab as an equal.

FAHED. I'm not talking about your views. I know you're anti-racist. But precisely because of your views, you fall into the trap. You don't want to present an Arab who behaves dishonourably.

BENESH. I'll grant you that much. The way things are now, with the anti-Arab racist attitudes, I'm about to present an Arab whose behavior is liable to make people feel contempt or scorn.

FAHED. I categorically disagree with you, even though I am an Arab. Maybe that's what we should be showing: that the dishonourable situation that people are forced into makes them behave dishonourably? *(addressing everyone)* As Jews, don't you understand that? *(to BENESH again)* Why do you want to make this film about Samira anyway? Just because you happened to meet Samira on a flight from London to Israel and she told you her story? Why not make a film about yourself and your own situation?

BENESH. This is a film about me and my situation.

FAHED. I don't get it.

BENESH. Samira had the guts to fight for the freedom she didn't possess, the freedom everyone was trying to deprive her of. I don't have the guts to follow through on the freedom I do possess.

FAHED. What do you mean by the guts to follow through on your freedom?

BENESH. It's the guts to give freedom to those who depend on you.

UDI. Are you talking personally or in the political sense?

FAHED. Hold it. Let's leave politics out of this. Look at us. I'm an actor, you're a director. I depend on you. Have you got the guts to give me my freedom?

BENESH. Just what do you mean by that?

FAHED. Let me release Adnan from your concept of him.

YONAH. And enslave him to yours?

FAHED. Stop philosophizing. *(to BENESH)* I'm Adnan. Give me the freedom to be the way I feel. Let me do an improvisation on the scene.

BENESH. *(to DAHLIA)* Are you game?

DAHLIA. What the hell… let's try it… what could happen?

BENESH. Go ahead. Let me know when you're ready.

FAHED walks off the set. DAHLIA is about to leave too.

Where to, Dahlia?

DAHLIA. To the john. Call me when you're ready. *(exits)*

HAVKIN. Just a minute. Just a minute. Are we adlibbing?

ADA. As part of the scene, Havkin. As part of the scene.

HAVKIN. What's part of the scene…. Who's part of the scene…. If it's freedom we're after, then let's have freedom all the way. There's no half-freedom, just like there's no half-love.

BENESH. Havkin, we're trying something out.

HAVKIN. Trying something out? Of course we're trying something out. You think I'm in the theatre since yesterday? You think I'd force my way in just to steal a scene? I'm just asking if I can join in when I feel the time is right, or should I go on sleeping?

YONAH. How can you join in when the scene is taking place in Jerusalem, and you're in London?

HAVKIN. Who's in London?

YONAH. Herbert!

HAVKIN. What does my being in London have to do with it? *(to BENESH)* Didn't you explain to me that all of the scenes take place in my London studio?

BENESH. Yes, but in Magda's memory.

HAVKIN. Yes, in Magda's memory…

BENESH. And this scene took place in Jerusalem.

HAVKIN. So…

YONAH. You know what, Havkin, just go on sleeping.

HAVKIN. You go on sleeping! I don't understand…

BENESH. Shh... shh.... Enough! We're starting.

HAVKIN. *(as he steps aside and FAHED enters as ADNAN)* I don't understand.... There's something here I don't understand.

Scene 3

FAHED enters dressed as a Hasid from Me'ah She'arim, an ultra-religious neighbourhood in Jerusalem. This includes a black robe, a fur hat, a beard and sidelocks. He is holding a prayer book and is absorbed in his prayers, swaying like a branch in the wind.

BENESH. *(to the cameraman)* Roll VTR!

YONAH. VTR rolling.

The cameraman dollies in towards FAHED who is swaying to and fro in fervent prayer. DAHLIA returns from the bathroom. She enters unwittingly, humming a song from the European hit parade, not realizing that they've started shooting. Suddenly, she sees the Hasid praying and bursts out spontaneously.

ADNAN. Shabess! Shabess!

DAHLIA. What's this?

ADNAN. Shush, you heathen.

DAHLIA. *(to everybody)* Who is he? David?

Suddenly she realizes that the camera is rolling and she cries out in dismay.

Oh, no.... You're shooting!

SAMIRA. Improvising.

ADNAN. *(whispering to her)* Magda.... Magda...

She gives the others a perplexed look. BENESH nods to her and signals her to continue. She assumes the role of MAGDA and starts improvising.

MAGDA. Adnan?

ADNAN. Magda...

MAGDA. Adnan, I'm coming. What's this? Have you converted?

ADNAN. I heard you were in the hospital. I went to visit you but they told me you'd been discharged already.

MAGDA. What's this get-up?

ADNAN. I'm appearing in a film.

MAGDA. What film?

ADNAN. A piece of nonsense. The Jews are doing another production about the Arabs to calm their crummy conscience.

MAGDA. Any money in it at least?

ADNAN. Money, my foot! A bunch of down-and-outs making a two-bit video film.

MAGDA. Where've you been all this time?

ADNAN. Anyone ask about me?

MAGDA. Who should have asked?

ADNAN. The police.

MAGDA. The police? What're you talking about?

ADNAN. Didn't they question you?

MAGDA. About what?

ADNAN. About our Independence Day performance.

MAGDA. Of course not. What's got into you? They've forgotten all about it.

ADNAN. Damn that Fahed! If I catch him, I'll break every bone in his body. Boy, did he put one over on me, the bastard. "Watch out, Adnan, don't show your face. The whole security service, the whole police force is after you…"

> YONAH and PAUL enter the improvisation as BARRY and AVI. They walk onto the set, smoking cigarettes.

BARRY. *(to AVI)* Look at her. Don't we know her from somewhere?

AVI. Isn't she from the university?

BARRY. Say, where do I know you from?

ADNAN. *(bursts in as a Hasid)* Shabbess! Shabbess!

AVI. What do you want?

ADNAN. Cigarettes on the Sabbath in our Holy City? Heretics!

BARRY. What's gotten into you man?

ADNAN. *(begins ranting and raving)* "And if ye will not for all this hearken unto Me, but walk contrary unto Me, then I will walk contrary to you also in fury. And I, even I, will chastise you seven times for your sins. And ye shall eat the flesh of your sons, and the flesh of your daughters shall ye eat… and cast your carcasses upon the carcasses of your idols…"

AVI. Lunatic!

BARRY. Leave him alone. Come on.

ADNAN. TFU! "And I will scatter you among the heathen… and your lands shall be desolate and your cities waste, and ye be in your enemies' land and ye shall perish among the heathens and the land of your enemies shall eat you up, and they that are left of you shall pine away in their iniquity in your enemies' lands." Tfu!

AVI. Lunatic!

BARRY. Leave him be. Let's go..

They leave and ADNAN shouts after them.

ADNAN. "I will even appoint over you terror, consumption and the burning ague and cause sorrow of heart. And ye shall be slain before your enemies. And I will bring a sword of vengeance upon you and I will send the pestilence among you and ye shall de delivered into the hand of the enemy." *Paskudniakees.*

MAGDA. Stop it, enough, they're gone. Calm down. "I will even bring a sword of vengeance upon you and I will send the pestilence among you and ye shall be delivered into the hand of the enemy…"

ADNAN. What?

MAGDA. You're not the only one they forced to study Bible. I went through that too.

ADNAN. Are they the ones that hit you?

MAGDA. No, someone else.

ADNAN. Who?

MAGDA. What's it to you?

ADNAN. Am I your boyfriend or not? Tell me who beat you up and we'll finish him.

MAGDA. Haven't enough people been hurt? Do we have to have more?

ADNAN. A Jewish fascist beat you up and you want me to take it easy?

MAGDA. What's hurting you, your sense of honour?

ADNAN. You don't know what that means, do you?

MAGDA. All I know is this: when they were beating me up, you ran.

ADNAN. The only language they understand is the language of force. Tell me who it was and I'll finish him off.

MAGDA. I don't want to finish him off.

ADNAN. Why are you covering for him? I'll find him myself.

MAGDA. God help you if you lay a hand on him. You know me and you know what I can do.

ADNAN. What's this all about? You haven't fallen in love with him by any chance, have you?

MAGDA. It so happens I have.

ADNAN. With a Jew? The one who beat you up?

MAGDA. He didn't know what he was doing. When we're together, I'm not an Arab, and he's not a Jew. We're two people who've discovered one another.

ADNAN. You're the sharpest woman I know, but you don't have the slightest bit of political awareness. Politically you're no more than an infant.

MAGDA. And you. You're so smart but sometimes you're such a fool. Still, I'm not mad at you. You're jealous. That's human and natural. Politically or otherwise, the man in you is what's been hurt. I understand you.

ADNAN. I understand you too, woman. Power, that's what attracts you in a man. And as soon as you smell weakness, you spit and scratch and lick. In that area, when you match me up against your new man, I'm bound to lose. How attractive can the victim be, compared to the sex appeal of the hangman? He can walk around with a gun, in uniform, standing tall, head up high. And me, I've got to castrate myself, to lower myself, to bow my head and to keep out of sight so that he might condescend to give me a fraction of the right to exist. He's the master of the land, the king. And what am I? A servant, a beaten dog. Look at me: a lousy joke of a human being. I can understand your choice.

> *HAVKIN jumps up and joins the scene.*

HAVKIN. That's not true. What utter nonsense! First you be a victim for two thousand years, then you'll understand how much sex appeal there is in weakness.

ADNAN. What are you doing here?

HAVKIN. *(embarrassed)* What?

> *Realizing he has entered a scene where he doesn't belong, HAVKIN becomes HERBERT and introduces some anger into the character.*

HERBERT. What are you doing here?! You're in my studio.

ADNAN. We're in Jerusalem, Sir.

HERBERT. *(pointing at MAGDA.)* In her memory you're in Jerusalem. You only can exist in her imagination. But she's in my studio in London.

ADNAN. *(Actually FAHED, who doesn't know how to continue the improvisation, indicates this directly.)* Sorry, I don't know you and I have no interest in knowing you.

HERBERT. So fuck off! *(to MAGDA)* You've got company. I've got to tell you he's an intruder in my house and he's got the gall to tell me he doesn't know me!

FAHED. A victim for 2,000 years. They've slashed off three zeroes, in case you don't remember.

MAGDA. I though you were asleep...

HERBERT. How can anyone sleep with him standing there carrying on at the top of his lungs?

> *He's stuck, trying to figure out a way to end his part of the scene. He then finds a solution.*

Incidentally, I think someone is looking for you.

MAGDA. For me? Now?

HERBERT. Yes. Someone came, knocked on the door. I open up and ask "What do you want?" "To see her." "Who?" "The girl who's living with you." What should I tell him?

MAGDA. Tell whom?

HERBERT. The guy who's looking for you.

MAGDA. Nobody is looking for me at 3 a.m. on Christmas Eve in London.

HERBERT. Come, let me walk you to your bed.

> *DAHLIA wants to get out of the scene too and to end the improvisation, but now BENESH enters in the role of RODNEY, surprising them both.*

RODNEY. Magda?

MAGDA. Rodney?

RODNEY. I've been looking for you everywhere. I knocked on this door out of sheer desperation.

HERBERT. Oh, there he is. *(to RODNEY)* She didn't want to believe me.

MAGDA. Why are you chasing me?

HERBERT. He wants you. That's obvious.

MAGDA. *(to RODNEY)* I told you it was all over between us.

HERBERT. I guess you didn't sound very convincing.

MAGDA. So what brings you here at such an hour? Your wife fall asleep again?

RODNEY. I'm in the middle of filming a new television play.

HERBERT. Are you married?

RODNEY. Would you mind excusing us?

HERBERT. Sir, I don't know you. If anyone has any excusing to do, surely it's your wife. Want to call her and apologize?

RODNEY. *(to MAGDA)* Can we go somewhere private?

HERBERT. Don't worry. I don't see very well.

RODNEY. Sorry, Sir. We have something private to discuss. Would you mind leaving us alone?

HERBERT. By all means. *(turns to go)*

MAGDA. No, Father, you stay here.

RODNEY. "Father."

MAGDA. I'd like to introduce you. My spiritual father, Herbert. My ex-lover, Rodney.

HERBERT. Hello, ex-lover.

RODNEY. Hello, spiritual father.

HERBERT. You, I haven't adopted yet.

RODNEY. What's this supposed to be?

MAGDA. Recreation. Like your love.

HERBERT. If you're not in a hurry to get home to your wife, you're invited.

MAGDA. He's never in a hurry to get home to his wife before he sleeps with me. Only after.

HERBERT. The old story.

MAGDA. The old story.

RODNEY. Hah, hah. I love jokes, you know.

MAGDA. Sure, I know. Wasn't I your last joke?

RODNEY. That's not true. You weren't my last joke.

MAGDA. Wasn't I? Is there a new one? What's her name?

RODNEY. I knew you wouldn't go back to Israel. I'm awfully glad you've stayed.

MAGDA. I know you're glad. You think everything will go back to being just the way it was. You'll come over, spend an hour with me, then you'll begin stealing looks at your watch.

RODNEY. No, that's over.

MAGDA. That's right. As far as I'm concerned, that miserable chapter is over.

HERBERT. *(taking over the role from RODNEY)* We'll open up a new leaf.

MAGDA. How well I know these conversations.

HERBERT. Let's draw a line over everything that's happened.

MAGDA. Let's forget the past.

HERBERT. Fine. I've forgotten already. Don't you believe me?

MAGDA. I believe you. I believe every word you say.

HERBERT. The past is dead.

MAGDA. Dead and buried.

HERBERT. I'm going to cut off all my other ties. It'll take a week, two weeks… then I'll be all yours. We'll go out together, we'll have a good time, we'll live together. *(to RODNEY)* Forgive me for stealing your text.

RODNEY. Steal away if it makes you happy.

HERBERT. It isn't only yours, and stealing from a thief doesn't count. *(to MAGDA)* Want to dance?

MAGDA. By all means!

> *HERBERT motions with his hand. PAUL sits down at the piano and starts playing Edith Piaf's "Rien de Rien." The singer joins in. HERBERT and MAGDA dance. RODNEY leans against the door, watching them.*

RODNEY. Bravo, bravo! Like a couple of lovebirds. Let's go out Magda. Let's go get something Chinese in the Soho.

MAGDA. Maybe something Middle Eastern?

RODNEY. Fine, just say where.

MAGDA. In one of the restaurants of the Old City or in Eastern Jerusalem?

RODNEY. What are you talking about? What's the matter with you?

MAGDA. In Jerusalem, in my own apartment.

RODNEY. And I'm at the North Pole.

MAGDA. I can feel the cold all the way to here.

RODNEY. What's happening to you?

SAMIRA gets up. She walks over to face the camera and talks.

SAMIRA. I'm in my room, in Jerusalem. I'm having a conversation with my boyfriend Adnan. David is on reserve duty in Lebanon. I went down to the pay phone because I'd set a time with David. That's when I met Adnan and took him to my room. Do you remember him? You met him a year-and-a-half ago, at the Independence Day party at the university.

He's in jail now. Got ten years as an accomplice to a murder. They killed the Jewish thug who kicked me in the stomach and killed my baby. Mine and David's.

David was a total wreck. He's in some yeshiva in the ultra-religious neighbourhood. A born-again Jew. I saw him right after I got out of the hospital. I was in for a long time. He wanted me to convert and then we'd get married. He loves me. Adnan's willing to forgive me too. Everyone's willing to forgive me. One says to convert, the other says to come back to Islam, the third one coaxes me to London, to be European. All I needed was to fall in love with someone from India. I'm much in demand, what can I do? I was a wreck when I got out of the hospital. I headed for London. You remember how you invited me when we met at the university. That's when I came to you, Rodney. You said you were a confirmed believer in the Palestinian cause. You promised to help me find a job. I was a real mess when I first arrived. I tired to pull myself together, but you got me this room in Covent Garden and made me your mistress. Except that now we're in Jerusalem with Adnan.

MAGDA. *(actually DAHLIA to BENESH, directly)* Between you and me, it's the same story with us, give or take a few minor details.

RODNEY. *(actually BENESH, who is trying to stop the improvisation now that the earth is beginning to burn under his feet)* That'll do. Why don't we stop there?

DAHLIA. No. This time I'm going to tell you everything.

BENESH. Wouldn't you rather save it for some other time, in private?

DAHLIA. You're not going to get another chance. I can see exactly how things are between us. Right now! I'm going to tell you everything right now!

BENESH. You can't do this…

DAHLIA. Can't I? Why not? Because that's the way the master wants it? I certainly can and I will! Just what do you think I am, another character in one of your dramas?

BENESH. No. I don't have any characters that vulgar in my dramas.

DAHLIA. So this time you will, and I'll show you just what vulgarity really is. I'll pick up the phone to your wife.

BENESH. You'll do no such thing.

DAHLIA. Just you try me.

BENESH. That'll be the end. I mean it. You know I'm capable of throwing you out, just like that. Which would be a pity. You know that no man ever loved you like I did and no man ever will.

DAHLIA. You've done a good job. "Be sociable. Have a Pepsi." And go.

HERBERT. Do you know the way out, or do I have to show you?

BENESH. *(briefly resuming the role of RODNEY)* Thanks. I'll find my way out.

> *He steps off the set, then takes a cigarette. His hands are shaking with excitement as he lights up. DAHLIA is crying, her face buried in her hands. HERBERT hurries over to her side, takes a long elegant coat off a hanger in his apartment and wraps it around MAGDA. Meanwhile, YONAH is preparing to hand the director's baton back to BENESH.*

YONAH. Benesh…

BENESH. Keep going, keep going… I need a cigarette.

> *YONAH continues to serve as director, pointing the cameramen in the right direction from behind. Meanwhile, the scene between HERBERT and MAGDA continues.*

HERBERT. *(trying to comfort DAHLIA; i.e., MAGDA.)* There, there. Take it easy.

> *He wraps the coat around her, takes a period hat from the thirties and puts in on her head. She continues crying.*

There, there…. Come on…

> *He leads her to the mirror, facing her reflection. DAHLIA is surprised to see herself dressed up as an elegant Viennese lady from the thirties. She starts laughing through her tears. HERBERT is encouraged by her laughter. He hands her a pair of long gloves. She puts them on. He wraps a beautiful old cape around his shoulders, a white shawl around his neck, a top-hat on his head. He stands at her side and the two of them look like a glamorous Viennese couple from the thirties. PAUL draws inspiration from the picture and begins picking a tune on the piano—a nostalgic Viennese waltz. The singer scats to the music. The dance starts out softly but gradually grows into a shattering, burning waltz.*

Viens, mon amour!

He leads DAHLIA into a dance to the beat of the waltz. As they dance, HAVKIN forgets about HERBERT, and what we see are DAHLIA and HAVKIN laying their souls bare.

DAHLIA. Why are you dressing me?

HAVKIN. Isn't it pretty?

DAHLIA. Who are you, really?

HAVKIN. I'd like to be the story of your life. No man has ever loved you the way I did, and no man ever will.

DAHLIA. What would I do without you at such a terrible time in this strange place?

HAVKIN. We were bound to meet. It was the inevitability of chance.

DAHLIA. I don't understand you.

HAVKIN. Every meeting takes place by chance, but when you meet the right person, the inevitable happens.

DAHLIA. *(suddenly stops dancing)* I'm all alone. You have no idea how lonely I am. I haven't a soul in the world.

HAVKIN. That's not true.

HAVKIN embraces her. He kisses her on the lips passionately, like an ardent young lover.

DAHLIA. What's come over you?

HAVKIN. You've done a good job. "Be sociable. Have a Pepsi!"

DAHLIA. I'm sorry… *(reaches out to stroke his face, but he pulls back)*

HAVKIN. *(one by one he removes the items of Viennese clothing. He bends over.)* I'm an old man. I know that. I'm not asking what I would have asked thirty or forty years ago. Now let me crawl quietly back into my corner. By myself. I haven't a soul in this world. Good night…

HERBERT walks away from the set.

YONAH. Cut!

All those present burst into spontaneous applause, gather around HAVKIN and lavish their praise on him. He is very excited.

BENESH. Let's take a break, everybody!

They all amble out. Remaining on the set, in separate corners are UDI and SAMIRA. Also on the set are DAHLIA and BENESH.

Scene 4

BENESH walks over to DAHLIA.

BENESH. Dahlia…

DAHLIA. Leave me alone. *(turns to leave)*

BENESH. Wait a minute, Dahlia…

DAHLIA. Don't worry. I won't tell your wife. I'm not that vulgar.

She leaves. BENESH follows her.

BENESH. Dahlia, I'll wait for you in the cafeteria. *(exits)*

UDI, holding a cigarette, walks over to SAMIRA.

UDI. Got a light? *(She lights his cigarette, and one for herself.)* Thanks. What's with your apartment?

SAMIRA. What do you mean?

UDI. I heard you were having some problem.

SAMIRA. No, that was a white lie. I was looking for an excuse to get away from here for a while.

UDI. Why?

SAMIRA. Because of Dahlia. She thinks I have something going with Benesh.

DAHLIA. Well, don't you?

UDI. Everyone thinks you do.

SAMIRA. After that business with Howard, I keep away from married men.

DAHLIA. Who's Howard?

SAMIRA. That's Rodney, in the script.

DAHLIA. Did it happen just that way?

SAMIRA. Not exactly. But pretty much. Benesh apparently put a lot of himself into the part of Rodney.

DAHLIA. What's it like seeing your own story being filmed?

SAMIRA. It isn't exactly my story. Dahlia puts a lot of herself into Magda too.

DAHLIA. So what's it like to see others hitching a ride on your story?

SAMIRA. Interesting. Suddenly you realize that we're not so different from one another.

UDI. And me? Do I remind you of David or isn't it the same story at all?

SAMIRA. You'd be surprised. You're very much like him. You even look like him. Sometimes when I look at you, I see him.

DAHLIA. Are you still in love with him?

SAMIRA. No. I feel sorry for him.

UDI. Why?

SAMIRA. David is a man who'll never know who he is.

UDI. Is there such a thing?

SAMIRA. Sure there is. A person who never comes to terms with moral questions. A person who only acts on his emotions.

UDI. That's someone spontaneous, isn't it?

SAMIRA. Are you developing the character or are you talking with me?

UDI. Both...

SAMIRA. He's a person who's torn between conflicting desires.

DAHLIA. You talk a lot about morals.... That subject's on your mind a lot.

SAMIRA. If you were the target of repression and exploitation, you'd be sensitive to people's moral or immoral behavior too and it would be on your mind a lot.

DAHLIA. It's damned hard getting near you...

UDI. Yes, it really is.

SAMIRA. Are you sure you want to?

UDI. In order to know that, I have to try, don't I?

SAMIRA. Go ahead and try.

UDI. Would you be willing to help me?

SAMIRA. How can I help you?

UDI. Let's begin with that scene of the phone-call from Lebanon.

SAMIRA. How can I help you?

UDI. I'll do my text and you throw in Magda's.

SAMIRA. No problem. *(She takes the text, opens on the relevant page.)* Go ahead.

UDI recites DAVID's text. SAMIRA recites MAGDA's.

DAVID. Hello. Hello. Magda?

SAMIRA. *(reading from the script)* David? Where are you calling from?

DAVID. *(half acting)* From the outpost. We've got a phone connection for half an hour. Lucky I caught you. How are you doing?

SAMIRA. I miss you.

DAVID. I miss you too. Terribly.

SAMIRA. What? I can't hear you.

DAVID. I miss you too. Terribly. How's our apartment doing?

SAMIRA. It's empty. It's awfully empty without you. Last night I woke up and looked for you in bed, everywhere, even in the bathroom. Then I suddenly remembered you're in Lebanon. What are you doing?

DAVID. Dying.

SAMIRA. What?

DAVID. Dying to see you.

SAMIRA. I want you here next to me. Can you hear me? Now!

DAVID. I keep picturing you. It takes so much out of me emotionally.

SAMIRA. What? I can't hear you. What did you say?

DAVID. I said it uses up such a lot of energy to create a picture of you in my mind.

SAMIRA. Yes, it's crazy.

DAVID. What a tremendous waste of energy. I know just when my energy is going to run out. If I don't get to see you by then, I'll start to die. You hear me?

SAMIRA. I hear your voice, but I can't see you. I miss you so much. I can't touch you. You took everything I love with you. But I can still feel you.

DAVID. Go on. I hear you.

SAMIRA. Everything in the apartment reminds me of you. It's so hard being without you, and I want you back right now. I want to feel you. How are you?

DAVID. A soldier in my platoon was killed two days ago.

SAMIRA. You've got to come back to me, you hear me? I want you back safe and sound, beside me.

UDI. *(abandoning his impersonation of DAVID)* Lebanon was an eye-opener for me too.

SAMIRA. Did you take part in the war?

UDI. No. I was in an entertainment troupe with two other actors from the theatre. We had nothing to give. None of us was an entertainer. So we put on segments from Kafka's *The Trial.* One day they sent us to some godforsaken spot. When we got there, it turned out to be a makeshift POW camp. A kind of small, improvised barbed-wire pen. We appeared on a small platform, concocted out of some ammunition crates. The audience consisted of a dozen oddballs whose job was to interrogate the prisoners. They sat there in front of the fence. Behind it, on the ground were the prisoners.

A few dozen men—filthy, unshaven, their hands tied and their eyes covered. I can picture it all as if it were happening right now: there I am on the platform, recounting the story of the gates and the guards while those investigators sit there across from me, staring, their eyes red from sleepless nights. Behind them was the fence, and behind it the prisoners, with strips of rags on their eyes. And there I stood, spitting out those words by Kafka…

SAMIRA. And what did you do?

UDI. Nothing. What did I do? I finished and got off the stage. What could I do?

SAMIRA. You could have said what you thought.

UDI. I wish I knew what I thought. We live in a fog. Nothing's clear-cut.

SAMIRA. And that suits you fine.

UDI. No. Why do you think that suits me?

SAMIRA. Why are you taking part in this film?

UDI. It's an important film…. It's important for the public to know the truth…

SAMIRA. Are you discovering any truth in this file that you didn't already know?

UDI. Look… the very fact that we're dealing with this subject…. Jews, Arabs…. It's a subject that our whole future depends on…

SAMIRA. Why don't you think things through?

UDI. Wait a minute. In your story do you discover any truth that you didn't know before?

SAMIRA. No. I'm afraid I've failed. I admit it. When I was immersed in my work, I didn't notice. Now that I'm sitting on the sidelines watching the results, I can see the whole story's there but the truth doesn't come through.

UDI. If I were you…

SAMIRA. What would you do?

ADA. *(peeping out behind the set)* Udi? Is that where you are? They're looking for you. Come and get dressed.

UDI. In a second.

ADA. With you, a second is half an hour.

UDI. Lay off, Mother. Just a second. I'll be right there. *(to SAMIRA)* My mother was all I needed here. What did I bring her into the production for, anyway?

SAMIRA. I don't know. I didn't bring my parents in.

FAHED appears, holding the script. He is memorizing the text.

FAHED. Sorry. Am I interrupting anything?

SAMIRA. No, we were working on the text.

ADA. *(offstage)* Udi!

UDI. I'm coming! *(exits)*

FAHED. Would you work with me too?

FAHED is eating nut chocolate throughout the scene.

SAMIRA. *(taking the text)* Where from?

FAHED. *(pointing to the line in the text)* Where he stopped.

SAMIRA. *(reading from the text)* What's up? Am I being blackballed?

FAHED. Hold it. Just where is this happening?

SAMIRA. In the street. He's been avoiding me. I run into him in the street. He's just walking by, reading a book.

FAHED. In the street?

SAMIRA. Yes. He'd always walk with a book in his hand, immersed in it, paying no attention to what was going on around him, living in a dream world. It was Da'ud.

FAHED. Da'ud?

SAMIRA. Yes. Adnan in the script.

FAHED. I see… well, let's begin. *(He takes the text and walks as he reads.)*

SAMIRA. What's up? Am I being blackballed?

ADNAN. *(lifting his head from the text)* Oh, it's you? When are you converting?

SAMIRA. I'm not converting.

ADNAN. Is the fascist planning to become a Moslem?

SAMIRA. There's no need. There are enough Moslem fascists without him.

ADNAN. So how will you work it out? Are you going to have a progressive Jewish lawyer draw up a contract allowing you to live together?

SAMIRA. We don't need a contract. We'll go on the way we've done until now.

ADNAN. And when there is a baby, are you going to raise him as a Jew? As an Arab?

SAMIRA. When there's a baby, we'll try and raise him as a human being.

ADNAN. That fascist has turned you into a cosmopolitan. You're half-Jewish already.

SAMIRA. That fascist is no fascist and I'm not half-Jewish.

ADNAN. You're naïve. You don't know what you're doing. Politically, what you do is meaningless.

SAMIRA. Why bring politics into this?

ADNAN. I don't know. I'm talking nonsense. You're getting me mad and you're making me talk nonsense, which only gets me madder…

SAMIRA. Why don't you come and visit us, Adnan.

ADNAN. No way! Absolutely not…

SAMIRA. Do we have the plague?

ADNAN. Listen…. Maybe I'm not so free-thinking, so liberal… *(in an outburst)* I'm sick and tired of following the cultivated rules of western civilisation.

SAMIRA. Why "western civilisation" all of a sudden?

ADNAN. I don't know. I don't want to see you with him. I'm jealous, okay?

SAMIRA. That's a shame. I happen to be very fond of you, as a human being.

ADNAN. "As a human being." Boy, you sure know how to turn the knife…

SAMIRA. Adnan…

ADNAN. Forget it. Go to him. He'll make you feel better.

SAMIRA. He's in Lebanon.

ADNAN. Here's hoping he never comes back.

SAMIRA. Adnan!

ADNAN. What's got into me!

SAMIRA. What do you think of the script?

FAHED. One hell of a script.

> *Gathering up the chocolate crumbs from the aluminum wrapper and licking his fingertips.*

SAMIRA. I'm asking seriously.

FAHED. Seriously, I can't tell you.

SAMIRA. Why not? Afraid of hurting my feelings?

FAHED. Don't be silly. I simply haven't read it.

SAMIRA. You haven't read the script?

FAHED. No. Why are you staring at me like that? Don't take it to heart. I never read scripts. I just read my own part.

SAMIRA. Terrific. And even that, only at the last minute, I see.

FAHED. If I have no choice.

SAMIRA. You probably even make an ideology out of it—arriving nice and fresh for the actual shooting...

FAHED. Who's fresh? Can't you see how tired I am?

SAMIRA. And you think you're going to change things that way?

FAHED. Who has any intention of changing things? Lady, things have changed me. I used to be all gung-ho once, like you, but now... for years, I've been too tired. Boy, am I tired. *(laughs)* But don't worry. Your script isn't the only thing I haven't read. You're in good company. I haven't read Shakespeare in years either. Or Ibsen. Or Chekhov. Actually, since I graduated university I haven't read a single play, except the ones I took part in. I'm in the actors' guild at the theatre. What do you think we talk about at meetings? Work-hours, premiums, promotions.... Who has the time to read anything.... At our last meeting, someone suggested that the actors should have a say in deciding on repertoire. Why shouldn't they put on a play by Wedekind? Everyone was in favour. Me too, even though I'd never read a single work of his and I got the impression the others hadn't either. Still, the name has a nice ring to it. Wedekind. That's a playwright's name for you. When did he live?

> *Enter BENESH and YONAH followed by the entire cast, just back from their break. YONAH is in the middle of a sentence.*

YONAH. You can take it from me, I tell you. If you go on at this pace, we'll be through shooting by 5am and by 8 you'll be able to give them back the studio the way we said we would.

BENESH. Take the cast and set them up for the scene. *(As YONAH goes about organizing the next shots, BENESH turns to SAMIRA.)* Samira, get ready with the lead-in for scene 12.

SAMIRA. Aren't you doing a re-take of the phone-call from Lebanon and the meeting with Adnan?

BENESH. No. We saw yesterday's rushes and decided to do without it.

SAMIRA. There were quite a few inaccuracies in the text…

BENESH. Never mind, it comes across clearly.

SAMIRA. I was sure we'd re-do those shots. You said…

BENESH. We'll see. We'll see…. If we have any time left over, then maybe…. How's it going, Yonah?

YONAH. All ready. Let's begin.

BENESH. *(to SAMIRA)* Do you need to go over the text?

SAMIRA. No, no. I remember it. *(She walks over to the camera and begins talking.)*

Scene 5

SAMIRA is talking to the camera.

BENESH. Roll VTR.

YONAH. VTR rolling.

SAMIRA. David got back from the army on the night of Purim. He had a beard. He was in a strange mood. "Do you mind my uniform" he asked. I don't care what you've got on. He suggested that we go out right away to "meet the two criminals who are to blame for my existence." He was referring to his parents. He always called them by all sorts of strange names instead of simply referring to them as "my parents." I asked him if he'd told them yet that I was an Arab. "No" he said. "They'll find out the hard way." I said I didn't want to go to see them because I didn't want any part in his games with his parents. To which he replied that they would be a part of our game. He insisted that we dress up as a couple of born-again religious Jews. I told him, "David, hold it." We got to David's parents' house very late at night.

> *MAGDA and DAVID go in. MAGDA is dressed in the modest garb of a very religious girl, with a kerchief on her head. DAVID is in uniform. He has a beard and is wearing a skullcap. SAMIRA continues with her story.*

The apartment was very dark. David rang but there was no reply. He used his own key to unlock the door, and we went in. We waited more than an hour for them to arrive. They'd been to a Purim masquerade party put on by the drama club where David's mother served as an instructor.

MIRIAM. David? Dudale.

DAVID. Hi, Mom. Hi, Dad.

EPHRAIM. Hi, Son.

DAVID. Let me introduce you. Magda.

MIRIAM. Delighted. Miriam.

EPHRAIM. I'm Ephraim. Nice to meet you. You're still in the reserves?

DAVID. I'm through.

EPHRAIM. Welcome.

MIRIAM. Duvidel. You've lost weight.

DAVID. No I haven't.

MIRIAM. Hasn't he?

EPHRAIM. No. Yes. Maybe a little.

MIRIAM. Have you eaten anything?

DAVID. I'm not hungry.

EPHRAIM. He's not hungry.

MIRIAM. There's fish in the fridge.

DAVID. I told you, Mother. I'm not hungry.

EPHRAIM. Sit down. Why are you standing?

DAVID. How's business, Dad?

EPHRAIM. Pretty good. Can't complain. How's school?

DAVID. Okay.

MIRIAM. You met at the university?

DAVID. That's right.

MIRIAM. Good. Then I'll get the fish.

EPHRAIM. Yes, yes, get the fish. Are you staying over?

DAVID. We'll see.

EPHRAIM. Don't go back to Jerusalem tonight. Stay here.

DAVID. We'll see.

MAGDA. We'll see.

MIRIAM. You prefer gefilte?

MAGDA. I prefer fish.

MIRIAM. Gefilte is fish, stuffed fish.

MAGDA. I see.

MIRIAM. The non-gefilte kinds has lots of little bones in it.

MAGDA. I'll have gefilte.

MIRIAM. Ephraim prefers the non-gefilte kind. But he's an expert. You should see him clean a head. David, I'll give you some...

DAVID. Gefilte, gefilte. Magda and I have known each other for almost a year.

EPHRAIM. Is that so? Is it serious between you two?

DAVID. You might say so.

EPHRAIM. Good, good. Well, go ahead and eat.

DAVID. We met at the Independence Day Ball at the university.

EPHRAIM. That's a nice occasion for meeting people.

DAVID. Remember the fight at the ball that night?

EPHRAIM. The fight? No… what about?

DAVID. Arabs students started a provocation.

EPHRAIM. Oh… well, no wonder there was a fight.

MIRIAM. Your name is Magda, right?

MAGDA. Yes, Magda.

MIRIAM. So how do you like the fish, Magda?

MAGDA. A bit… sweet.

MIRIAM. Not sweet enough?

MAGDA. No, no! It is sweet enough.

MIRIAM. That's the way my mother used to make it.

MAGDA. Really? It's very… special…

EPHRAIM. Magda…

MAGDA. Yes?

EPHRAIM. I knew a girl called Magda once.

DAVID. Really? You never told me.

EPHRAIM. Her real name was Magida. She was the great-great-granddaughter of the renowned rabbi, the Magid of Mezerich, so they named her after him. Magida, Magda.

DAVID. Magda is not related to the Maggid of Mezerich.

EPHRAIM. She isn't?

DAVID. No, she's not a member of the Maggid's family.

EPHRAIM. I'm no great admirer of the Maggid.

MIRIAM. What are you studying?

MAGDA. Acting.

MIRIAM. Oh, that's nice. I teach creative drama.

MAGDA. Do you like your work?

MIRIAM. Yes, very much.

DAVID. We're thinking of getting married.

EPHRAIM. When?

DAVID. We haven't set a date yet.

MIRIAM. As far as we're concerned, you can live together without getting married.

EPHRAIM. Sure, we're free-thinking people.

MIRIAM. If I were your age, I wouldn't dream of getting married. I'd go for free love, living with whoever I love. Marriage? That institution hasn't a foot to stand on.

EPHRAIM. It hasn't any feet at all.

MIRIAM. I'm surprised at you two.

DAVID. But we want to get married.

MIRIAM. If it's what you want, go ahead.

EPHRAIM. Sure. Go ahead if you want to.

DAVID. Do you want to meet Magda's parents?

EPHRAIM. No.

DAVID. No?

EPHRAIM. No, on the contrary, why shouldn't we?

MIRIAM. I suppose we'll have to eventually, if you decide to get married.

EPHRAIM. Sure we will. Sooner or later.

MAGDA. Isn't it funny how a fight can lead to a wedding.

EPHRAIM. Well, life is full of surprises.

DAVID. We were in a fight together.

EPHRAIM. Well, you know what they say—the first step is always the hardest.

MIRIAM. I'd be happier if you stayed away from that sort of thing.

DAVID. Why's that? You think we should just let the Arabs make a mockery of the holiday?

MIRIAM. Dudaleh, you're a student now. You should concentrate on your studies. If there's any unrest, there are people in charge of keeping the peace.

DAVID. What do you think, Dad?

EPHRAIM. Just a minute. Got a bone here. What did you want to know?

DAVID. If you think we should let the Arabs make a mockery of the holiday.

EPHRAIM. Listen, I don't spend all day thinking about it. There's law, there's law enforcement, there's the security forces.

DAVID. My parents are very moderate people. They belong to what's called the Silent Majority.

EPHRAIM. That's how it is.

MAGDA. I don't get it. *(Everyone freezes, looking at her.)* I don't get it.

MIRIAM. What don't you get?

MAGDA. He calls you "the two criminals." *(laughs)* The two criminals who are to blame he's alive...

EPHRAIM. *(laughs)* We like using nicknames in our family—Miruskah, Dudaleh, Froilech.

DAVID. Hold it, Dad. I want to get this straight. A bunch of Arab students use the Independence Day celebration to make fun of the holiday…

MAGDA. What do you want him to do?

EPHRAIM. No, really, what do you want me to do? Did I send them?

DAVID. Are you on drugs, Dad?

EPHRAIM. On drugs? What do you think I'm taking?

DAVID. Do I know? Hash? Marijuana?

EPHRAIM. We're on fish.

DAVID. You're behaving as though you're on a trip.

EPHRAIM. *(still containing himself, but only barely)* Trip…. Shmip…

MIRIAM. Ephraim, you're eating the fish with the bones.

EPHRAIM. The hell with the fish. The hell with the bones.

MIRIAM. Ephraim, the boy's home on a visit.

EPHRAIM. Home? Does he have any idea what a home is?

MIRIAM. Ephraim, we decided something.

EPHRAIM. You decided!

DAVID. What did you decide? What about?

MIRIAM. Dudaleh!

DAVID. Don't you call me Dudaleh anymore. Got that? Don't you dare call me Dudaleh. David! David!

EPHRAIM. You decided! Freedom! Now look what your freedom's got you! A guy tries to hold on to his sanity, and they tell him he's on hash! A trip! He just doesn't know where to stop. That's the result of your freedom. A house that's free is no place to be.

DAVID. Wait a minute. What did you decide?

MIRIAM. Nothing.

EPHRAIM. The boy's home on a visit…. Don't I know this character? You got yourself out on a limb; now don't expect me to pull you down. Got that?

DAVID. What are you talking about?

EPHRAIM. I'll tell you just what I'm talking about. Light and darkness can't live together. And if you think you're so smart, it's because nobody ever told you "no" on account of that genius who brought you up by the book instead of giving you a few sound spankings when it might still have done some good, damn it!

MIRIAM. Ephraim, have you gone mad?

EPHRAIM. You've gone mad yourself. Go find your Dr. Spock now!

DAVID. I want to know just what you decided!

MIRIAM. He's stoned out of his mind. He doesn't know what he's saying. Wasn't it bad enough the way you embarrassed us before the entire faculty and student body?

EPHRAIM. You wanted a clown? Fine! She forced me into this get-up.

MIRIAM. He gets right up there on the stage and starts singing the funeral hymn… unbelievable.

EPHRAIM. She thinks she can just get the whole world to do what she wants! Why blame me when it's your dumb students that insisted on wearing pajamas? Death makes me laugh, it's not my fault.

MAGDA. Not me. Death doesn't make me laugh.

DAVID. Just wait a minute. Who went out on a limb?

EPHRAIM. You did!

DAVID. I went out on a limb?

EPHRAIM. Who else?

MIRIAM. Ephraim…

EPHRAIM. Always smoothing things over. You think you can smooth everything over. You've stuffed the fish, now eat them yourself.

DAVID. I stuffed the fish?

EPHRAIM. And how you did! Nobody's going to eat them for you. Running from one extreme to another. First a pacifist…

DAVID. He's digging up archaeological finds.

EPHRAIM. And now a pacifist. A conscientious objector, no less. A draft dodger.

MIRIAM. He was rebelling against his father. Ephraim was a company commander in the Armoured Corps then.

EPHRAIM. With him everything is a rebellion. He's so busy rebelling that he'll marry the daughter of the Rabbi of Lubavitch.

DAVID. Me marry the daughter of the Rabbi of Lubavitch?

EPHRAIM. Yes, you marry the daughter of the Rabbi of Lubavitch.

DAVID. Me?

EPHRAIM. You'd marry the Rabbi of Lubavitch himself. You haven't by any chance joined some Indian sect or become a vegetarian, have you?

DAVID. No, but I'll tell you what I have done.

EPHRAIM. What?

DAVID. I've come to the conclusion that Arabs and Jews can live together in this country.

EPHRAIM. You don't say? What ever made you think that? The Lebanese experience?

DAVID. That too.

EPHRAIM. And what else?

DAVID. Magda. She's opened my head.

EPHRAIM. Is that so? Is that what you think too?

MAGDA. Yes, me too.

EPHRAIM. Fascinating. And just what opened your head? The beating he gave you on Independence Day?

MAGDA. What? What did you do?

EPHRAIM. I've always said the only thing the Arabs understand is force.

MAGDA. Leave them alone, David. Let's get out of here.

DAVID. I didn't tell them.

EPHRAIM. What did you think, kid? That you could keep us from finding out that you're shacking up with an Arab? Your friends told us everything.

DAVID. You knew. You've known the whole time…. And still you've been acting it out, with your hypocrisy…

EPHRAIM. What did you think, kid? That we still get all shook up by your nonsense? What did you think, that you can still impress anyone with those whims of yours?

DAVID. *(to MIRIAM)* That's your doing. "It's just a stage." I can just hear you: "It'll pass…"

EPHRAIM. Yes, that's right. Just like all the other whims passed eventually. You'll live with an Arab, you?

MIRIAM. Ephraim, don't answer him!

EPHRAIM. *(mimicking her)* "Don't answer him. Don't answer him." *(to DAVID)* Don't I know you by now? You got scared by your own nerve! Just look at the hero who's going to go living with an Arab. I could see straight through you from the very beginning. Coming home when it got to be too much: Mommy, Daddy, help!

DAVID. Hah! Hah! So you've finally come out of your holes.

EPHRAIM. A big mouth, that's all you've got.

DAVID. It stinks, eh? It stinks! At long last. So you're opening your filthy trap for once! Go ahead! Have a field day while you're at it! A free house! A tolerant house! Say it! An Arab! Scared you, didn't it? Of course it did. Bringing a monster into your cozy little nest? Shitting into your homemade soup. That's the truth, isn't it? A filthy Arab! Go ahead and say it! Gefilte! Gefilte! Are you going to ostracize me or what? Going to go into mourning over me? Disinherit me? I don't give a shit about your money! Wouldn't take a penny from you anyhow! You can stuff it with your stinking money! Get your Dr. Spock to have me committed! Scum, that's what you are. You rotten old pair of no good… *(pulls back, grabbing his gun)* You'll pay for this… you'll pay for this! *(runs off)*

ACT THREE

Scene I

MAGDA is nestled in HERBERT's arms. He is wrapped up in an old coat. The two of them are on the old sofa, deep in a haunted sleep. The scene is accompanied by Schoenberg's "Verklärte Nacht" played softly by PAUL on the piano with the singer scatting along. BENESH is in charge of the filming.

MAGDA. *(in her sleep)* David.

HERBERT. *(patting her head in his sleep and muttering in German)* Ruhig, ruhig Heloise.

MAGDA. My love.

HERBERT. *Ruhig, mein Kind.*

MAGDA. So good.

HERBERT. *Schlaf ein, mein Kind.*

MAGDA. Don't leave me again.

HERBERT. *Ja ja, mein Kind. Schlaf ein,* Heloise. *Schlaf ein.*

MAGDA. *(wakes up, looks around)* Where am I?

HERBERT. *(in German) In der Fremde.*

MAGDA. What? Where? Mama!

HERBERT. *Wo ich Mutter rufe, bin ich alein.*

MAGDA. Herbert.

HERBERT. Hmm? *(wakes up)* Oh, pardon. *(tries to get up)*

MAGDA. No, don't go. *(She cuddles in his arms.)* Who is Heloise?

HERBERT. A little girl.

MAGDA. Yours?

HERBERT. Yes.

MAGDA. Where is she?

HERBERT. Gone.

MAGDA. I'm sorry.

HERBERT. You're not to blame. Alma didn't want to leave the theatre.

MAGDA. Your wife?

HERBERT. I told her: I'm going to Paris to line up a place for us. You're crazy, Herbert, she told me. Then it was too late.

MAGDA. You never saw her again?

HERBERT. I did.

MAGDA. When?

HERBERT. Recently.

MAGDA. Where?

HERBERT. Sitting on the sidewalk near the railroad tracks.

MAGDA. Where?!

HERBERT. In Grossman's album.

MAGDA. Who's Grossman?

HERBERT. A photographer. He took pictures of it. Of everything.

MAGDA. Where was it?

HERBERT. In Lodz. In the ghetto.

MAGDA. Not in Vienna?

HERBERT. There was a transport.

MAGDA. Are you Jewish?

HERBERT. In the Nazi sense, not in the Jewish one.

MAGDA. Only your father was Jewish?

HERBERT. My father was a snapshot on the wall. A young man in an officer's uniform with a sword. In a black frame. And brass letters on a wooden board: "Lieutenant Fredinand Birger. Fell in the field of honour, in the service of his Majesty the Emperor." But my mother never told me.

MAGDA. That he was killed?

HERBERT. That he was Jewish.

MAGDA. How did you find out?

HERBERT. Thanks to her legs.

MAGDA. Your mother's?

HERBERT. No. Although she had nice legs too. I fell in love with a girl. At sixteen. Because of her legs. She had very beautiful legs. Well shaped. Like yours. *(He stokes her legs.)* One day we sat by the river. It was a warm summer day. I was stroking her legs when suddenly she said: aren't you Jewish?

MAGDA. How did she know?

HERBERT. Her mother told her.

MAGDA. What did you do?

HERBERT. I ran away. Into the forest.

MAGDA. David ran away too.

HERBERT. People can't take too much reality.

MAGDA. I was left alone.

HERBERT. You can't run away from yourself.

MAGDA. I was in my fourth month. I'd looked for him everywhere for a week. At night I'd lie in our bed, listening to every sound on the stairway, waiting to hear his key in the door. I'd picture him beside me. I'd take his hand. *(She takes HERBERT's hand.)* I'd put it on my stomach and let him feel the baby.

HERBERT. *(His hand is on her stomach.)* Yes. I remember.

> *They are quiet. Waiting. Feeling somewhat awkward. BENESH bursts in, angry.*

BENESH. Cut! Samira, what about your part? *(no reply)* Samira? Where is Samira? Does anyone know where she is?

FAHED. I saw her during the break. She was chatting with Udi.

ADA. Udi? *(no reply)* Udi! *(She turns to leave.)*

BENESH. Where are you going?

ADA. To look for him.

BENESH. No one is going to look for anyone.

ADA. I knew it would happen to him. It's always like that. Just when you need him, he's gone.

DAHLIA. He doesn't need him. He needs her.

BENESH. Shit. *(He paces the floor, suddenly letting loose a strong kick at the crate. The others barely control their laughter. BENESH, whose kick helped him unwind, issues the order in a very soft voice.)* Carry on!

DAHLIA. How can we?

BENESH. Go straight into the phone-call scene.

DAHLIA. No lead-in?

BENESH. No.

DAHLIA. How will they know David's been gone for a week, without a sign?

BENESH. I don't know.

DAHLIA. Then think.

ADA. I can fill that in, as Udi's mother.

BENESH. No.

DAHLIA. David's. She means David's mother.

ADA. Yes, as David's mother. Did I say Udi's?

BENESH. No. Out of the question. We'll tape her later, separately.

DAHLIA. It won't be spontaneous.

BENESH. You got any other problems?

DAHLIA. I thought it was your problem.

BENESH. You let me decide which problem is mine and which isn't, okay?

DAHLIA. Okay.

ADA. I really don't understand what's got into Udi. Maybe I ought to—

BENESH. No! I said no! Now get with it! Start the scene.

Scene 2

> *DAHLIA rushes to a street telephone cabin. ADA walks over to MIRIAM's place.*

MIRIAM. Hello? Magda?

MAGDA. Speaking.

MIRIAM. It's Miriam. How are you, Magda?

MAGDA. Have you heard from David?

MIRIAM. Yes, Magda. Of course.

MAGDA. Is he at your place?

MIRIAM. No. Magda. He's not here.

MAGDA. Where is he?

MIRIAM. He's all right.

MAGDA. Where is he, I asked.

MIRIAM. Why don't you come over?

MAGDA. Can't you tell me over the phone?

MIRIAM. No, Magda. It's not a subject to discuss over the phone. Come over just before three. I'll be at home alone.

MAGDA. Before three, you said.

MIRIAM. I'm sure we can be of use to one another.

MAGDA. I'll be there.

> *They stop, having reached the end of the scene, where SAMIRA's next lead-in was supposed to be. BENESH checks his anger.*

BENESH. Cut. Let's go on with the next scene. Go.

Scene 3

> *MAGDA and MIRIAM move to a different corner of the set, the inside of the Bendor home. The sound of a doorbell. MIRIAM goes to open it. MAGDA enters.*

MIRIAM. Oh, Magda, I'm very happy to see you. Come in.

MAGDA. I just want to know where he is. Do you know or don't you?

MIRIAM. If you help me, we might find him.

MAGDA. You don't know where he is. Why did you ask me to come?

MIRIAM. He called home twice.

MAGDA. Where from?

MIRIAM. He didn't say.

MAGDA. When did he last call?

MIRIAM. Yesterday. At three in the afternoon. And the day before also. At three. I'm hoping he'll call today too. Maybe any minute now.

MAGDA. Are you telling me the truth, or are you simply trying to hold me here?

MIRIAM. Why would I want to do that?

MAGDA. I don't know. I don't understand the way you think.

MIRIAM. Look, Magda, in times like this the best thing is to work together. If David means a lot to you—

MAGDA. If David means a lot to me!

MIRIAM. If you cooperate, we stand a chance of finding him. But if you don't believe me, I'm not going to hold you here against your will.

MAGDA. What did he say when he called?

MIRIAM. Nothing.

MAGDA. What do you mean?

MIRIAM. He calls, I pick up the receiver, I talk to him, he doesn't answer. He holds the receiver for a while, then he hangs up. Without saying a word.

MAGDA. How do you know it's David?

MIRIAM. I know my son. It's definitely him. Maybe if it was you talking, he'd answer. If you don't mind waiting.

MAGDA. Of course I'll wait.

MIRIAM. Would you like something to eat? *(MAGDA shakes her head.)* A drink?

MAGDA. No, thanks, nothing.

MIRIAM. You're pregnant.

MAGDA. Yes.

MIRIAM. I noticed it. The first we met.

MAGDA. I don't try to hide it.

MIRIAM. Why weren't you careful?

MAGDA. Is that all you can think of asking me now?

MIRIAM. Sorry. May I talk to you woman-to-woman?

MAGDA. Talk to me any way you want.

MIRIAM. You're trembling.

MAGDA. I'm cold.

MIRIAM. Take this. *(wraps her sweater around MAGDA)*

MAGDA. Thank you.

MIRIAM. Can I ask you to keep this conversation strictly between us?

MAGDA. David and I never kept anything from one another and we never will.

MIRIAM. All right. I'll tell you what's on my mind. You do whatever you think is right.

MAGDA. Yes, that's clear.

MIRIAM. You seem to be a honest girl, and very sharp.

MAGDA. What do you want?

> *UDI and SAMIRA enter. They notice that they've walked in while the filming is under way. They freeze. Everyone notices them. ADA senses what's happening to UDI and what has gone on between him and SAMIRA. She continues as MIRIAM.*

MIRIAM. Believe me, it's not easy for me to say this. David is my son. Honestly, he's not for you.

MAGDA. Oh, spare yourself that rubbish.

MIRIAM. You're in much too complicated and difficult a situation. Believe me. We're not living in France or America.

MAGDA. You don't say!

MIRIAM. A mixed couple has to be strong as steel to hold on in a society like ours, and my son just doesn't have the strength of character it takes.

MAGDA. How can you talk that way about your son?

MIRIAM. I know him.

MAGDA. And I love him.

MIRIAM. Listen to me. David is like his father, and he's someone with a weak character too.

MAGDA. Your husband doesn't interest me.

MIRIAM. My son is always getting himself into a bind, but he never knows how to stick it out. He's a good kid, a nice person, I know, but he's the kind of man who always backs out just when the going gets tough. He's one of those men who simply disappears just when you need him the most.

MAGDA. He's not "one of those men." For me he's David.

MIRIAM. Where is he now? Look at the state he left you in. Why did he run off? Why did he just disappear?

MAGDA. You have the nerve to ask? Don't you even realize what you've done to him? You stripped him bare right in front of me, like he was a baby. You simply murdered him.

MIRIAM. Don't you talk like that.

MAGDA. Why do I even bother talking to you? What am I doing here anyhow? You lied to me about the phone call. You tricked me into this disgusting and degrading conversation, and me—I was gullible enough to fall for it.

MIRIAM. I swear to you on my life.

MAGDA. What did you expect him to do? You think I don't know things are tough for us in this unhappy country, with its two screwed up peoples? What's the point of telling me we're not in France or America? What's the point of telling me about your husband? Do I tell you about my problems? With my parents? With my brothers? With my Palestinian friends? Did I come to tell you about the sign they painted in black on our door, "Death to the traitors. You are doomed."

MIRIAM. Who wrote that on your door?

MAGDA. Do I know who? My friends, his friends. Are we short of lunatics in this country? And you, instead of helping your son, instead of standing behind him and giving him full support in such a difficult situation, what did you do to him? You went behind his back and worked against him. You pulled the carpet out from under him. And why? Because he loves an Arab girl like me.

MIRIAM. That's not true.

MAGDA. It is true. At least have the decency not to lie. What kind of garbage are you trying to sell me? He's not for me, he is for me. You're your son's worst enemy, do you know that? I just pray that what you did to him can still be undone somehow.

> *The telephone rings. MIRIAM picks up the receiver.*

MIRIAM. Hello? David? Is that you? Magda's here. I'm putting her on. Don't hang up.

MAGDA. *(taking the receiver)* David? Yes, it's me. I do too. How can I? Then come. I'm waiting for you in our room. I miss you too. Terribly.

> *Hangs up. The camera shifts to the spot where SAMIRA's lead-ins are being shot. SAMIRA does not step onto the podium.*

BENESH. *(prodding her)* Samira. Samira!

Scene 4

SAMIRA. Stop shooting.

BENESH. Cut. What's the matter?

SAMIRA. I can't go on.

BENESH. What do you mean you can't go on?

SAMIRA. The further you shoot, the more this film has turned into something altogether different from what it was supposed to be. People improvise, people interpret the characters anyway they feel it.

BENESH. That's the way I work.

SAMIRA. That's your problem. People change the text without a second thought.

BENESH. Is the text the most important thing to you? What's this supposed to be: a classical drama? Shakespearean language? People change texts.

SAMIRA. I wouldn't say a thing if it were done seriously, with some thought. But people here just feel free to adlib dialogue without so much as reading through the text a single time! I don't recognize my story anymore.

BENESH. Who hasn't read the text?

SAMIRA. I haven't cross-examined everyone.

BENESH. Everyone's read the text.

SAMIRA. Have you asked everyone?

BENESH. I don't have to.

SAMIRA. Then don't declare that they have. It simply isn't true.

BENESH. Who hasn't read it?

SAMIRA. If the shoe fits, wear it.

DAHLIA. That's not fair. You're throwing out accusations. Let's hear you back them up with some facts.

SAMIRA. Fahed hasn't read it. All right?

FAHED. Got any complaints about the way I do my part?

SAMIRA. You do the part just fine, except that any resemblance between your performance and Adnan is sheer coincidence.

FAHED. I don't need to read the whole script to know Adnan.

BENESH. I want him to play the Adnan he knows, not some paper character.

SAMIRA. Listen, Benesh, all sorts of personal relationships that don't belong in this story worked their way into it.

DAHLIA. You're generalizing. Just what kind of relationships are you talking about?

SAMIRA. The one between you and Benesh, for example. It's completely superseded the one between Magda and Rodney.

DAHLIA. I don't know how you understand real acting, but—

BENESH. We are not about to start a theoretical debate about acting. We have exactly two hours to finish shooting and not one minute to spare for bull sessions. Are you going to continue, yes or no?

SAMIRA. There's no truth in this film anymore.

HAVKIN. Is your whole life nothing but truth?

BENESH. Havkin…

HAVKIN. No, I want to understand. *(to SAMIRA)* Is there really that much truth in your life? Or maybe your life, like all our lives, is an ocean of trivial moments with you jabbering on about this and that and doing thousands of meaningless things. That's what I'd like to know…

SAMIRA. If you really want to know, the part of Herbert wasn't even supposed to be in the story.

BENESH. Lay off of that now!

SAMIRA. Why? 'Cause it makes you uncomfortable?

HAVKIN. Wait a minute. What's the problem with Herbert?

SAMIRA. There never was such a person.

HAVKIN. What do you mean there never was?

SAMIRA. Herbert is a brainstorm of Benesh's.

DAHLIA. But look how much colour he adds…

ADA. And meaning…

SAMIRA. That wasn't why Benesh put him in.

HAVKIN. What was the reason then?

SAMIRA. Ask him.

BENESH. What difference does it make now?

SAMIRA. You're not prepared to back up the things you said.

BENESH. I'll back them up, I'll front them up, I'll side them up…

SAMIRA. Great. Go ahead and kid about it.

BENESH. I wanted your story to have one character with a bit of human warmth to it.

SAMIRA. That's a lie.

HAVKIN. And what's the truth?

SAMIRA. He wanted to find you something to do.

HAVKIN. What? What did you say? What did he want?

SAMIRA. He said you…

BENESH. Why don't you shut your ass!

HAVKIN. Hold it! Watch how you talk to her.

BENESH. You can shut up too.

HAVKIN. I don't get it. What did he tell you?

SAMIRA. He said he knows a desperate old actor…

BENESH. You stupid fool. You and your truth.

SAMIRA. Isn't that the truth?

HAVKIN. It is the truth…. I don't see why you have to argue about it. It's the exact truth…. To hell with it… "An actor…." What's an actor anyhow…. You think

I'm an actor... that I can play all sorts of roles... I can't even figure out the text... and I for one did read it... I read it!... But I don't understand it. I don't remember a thing.... For heaven's sakes.... The scene I just did... I don't know... twenty-five or thirty years ago I could.... Now I just don't get it... maybe I'm not a real person anymore... maybe I'm just pretending that I have arms and legs and a head... maybe I'm not alive anymore... maybe I just think that I'm actually walking and eating and sleeping... the devil only knows... it's all so pointless... and I've got a wife at home... if I just had a bottle here I'd get drunk...

DAHLIA. That's enough, Havkin, take it easy.

HAVKIN. Maybe none of us really exists. Maybe we just think we do...

DAHLIA. Take it easy, Havkin.

HAVKIN. It isn't me. I don't really exist after all. It's Doctor Chebutikin. I never did understand that monologue and now all of a sudden I do. There's a true giant, Chekhov...*(turns to SAMIRA)* In order to create truth, you have to destroy a truth.

> *Silence falls. They all stand around, their arms limp. SAMIRA turns to leave.*

UDI. Hey, Samira, where to?

SAMIRA. I'm a fool, haven't you heard?

UDI. Just a minute, Samira.

SAMIRA. You can stay here and finish up your part. It's an interesting one, isn't it, and that's what counts as far as you're concerned.

UDI. I'm going with you.

SAMIRA. You promised to back me up and you didn't say a word. You don't have an ounce of character.

UDI. I'm going with you, Samira.

> *YONAH dashes out in front of them, blocking their way.*

YONAH. Just a minute! Nobody's going anywhere.

SAMIRA. Get out of the way.

YONAH. *(pushing her to the centre of the set)* Get back in position facing the camera, you hear me?

UDI. How dare you raise a hand on her?!

YONAH. Shove off, before I smash your face in!

UDI. What?!

YONAH. You get back to the camera on the double! If there's any place in this world that I hold to be sacred, this is it. You're going back there. What did you have in mind—that you can just go ahead and spit on people? Truth, untruth... if it's truth you're looking for, suck it out of your ass. You got more truth there than you have in your heads. People put everything they've got into this story of yours. This guy is my friend and he has to face all of you naked at the end of his tether. And you have the gall to complain. He pulled Rodney in his direction? Rodney who, Rodney what? I don't give a shit about Rodney. You don't know who Yonah is yet. I'll break the bones of anyone who hurts him now. "The truth"! You're afraid of how your story is going to wind up. You get up there in front of the camera right this minute, you hear me?! *(He shoves SAMIRA, then shoves off UDI who tries to interfere.)* You too! Protecting her honour… do you have any idea what you're working on here?!… I've read your text… *(to UDI)* You think you're on some kind of pleasure trip, trampling on the pus and the guts of a disintegrating soul like David and keeping the precious integrity of your own sweet personality intact?! Protecting her honour, no less…. That man's life has been wrecked in this work. Where do you come off treating that part like it was some kind of windfall? What do you think, that a person can dig out all of the wickedness and rot buried deep inside him without being torn to bits and coming within a hair's breath of being put away? How dare you come to this job like you were in a pharmacy? How can you possibly expect to play your last scene in the kind of amiable mood you arrived in from that nature trip you took with her? Just what did you have in mind? Have you given any thought to the God-awful things you're going to have to bring to life in a few minutes or are you completely immersed in thoughts of how to escape the confusion and madness within you? Idiot! If that's what you want, then go ahead and hold hands with her , and make out and have a good time! Protecting her honour…. You should both be ashamed of yourselves, you stinking couple of bourgeoisie…. Tfu! You make me sick! Go ahead! Go back on the set! And if anyone so much as utters the word "truth" here, I'll break his bones! *(to the cameras)* Action! Go!

Scene 5

UDI stands stunned. DAHLIA enters as MAGDA. She is aware of UDI's condition. Ignoring the text, she walks over to him, touches him, hugs him, shows him her affection.

MAGDA. It's good to have you back. I've missed you. Don't talk. You don't have to say anything.

DAVID. I'm such a good-for-nothing.

MAGDA. Stop it.

DAVID. Laughable and good for nothing.

MAGDA. We're together. That's what counts. Let me help you.

DAVID. *(still Udi speaking about his own situation in the scene)* I can't…. Help me get out of sight…

MAGDA. I won't let you go away again.

DAVID. You're afraid I'll do something to myself…

MAGDA. You want a spanking? You love me. You've got me. You've got a baby in my belly. You've got enemies who want to hurt you. You've got things worth protecting. Why get out of sight?

DAVID. What did you think I was doing all this time?

MAGDA. Trying to get your head straightened out. Thinking about yourself.

DAVID. How? How does a person think about himself. How do you do it? You tell me.

MAGDA. Simple. You try to open your eyes to what's happening to you.

DAVID. Yeah, sure.

MAGDA. You ask yourself what you really want.

DAVID. What I really want. What I really want.

MAGDA. You try to find out what other people want from you. Who is trying to use you and how…. You focus on yourself… you're the object of your own life…. You…

DAVID. I can't think about myself. Ever. I try. But my thoughts run away with me. I tell myself: now you're going to think about yourself. Only about yourself. Nothing else. A minute later I find myself thinking about all sorts of other things. Everything except myself. I try to take myself in hand. To re-focus my thoughts on myself. I force myself to concentrate on it. I call out my own name… and I find myself looking out at the sea, the hills, the sky… feeling so empty… scared.

MAGDA. For years, you had all those different heads inside your own. Getting rid of them can't be easy.

DAVID. How did you manage? How? How?

MAGDA. Me… I told myself at a very early stage… I remember…. It was at night…. My mother was crying… softly…crying… then she fell asleep… she kept sighing in her sleep… I couldn't fall asleep… I lay there in the dark on my back… staring into the darkness…. Suddenly it was all clear to me… my whole existence…. Magda, I told myself…. Magda…. You've been brought into a world where you will be exploited… you won't be free… you'll be forced to stoop down… to serve the will of others all through your life… until you die… and that's the only life you'll ever have… never in all eternity will you have another… and it should mean everything to you, this life of yours… it should be more precious than anything else in the world… and nobody should use your life for his own ulterior motives… don't let anyone lie to you, you hear? Don't let anyone conceal his real intentions from you… *(Suddenly she turns sharply towards DAVID.)* What do you mean you can't think about yourself.

DAVID. I'm trying to tell you the truth.

MAGDA. I believe you.

DAVID. You know why I didn't come straight to you? I was ashamed. I was ashamed of running away. I was ashamed of exposing myself to you that way. Of all my stupidity. Like a spoiled child. Then, when I realized what I'd done, I was ashamed to come back to you. I said to myself: how are you going to be able to look her in the eye? I went into hiding. A whole week. I stayed out of sight. You know where? If I tell you, you won't believe me.

MAGDA. Forget it. You don't have to tell me.

DAVID. Yes, I do. I felt so wretched.

MAGDA. Let's drop it. I don't want you to expose yourself in such a humiliating way.

DAVID. I have the humiliation coming.

MAGDA. Don't start feeling sorry for yourself and don't try to drag me into feeling sorry for you, because I won't.

DAVID. You despise me. I know.

MAGDA. Don't tell me what I feel towards you.

DAVID. My running away was unforgivable. I should have been with you and I wasn't.

MAGDA. You should have been wherever you wanted to be.

DAVID. It's unforgivable.

MAGDA. Who has to forgive you except me, in order for you to forgive yourself?

DAVID. Now you're treating me like a psychologist.

MAGDA. Go to hell, will you.

DAHLIA. A human reaction at last.

MAGDA. You're sneaky, you know that? I have to watch out with you.

DAVID. Nobody takes me seriously. I run away with a gun and you're not even scared 'cause you know just what I'm worth. *(talks out into space, as if addressing everyone who has affected his life)* It won't do you any good. Some things just have to be punished.

MAGDA. And you're dying for me to punish you?

DAVID. Not you. It'll come. Don't worry.

MAGDA. The black writing on the door?

DAVID. I don't give a damn about that. I know my old friends: psychopaths. Morbid cowards who aren't satisfied unless they manage to scare others too. Their heroism is the heroism of miserable sadists who keep looking for a helpless victim to pounce upon so they can feel a little more powerful.

MAGDA. I'm scared.

DAVID. The black writing on the door? Don't be. I might not know how to think about myself yet, but I do know how to fight. Let them just dare come. God… they sure won't get out of here in one piece.

MAGDA. *(gasping and putting her hand on her stomach)* Ah!

DAVID. What happened?

MAGDA. It kicked me.

DAVID. *(patting her stomach)* Are you kicking? So tiny, and already kicking? You little rascal. I'll never do to you what my father did to me.

MAGDA. Couldn't we go to sleep somewhere else?

DAVID. No. This is our home. We don't have another. And this is the first time in my life that I know exactly what I'm going to be fighting for.

> As SAMIRA goes on with her story, YONAH, PAUL and ADA climb onto the set and tie up UDI and DAHLIA. DAHLIA lies down on the mattress. UDI sits on the floor. YONAH and PAUL are kneeling next to him.

Scene 6

SAMIRA. They took us by surprise while we were sleeping. They got in through an open window, sneaked up to our mattress and started beating us in our sleep… *(She stops talking, then turns to BENESH.)* I can't continue.

BENESH. Go on.

SAMIRA. You cut whatever you want out of the story. You'll cut it all out.

DAHLIA. She's right.

BENESH. Wait a minute. What are you missing? Which scene are you missing now?

SAMIRA. I'm not missing anything.

DAHLIA. Why don't you say anything? The scene where Magda and Rodney split up.

BENESH. Oh, is that the scene you miss?

DAHLIA. No, except that without it the whole character of Magda is meaningless.

BENESH. Is that scene the one with all the meaning?

DAHLIA. Yes.

BENESH. And I'm telling you that scene is totally unnecessary.

DAHLIA. Why? Because it talks about you?

BENESH. Yonah, do we have enough footage?

YONAH. Footage, yes.

BENESH. All right. We'll take that scene.

DAHLIA. I don't need that scene…

BENESH. *(resolute)* We're taking the scene.

YONAH. We have to put the London apartment set back up…

BENESH. Never mind the set. Do it in close-up, faces filling the screen, no background. *(to DAHLIA)* Let's go. Let's hear the lines without which the character has no meaning.

YONAH. Sound running! Shoot!

DAHLIA enters in the part of MAGDA.

MAGDA. You know, Rodney, I don't understand the point of this life I'm living in London. If you love me the way you say you do, why do I keep coming up against a wall of double entendres. Do you love me, or don't you? Be indifferent. Say your feelings are dead. That what we had between us can't be revived.

RODNEY. I do love you.

MAGDA. Why does your behaviour prove the opposite? No feeling, no hope…

RODNEY. Don't we have it good when we're together?

MAGDA. Our bodies touch one another and tingle but I don't even know if that's truth or untruth anymore…. How do you feel about me? *(shifts to DAHLIA)* The woman you got pregnant… the woman who miscarried…

BENESH. That's not your text.

DAHLIA. Those are the facts.

MAGDA. Rodney.

DAHLIA. Even if you'd rather avoid that memory…

MAGDA. Rodney.

DAHLIA. Those are the facts, and you were away from me just at the time when I was the most upset, the most vulnerable, the most frightened.

MAGDA. Rodney.

DAHLIA. And you can just carry on as though nothing has happened to you? Or to me? What a progressive person you are. A scathing critic of social injustice. A revolutionary. A Trotskyist. What not…. What do you feel about all the months we've put into one another and into our relationship? I came from Palestine for you…. "Come, just come, and I'll help you…." What am I to you? Some creature you can use when it suits you? You—a man who has everything, and give him more… just give him more… he takes, never asking who did the giving…. Don't you think I'm a whole human being? Don't I deserve whatever a person in love can give someone he loves? Or is there something wrong with me? Why—is it because I'm a woman? Or because I'm not English? Not European? Different? Or maybe you simply aren't really in love? Maybe you're just lying? Not only to me; to yourself too. But if you're lying to me, tell me. Don't try to put one over on me and don't make me play the fool for the rest of my life.

BENESH. Have you had your say? Are you satisfied now? Can we move to the next scene?

DAHLIA. Why don't you answer me? Are you that much of a coward?

RODNEY. *(i.e. BENESH who has made up his mind to hide completely behind the text SAMIRA has written for RODNEY.)* Listen, I'm a playwright. I write television plays and it's a shitty job. It's something that takes everything out of me. Sometimes, I catch myself red-handed, behaving abominably, and I say to myself: follow through on that, take it as far as it will go. But remember the details for the upcoming scene in your play. If I botch up a personal relationship, I splatter the dregs over my next play. When I find myself being inhuman, I tell myself: raw material for a scene. I can't help it. All I can do is work a new scene around the defective stuff I'm made of. I create, and my life melts away. I destroy and wreck everything around me, and I turn the story of that destruction into an episode of Hearthrug Theatre. I'm not trying to make excuses. Of course you're right in everything you've said. When I'm dying, there's one thing I'll regret: that I won't be able to use such an interesting setting in any scene of any play... I guess I'm the kind of person who has no real substance; I guess my life itself is just an illusion.

> *Suddenly he becomes genuinely enraged, no longer in the role of RODNEY, and makes his exit in an improvisation of BENESH.*

BENESH. It's all a fake. All false. What are you asking me to do anyway? You want me to give you all the time I've got left to live? You want all of me to yourself? What right do you have? Who's a Trotskyist? Who's progressive? You're fighting me! You want to take me over. To tame me. To turn me into your plaything. You want me to give in. Can't two people find some other way of sharing their lives? Does one always have to be the master and the other the slave.... And if the ultimate enslavement is death, can there be any life together without actually looking forward to the other one's death? Like that old couple playing the comedy of love, with all the niceties. Playing worn-out pranks on one another. Rehashing a textual cliche. So hackneyed. With each of the two clowns displaying flickers of independence for their awestruck friends in the audience. Each of them caught up in the same web that has entangled them together. That's what the play is: those two old rakes pretending to give each other what a person in love is capable of giving the one he loves, whatever time he has left to live... and at the very same time they keep stealing a glance at one another out of the corner of an icy eye, laying low and waiting anxiously and eagerly for the moment when the other one's eyes will look up to freeze all at once in sudden death and the comedy will be over... *(turns to DAHLIA through MAGDA)* What it means, you ask... what it means... after everything we've been through we still work together.... You're hurt. So am I. We may not be destroyed but we're badly hurt. And just look what we're doing with our wounds: working together. And you still ask what it means...

> *SAMIRA steps into position and speaks to the camera.*

SAMIRA. They broke in while we were asleep and started hitting us. When I came to, my head was roaring like an ocean. I could hear voices through the racket. I recognized David's. He was talking with two strange men. He was saying some terrible things. I thought it was a nightmare. I tried to move my arm and realized I was tied up. I opened my eyes. David was tied up beside me. He was talking with two thugs. I couldn't believe my ears. I wanted to scream at first but I guess I was too stunned to make a sound. I kept still. I pretended I was still unconscious.

Scene 7

The apartment in Jerusalem. A mattress on the floor. DAVID and MAGDA are tied up. MAGDA is pretending to be unconscious. DAVID is talking in a whisper with the two thugs, AVI and BARRY.

AVI. I don't believe you. I don't believe you.

DAVID. You really blew it, I'm telling you. What idiots! Do you know how long it took me to win this Arab chick over? And her friends too? Do you have any idea how touchy and complicated it's been? I'm just beginning to see some results and there you go, with your thick-headedness, throwing months of hard work down the drain!

AVI. If it's true, what you're saying, why haven't you said a word?

DAVID. Who to, you idiot, who to?

AVI. Don't you call me an idiot!

DAVID. Idiot! Who to?

BARRY. To one of our members.

DAVID. You're a real asshole, you know that? If I'd said a word to anybody, it would have leaked for sure and the whole thing would go to waste. That kind of work can only be done solo, see what I mean?

AVI. But you were seen kissing in the street.

DAVID. You moron! I'm telling you I've been putting on an act.

BARRY. But the guys don't understand!

DAVID. What's more important? For the guys to understand or for us to get a hold on the traitors who collaborate with them? "The guys don't understand...." Are we an underground or a youth movement?

AVI. But...

DAVID. Our members had better get used to the idea of not understanding all sorts of things. Carrying out orders, not asking questions.

AVI. I don't know whether or not to believe you.

DAVID. Go ahead… carry out your orders… suits me fine. *(silence)* Why didn't I rub out the writing on the front door? Figure it out for yourself. Couldn't I have just taken some paint and gone over it? Why didn't I? I was thrilled to bits when I saw that message. I told myself: they're finally helping me out.

AVI. What do you want me to tell the guys?

DAVID. Nothing! Got that? Not a word should leave this room.

BARRY. But she'll talk.

DAVID. Untie me and go. I'll untie her, I'll bring her to and I'll tell her I had it out with you.

BARRY. *(to AVI)* What do you say?

AVI. I don't know…

DAVID. Beat it quickly before she wakes up. Go and tell the guys that you really let us have it and that you were interrupted in the middle…. Sell them some bill of goods, what's the difference? When the time comes…. When I have the whole list, we'll gather all the guys and I'll tell them about the whole operation myself.

BARRY. What about her pregnancy?

AVI. That could be a problem.

DAVID. Don't worry about it! Are you her father? We'll take care of the pregnancy and everything else when the time comes. Just cool it. There's not going to be any baby if that's what you're worried about.

BARRY. Did you enjoy it at least?

DAVID. Want the details?

BARRY. You're a bastard, David. A real bastard!

DAVID. What did you think. With the kinds of methods our "leader" was using, you suppose we would have gotten anywhere?

BARRY. He's really turned soft.

DAVID. Holding demonstrations, making headlines. What we have here calls for completely different methods. You just wait and see. When the time is ripe, we'll throw the old fogy out and take things into our own hands. If anyone opens his trap then, we'll slash his face.

AVI. Listen… so help me… I don't know if I should believe you or not.

DAVID. Believe your ass, okay?

AVI. You're not human. You're a monster, you know that?

DAVID. Or maybe you think the Arabs are going to get on those trucks just because you ask them to. When the moment comes, we're going to have to be monsters.

AVI. I could never act like you. Not even to that Arab chick. She's human too, after all, isn't she?

DAVID. What do you think, that it's easy for me? Sure it's cruel, but we don't have a choice. If we want this country to be totally free of Arabs, we're going to have to learn to be cold as a stone.

BARRY. *(enthusiastic)* Sure! Cold as ice!

AVI. *Eiskalt.*

BARRY. *Eiskalt*, that's a terrific slogan.

DAVID. Scary, eh? If you'd seen the list of names I've got already and if you knew how many planted agents have been working from within our own ranks and who some of your so-called friends are, them you'd know what scary means.

BARRY. Who? Who's planted?

DAVID. You want to see the list?

BARRY. Of course I do.

DAVID. Then untie me and I'll show you something.

BARRY. Let him go.

AVI. You sure?

BARRY. Let him go. *Eiskalt.*

> AVI *cuts through the ropes;* BARRY *and* AVI *disappear.*

DAVID. Magda, are you alright?

MAGDA. Keep away from me.

DAVID. Let me set you free.

MAGDA. Don't touch me, you monster.

DAVID. What's with you?

MAGDA. I saw you.

DAVID. You don't understand.

MAGDA. I heard you.

DAVID. Listen a minute.

MAGDA. I understand perfectly.

DAVID. Let me explain.

MAGDA. I can't stand hearing your voice.

DAVID. You think I meant what I told them?

MAGDA. Get away from me.

DAVID. I was pretending.

MAGDA. I don't believe a word you say anymore.

DAVID. What did you want me to do, you moron.

MAGDA. You're sick. That's what you are.

DAVID. God. How can I convince you? I was just pretending. Don't you understand what pretending means?

MAGDA. You were not! I could see you and hear you. It was you... you.... More you than I've ever seen you.

DAVID. You don't understand a thing. You're a real idiot. You're all screwed up.

MAGDA. A screwed up Arab. Say it.

DAVID. You're nuts. Let me untie you.

MAGDA. Get away from me.

DAVID. Stop it. You're mad.

MAGDA. Mad. Sure I am. You drove me mad. I could die.

DAVID. Come on, stop it.

MAGDA. Kill me. Why don't you just kill me and finish off where your friends left off.

DAVID. Why do I deserve this? God, I deserve this. I did everything to save you. God, you've got to believe me.

> *AVI and BARRY reappear.*

AVI. Traitor. You thought you'd fool us.

BARRY. Traitor. We'll finish you off.

DAVID. Psychopaths. Come on, psychopaths.

MAGDA. David... behind you.

> *DAVID swerves towards BARRY and hits him. BARRY falls on the ground. Just then, AVI hits DAVID over the head from behind. DAVID falls over. AVI kicks him in the stomach, then in the head. BARRY gets up. His face is smeared with blood. He jumps on MAGDA.*

BARRY. You filthy whore, I'll show you!

> *He kicks MAGDA in the stomach. She gasps and lifts her still-tied hands to her stomach, then kneels and rolls over.*

Scene 8

> *As soon as MAGDA falls as a result of BARRY's kick, SAMIRA gets up and takes two or three steps towards the camera to give her lead-in. She mumbles something unclear. Her knees buckle and she turns full-circle, unsteadily, as though drunk. The lighting flickers to the rhythm of SAMIRA's movements, alternately blinding and fading. SAMIRA moves towards the corner of the stage. Everyone rushes to her. She falls to the ground.*

> *Blackout.*

A different light goes on. The light of a nightmare. The people in the nightmare are moving to the rhythm of a double-speed film. Their voices are high-pitched and screechy. Their speech sounds like a tape being played at twice the normal speed.

The whole scene gives the feeling of a film being screened at double-speed. If this effect cannot be achieved with live actors on stage, the scene can be shot for video and screened on the large video screen at double speed.

RODNEY. Hello where are you calling from oh Heathrow it's wonderful to have you here got a pen and paper take down the address then I've rented a flat for you no I'm not living there myself yet, that'll take another few weeks I'll explain when I see you this afternoon or tomorrow at the latest It'll be super believe me...

PSYCHOLOGIST. *(ADA in a white gown and nurse's cap)* Good morning Samira, did you have a good night you're looking wonderful here take these pills at the rate you're going, you'll be better and out of here in just two or three weeks. Meanwhile there's someone here who's very eager to see you you may come in Sir she's still in a very weak condition her defenses aren't too strong be gentle when you talk to her...

RODNEY. *(shows up in underwear and dresses at breakneck speed)* That was fabulous wasn't it where did I put my watch oh no it's six already With you time goes by so quickly sweetheart gotta run bye till next time darling...

ADNAN appears in the garb of an ultra-religious Moslem. He is holding a strand of prayer-beads and shuffling the beads at a mad pace. As he talks he also keeps falling to his knees and standing back up again, in a frenzied re-entry into the Moslem praying position.

ADNAN. Hello Samira don't you recognize me it's me Adnan what no I'm not hospitalized here I'm in jail we bashed in the head of the thug who killed your baby why are you laughing this is no get-up it's our national apparel.

ADA. *(in a flash-appearance of the PSYCHOLOGIST)* You've got to return to your national identity. As a psychologist and a Jew I can tell you that assimilation isn't the solution... *(vanishes)*

ADNAN. I'm willing to forgive you all of it despite everything you did and despite the loose lifestyle. I love you and I would marry you too. Of course, you'd have to change the way you live and say goodbye to your European habits...

RODNEY. *(in an affectedly casual style of dress)* I'm off to the film studio, darling, haven't managed to get you a job yet, but be patient... *(He disappears.)*

ADNAN. Cut out smoking completely, wine is out of the question, of course, not to mention those old clothes of yours... burn them all and start wearing our traditional outfits.... Living like a decent Moslem woman observing the religious laws and, of course, learning everything you need to now about religion and about the obligations of a Moslem wife... *(leaps up in an odd* *movement)* Why are you spitting, you lunatic? *(He jumps back and forth as if to avoid SAMIRA's spitting.)* You're crazy, stop it, you're crazy... *(vanishes)*

RODNEY. *(dressed to the teeth)* My wife's very vulnerable right now, emotionally I can't just leave her, she's human too you know, but it shouldn't take more than another two or three weeks, a month at the most, incidentally, about that job, there may be an opening for a small part in a television film this autumn...

> *DAVID is dressed as an ultra-orthodox yeshiva student. He is poring over a page of Talmud, jumping up to pray, laying phylacteries and removing them; in short, going through all the ritual motions preformed by an observant Jew in the course of a single day. Meanwhile, MIRIAM and EPHRAIM, in clown's outfits, have undergone a Jewish metamorphosis of sorts and have become Jewish-theatre clowns. They are carrying armfuls of dishes with various foods on them. EPHRAIM is juggling three bananas while MIRIAM is pulling bowls out of a basket and placing them before DAVID who is preforming the rituals.*

MIRIAM. David Davidarling Davidear have some broiled chicken and here are some meatballs and meatloaf with lots of onion and garlic the way you like it and here's some gefilte fish for the Sabbath meal...

DAVID. *(performing the rituals at breakneck speed)* Take away your sacrilege.

MIRIAM. David you've got to eat.

EPHRAIM. *(still juggling the bananas)* How does that line of yours go—without flour there is no Torah...

MIRIAM. I'm leaving you some apples and bananas too...

DAVID. I told you to take away your heathen abomination.

MIRIAM. It's all kosher all kosher we koshered our kitchen at home ask Daddy.

EPHRAIM. Kosher as can be and we put up mezuzahs on every doorpost including the bathroom you needn't be afraid to come home.

DAVID. *(He hurtles the dishes at his parents. They stagger and convulse in odd fits and jumps to avoid being hit. RODNEY suddenly finds himself in the middle of the scene.)* You can take your meatballs take your meatloaf take your fish...

EPHRAIM. Honour thy father and thy mother.

DAVID. She is not my mother and you are not my father.

RODNEY. *(ducking the flying meatballs)* In late July my wife will be getting a job in Portugal and then I'll move in with you at Covent Garden sweetheart see you next time.

MIRIAM. You've been through a difficult time we understand.

DAVID. Go away and don't let your feet profane this place.

RODNEY. *(appearing with an extravagant sweater tied around his neck, waving in the air behind him)* Yes darling autumn here is very long but you've got to admit it's the loveliest season of the year and that the afternoon hours are the most appropriate for lovemaking *l'amour l'apres-midi.*

MIRIAM. *(to SAMIRA who is out of sight)* Go to him I beg of you Samira... you he'll listen to you're the only one who can get this obsession out of him and give us back our son Samira go to him.

RODNEY. Why do you say concubine stop using such vulgar language the characters in my plays don't use such vulgar language are you short of money come on darling let's stop fighting I swear to you this Christmas we'll celebrate together in our apartment and by then I promise you'll have a passport and a job...

DAVID. *(all the while swaying back and forth in frenzied orgastic movements of a person praying)* Why did you come here Samira why I'm trying to get you out of my system and I can't sit here memorizing verses and I keep thinking of you Hear O Israel I say at night and think of you I love you go away from here go I told you there's no escaping retribution and now I know there's a connection between all the events and the coincidences and that there's a supreme pretext now I know don't go to London Convert we'll call you Ruth after Ruth the Moabite may she rest in peace and we'll be married in a proper Jewish wedding Samira.

RODNEY. *(appearing in festive winter clothing, dancing and singing as he waves a small gift-wrapped box)* Merry Christmas to you / Merry Christmas to you / Merry Christmas dear sweetheart / Merry Christmas to you...

MIRIAM. Go to him. Go Samira you're the only one who can bring our son back to us.

ADNAN. Get rid of cigarettes, the wine, learn the basic precepts of our religion.

DAVID. You'll become a proper Jew and we'll get married.

RODNEY. I can't stay now but I'll be back tonight she gets drunk easily and then she passes out for twelve hours I'll come and we'll have a wonderful time.

HERBERT. *(enters with a small Christmas tree)* I'm a Jew in the Nazi sense not the Jewish one.

RODNEY. Merry Christmas.

DAVID. Simply convert.

ADNAN. And learn the duties of a Moslem wife.

RODNEY. She gets drunk easily.

ADA. *(as the PSYCHOLOGIST)* Identity, Samira, Identity. Assimilation isn't the answer. You've got to find your identity again because without an identity you understand. Identity is...

SAMIRA. *(yelling as she comes to; as she yells, the light loses its nightmarish effect)* Go away! Go away! All of you! Go away! Leave me alone all of you! Go away! Go away! Go away, you and your filth! Go! Go! Go... *(She wakes up and sees the others all standing over her.)* What's going on?

ADA. You fainted.

UDI. How are you feeling?

SAMIRA. All right. Strange. Like after a good sleep. Was I out for long?

YONAH. Seconds. Maybe half a minute. Can you stand up?

SAMIRA. I'm okay. As far as I'm concerned, we can carry on.

BENESH. What do you mean "carry on"? We've finished the story...

SAMIRA. Finished?... Aren't you shooting the nightmare?

BENESH. Yesterday's rushes came out great. No need to do a retake.

SAMIRA. Then we're through.

BENESH. Yeah. That's it. We can start taking the set apart.

YONAH. Wait a minute. Who's taking things apart already? A job well done calls for a drink first! *(pulls the cork on a bottle of champagne and hands the bottle to BENESH.)* Take a sip, wet your whistle and say a few words man!

BENESH. *(passing the bottle on)* What can I say... I don't know what to say...

HAVKIN. Stop that nonsense. Don't listen to him. Nothing to say, my eye!

YONAH. Havkin!

HAVKIN. Ladies and gentlemen, don't take yourselves too seriously. We haven't exactly turned the world upside down. All we've done is tell a story and here's hoping we did a good job. Now we're excited and that's natural but we'll be splitting up soon, each one of us returning to his own life. And we'll discover that we haven't moved any mountains. On the other hand, we'll discover that no abyss has opened up either. We're not about to change the world, for better or for worse. So let's forget about words. Have you forgotten where you are—the studio of Herbert! Someone who never even existed! And in Herbert's studio, when you run out of words, you dance! Isn't that right, Benesh?

BENESH. Ausdruck-Tanz.

HAVKIN. Exactly. Ausdruck-Tanz. Paul—music!

> PAUL *sits down at the piano and begins to play Ravel's "La Valse".*
> *The singer scats along and everyone joins in the Ausdruck-Tanz. Their*
> *manner of dancing gives each actor the chance to express his own*
> *particular character.* HAVKIN *directs the dancing, brings the characters*
> *together and uses the dance to convey the essence of the play.*
>
> *The end.*

Reading Hebron

Jason Sherman

• Jason Sherman •

Jason Sherman's plays include *Three in the Back, Two in the Head* (first produced by Tarragon Theatre/Necessary Angel/National Arts Centre), *The Retreat* (Tarragon), *Patience* (Tarragon), *It's All True* (Tarragon), *An Acre of Time* (Great Canadian Theatre Company), *The League of Nathans* (Orange Dog Theatre/Theatre Passe Muraille), *Reading Hebron* (Factory Theatre), and *None is Too Many* (Winnipeg Jewish Theatre/Manitoba Theatre Centre). He has received the Governor General's Award for Drama (and been nominated three other times), and the Chalmers Canadian Play Award (twice, along with three other nominations). He lives in Toronto.

• Playwright's Notes •

I would advise against anything approaching naturalism in the staging. The play requires nothing more than a desk and a few chairs. Dany Lyne, who designed the first production, created a multi-purpose table accompanied by a bench and twin chairs which served all our needs—the bench, for example, was used as a seat in Mr. Big's office, a bed in the Boss' house, and a bookshelf in the bookstore.

Props, also, should be kept to a minimum. Other than books and papers, the play needs a bottle of wine here and a set of candlesticks there. The actors should wear the same costumes throughout (with an occasional accessory, if desired) so that the actors—not their outfits—create the different characters.

The line breaks and absence of punctuation in the Judges scenes are an attempt to slow down the testimony, to make the delivery more deliberate, less overtly emotional and almost devoid of interpretation. The more controlled the delivery, the more powerful the testimony. There should be a great contrast between these scenes and all the others.

Quotation marks around a character's name indicates that Nathan is imagining this part of the conversation in the midst of a real conversation; it's best if the audience thinks the conversations between Nathan and the Israeli Consulate receptionist and the Palestinian receptionist are continuous—no special lighting tricks to give the game away. After the library scene, where Jane is both a real and an imaginary person, the quotation marks are dropped, since, by now, it should be clear that Nathan is making things up.

Speaking of Nathan's fantasies—such as the ones he has in the library and the bookstore—these should be staged as seamlessly as possible, so that characters appear out of "nowhere."

Accents are entirely appropriate throughout—the more outrageous the better, except in the Judges scenes, where moderation would be prudent.

Edward Said's last name is pronounced sah-eed.

There is no intermission. Playing time should be about 85 minutes.

Stage directions have been kept to a minimum.

• **Production History** •

Reading Hebron was first produced by Factory Theatre, Toronto, in November/
December 1996, with the following company:

Michael Healey
Niki Landau
Alon Nashman
Earl Pastko
Felicia Shulman

Directed by Brian Quirt
Set and Costumes by Dany Lyne
Lighting by Paul Mathiesen

• **Characters** •

The actor playing NATHAN plays no other roles. Two men and two women are
needed for the remaining roles, as follows:

FIRST MALE	SECOND MALE	FIRST FEMALE	SECOND FEMALE
Judge 1	Witness 2	Witness 1	Judge 2
Consulate receptionist	Judge 3	Judge 4	Lotte
Witness 4	Lev	Jan	Witness 3
Witness 5	Judge 6	Judge 5	Mom
Witness 8	Witness 7	Randa	Witness 6
Said	Leibowitz	Judge 8	Judge 7
Clerk	Mr. Big	Jane	Boss
Rosenthal	Conspirator	Secretary	Ashwari
Excited Man	Lerner	Ex-wife	Mossad agent
Zaydie	Spielberg	Ozick	Settler 4
Mourad	Sternberg	Eliach	
Mossad agent	Dad	Bubbie	
Settler 2	Mossad Agent	Ben	
Rabin	Chomsky	Mossad agent	
	First Hasid	Second Hasid	
	Settler 1	Settler 3	
	Baruch	Noa	

• *Reading Hebron* •

Judges I

NATHAN's apartment. A desk, on top of which sits a telephone, and nothing else.

NATHAN enters with a stack of books, magazines, files, newspapers.

NATHAN. *(addressing the audience)* On February 25th, 1994, Dr. Baruch Goldstein, a settler from Kiryat Arba, committed a massacre at the Tomb of the Patriarchs in Hebron. On February 27th, 1994, the Government of Israel decided to appoint a Commission of Inquiry to determine whether Goldstein acted alone or with accomplices.

The telephone rings.

Hello?… No, I… I can't talk right now.

He hangs up.

The Commission heard most of the testimony in sessions that were open to the public.

The Commission held 31 sessions and heard evidence from 106 witnesses, some of them at the Commission's initiative and some at their own request.

The complete or partial testimony of 16 witnesses was heard behind closed doors.

The Commission made a public announcement requesting that anyone who wished to testify before it or present it with documents or exhibits, make their intention known to it in writing.

The placement of the JUDGES and WITNESSES is up to the director— the first production had them at windows behind an upstage wall that extended from one side of the stage to the other.

JUDGE 1. The witness
is a settler
from Kiryat Arba
near Hebron
You are a reservist
with the Israeli Defense Forces

WITNESS 1. Yes

JUDGE 1. And you were on active duty
the morning of the massacre

WITNESS 1. Yes
I was at a

communications headquarters
in Kiryat Arba
At 5 a.m. I received a call
from Dr. Goldstein
He asked that I meet him
at his clinic
and take him down
to the Tomb of the Patriarchs

JUDGE 1. Did he give any indication
of what he was about to do

WITNESS 1. No hint
No
We talked a little
about ambulance supplies
for the settlement
Oh
I proposed a way
to keep intravenous infusions warm
He said
"I hope there won't be any more need
for infusions"
He cared very much
about human life

JUDGE 2. The witness is
the army commander
for the West Bank

WITNESS 2. For Judea and Samaria
that is correct

JUDGE 2. Would you tell us what happened
at the Tomb of the Patriarchs
on February 25th, 1994

WITNESS 2. At 5.20 a.m.
Dr. Goldstein entered the mosque
in his army uniform

JUDGE 2. He carried his weapon
in plain view

WITNESS 2. Jews
Only Jews
are permitted to bring in weapons with them

JUDGE 2. He carried a bag with him

WITNESS 2. Yes
We can assume that it contained
the ammunition magazines

JUDGE 2. Why was the bag not checked

WITNESS 2. It is policy
not to inspect bags
carried by Jews

JUDGE 2. Even though it is standard
in almost all public buildings in Israel
for people to be asked
if they are carrying weapons
and to have bags searched

WITNESS 2. Dr. Goldstein did not receive special attention
didn't arouse suspicion
He told an officer who knew him
that he was on reserve duty
In a section of the Tomb known as the Isaac Hall
400 to 500 Muslims
were beginning their Ramadan Friday prayers
In the adjacent Abraham Hall
13 Jews were reciting prayers for Purim
Dr. Goldstein entered the Isaac Hall
through the first of three doors
then fired into the worshippers
from different locations at the back of the hall

JUDGE 2. Where were the Israeli soldiers
who were supposed to be on duty

WITNESS 2. Three of them had slept in
and arrived when it was all over
A regular policemen was also not there
and another soldier
had been sent by a superior officer
to switch places with a soldier outside

JUDGE 2. So only one of the six Israelis
assigned to the security detail
was in place

WITNESS 2. That is correct

JUDGE 2. How did he react to the gunfire

WITNESS 2. He tried to make his way into the hall
but was pushed back by the crowd
trying to escape
He finally made his way into Isaac Hall

but it was too late
He found Dr. Goldstein dead
in a corner
beaten by the Palestinians
with a fire extinguisher

JUDGE 2. Can you tell us General
why Jews are permitted
as a matter of routine
to bring weapons to the cave
when Palestinians do not enjoy
the same privilege

WITNESS 2. It dates back to 1980
after an Arab attack
that killed six Jews in Hebron

JUDGE 2. What do you make of the policy

WITNESS 2. I think it makes sense
The firearms have been a deterrent
to Arab violence

JUDGE 2. Why this discrimination

WITNESS 2. I would not draw conclusions
from an extraordinary case
of a lunatic
God forbid
I could have found myself testifying
before a commission
after Jews were butchered
by 500 inflamed Muslim attackers
Then the question would have been
why weren't the Jews armed
when they were praying
so close to 500 Muslims

JUDGE 2. I do not understand why people
who are coming to pray to God
have to take weapons with them

WITNESS 2. I don't have an answer to that
Those were the decisions
The thing that is hard for me to imagine
is that in a place where there are armed soldiers
a Jew
an Israeli
would do such a thing

Paranoia

NATHAN makes a telephone call; the CONSULATE receptionist answers.

CONSULATE. *(on the telephone)* Shalom, Consulya Israel.

NATHAN. Oh, oh. Hebrew.

CONSULATE. Israeli Consulate, hello.

NATHAN. *(on the telephone)* Oh, hello. I'm looking for information about the Hebron Massacre.

"CONSULATE". Why?

NATHAN. Um. I'm a… rabbi and. It's a research project.

"CONSULATE". *(outrageous Israeli accent; over the top)* BULLLLLL-SHEEEEEEEEEEET!

NATHAN. Okay. Look. I'm a Jew. I'm *interested*. I'm worried the whole thing's gonna be passed off as the work of a madman.

"CONSULATE". It *was* the work of a madman. Goldstein was a foreign implant, a Brooklyn Jew who went to Israel to kill Arabs.

NATHAN. But—

"CONSULATE". You think you're the only Jew disgusted by what he did?

NATHAN. No, but—

"CONSULATE". There are plenty of Jews hanging their heads in shame and remorse over this unforgivable atrocity. But do we go around trying to slander the whole Jewish race?

NATHAN. I'm not trying to—

"CONSULATE". You're out to *prove* something, admit it.

NATHAN. No, I just want to make sure I understand it all.

"CONSULATE". Understand it all? If you want to understand it all, you better do more than read about Hebron. You can't take some isolated event, forget about history, ignore the fact that a month before the massacre, Goldstein watched a close friend of his die at the hands of an Arab terrorist.

NATHAN. The Palestinians are an occupied people.

"CONSULATE". And that gives them the right to *kill Jews*?

NATHAN. I'm not condoning terrorism on either side.

"CONSULATE". Then why pick on the Hebron Massacre? Read *today's* paper. Any more suicide bombings? You ought to be ashamed of yourself, ashamed to call yourself a Jew. What is it with you, why is it every time an Arab dies you run screaming bloody murder, and every time a Jew is killed you call it self-defense. What is wrong with you?

NATHAN. I don't have an answer to that.

CONSULATE. Sorry to keep you waiting. Can I help you?

NATHAN. Yes. I was wondering, is there someone there who could help me get some information about the inquiry that was held recently into the massacre at Hebron.

CONSULATE. Yes, I can help you. What were you looking for?

NATHAN. Oh. Just. Do you have a copy of the report?

CONSULATE. I have a copy of excerpts, in English. You're more than welcome to it. Do you have a fax?

NATHAN. No. Could I pick it up?

"CONSULATE". Certainly. I'll leave it at deception.

NATHAN. Sorry?

CONSULATE. Certainly. I'll leave it at reception. Your name?

NATHAN. My name. Is. Nathan Abramowitz.

"CONSULATE". I *figured* as much. Hey, Lotte.

"LOTTE". Yeah?

"CONSULATE". I got Abramowitz on the line. Don't worry, *Nathan*, we've got a *file* on you. We know who you are, anti-Semite, self-hating Jew…

"LOTTE". *(checking the file)* Kapo.

"CONSULATE". Kapo…

"LOTTE". Sondercommando.

"CONSULATE". Sondercommando…

"LOTTE". Betrayer of your race.

"CONSULATE". Betrayer of your race.

"BOTH". …ASSIMILATIONIST!

NATHAN. What?

"CONSULATE". Married a shiksa didn't you? Two boys, neither one circumcised.

NATHAN. That was for medical reasons!

"CONSULATE". Christmas trees? Easter egg hunts? Are those for medical reasons, too?

NATHAN. I'M STILL A JEW!

CONSULATE. …Alright, Mr. Abramowitz. I'll leave it at reception. When will you pick it up?

NATHAN. Today. Four o'clock?

CONSULATE. We close at three today. It's shabbas.

NATHAN. Of course it is. Yes. Two o'clock then.

CONSULATE. It'll be waiting for you.

He tosses the report to NATHAN.

Judges 2

JUDGE 3. The witness
was a soldier at the Tomb
We heard testimony
that you were stationed by a door
in a passageway
and that as worshippers fled
you fired six or seven shots
into the air

WITNESS 3. We fired not only into the air
but also at the door

JUDGE 3. How many shots
did you fire at the door

WITNESS 3. At least four

JUDGE 3. How high

WITNESS 3. Some were chest high
But no one was hit
by our bullets

JUDGE 3. How can you be certain

WITNESS 3. The worshippers
hadn't reached the door yet
If I'd hit somebody
I'd have seen him fall

JUDGE 3. Why did you fire

WITNESS 3. At first
we thought that a Palestinian was shooting
inside the mosque
and we wanted to stop him from reaching us
They would have trampled us
So we shot at the door
before any of the worshippers got there
We wanted to create a jam at the door
We were afraid that the shooter
if he was an Arab
would come outside and hurt us
We stopped firing
when we saw a wounded man stagger out of the mosque
He was full of blood
We understood
that a Jew was firing inside

not an Arab
and that they were fleeing for their lives

JUDGE 4. The witness
was in the Jewish prayer area
Can you describe what you heard

WITNESS 4. I heard several closely-spaced bursts of gunfire
The bursts sounded like they were coming
from the same weapon
We
the Jewish worshippers
took cover
We were afraid of an Arab attack
or fighting among the Muslems
Some of us fled
But the army told us to go back
So we went back
and continued our services

JUDGE 4. You continued your prayers

WITNESS 4. Yes
For an hour
It was Purim
after all

JUDGE 4. Did you
or any of the others
know
what had happened in the mosque area

WITNESS 4. No
I didn't
When I got back home
I heard what had happened on the radio

JUDGE 4. Thank you

WITNESS 4. May I say
that I am grateful
that no other Jews were hurt
in the incident

JUDGE 4. No other Jews

WITNESS 4. In addition to Dr. Goldstein
Thank God
it all ended well

Hi Mom

The telephone rings.

NATHAN. Hello?

MOM. Hello, darling.

NATHAN. Hi, Mom.

MOM. What's doing?

NATHAN. Same as yesterday when you called.

MOM. So: what time you coming Tuesday?

NATHAN. Tuesday?

MOM. Passover. You forget or something?

NATHAN. No.

MOM. I want to sit by seven.

NATHAN. Alright.

MOM. So you'll come when?

NATHAN. Seven?

MOM. So late?

NATHAN. Six-thirty?

MOM. Your cousin Jan's gonna be here.

NATHAN. Jan…

MOM. From Israel. With Lev.

NATHAN. Who?

MOM. Her husband. They're very anxious to talk to you.

NATHAN. Oh?

MOM. They know how interested you are in Israel.

NATHAN. Uh huh.

MOM. So come a little early.

NATHAN. What are they um… anxious about?

MOM. They didn't… they just… they want to talk to you.

"LEV". You got no right to say ONE WORD about ISRAEL!

"JAN". Lev, please…

"LEV". NEVER MIND "Lev please." You think we need your lousy money? Mr. Big Shot North American Jew.

"JAN". Don't make trouble.

"LEV". Who's making trouble, I'm talking. You try living with Hezbollah rockets landing in your backyard, wondering are your children going to be blown up.

We're building a country here for the Jewish people and the day you make aliyah is the day you'll be a Jew, and not before.

NATHAN. Alright, I'll come up at six.

MOM. Don't do me any favours.

NATHAN. Mom...

MOM. I wouldn't mind a little help setting up.

NATHAN. Five-thirty.

MOM. We got 15 people coming.

NATHAN. Five o'clock.

MOM. The way my back's feeling, I don't think I'm gonna be able to stand long...

NATHAN. Uh huh.

MOM. ...make the matzah balls...

NATHAN. Yeah.

MOM. ...carve the brisket...

NATHAN. Mmhm.

MOM. ...vacuum.

NATHAN. Why don't I come up Monday and sleep over?

MOM. Alright.

NATHAN. I'm kidding, Mother. Okay, look. I'll come up at four.

MOM. Four...

NATHAN. I'm working next Tuesday.

MOM. You're gonna work Yontif?

NATHAN. 'Scuse me. (*silent scream*) Mom. The office closes at three. I'll be up at four.

MOM. Fine. Are you bringing the boys?

NATHAN. I don't think so.

MOM. Why not?

NATHAN. It's better this way.

MOM. Mm. Well, it's up to you.

NATHAN. I gotta go.

MOM. If it was up to me.

NATHAN. I really gotta go. Goodbye.

MOM. Goodbye.

They hang up.

Judges 3

JUDGE 5. The witness
　　was at prayer in the mosque
　　What can you tell us about the attack

WITNESS 5. It began with an explosion that shook the hall
　　Then there was gunfire
　　and another blast
　　We heard more than one source of shooting

JUDGE 5. In your earlier statement
　　to investigators
　　following the massacre
　　you made no mention
　　of multiple sources of gunfire

WITNESS 5. When Goldstein took out an empty clip
　　firing continued
　　from another source

JUDGE 5. Did you in fact see a second shooter

WITNESS 5. No
　　I was shot
　　I was lying on the floor
　　waiting to be carried out
　　Also the overhead lights had been shot out
　　so the room was in darkness
　　People were trying to get out
　　some wounded
　　others
　　carrying the bodies of the dead
　　They reached the passageway
　　screaming for help
　　trying to pull soldiers inside
　　to help the wounded and dying
　　When I was carried out
　　there was shooting
　　from many directions
　　from many sides

JUDGE 6. The witness
　　was in the women's section of the mosque

WITNESS 6. When I got out of the women's section
　　I tried to get into the room
　　where the massacre had taken place
　　I could see the three soldiers by the door

with their guns
I could not get into the mosque
There were too many people
Suddenly
I heard gunfire
and I saw one of the soldiers
firing at the people
I saw one man
run toward a soldier
and yell
"God is great"
The soldier shot him

JUDGE 6. That is all

WITNESS 6. I want to say
something else
There are
half a million Arabs
in the Hebron area
Either they will have to go
to the Arab states
or the troublemakers
the settlers
will have to be moved out

JUDGE 6. Thank you

WITNESS 6. I hope the commission
will be neutral
and that it will achieve
positive results

Palestine House

NATHAN makes a telephone call.

RANDA. Palestine House.

NATHAN. Yes. Hello. Is that Palestine House?

RANDA. Yes.

NATHAN. Good. Um. Do you have a library or a resource centre of any kind?

RANDA. We have a small library, yes.

NATHAN. Good. Because I'm looking for documents related to the… Hebron Massacre? Have, have you heard of the Hebron Massacre?

"RANDA". Of course. What do you know about it?

NATHAN. Well. Just what I've read.

"RANDA". Precisely. What you've read. You have no experience with our situation. You would shit your pants if you ever had to leave the comfort of your cozy world and live amongst us.

NATHAN. I don't deny that for a second. The point is…

"RANDA". The point is that for you, it's an intellectual pursuit. "The effect of the massacre on the soul of the Jewish people. How could a Jew commit this stain upon us?" To think that a Jew, who is essentially a good person, could commit such a crime. Now an Arab, well, naturally, an Arab, who is essentially a violent person, would do this. But a Jew?

NATHAN. No. Look. You've got this all wrong. What I'm saying is, let's not whitewash the Hebron Massacre, let's not write it off as another action of a deranged madman, but look at it as proof of Jewish racism, and and and deal with that, I mean, let's take a good hard look at ourselves for once, and drop the rhetoric and the bullshit and for once, for once leave the Holocaust out of it and say, "Look, a great injustice has been done, we took another people's land, we have become the oppressor, we have murdered, we have tortured, we have lied, and it is time to DO SOMETHING ABOUT IT."

RANDA applauds. The others join in.

NATHAN. Thank you. Thank you. No. No, please.

"RANDA". Nathan Abramowitz, ladies and gentlemen!

NATHAN. Thank you. No, no, thank *you.*

"RANDA". Nathan Abramowitz! Saviour of the Palestinian people!

NATHAN. Alright.

"RANDA". You see, Nathan, you are not truly interested in the plight of the Palestinian people. We are merely a pet project; you think you are a humanist, that you believe in justice for the underdog, so you point fingers in the direction of a land to which you have never been, and you say "That is no way to act." And this, despite the fact that you would act no differently if it were you.

NATHAN. That's not true.

"RANDA". Isn't it? The revolution begins in your own home, Nathan. Do you treat those around you with respect and dignity?

NATHAN. So let me see if I got this straight. You have no reports or documents or…

RANDA. We only have a small library here. Have you tried the Metro Reference?

NATHAN. Metro Reference.

RANDA. Or the Israeli Consulate?

NATHAN. Uhh…

"RANDA". Why don't you try them. You see we're just a welcome house for terrorists.

NATHAN. Sorry?

RANDA. I say, we're just a welcome house for immigrants. So we don't really have anything about the Hebron Massacre here.

NATHAN. Yeah. Well, that's typical. You know how hard it is for me to find Palestinian literature? You know, you people have to do a better job of getting the message out.

"RANDA". I know, but we are so stupid.

NATHAN. Apparently.

"RANDA". And badly organized.

NATHAN. This too is true.

"RANDA". All we know how to do is blow up buses. I don't know why we don't just go and live in Jordan. That is our country. But no. We stay. We want to spend our lives making bombs and living in squalid refugee camps, with shit and piss running through the streets. We are cowards; we are not to be trusted; we stink; we are ugly; we don't even exist, really. Why, if it were not for the work of good people like you, we would disappear altogether. I say, "Thank Allah for people like Nathan, without whom the Palestinian people would be helpless. We are so grateful to you, Nathan, for wanting to help us."

> *Pause.*

NATHAN. Thanks, I… thanks.

RANDA. Sorry I can't be of more help. Why don't you leave me your name and number and if I find anything I'll—

NATHAN. No, that's okay, thanks. I'll try the library.

> *He hangs up.*

Judges 4

JUDGE 7. The witness
   is a senior noncommissioned officer in Hebron
   What did you understand your orders to be
   regarding shooting at settlers

WITNESS 7. My orders were never to fire at a settler
   even if he is shooting at other people

JUDGE 7. What would happen
   if you saw a settler
   shooting a woman

a child
a civilian

WITNESS 7. It depends on the situation
If I had seen him shooting
one or two shots at someone
I wouldn't have shot to kill him
immediately
But if it was a
massacre
or something
it depends
The directive says not to shoot

JUDGE 7. Even if you see that it is a massacre

WITNESS 7. Even if I see that it is a massacre
the directive of the brigade commander
is not to shoot

JUDGE 7. What do you think of this directive

WITNESS 7. I find it
surprising

JUDGE 8. The witness
was West Bank commander in 1992 and '93
We have heard from several witnesses
that Israeli forces in the West Bank
have standing orders not to fire at settlers
even if they are shooting at Palestinians or troops

WITNESS 8. On the question of firing at Jews
in connection with disturbances
the answer was perfectly clear
It discriminated between
Jews and Arabs
Absolutely clear discrimination
which is also understandable
Arab riots often endangered soldiers' lives
so they were allowed to fire
in some cases
Regarding Jews
of course there is discrimination
Even in the most serious confrontations
between soldiers and Jews
it did not occur to anyone
I hope
that a Jew would even injure a Jewish soldier
So in cases of disturbances

there was an absolute prohibition to open fire
Even shooting tear gas
to disperse a Jewish demonstration
required the approval of the division commander

JUDGE 8. What if a soldier
were to see
a settler firing

WITNESS 8. Army orders
were that the soldier was not to shoot
because the natural situation
is that a Jew is defending himself
against Arab attack
No-shoot orders did not apply
by the way
to murderous Jewish assaults

JUDGE 8. Is it possible
that the orders were interpreted
in that way by soldiers

WITNESS 8. It should be clear to soldiers
that they must open fire
if necessary
to prevent life-threatening crimes
However
no such directive was drawn up for such situations
because nothing like this massacre
could have been anticipated

Nathan at Work

*NATHAN is now at his office job. The first two times the BOSS calls for
NATHAN can be overlapped with WITNESS 8's last speech.*

BOSS. Nathan. Nathan. Hey, Nathan.

NATHAN. Huh?

BOSS. You still here?

NATHAN. No. I'm a hologram.

She laughs.

BOSS. The office is closed.

NATHAN. Right. I just, uh, I wanted to type up those minutes for ya.

BOSS. Forget about the minutes.

NATHAN. Tomorrow's my last day.

BOSS. Forget about the minutes.

Pause.

BOSS. Lemme ask you something. I mean, do you mind…?

NATHAN. No, no.

BOSS. Well. You're Jewish, right?

NATHAN. Right.

BOSS. What are you doing for Passover?

NATHAN. I'll, I'm going to my mom's house for dinner.

BOSS. Oh yeah? That's nice.

NATHAN. Yeah.

BOSS. Yeah.

NATHAN. Yeah yeah… well, goodnight

BOSS. Nathan.

NATHAN. Uh huh?

BOSS. I was wondering if. Well. You do good work. You're punctual and pleasant and everybody around here seems to like you.

NATHAN. I hardly know what to say.

BOSS. You came in, you told a joke or two. Really lifted the place up.

NATHAN. I'm blushing all over.

BOSS. All over?

NATHAN. Tick tock.

BOSS. What I'm getting at is this: how'd you like to stay on, full time? A regular salary. Bonuses. The whole schmeer.

NATHAN. I don't think so.

BOSS. Are you telling me you'd rather temp all your life? Go from one job to the next, never settle?

NATHAN. I don't like staying in one place too long.

BOSS. Why's that?

NATHAN. I'm sensitive to smells.

BOSS. So what are you gonna do?

NATHAN. I don't know. Travel.

BOSS. Really? Where to?

NATHAN. Israel.

BOSS. I love Israel. Oh my God, so much history.

NATHAN. So I've heard.

BOSS. And the people. They really, they know who they *are,* you know? So confident. They really live in the moment, you know? Nathan?

NATHAN. Mm?

BOSS. You ever been?

NATHAN. To Isra—no.

BOSS. Hold old are you, Nathan?

NATHAN. Early thirties, I'd say.

BOSS. Uh huh. Married?

NATHAN. I think I was.

BOSS. I don't get you.

NATHAN. Me neither. I should go now.

BOSS. Nathan. What is it? What's on your mind?

NATHAN. It's hard to pin down. Oh wait, I remember now. Endless human suffering. Gets me right here. I'm torn between wanting to change the world and wanting to blow it up.

BOSS. What are you gonna do about it?

NATHAN. Worry.

BOSS. And?

NATHAN. Complain.

BOSS. What are you doing tonight?

NATHAN. Tonight? Going to bed.

BOSS. And after that?

NATHAN. Waking up. Going to bed. Waking up. It's endless.

BOSS. Nathan. My home number. *(stuffing a piece of paper into NATHAN's shirt pocket)* Call me if you get lonely.

> *BOSS exits.*

NATHAN. *Get?*

The Library

> *NATHAN goes to the Metro Reference Library.*

JANE. Can I help you?

NATHAN. Yes, I was wondering if—

> *The telephone rings.*

JANE. 'Scuse me.

Metro Reference.... You want the history department, I'll put you through. *(to NATHAN)* Can I help you?

NATHAN. Yes, I was wondering if you could tell me—

The telephone rings.

JANE. Metro Reference... thirteen. Okay. *(to NATHAN)* Can I help you?

NATHAN. Yes, I was wondering if you could tell me why the Hebron Massacre is different from all other massacres.

JANE. ...The what.

NATHAN. The Hebron Massacre.

JANE. Spell it.

NATHAN. Uh. N-A-T-H-

JANE. What?

NATHAN. Oh. Sorry. H-E-B-

The telephone rings.

JANE. Metro Reference... what?... no we don't. *(She hangs up.)*

"JANE". *(taking an interest in NATHAN)* Hi.... Can I... help you?

NATHAN. Yes. I'm looking for information about the Hebron Massacre.

"JANE". Oh. You interested in...?

NATHAN. Well I'm. I've been following it in the papers...

"JANE". *Papers...*

NATHAN. Yeah, *The New York Times* had—

"JANE". *New York Times,* are you kidding, that lapdog of the rich and powerful, for*get* it, if you want the *real* story, you have to get your hands on as much information as you can. You have to dig *deep.*

NATHAN. I already *have* a lot of information. I just, I feel like there's something I'm not *getting.*

"JANE". Have you read Edward Said?

NATHAN. No.

"JANE". Oh, you have to. *The Question of Palestine?* Brilliant insights into the nature of Palestinian identity.

SAID. *(appearing out of nowhere)* Please, you flatter me.

"JANE". Professor Said. May I introduce...

NATHAN. Nathan Abramowitz. Pleasure to meet you, sir.

SAID. Not at all.

"JANE". Nathan's looking for information on the Hebron Massacre.

318 • *Modern Jewish Plays*

SAID. I see. Well. I was not surprised by it. I visited Hebron two years before the massacre, and was shocked to find, even then, heavily armed Israeli soldiers inside the mosque. I felt that a Muslim holy place had been violated, deliberately, and that Hebron was simply waiting to explode.

NATHAN. I'm so glad to talk to you. I've been trying to get the Arab…

JANE. Ahem.

NATHAN. I mean Palestinian, point of view. But I haven't had much luck.

SAID. Of course not. Arabic literature is heavily censored in the democratic West; as for Palestinian writing, well, I'm afraid we haven't done a very good job of creating our own narrative.

"JANE". Why don't you ask Professor Said a question?

NATHAN. Professor Said, if and when you are invited to speak to Jewish audiences, what will you tell them about the future of Jews in Palestine?

SAID. My goodness—what a powerful question that is! It is very difficult for me to talk about the future of another people, which feels itself, for the most part, to be so different from the Arab Palestinians. But the Palestinian experience is a struggle to achieve a mode of coexistence. Over the last generation a strong bond has been formed between the Israeli and the Palestinian on the basis of fear.

ASHWARI. I think the Israelis have allowed themselves to fall victim to the psychology of the occupier, where you study the occupied only for the purposes of domination and control.

"JANE". Nathan, may I introduce Hanan Ashwari, Minister of Education for the Palestinian Authority.

NATHAN. Ms. Ashwari.

"JANE". Oh, and you should read *The Fateful Triangle*.

SAID & ASHWARI. Ahh…. Chomsky.

"JANE". And there's an interview with Yeshayahu Leibowitz in *Tikkun*…. Mr. Leibowitz won the Israel Prize, "for a lifetime of original thought and social criticism," but he turned it *down*.

LEIBOWITZ. The reasons were personal, not ideological. I was fed up with the uproar. People were upset about my positions.

"JANE". Tell him.

LEIBOWITZ. Israel is going through a Nazification process. The problem we face is that there are many people who are enamoured of being Jewish, of their Jewishness—but for them this has no connection with Judaism. So this becomes a nationalism that quickly falls into idolatry and self-deception. Israel is not a state of Judaism—it is simply a secular state whose problems have nothing to do with Judaism.

The telephone rings; JANE goes to get it.

NATHAN. Wait. Don't answer that.

"JANE". Why not?

NATHAN. I need some answers.

"JANE". There are no answers, Nathan. Only positions. What's yours? *(They all stare at NATHAN, waiting for an answer; the telephone rings.)* Metro Reference… let me check. Can I help you?

Mr. Big

The scene switches to the office of MR. BIG (in fact, a loan officer at NATHAN's bank). For the switch JANE can hand the library telephone to the actor playing LEIBOWITZ, who then becomes MR. BIG. NATHAN's first line is then in response to JANE's last line.

NATHAN. I'm here to see Mr. Big.

SECRETARY. I'll see if he's in.

NATHAN. Never mind, sister.

SECRETARY. Hey! Stop! You can't go in there! Security!

> *NATHAN bursts in on MR. BIG, who's on the telephone, chomping on a cigar.*

NATHAN. Put the telephone down.

MR. BIG. *(into the telephone)* Hold on a second, will you Bill?

SECRETARY. I'm sorry, Mr. Big, he just walked right past me.

NATHAN. I said put the phone down, now.

MR. BIG. It's alright, Lotte. I've been expecting you, Nathan.

NATHAN. Expecting me?

MR. BIG. Have a seat. Go back to your desk, Lotte.

> *She exits.*

Nathan, please. Sit. I'll be right with you.

> *NATHAN sits; MR. BIG returns to his telephone call.*

Mr. President? Listen, I have to go, I've got Abramowitz here… that's right… that's right… oh don't you worry about that… a ha ha ha… you just worry about those loan guarantees… uh huh… well, if you think losing Israel as a strategic ally is… then you know what to do… alright… I'll wait for your call. Love to Chelsea.

> *He hangs up.*

Drink?

NATHAN. No thanks.

MR. BIG. I'm surprised it took you this long to find me.

NATHAN. It wasn't easy. I had to read *The Fateful Triangle*.

MR. BIG. Ah…. Chomsky.

NATHAN. Israel, the United States and the Palestinians: the fateful triangle.

MR. BIG. Yes, I've read it. Let me see: Israel is a client state of the U.S.; they have a symbiotic relationship—Israel gives the U.S. a strategic presence in the Middle East, originally as a buffer against Soviet aggression, later to stem the tide of Islamic terrorism; the U.S., in return, pours billions of dollars of military and economic aid into Israel and protects it from international censure; thus, U.S. interests are served, Israel self-destructs and the Palestinians get it in the neck. That about it?

NATHAN. A little simplistic, but…

MR. BIG. But essentially, that's it?

NATHAN. Yes.

MR. BIG. And since the government of the United States is nothing more than a puppet regime for those who own the country—General Motors and the like—the Middle East situation is the result of market forces too complex for most people to understand.

NATHAN. They'd understand it if the media had the guts to point it out once in a while.

MR. BIG. Oh sure, sure kid, the media, yeah, I-I-I forgot, they're all part of this, too. But ultimately, the bloodshed is the result of the Chairman of General Motors serving the needs of his stockholders.

NATHAN. Damn right.

MR. BIG. The Israelis, the Palestinians, they're all pawns in the game.

NATHAN. Precisely.

MR. BIG. Well. You have connected the dots quite thoroughly. There's only one dot you've left out.

NATHAN. Oh?

MR. BIG. Yours. After all, you have a decent life.

NATHAN. Some would say.

MR. BIG. You seem to work fairly regularly.

NATHAN. Often as I can.

MR. BIG. You support two children.

NATHAN. I do.

MR. BIG. Yet you have no stocks or bonds.

NATHAN. None.

MR. BIG. RRSP?

NATHAN. Negligible.

MR. BIG. Mutual funds?

NATHAN. Morally opposed.

MR. BIG. Short term investments.

NATHAN. Zip.

MR. BIG. I see.

NATHAN. You see?

The telephone rings.

MR. BIG. Yes?

SECRETARY. David Frum on two.

MR. BIG. Take a message. Still, you have all the necessities.

NATHAN. True.

MR. BIG. A standard of living most of the world envies.

NATHAN. A standard of living made possible by exploiting most of the world.

MR. BIG. I suppose you'd be happy in a shack. Guilt, Nathan. That's all it is. You
  know, I don't think we're all that different, you and I.

NATHAN. Except I'm sitting on this side of the desk and you're sitting on that side
  of it.

MR. BIG. Would you like to sit on this side?... Please. Just for a moment.

They switch seats.

How's that feel?

NATHAN. Not so bad.

MR. BIG. You're in control now, Nathan. Go ahead. Fix it. Give the world
  a makeover. What are you gonna do first?

NATHAN. Redistribute the wealth.

MR. BIG. Good.

NATHAN. End corporate welfare.

MR. BIG. Uh huh.

NATHAN. Establish a Palestinian homeland.

MR. BIG. Of course.

NATHAN. And Native self-government.

MR. BIG. Why not hand the whole country back to the Indians? After all, we stole
  it from them, herded them into camps, infected them with diseases, destroyed
  their culture, reduced them to streetcorner drunks.

NATHAN. Now you're talking.

MR. BIG. Fine. Well. That's it then.

NATHAN. What a day.

MR. BIG. There's just one more thing you ought to do.

NATHAN. Uh huh.

MR. BIG. Change human nature. Take away our awareness of death. Our instincts for envy, hate, greed, revenge, power.... Go on, Nathan. Rage against the machine. Sign a petition. Go on a march. Get yourself a foster child. Listen. The day you walk in here ready to acknowledge that you are motivated by your very real fear of being alone, and not by some vague hope for solidarity, that is the day I will break bread with you. On that day, I will call you friend. And give you anything you ask for. Anything else, Mr. Abramowitz?

> *MR. BIG becomes the loan officer at this point—his cigar now a fountain pen—as NATHAN snaps back to reality.*

Mr. Abramowitz?

NATHAN. No.

MR. BIG. It's not that I don't *want* to extend your line of credit.

NATHAN. It's just a thousand dollars.

MR. BIG. I understand that but, Mr. Abramowitz, look at it from where I'm sitting. You haven't held a steady job in five years. You have no assets.

NATHAN. There are no steady jobs, Mr. Loan Officer. I'm doing the best I can. I temp.

MR. BIG. It's unpredictable.

NATHAN. So's life.

MR. BIG. Pardon?

NATHAN. For example.

> *NATHAN strangles the loan officer.*

Die. Die. Die.

MR. BIG. I'm afraid I can't do that.

> *NATHAN leaves.*

Israel's Books

> *NATHAN goes to a Jewish bookstore.*

CLERK. Can I help you find something?

NATHAN. Yes. I'm looking for anything to do with the Hebron Massacre.

CLERK. Which one?

NATHAN. Which... one?

CLERK. There've been so many. In 1929, the Arabs murdered 60 Jews.

NATHAN. I was thinking about 1994.

CLERK. Of course you were. Well. There aren't any books that deal specifically *with* that. Amos Oz wrote an essay about it, and there are a couple of others that mention it in passing.

NATHAN. Alright.

CLERK. That's the problem with Israel. You talk about one event, you wake up the next day, they're onto something else

NATHAN. *Plus ça change.*

CLERK. If you're interested in the wider context of the Palestinian question, I could recommend a few titles.

NATHAN. Sure.

> *The telephone rings.*

CLERK. One second. *(picking up)* Israel's Books and Tapes.... Lotte? Just a second... *(to NATHAN)* I'll just be a minute, why don't you have a look around... *(into telephone—this continues under following, diminishing in volume until it fades right out; as he speaks, the CONSPIRATOR enters, loaded down with books)* Well I just talked to him... I don't know what he's looking for... he seems very confused... uh huh... and the children?... what, he's going to turn them against us, too?... it's terrible...

CONSPIRATOR. Pssst.

NATHAN. Hm?

CONSPIRATOR. You interested in Hebron?

NATHAN. Yeah, I—

CONSPIRATOR. Keep your voice down.

NATHAN. Yes. I'm interested.

CONSPIRATOR. I happen to know a thing or two about it.

NATHAN. Uh huh.

CONSPIRATOR. Come over here... you can't be too careful. You hear about Yayha?

NATHAN. Who?

CONSPIRATOR. *Yayha.* From Hamas. The one who planned the suicide bombings. Mossad got him. Blew his head off. With a cell phone.

> *He has a big laugh as he looks around the room.*

They can get you anywhere. Now listen. This Hebron thing. You don't understand.

NATHAN. I know, I'm trying—

CONSPIRATOR. Shhh. Listen. It's bigger than Hebron. Goldstein, he's nothing you understand? He's like the Watergate plumbers. The inquiry, the judges, they're going to pass him off as a madman. If you ask me, it's the judges who are crazy, if they—

A customer passes by.

IF THEY THINK THE LEAFS ARE GOIN' *ANYWHERE* THIS YEAR THEY'RE CRAZY. THEY'RE NUTS THEY'RE...

The customer has left.

The settlers think they're following their destiny as laid out in the Bible.

NATHAN. That's why they call the West Bank Judea and Samaria.

CONSPIRATOR. Ten points, bubbie. For them everything has biblical significance. They're fighting a holy war. See? It's not political; these fuckers are serious. They think the West Bank is theirs from thousands of years ago. And it's not just the settlers. This goes back to Ben Gurion. The Zionist dream was to reclaim all the of ancient Israel. The Israelis don't care that they've displaced the Palestinians. As far as they're concerned, the Palestinians were never there. Golda Meir said, "they did not exist."

The customer who passed by earlier, who has been looking at NATHAN, turns out to be cousin JAN.

JAN. Nathan?

CONSPIRATOR disappears behind a bookcase.

Oh my God! Lev! Lev, it's Nathan.

LEV. *(emerging from behind the bookcase; awkwardly)* Hello.

JAN. You don't remember me? What's my name? What's my name? Cousin...

NATHAN. Cousin...

NATHAN & JAN. Jaaaaaan!

JAN. Nathan, this is my Lev, my husband.

Pause.

LEV. We hear so much about you.

Pause.

JAN. Well, we have to run.

NATHAN. Me too.

LEV. I'll bring the... the... *(indicates car)*

He exits behind the bookcase.

JAN. We'll see you at your mom's?

NATHAN. Absolutely.

> *She exits. CONSPIRATOR reappears.*

CONSPIRATOR. "Cockroaches," that's what Sharon called them. "Two-legged beasts." "Palestinian" is synonymous with "terrorist." All Goldstein's doing is carrying the policies of Israel to their logical conclusion. And those of us who watch it happen are as guilty as Goldstein, because we're allowing it to happen.

NATHAN. What can we do?

CONSPIRATOR. That depends. Are you prepared to be called an anti-Semite? That's how they get you.

NATHAN. I'm ready.

CONSPIRATOR. Alright.

> *The CLERK has snuck up behind them.*

Don't look at me. Look ahead. They're watching us.

NATHAN. Who?

CONSPIRATOR. Mossad, schmuck.

NATHAN. Where?

CONSPIRATOR. Look ahead. Laugh. Ha ha ha.

NATHAN. Ha ha.

CONSPIRATOR. Now. What's the root word of Hebron?

NATHAN. Um um um

CONSPIRATOR. Haver.

NATHAN. Haver.

CONSPIRATOR. Haver. And what did Clinton say on hearing of the death of Rabin?

NATHAN. Um um um.

CLERK. Shalom Haver.

CONSPIRATOR. So Shalom Haver means?

NATHAN. Hello Hebron.

CONSPIRATOR. Or?

NATHAN. Peace Hebron.

CONSPIRATOR. Or?

NATHAN. Goodbye Hebron.

CONSPIRATOR. Exactly!

NATHAN. Goodbye Hebron!

CONSPIRATOR. Now—who signed the Oslo Accord?

NATHAN. Arafat.

CONSPIRATOR. And?

NATHAN. Rabin.

CONSPIRATOR. Good. And the Accord calls for Israel to pull out of Palestinian towns, right?

NATHAN. Right.

CONSPIRATOR. And what's the last town from which the army was to pull out?

NATHAN. Hebron.

CONSPIRATOR. Right again. And who stalled that pullout? Don't look at me!

NATHAN. Sorry!

CONSPIRATOR. Laugh.

NATHAN. Ha ha.

CONSPIRATOR. Well?

NATHAN. Netanyahu.

CONSPIRATOR. Good. And what is his nickname?

NATHAN. Bibi.

CONSPIRATOR. And what do you think of when you think of the word "bibi"?

NATHAN. A gun?

CONSPIRATOR. Exactly! You see! It all fits! You must take a gun, go to Hebron and kill Benjamin Netanyahu. Only then will there be peace. Go, Nathan. Kill Netanyahu.

The CLERK grabs the CONSPIRATOR from behind.

CLERK. One more word and you die. You feel that? One more word and I shoot you through your self-hating Jewish heart.

CONSPIRATOR. It's up to you now, Na—

CLERK. I said shut up. Let's go. You first. Nice... and slow, see... that's... the way to do it... nice... and slow.

They exit. The CLERK returns.

Did you find what you were looking for?

NATHAN. Uh huh.

CLERK. (*looking at the books NATHAN picked up*) Israel: A Colonial-Settler State. A classic in the field. *Zealots for Zion.* Very revealing. *Chronicles of Dissent.* Ah. Chomsky. A brilliant man. But between you and me? Self-hating Jew.

NATHAN. Thanks. I'll take 'em.

Moral Equivalence

NATHAN returns to his apartment, with an armful of books and magazines. The telephone is ringing.

NATHAN. Hello?

EX-WIFE. It's me. Your ex-wife.

NATHAN. Yes?

EX-WIFE. Not that I'm desperate to speak with you.

NATHAN. Uh huh.

EX-WIFE. But if you could return just one of my phone calls.

NATHAN. I've been a little busy.

EX-WIFE. With what?

NATHAN. Things.

EX-WIFE. Things, right, and I guess these "things" are more important than Ben and Andrew.

NATHAN. What are you talking about…

EX-WIFE. I'm talking about…

NATHAN. …they were just here.

EX-WIFE. Yeah, watching cartoons.

NATHAN. They watched "Pinocchio" a couple times, what's—

EX-WIFE. Uh huh.

NATHAN. What's wrong with that?

EX-WIFE. Nathan, you've—

NATHAN. What is wrong with *that?*

EX-WIFE. You've got to spend time with them.

NATHAN. I.

EX-WIFE. You want them to grow up without knowing you?

NATHAN. Look—*no.*

EX-WIFE. Then?

NATHAN. I can't talk about this right now.

EX-WIFE. You can never talk about *this* right now. You think just because you moved out it's all gonna go away?

NATHAN. That was the plan, yes.

EX-WIFE. You can't pretend I don't exist. I mean we lived together a long time, Nathan. We had kids together for Christ's sake.

ASHWARI enters. In the first production, she entered at an upstage window.

ASHWARI. Think of the terrible effect this is having on our children.

NATHAN. Don't *use* the kids, *please.*

ASHWARI. They suffer. I begin to feel responsible for all the children killed by the Israelis.

NATHAN. Okay, look. I'll spend more time with them.

EX-WIFE. That's all I'm asking. You going to your mom's tomorrow?

NATHAN. Yeah.

EX-WIFE. Say hi to everyone.

NATHAN. Will do.

EX-WIFE. I'm gonna miss it this year.

NATHAN. Goodbye.

He hangs up; starts sorting through the material he's picked up on his travels—there should be an overwhelming amount it. After a while:

Step up to the microphone, please. State your name.

As he flips through the books and magazines, people appear out of nowhere. Stars of David are lit against the back wall, and gaudy music— a bar-mitzvah band's "Hava Nagila", perhaps—plays throughout. Or not.

LERNER. Michael Lerner.

NATHAN. And what do you do?

LERNER. I'm a writer. I edit a magazine called *Tikkun,* which is a journal of opinion on Jewish uhh matters.

NATHAN. A left-wing journal, would it be safe to say?

LERNER. Left-wing, yes, alright.

NATHAN. Alright, Mr. Lerner, and you have something to say about the Hebron Massacre?

LERNER. Yes. Yes, I do.

NATHAN. Alright. And the title of your speech?

LERNER. Is "Disarm the West Bank Settlers."

NATHAN. You'll be judged on originality, economy of language and humour. You'll have thirty seconds to make your points. At the twenty-five second mark, you'll hear this sound *(He imitates the sound of a bomb whistling to its mark.)* at which point you'll be asked to wrap up. If you exceed the five-second mark, you'll hear this *(The bomb explodes.)* at which point you'll have to stop. Alright?

LERNER. Got it.

NATHAN. Michael Lerner, with "Disarm the West Bank Settlers." Thirty seconds, starting... now.

LERNER. *(quickly)* The murder of more than 40 Palestinians at Ramadan prayer in a mosque in the West Bank town of Hebron yesterday cannot be dismissed as the action of a psychopath and nothing more. Yes, Dr. Baruch Goldstein, a religiously observant Yeshiva University graduate who was armed with an automatic rifle, was crazy. But his craziness mirrors a climate of hatred nurtured by right-wing Jews who, raised on a steady diet of Holocaust stories and anti-Arab racism, are determined to show that Jews can be powerful— even if that power can be exercised only against an unarmed and essentially defenseless Palestinian population. North American—

The sound of a whistling bomb.

NATHAN. Five seconds.

LERNER. North American Jews who wish to dissociate themselves from the extremists must insist that the Israeli Army disarm all West Bank and Gaza settlers.

NATHAN. Well done, Michael Lerner. We'll see you again for the quick-fire round at the end of the show. Next speaker, step up to the mike. Your name?

ROSENTHAL. A.M. Rosenthal.

NATHAN. A.M.? Does that mean you're a morning person?

ROSENTHAL. What?

NATHAN. A morning.... Never mind. What do you do, sir?

ROSENTHAL. I'm a columnist with *The New York Times.*

NATHAN. Very good.

ROSENTHAL. I used to edit *The New York Times.*

NATHAN. Alright, and you've got a thing or two to say about the Hebron Massacre.

ROSENTHAL. Damned right I do.

NATHAN. Alright, and the title of your speech?

ROSENTHAL. It's called "The Worth of Israel."

NATHAN. "The Worth."

ROSENTHAL. "The Worth of Israel."

NATHAN. Very good. You heard the rules?

ROSENTHAL. Uh? Yeah, I heard.

NATHAN. Alright, then, A.M. Rosenthal of *The New York Times,* you've got thirty seconds, starting... now.

ROSENTHAL. *(taking his time)* Baruch Goldstein committed a monstrous act of terrorism that cannot be softened by talk of his rage. But Israelis denounced the crime; some even saw it as a time for national contrition. After the massacre, the President of Israel went to Hebron to bow his head. And now, it is healthy and wise to ask some questions. When Pan Am 103 was bombed out of the sky, did Arab states immediately begin an investigation?

Whistling bomb.

NATHAN. Wrap it up, please.

ROSENTHAL. When 22 Jews in an Istanbul synagogue were murdered at prayer—

Explosion.

Damn.

NATHAN. I'm sorry, Mr. Rosenthal. Would our last speaker step up to the mike. Your name?

OZICK. Cynthia Ozick.

NATHAN. And you are?

OZICK. A writer and critic. I mainly work in prose, but right now I'm working on a play.

NATHAN. A play.

OZICK. Yes.

NATHAN. Can you tell us a bit about it?

OZICK. Well, it's about denial of the Holocaust.

NATHAN. Very good, very good. Oughta do well for you. You can't really go wrong with the Holocaust. There's no business like Shoah business. Isn't that right, Mr. Spielberg?

SPIELBERG. I'd like to thank the Academy for this award. It means a lot to me. I owe so many thanks to so many people, but there's one man in particular without whom this picture could never have been made.

NATHAN. Hitler. Alright, where were we?

OZICK. Over here, tatala.

NATHAN. Alright, Ms. Ozick, and what is the name of your speech?

OZICK. "Mutual Sorrow, Mutual Gain."

NATHAN. "Mutual Sorrow, Mutual Gain," very nice, very nice. Alright, then, Cynthia Ozick, writer, critic and, what the hell, playwright, you have thirty seconds to talk about the Hebron Massacre, starting... now.

OZICK. *(very quickly)* Always and always, the deaths of Jews and Arabs are paired. To pair murders is to count heads, and to count heads is to quantify killing, and to quantify killing is to denigrate the sacred meaning of a single human life. The idea of "extremists on both sides" leads to that tired old sleight-of-hand known as moral equivalence. Suddenly the mathematics of atrocity is back in place. Here is a massacre, by a Jew, of Arabs. Here are the murders, by Arabs, of Jewish employers, a Jewish father and son in Hebron, a pregnant Jewish housewife. If there is to be an equality of blame—

Whistling bomb.

NATHAN. Five seconds.

OZICK. —shouldn't there also be an equality of contrition? Consider the power of contrition alone, as a primary assertion of effective leadership.

Explosion.

OZICK. I mean the political power of sorrow, shame and grief.

NATHAN. Ms. Ozick...

OZICK. What needs to be paired are not criminal acts of murder—

NATHAN. Ms. Ozick, I'm afraid your time...

OZICK. —shut up—

NATHAN. You've exceeded your—

OZICK. ...but demonstrations of contrition. Mutual contrition is above all a political act, and it is the right way back.

NATHAN. Alright, Ms. Ozick. You went far past your allotted time, and so we're going to have to allow for rebuttal. Would anyone in the audience care to rebut Ms. Ozick's position? Anyone at all? Just step right up.

STERNBERG. Yes, I have something to say.

NATHAN. Your name, sir?

STERNBERG. Rabbi Shlomo Sternberg, from Cambridge, Massachusetts.

NATHAN. Can you say that five times fast.

He starts. NATHAN interrupts.

Rabbi.... Rabbi.... Tawk to me.

STERNBERG. What Ms. Ozick refuses to confront is our shared responsibility — hers and mine — in these atrocities. Baruch Goldstein received his education from within the "modern orthodox" community. From all accounts, Dr. Goldstein was a paragon of self-sacrifice and devotion to others. It is hard to believe that such a person could become a mass murderer. It must take years of training. Dr. Goldstein was a model student at the Yeshiva of Flatbush, Yeshiva University and Einstein Medical School. I have yet to hear public statements of contrition from the leaders of these educational institutions.

NATHAN. Anyone else?

ELIACH. I'd like to respond to Rabbi Sternberg's rebuttal.

NATHAN. And you are?

ELIACH. Dr. Sarah Eliach, from Brooklyn.

NATHAN. Make it sing.

ELIACH. Rabbi Sternberg asks for a public statement of contrition from Baruch Goldstein's former teachers and principals. While we all deplore and condemn the senseless murder of innocent individuals, we cannot comply with his request for acquiescence in his libel of Orthodox Jewish education.

EXCITED MAN. Rabbi Sternberg surely knows that there is no line that goes from Orthodox Jewish education to Hebron. Some of our alumni who move to Israel live in Judea. Others have a different political position. They all received the same education that Baruch Goldstein did.

> *NATHAN has had enough. He cuts off the music and kicks everyone out. He finds the piece of paper containing the BOSS' telephone number. Calls her.*

Torture

> *NATHAN and the BOSS, at her place.*

NATHAN. I don't speak Hebrew. Don't read it, neither. Neither do I read it. Used to, though. Used to be able to read Hebrew. Like, when I was thirteen.

NATHAN AT 13. *(singing)* Ma nish-ta-naw ha-lai-law ha-zeh mee-kawl ha-lay-lot? Mee-kawl ha-lay-lot?

THE RELATIVES. *(applauding)* Awwwwwwww!
Good singing, Nathan!
He's so cute!

NATHAN. I was the youngest, so I asked the four questions. Why is this night different than all other nights?

MOM. Ask the first question, Nathan.

NATHAN AT 13. She-b'chawl ha-lay-los aw-nu o-ch'leen chaw-maytz u-ma-tzaw, ha-lai-law ha-zeh ku-lo ma-tzaw?

NATHAN. When my Zaydie led the ceremony, it seemed to go on forever.

> *ZAYDIE, BUBBIE and NATHAN at 13 at the seder. ZAYDIE wears a hat.*

You could smell the chicken soup simmering in my bubbie's kitchen. The kids would giggle and jostle. My zaydie took the ceremony very seriously. He wore a hat, not a yarmalke, and he stood as he recited the prayers. In Hebrew.

ZAYDIE. *(chanting)* Haw lach-maw an-yaw dee-a-chaw-lu a-vaw-haw-saw-naw b'ar-aw...

NATHAN. We did the entire Haggadah, including the songs.

THE OTHERS. *(robustly)* Di-di-ay-nu, di-di-ay-nu, di-di-ay-nu, dianu dianu!

NATHAN. When Zaydie died, Dad took over the ceremony. He made a few changes.

> *ZAYDIE turns into DAD, BUBBIE into MOM.*

DAD. Listen to this, Nathan. It says here, "Now we are slaves in a foreign land; next year may we be free in Jerusalem."

NATHAN. Right...

DAD. *I'm* not a slave. That's number one. Second, I don't want to go to Jerusalem. What are they, nuts? And get my head blown off?

NATHAN. So when he got to that bit:

DAD. Now we live in a free land; next year, may all those who want to go to Jerusalem, *go.*

NATHAN. As the years went by, he got bored.

DAD. This year, I'm going for a new record. Ready?

NATHAN. Ready... and... *now...*

DAD. *(very quickly)* BlessedartthouOeternalourGodKingoftheUniverseCreatorofthefruitofthevine.

NATHAN. Three seconds.

DAD. Drink the first glass of wine.

NATHAN. We went from reading the whole book, singing the songs, the whole bit.

ALL. *(trying to find the words)* Di... di... aynu?

MOM. I'll get the fish.

NATHAN. We got it down to a couple of blessings and a token reading of the story of how the Jews escaped from Yul Brynner. Oh, and the spilling of the drops of wine, to represent each of the ten plagues:

DAD. Blood.

THE OTHERS. Blood.

DAD. Frogs.

THE OTHERS. Frogs.

DAD. Vermin.

THE OTHERS. Vermin.

DAD. Aunty Yetta.

THE OTHERS. Aunty Ye—

NATHAN. Passover went from something meaningful in a language I didn't understand, to something meaningless in a language I did. Then my dad died. Now it's my turn to lead the seder.

They begin to make love, a young Palestinian boy appears:

MOURAD. From the moment I was arrested,
they put me in an atmosphere of fear and violence.
Five to ten of them invaded my house
smashing furniture, pictures and personal things
They kidnapped me from my bed.

and started beating me
even before they asked me my name.
They put me in an isolated cell
where they covered my head
with a hood
that had been soaked in urine.
They told me to lie on my back
and
with my hands tied
they hit
and kicked my testicles
Twice they strangled me
for up to a minute at a time,
beat me on the head
with a metal bar covered with rubber
They tied me to a stool
and with my head and legs on either side
beat me on the stomach
After this
they took me to be in the *shaba*
a long dark thin closed cupboard
where I was left
half conscious.
This continued for a month
during which time
I was not allowed to shower
or change my clothes
They arrested my aunt
who brought me up.
They know that I love her very much.
They told me they had to arrest her
because I would not confess.
They lifted me up
so I could see her
through a small window.
They told me my father was so sick
that I could not see him.
I was sentenced
to thirty months
for throwing stones.
The judge recognized
that this was to prevent the violence
they said
I would commit
against Israel.

This trial took place
when I was thirteen.

Morning

The next morning. NATHAN is reading the paper.

BOSS. Nathan?

NATHAN. Asshole.

BOSS. What?

NATHAN. Morning.

BOSS. Whatcha doing?

NATHAN. Reading.

BOSS. Uh?

NATHAN. *The New York Times.*

BOSS. It's Sunday? It isn't Sunday.

NATHAN. No.

BOSS. It can't be Sunday. I'm going to shul.

NATHAN. It's Saturday.

BOSS. You read *The New York Times* on Saturday?

NATHAN. I read it every day.

BOSS. Why?

NATHAN. I like to start my morning with the Big Lies. It makes the little ones
a little more palatable.

BOSS. Lies, like what?

NATHAN. Like A.M. Rosenthal. He writes an entire column about Hebron, making
sure to mention the 1929 massacre of Jews by Arabs, totally ignoring Goldstein's
massacre. It doesn't exist, because it gets in the way of his theory, which is that
the poor 400 Jews who squatted in Hebron need to be protected from the
100,000 Palestinian terrorists who have the temerity to live their squalid lives
there.

BOSS. Don't you think they need to be protected?

NATHAN. Is that coffee I smell?

BOSS. You sure you don't want to come to shul?

NATHAN. I'm sure.

BOSS. I got box seats. Going once… going twice…

NATHAN. Why do you go?

BOSS. …Because it's there.

NATHAN. You feel anything for it?

BOSS. I love the music.

NATHAN. Right.

BOSS. It's important. I don't want to lose touch with who I am.

NATHAN. You mean, with who you were.

BOSS. No. Who I am.

NATHAN. And who's that?

BOSS. It's a little early to play Who Am I, okay?

NATHAN. Okay…. You donate money to Israel?

BOSS. What?

NATHAN. Do you—donate—

BOSS. Yeah.

NATHAN. "Yeah."

BOSS. What's wrong with that?

NATHAN. Nothing. If you want to support murder and oppression.

BOSS. Oh puh-leez. What, did you wake up with your morals in a knot? "Support murder and…" I am supporting schools, hospitals…

NATHAN. Border closings.

BOSS. Border cl—Look. You don't know what you're—don't accuse me of "oppressing" anyone. I don't want to talk about this anymore, okay?

NATHAN. Okay.

BOSS. Thank you.

NATHAN. The thing is.

BOSS. Oh Jesus.

NATHAN. You send money to Israel. They use that money to build settlements. Some crazy fuck comes along with a machine gun, mows down a buncha dirty Arabs. It doesn't just happen. He shouldn't'a been there in the first place. Why is he there? Because of your money. Our money.

BOSS. Uh huh. It's funny, isn't it, how everything we do is wrong.

NATHAN. I'm not saying that.

BOSS. No, no. You, you spend all your time reading about Isr—kvetching about Israel, and what it is to be Jewish, and and…. What is wrong with you? You have no idea. How lucky you are. How lucky all of us are, to have Israel. For 2,000 years, Nathan, we were persecuted.

NATHAN. And now it's time to return the favour?

BOSS. Nathan, you can't. Listen. I want to tell you something. Because I don't think you understand. The first time I went to Israel, I went to the Holocaust Memorial. Yad Vashem. You know?

NATHAN. Yeah.

BOSS. I mean nothing can prepare you for that, Nathan. To see those pictures. Especially of the children. What they did to the children. How they suffered. Um. One of the photos was of a little boy, with his arms up and… he um, had this hat, this uh, he was wearing this hat… they shot him because of who he was. When I saw that picture, Nathan, I knew that we needed this country. And I am sorry for the Palestinian people, truly I am. But there is nothing I will say, not a word will I say, against this country. Can you understand that?

NATHAN. Yes. Because you love Israel.

BOSS. I do. I feel it.

NATHAN. People like you scare the shit outta me. You stand there and use those children to justify what we've done to the Palestinians. How can you do that?

BOSS. Fuck you.

NATHAN. Gesundheit.

BOSS. You accuse me of… you're saying that because I want to make sure that what happened to us never happens again, that I'm worse than Baruch Goldstein? Is that what you're telling me? I don't believe that. You read it somewhere. It sounded good so you added it to your armour. It doesn't mean a fucking thing, none of it, because you don't believe it. What do you believe?

NATHAN. I believe… you're late for shul.

EX-WIFE appears.

BOSS. Why are you doing this?

NATHAN. What?

EX-WIFE. Pushing me away.

NATHAN. I don't want you should be late.

BOSS. Answer the fucking question.

NATHAN. I vant to be a loner.

EX-WIFE. Good. Then get out.

NATHAN. Get out?

EX-WIFE. I packed your suitcase. Go on.

NATHAN. I don't want to go.

EX-WIFE. Fine. Then I will.

NATHAN. Just stay a minute.

BOSS. I can't. I'm late. *(starts to go)* Would you do me a favour?

NATHAN. Walk your dog?

BOSS. I don't have a dog.

NATHAN. Then yes.

BOSS. Would you hold me?

NATHAN. Hold you.

EX-WIFE. You know what that is?

NATHAN. Uh huh.

EX-WIFE. Then?

NATHAN. I don't think so.

BOSS. What?

NATHAN. I said I don't think so.

BOSS. You prick. You talk about compassion for people halfway around the world,

EX-WIFE. and you can't even give it to someone halfway across the room.

BOSS. You know what? I didn't want it. I was testing you.

NATHAN. I knew that. I detected the insincerity.

BOSS. Why did you come here?

NATHAN. Hm?

BOSS. Are you listening to me?

NATHAN. No.

BOSS. Why did you sleep with me?

NATHAN. You asked me to.

BOSS. You didn't want to?

NATHAN. Not especially. To tell you the truth, you disgust me. I can't stand the smell of you. I want to take a shower. I wish I could chop off my fingers, my tongue, my dick. I'll probably die of some disease you gave me.

BOSS. Are you listening to me?

NATHAN. Yes.

BOSS. Why did you sleep with me?

NATHAN. I wanted to be with you.

BOSS. Do you still want to be with me?

NATHAN. Yes. I'm sorry.

EX-WIFE. Are you?

NATHAN. No.

BOSS. Christ.

NATHAN. I mean yes.

EX-WIFE. I think you should go.

NATHAN. That is to say.

BOSS. Will you go please?

NATHAN. Uh.

EX-WIFE. Will you go?

NATHAN. Um. Er. Uh.

BOSS. Get out of my house.

> *He leaves, taking his paper with him.*

The Seder

> *NATHAN returns to his apartment. He pours a cup of wine, holds it up.*

NATHAN. Blessed art thou, O Lord our God, Ruler of the Universe, Creator of the fruit of the vine.

> *Pause.*

Amen.

> *Drinks.*

On February 25th, 1994, Dr. Baruch Goldstein, a settler from Kiryat Arba, committed a…

> *He shoves the books off his desk in one motion; takes a moment to recover.*

massacre at the Tomb of the Patriarchs in Hebron.
The Government of Israel decided to appoint a Commission of Inquiry to determine whether Goldstein acted alone or with accomplices.
(finds a Haggadah) Blessed art thou, O Lord our God, Ruler of the Universe, Who has chosen us from all peoples, and exalted us above all nations—

> *The telephone rings.*

Hello?

MOM. Hello, darling.

NATHAN. Hi, Mom.

MOM. How you doing?

NATHAN. Same as yesterday when you called.

MOM. So: you were gonna let me know about the boys?

NATHAN. I was?

MOM. Are you bringing them to the seder?

NATHAN. No.

MOM. Oi. I'm worried about you.

NATHAN. That's odd.

MOM. The first year without Pat and the boys.

NATHAN. I'm fine.

MOM. I just—

NATHAN. I'm fine.

MOM. I—

NATHAN. *I'm*. Fine.

MOM. Fine. So goodbye.

NATHAN. Goodbye.

> *They hang up.*

(*returning to his seder*) Blessed art thou O Lord our God Ruler of the Universe Creator of the fruit of the vine.
Amen.
Blessed art thou O Lord our God Ruler of the Universe, who has chosen us from all peoples, and exalted us above all nations, and sanctified us with—

> *The telephone rings.*

Hello?

EX-WIFE. It's me. Your ex-wife.

NATHAN. Yes?

EX-WIFE. Did Ben take his medicine?

NATHAN. (*cartoon voice*) Yes, dear.

EX-WIFE. You forgot to give it to him last time.

NATHAN. (*cartoon voice*) Yes, dear.

EX-WIFE. Did you give it to him?

NATHAN. (*cartoon voice*) Yes, dear.

EX-WIFE. Such an asshole.

> *They hang up.*

NATHAN. Blessed art thou O Lord our God Ruler of the—

ZAYDIE. (*appears*) This is your seder?

NATHAN. Zaydie?

ZAYDIE. Where are the boys?

NATHAN. Sleeping.

ZAYDIE. What happened to the seder? Where is the family?

NATHAN. I don't have an answer to that.

ZAYDIE. You could at least read in Hebrew, maybe?

NATHAN. Baruch ata adonai, elohaynu melech haolum.
Baruch ata adonai…
Barucha Goldstein adonai…
Baruch Goldstein got annoyed…
Baruch Goldstein shot some Arabs…

BEN runs out.

BEN. Bang!

NATHAN. Jesus!

BEN. Sorry, Daddy.

NATHAN. You know you're not supposed to play with guns.

BEN. It's not a gun, it's my finger.

NATHAN. What are you doing out of bed?

BEN. I'm not tired. Can you tell me a story?

NATHAN. No. I'm not telling you another story.

BEN. FINE! THEN I WON'T BE YOUR FRIEND!

NATHAN. Lower your voice. I don't want you waking up your brother.

BEN. He's dead.

NATHAN. Pardon me?

BEN. We were playing Arabs and Jews and he's an Arab and I shot him.

NATHAN. "Arabs" and "Jews". Where did you learn about "Arabs" and "Jews"?

BEN. From Mummy. She told me you were Jewish.

NATHAN. Uh huh. What did she tell you?

BEN. That the Arabs are bad guys and they want to kill the Jews.

NATHAN. It's a little more complicated than that.

BEN. Tell me, Daddy.

NATHAN. It's time for bed.

BEN. Nooooo, tell me.

NATHAN. Well. Alright, let's say some people came in here and said, "This is our house. You have to leave."

BEN. But it's our house.

NATHAN. But what if they said it was their house a long time ago.

BEN. But…

NATHAN. What would you do? How would you get your house back?

Beat.

BEN. Bang!

NATHAN. Exactly. Alright. Bedtime.

BEN goes off. NATHAN returns to the seder, realizes he needs something, goes off. Mossad agents come in, rearrange things on the desk, creating a more traditional looking seder table; then, they hide under the desk.

NATHAN brings back a box of crackers. He's wearing his grandfather's hat.

NATHAN. Drink the first cup of wine.

He drinks it.

Blessed art thou, O Lord our God, Ruler of the Universe, Creator of the Fruit of the Loom.

He takes out a cracker.

This matzah we eat.

He breaks half of it.

NATHAN. Nobody look. Nobody look. I'm hiding the afikoman. Hiding the afikoman.
This is the bread of affliction which our ancestors ate in the land of Egypt. All who are hungry—let them come and eat. All who are needy let them come and celebrate the Passover with us.

ZAYDIE comes out from under the table. They look at each other. NATHAN gives him his hat.

ZAYDIE. The Torah tells of four sons. One who is wise, and one is contrary; one who is simple and one who does not even know how to ask a question.

ASHWARI appears.

Who's here already?

NATHAN. Sorry. Hanan Ashwari, my grandfather.

ASHWARI. I am honoured to meet you.

ZAYDIE. Mm hm.

NATHAN. And this is Noam Chomsky, professor of linguistics at MIT.

CHOMSKY. Good Pesach.

ZAYDIE. A nice Jewish boy.

NATHAN. Wait'll he talks about Israel.

JANE. Hi, I'm Jane.

ZAYDIE. Mm hm. "Jane," this is a name for a Jewish girl?

JANE. I'm not Jewish, but I love the Jewish people. When I was a little girl, I wanted to be Jewish so badly. You people are so persecuted? I remember reading The Diary of Anne Frank and thinking, I wish *I* was Jewish.

Pause; the five are now gathered round the seder table.

ZAYDIE. The wise son asks, What is the meaning of the laws and customs which the Lord our God has commanded us? To him you shall explain all the laws of the Passover, to the very last detail of the afikoman. Did you hide the afikoman?

NATHAN. Yes, I did. And I've written the answer to the Middle East question on the afikoman, so whoever finds it gets an extra special treat.

JANE. I was at a seder once, and *I* found the afikoman. Me!

> *Pause.*

ZAYDIE. The contrary son asks:

NATHAN. Zaydie.

ZAYDIE. Be quiet, I'm talking.

NATHAN. I know that, but...

ZAYDIE. The *contrary* son asks...

NATHAN. You jumped ahead. We didn't ask the four questions.

ZAYDIE. So? You didn't light the candles either.

JANE. I brought candles! Hanan, would you help me do the blessing?

ASHWARI. I don't know it.

JANE. You read Hebrew, don't you?

ASHWARI. Of course.

JANE. I'll start; you follow.

> *They light the candles; NATHAN finds himself deeply moved by the traditional singing of the blessing.*

ZAYDIE. That brings us to the Four Questions.

NATHAN. Zaydie. It's my turn to lead the seder.

> *After a moment, ZAYDIE passes his hat to NATHAN, who puts it on and begins:*

Now it is written, I don't know where exactly it is written but it must be written somewhere, that it is our duty to retell the story of the Exodus. Why? So that we, the Jews, the Chosen Ones, the the the...

JANE. A Light Unto...

NATHAN. A Light Unto Nations, thank you Jane, A Light Unto Nations, so that we can recall what was done *for* us in our time of *need.* Thus we read of our oppression, and our deliverance. *Yet* we do not see. That we have become the oppressors. How has this happened? Let us ask some new questions, pertinent questions.... How is this country—Israel—different than all other countries? Noam Chomsky.

NOAM. I'm sorry?

NATHAN. Listen up, Noam. How is this country diff—

NOAM. Yes. I uh, I heard the question. I thought I told you once but, uhh alright. Israel is different because no other country is permitted to commit such terrible rights abuses and at the same time is revered as a paragon of moral rectitude.

NATHAN. Thank you.

NOAM. Much to its own detriment.

NATHAN. Right.

NOAM. I thought we'd covered this.

NATHAN. Now, how did the early Zionists rationalize the creation of a Jewish state in Palestine? Hanan Ashwari.

ASHWARI. Yes?

NATHAN. The Answer.

ASHWARI. Yes, alright. By claiming that no one lived there. *You* know, as in the slogan, "A country without a people for a people without a country."

NATHAN. Right. And that is despite the fact that it had been inhabited for—

ASHWARI. Yes.

NATHAN. Centuries.

ASHWARI. Clearly.

NATHAN. Good. Alright. I think we're getting somewhere. Um. How did the inhabitants of Palestine react to massive Jewish immigration? Jane.

JANE. They resisted.

NATHAN. Would you care to elaborate?

JANE. Again?

NATHAN. I don't follow.

JANE. Apparently not.

NATHAN. Okay. Professor Said, if and when you are invited to speak to Jewish audiences, what will you tell them about the future of Jews in Palestine?

      Pause.

Professor Said... future... of the Jews... in Palestine.

SAID. I have already answered this question.

NATHAN. You have.

SAID. In the library. Look, Nathan. We've been through all this. Now look. What exactly what do you want?

NATHAN. I j—I have some questions.

CHOMSKY. You've already asked them.

JANE. Besides, you're not really listening to the answers.

NATHAN. Of course I am.

SAID. Why did you invite us? To share your ceremony?

CHOMSKY. What do you want from us?

ASHWARI. You fall in love with an idea the way you fall in love with a woman.

SAID. And when our ideas are no longer attractive…

ASHWARI. You will push us away.

NATHAN. I'm asking questions.

SAID. The wrong questions.

NATHAN. The same questions you ask.

ASHWARI. Precisely. But they are not your questions.

JANE. You think you are the wise son.

CHOMSKY. In what way wise?

JANE. You think you are the contrary son.

SAID. Contrary to what?

JANE. You think you are the simple son.

ASHWARI. It is not so simple.

JANE. In fact, you are the son who does not even know how to ask a question.

> *A huge explosion; all hell breaks loose… two HASIDIM—right out of Vaudeville—appear:*

1ST HASID. Don't step there!

NATHAN. Where?

1ST HASID. What's the matter with you? That's somebody's skin.

NATHAN. Where?

2ND HASID. Under your foot. Move.

> *NATHAN moves. 2ND HASID scrapes the skin up, puts it in a bag.*

NATHAN. Where am I?

1ST HASID. Jerusalem. Hamas blew up another bus today. We're collecting the blood and skin and brains of the innocent.

2ND HASID. No one can be buried unless they are whole.

1ST HASID. That way, comes Moshiach, they'll be holy.

2ND HASID. You slay me, Hershel.

1ST HASID. Never mind. Hold this.

> *1ST HASID hands 2ND HASID the bag; scrapes something up; puts it in the bag.*

2ND HASID. Is that a finger or a…

1ST HASID. Oi!

2ND HASID. That's what I thought.

1ST HASID. I got news for you.

2ND HASID. What's that?

1ST HASID. It's not even kosher.

2ND HASID. Oi! It must be Nathan's!

The telephone rings.

NATHAN. Hello?

CONSPIRATOR. Did you do it?

NATHAN. Do what?

CONSPIRATOR. Kill Netanyahu?

NATHAN. Look...

CONSPIRATOR. What are you waiting for? There's gonna be a civil war. You have to do something. Forget about the massacre already. It's done, it's over; you think the Jews and Arabs are waiting for a history lesson? Don't get stuck on Hebron. You gotta move with the times. Move! Move! Move!

The telephone rings.

NATHAN. Hello?

MOM. Nathan, did you hear?

NATHAN. Hear what?

MOM. They shot Rabin.

NATHAN. Who did?

MOM. At a peace rally. They shot him.

NATHAN. Is he dead?

MOM. No. They took him to the hospital. They say it was a Jew. A Jew!

He hangs up. Orthodox Jews enter, dancing and singing.

SETTLER 1. Hero of Israel! Hero of Israel! There should be more like him!

SETTLER 2. *(his head covered in a white shawl)* This is the tallis of Goldstein! Put it on! It is like touching the saint.

NATHAN. Saint!

SETTLER 3. He is a saint! He has saved us! We came here to salute this righteous man.

NATHAN. He killed 29 men at prayer!

SETTLER 4. It says in the Torah that with those who want to kill you, you must kill them first.

NATHAN. Listen... there are only 450 of you here, and a hundred thousand Palestinians. You have to move somewhere else.

SETTLER 2. Our return to Hebron is not open for discussion. If Hebron falls, Jerusalem falls.

SETTLER 4. This is the most perfidious government that ever existed.

ALL. Death to Rabin! Death to Rabin! Death to Rabin!

> *The telephone rings.*

NATHAN. Hello?

MOM. Nathan, did you hear what happened in Hebron?

NATHAN. What?

MOM. The Jewish underground murdered three students at the Islamic College.

> *He hangs up.*

SETTLER 1. You don't "understand" Hebron.

NATHAN. I'm trying to.

SETTLER 1. You never will. Listen. The Arabs think it's theirs; it's ours. We got there first. Abraham bought it. Abraham, our father.

NATHAN. The Arabs call Abraham father too.

SETTLER 1. You are a Jew. And you are either with us or against us. If you choose to go with the Arab, you will be against your own people. Do you think the Arabs will take you in? No! Once they have used you, *used you to get what they want,* they will throw you into the sea.

> *The telephone rings.*

NATHAN. Hello?

MOM. Nathan, are you watching?

NATHAN. What?

MOM. Rabin's funeral. His granddaughter's doing the eulogy. You should listen.

> *NOA, Rabin's granddaughter, enters.*

NOA. Forgive me if I do not want to talk about peace. I want to talk about my grandfather. You always awake from a nightmare, but since yesterday I only awake into a nightmare—the nightmare of life without you, and that is impossible to fathom.

NATHAN. Noa Ben Artzi-Pelosoff?

NOA. Yes?

NATHAN. My name's Nathan Abramowitz.

NOA. Yes?

NATHAN. I understand you're writing a book about your grandfather.

NOA. Yes.

NATHAN. I hear you're getting a million dollars.

NOA. That's right.

NATHAN. I'd love to get a look at it.

NOA. On the ground, pig!

> *She starts to make love to him.*

NATHAN. Oh my God. Yes. Noa. Yes.

NOA. Come on, Nathan. Live in the moment, just like we do in Israel.

NATHAN. I'm living, I'm living.

NOA. You want to touch my gun? I'm in the army you know.

NATHAN. Yes, your gun, your gun.

NOA. You like this?

NATHAN. Uh huh.

NOA. What about that?

NATHAN. You read my mind. Tell me, what do you think of the peace process?

NOA. I think it's very good.

NATHAN. Uh huh?

NOA. I want to say to the Arabs, we want peace with you. But if you so much as think about invading us again, we will destroy you as surely as we annihilated the Amalekites.

NATHAN. Okay, that's clear. What do you think about a pull out?

NOA. No! Don't stop, don't stop.

NATHAN. Oh God. Do the eulogy.

NOA. What?

NATHAN. The eulogy, the eulogy.

NOA. You sick bastard, I want to fuck you all night.

NATHAN. Do it!

NOA. Grandfather, you were and still are our hero.

NATHAN. Oh yes, oh yes.

NOA. I wanted you to know…

NATHAN. Mm…

NOA. …that every time I did anything…

NATHAN. Yeah, yeah.

NOA. I saw you in front of me.

RABIN/ZAYDIE. Stop this!

NATHAN. Zaydie?

NOA. Grandfather!

RABIN/ZAYDIE. You ought to be ashamed of yourself!

NOA. Pull out! Pull out!

The telephone rings.

CONSUL. You defile the memory of the dead.

NATHAN. Not true.

CONSUL. Did you weep at the funeral of Rabin?

NATHAN. No.

CONSUL. You see!

NATHAN. But I wanted to.

CONSUL. Liar.

NATHAN. It's true.

CONSUL. Then why didn't you?

NATHAN. I felt manipulated.

CONSUL. By the death of a man of peace?

NATHAN. Peace! He ordered the bombing of Lebanon!

CONSUL. He shook the hand of his enemy! He was a Jew. And you didn't weep?

NATHAN. I wanted to.

CONSUL. Then weep!

He hangs up.

NATHAN. Spill a drop of wine for each of the ten plagues. Blood.

Pause.

JANE. At the library, you asked me:

SAID. Why is this massacre different.

NATHAN. Frogs.

JANE. You felt revulsion.

SAID. Disgust.

ASHWARI. Pity for the victims.

CHOMSKY. Revulsion that one of your own.

JANE. That a Jew.

ASHWARI. That an Israeli would do such a thing.

NATHAN. Lice.

SAID. When you heard that Goldstein had been beaten to death.

CHOMSKY. Beaten to death by the Palestinians.

JANE. You felt horror, too.

SAID. At the death of Goldstein.

CHOMSKY. Because his life means more.

ASHWARI. Than the life of an Arab.

SAID. Of 29 Arabs.

NATHAN. Wild beasts.

SAID. "It was Purim after all."

JANE. "The answer was perfectly clear."

ASHWARI. "Thank God it all ended well."

CHOMSKY. "The natural situation."

NATHAN. Pestilence. Boils.

SAID. You want to help us?

ASHWARI. You want us to have a state?

NATHAN. I.

JANE. Yes?

NATHAN. Well. I.

SAID. Yes, Nathan?

NATHAN. Hail. Locusts.

SAID. You're running out of plagues, Nathan.

ASHWARI. The Arab is a murderous thief.

SAID. "You cannot trust the Arab."

CHOMSKY. "Even when he appears to be civilized."

SAID. The plane went down.

ASHWARI. Arab terrorists.

CHOMSKY. Or perhaps mechanical failure.

SAID. Arabs is better.

JANE. The building blew up.

ASHWARI. Arabs.

CHOMSKY. Or perhaps the militia.

JANE. Arab terrorists.

ASHWARI. Cockroaches.

SAID. Exterminate them.

CHOMSKY. Erase them from history.

NATHAN. Darkness.

ASHWARI. We don't exist.

NATHAN. Slaying of the first born.

SAID. You have run out of plagues.

ASHWARI. Ask your questions, Nathan.

The telephone rings.

NATHAN. Hello?

MOM. Hello, darling.

NATHAN. Hello, Mother.

MOM. What's doing?

NATHAN. Nothing.

MOM. Good Pesach.

NATHAN. Same to you.

MOM. We're going to the Bernbaums.

NATHAN. Uh huh.

MOM. The Bernbaums. You remember. With the son.

NATHAN. Oh yeah.

MOM. So what are you doing?

NATHAN. Oh you know.

MOM. Did you hear what happened in Hebron?

NATHAN. No, what.

MOM. Abraham bought a cave.

NATHAN. That's nice.

MOM. So how's things with you?

NATHAN. Not bad. How were the Bernbaums last night?

MOM. Oh fine. We didn't eat 'til midnight.

NATHAN. Really.

MOM. Their son made such a fuss.

NATHAN. Uh huh.

MOM. Did you hear what happened in Hebron?

NATHAN. No, what.

MOM. The Arabs built a mosque over the cave.

NATHAN. Really.

MOM. So, what's with you?

NATHAN. Oh, not much.

MOM. How are the boys?

NATHAN. Fine.

MOM. When's the graduation ceremony?

NATHAN. End of the month.

MOM. I can't wait. Did you hear what happened in Hebron?

NATHAN. No, what?

MOM. Some crazy settler murdered 29 Arabs.

NATHAN. Really.

MOM. It's crazy. And how are you?

NATHAN. Oh fine.

MOM. Mrs. Bernbaum died.

NATHAN. Oh well.

MOM. How are the boys?

NATHAN. Divorced.

MOM. What a shame. Did you hear what happened in Hebron?

NATHAN. No, what?... What happened?... Mom?... Mom?

> *He hangs up.*

My questions.
Did I help Baruch Goldstein murder 29 Palestinians?
Am I at the side of Baruch Goldstein?
Am I Baruch Goldstein?
Do I believe, I mean really believe, that Jews have a greater right to live than do Palestinians?
Do I believe, against all my best instincts and hopes and understanding of the way the world works, that my life is more valuable than the life of a Palestinian? Of an Arab? A filthy Arab?

> *The guests start to pack up.*

A terrorist who would stab me in the back the first chance he got? A Jew hating, smelly, hummous eating—. Wait. Um. No. Those aren't the questions. What am I doing?

> *The others are ready to go.*

Don't go. Those aren't the questions. Find the afikoman.

> *There is a knock at the door.*

Come on, Hanan, *look* for the matzah.

> *The knocking continues.*

Jane, find the matzah.... What happened to the seder?... Keep looking.

> *Loud knocking.*

Yes? Who is it?

> *NATHAN opens the door; a young boy stands there.*

Are you hungry?... "All who are hungry. All who are needy." Well, that's pretty much all of us, isn't it? Come in.... Everyone, this is Baruch Goldstein.... He's 13 years old.... A student at the Yeshiva of Flatbush in Brooklyn, New York.

Come in. He wants to say something to us. Come in… come in… alright,
Benjy… go ahead…

> *The others are sitting at the dismantled seder table; GOLDSTEIN*
> *addresses the audience; he wears a* tallis.

BARUCH. Protest Against War
War is a threatening and fearful thing
with murder,
killing,
shedding of blood,
cruelty
and a burden to the wounded.
War causes much distress for the country,
soldiers
and their families.
Many people die in war
and leave behind
bereaved families,
bereaved parents,
young orphans,
and a nation that,
standing back,
sees all that occurred
and is sad
in its heart.
Also,
according to the Jewish religion,
war is prohibited.
One of the important things in the Torah is
"do not murder"—
and in war
many people are murdered.
In the Torah
it is written
"do not covet."
War is caused, according to most,
from this—
that a country covets the land of another country
or its resources.
The Jewish nation always wants peace
and always wanted peace and,
in prayers,
one says that God will make peace
over all of Israel
and there will be no war in the land.

Who will give something
to bring about
a situation such as this—
that all human beings will live in peace,
will not murder
and will not covet the land
of one's neighbour,
and peace will prevail in the entire world?
Who will give to bring this about?

NATHAN. I found it. I found it, Zaydie.

> *NATHAN goes to GOLDSTEIN; holds him in an embrace. GOLDSTEIN backs away, joins the others at the table, where they become the JUDGES of Israel.*

Judges 5

JUDGE 1. The witness
is a visitor
from Canada

NATHAN. I would like to thank
the commission
for allowing me
the opportunity to speak

JUDGE 4. You mentioned in your letter
that you felt concerned
about the implications of the massacre
for Jews outside of Israel

NATHAN. Yes
I followed the news reports
about the inquiry
and became convinced that you
the Judges of Israel
would find the courage
to tell the truth
about this massacre

JUDGE 4. The evidence is clear. Dr. Baruch Goldstein bears direct responsibility for
the massacre.

NATHAN. The massacre was not
merely the action of one
deranged man

but the inevitable
I might even say logical
consequence
of Israeli policy
toward the Palestinian people

JUDGE 1. Have you been to Israel
before

NATHAN. No
This is my first time

JUDGE 1. How long do you intend to stay

NATHAN. Long enough
to get a feeling
for the country

JUDGE 1. What does that mean

NATHAN. It means that
up until this moment
my only experience of Israel
has been a vicarious one
I suppose you could say that
for me
Israel is an abstract idea

JUDGE 1. An
Abstract idea

NATHAN. I love the Jewish people
and this country which
I have never seen
with my own eyes
I visit it through books
newspapers
television
and radio
and through the experiences
of friends and relatives
who have lived here
or visited
Israel is
my lover, my wife, my friend my
child
parent
grandparent and
teacher
I love you O Israel
I would never harm you

never wish to see harm done to you
nor
by you
I fear that
if the Jewish state
and the Jewish people
continue to act as we do
we will disappear as surely
as the Palestinian people
whose homes we have taken
whose families we have dispersed
whose dignity we have denied
whose dreams we have ended

JUDGE 1. Well
Mr. Abramowitz
may I say that
I have lived in Israel
my entire life
and that for me
and for my friends
and for my family
and for the people who live here
and who struggle daily with
these questions
that Israel
is not an abstraction
but a very real place
We appreciate your comments
and your observations
But they are of no concern
to those of us who live here

JUDGE 2. The evidence is clear. Dr. Baruch Goldstein bears direct responsibility for the massacre because the evidence unequivocally indicates that he carried it out. All stages of the event, including his preparations and behaviour on the morning of February 25th, 1994, indicate that his actions were premeditated.

JUDGE 1. We were asked to investigate the massacre and to determine findings and draw conclusions regarding the circumstances related to it.

JUDGE 4. We recommend, first and foremost, that arrangements intended to create complete separation between the Muslim and Jewish worshippers be adopted, in order to ensure the safety of all worshippers, and to prevent friction, disputes and acts of violence.

JUDGE 3. Separate entrance gates will be set aside for Muslim and Jewish worshippers.

Members of one religion will not be permitted to enter into an area in which prayers of the other religion are taking place at that time.

JUDGE 2. The massacre at the Tomb of the Patriarchs in Hebron was a base and murderous act, in which innocent people bending in prayer to their maker were killed.

JUDGE 4. We presented the lessons which must be learned from this tragic incident so that, as far as possible, the repetition of criminal acts such as these can be prevented. We made a series of recommendations meant to assist in returning things to normal both in the Tomb of the Patriarchs in particular, and generally in Hebron.

JUDGE 1. Let us hope that our inquiry and our report will indeed contribute to that end.

NATHAN. Drink the last cup of wine
Now we are slaves
Next year may we be free.

He exits.

The end.

• Glossary of Words and Phrases •

There's a saying that if you put ten Jews in a room you get eleven opinions; the theory holds true for word pronunciation. Consult your local Rabbi or use your best judgment.

afikoman - a piece of matzah hidden before the Passover meal begins; the lucky child who finds it gets a reward, often monetary.

aliyah - the greatest thing a Jew can do, we are told, is "return" or "ascend" to the land of Israel; this is called making aliyah. The second best thing a Jew can do is marry another Jew; this is called making your mother happy.

Amalekites - bad guys in the Old Testament, wiped out by the Israelites; the most vicious of the Wild West Bank settlers often refer to non-Jews as Amalek.

Baruch ata adonai, elohaynu melech haolum - "Blessed art thou, O Lord our God, Ruler of the Universe." The start of many prayers.

brisket - a huge, cheap cut of beef which, after being pickled or marinated, becomes pastrami, roast beef, smoked meat or, in extremely hot ovens over a long period of time, Jewish pemmican.

bubbie - grandmother.

the four questions - The Passover story begins when the youngest child at the table asks the four questions, which all begin "Why is this night different than all other nights?" and continues by pointing out that only on this night do we eat matzah; sit in a reclining position, etc. The story of the Exodus is then told as the answer.

hagaddah - book which tells the story of the Exodus, with commentary and songs; see Passover.

Hamas - depending on how you look at things, either a Palestinian charity organization attempting to raise funds for schools, orphanages and other worthy causes, or a group of terrorists whose favourite weapon, the suicide bomb, blows up with great regularity on Israeli buses. Or both. A thorn in the side of Yassir Arafat, Hamas may be Israel's own undoing—the state is said to have supported the group as a way of providing opposition to Arafat's group, Fatah.

Hezbollah - depending on how you look at things, either a group of freedom fighters trying to force the Israeli army out of the so-called security zone it occupies in Southern Lebanon, or a group of terrorists backed by Iran whose favoured weapon, the Russian-made Katyusha rocket, lands with great frequency on innocent farmers in Northern Israel. Or both.

Judea and Samaria - biblical names of the region known less zealously as the West Bank.

Kiryat Arba - Israeli settlement on the outskirts of Hebron.

kvetching - complaining.

matzah - unleavened bread... you know, crackers; the idea is that the former slaves fleeing Egypt had no time to sit and watch the dough rise, so the least we can do to remember their time in the desert is to eat what they did for eight days.